Years of Minutes

ANDY ROONEY

YEARS OF MINUTES

PublicAffairs

NEW YORK

BOOK DESIGN AND COMPOSITION BY JENNY DOSSIN

TEXT SET IN ADOBE MINION

Library of Congress Cataloging-in-Publication data
Rooney, Andrew A.
Years of minutes / Andy Rooney.— 1st ed.
p. cm.
Essays adapted from the author's commentaries
on the television news program, 60 minutes.
ISBN 1–58648–211–4
I. 60 minutes (television program) II. Title.
PN4874.R565A25 2003
791.45'72—dc22
2003062341

FIRST EDITION

1 3 5 7 9 10 8 6 4 2

Contents

Foreword

Forewords, prefaces and introductions are usually self-serving little essays that the writer puts at the front of a book describing how it was done, why it was done and who deserves all the credit. This is some of that but its also a plea for help.

Everything in this book was originally written by me to read aloud on television by me. Because no one speaks as he writes and no one writes as he speaks, words put down on paper to be read aloud are written in a different style than words to be read in silence by eyes alone. A speaker can add nuances of meaning with inflections in his or her voice or put in pauses and stops for which there are no adequate punctuation marks. For this reason I ask you to try to hear these words as you read them.

When these commentaries were shown on television as part of *60 Minutes*, they were always accompanied by pictures. Usually viewers would see me saying something general about a subject and then, when I got specific, the editors, Bob Forte and after 1997 Keith Kulin, would put images on screen that illustrated or emphasized the point.

The one thing I know that a lot of writers dont know, is how satisfying it is to put down words that are accompanied by pictures. Its fun. When the pictures and the words supplement each other, the impact on the viewer/listener is more than it would be with words or pictures alone.

There are times when the words dont need pictures but other times when the pictures dont need words and that doesnt come off very well in a book of words.

The one affectation I have forced on the publisher, Peter Osnos, the editor, Kate Darnton, my assistant, Susan Bieber, and the anonymous proofreaders are my apostrophe-free elisions. Because I write my scripts to read myself, I dont spell "don't" with an apostrophe. I spell it "dont." We all know the word and it seems foolish to put in an extraneous apostrophe. Punctuation marks are devices we use to make the meaning of sentences clear. There is nothing confusing about a word like "dont" printed without an apostrophe to indicate an omitted letter. Thats not true for all words that usually have apostrophes. Its difficult to make a general rule because there are places where leaving out the apostrophe doesnt work. If I wanted to elide "I will" without the apostrophe it would come out "Ill." That's another word altogether so I make an exception and spell it "I'll." Exceptions are based on nothing more than what I think might be confusing to me as I read the script aloud. Following is a list of elisions in which I dont use an apostrophe: arent, cant, couldnt, didnt, doesnt, dont, hadnt, hasnt, havent, Im, isnt, its, Ive, shouldnt, thats, theres, theyd, theyve, theyre, wasnt, werent, wont, wouldnt, youd, youll, youre, youve. That wont bother you, will it?

1982

True/False Test

Kids in school love true-or-false tests because they have a 50–50 chance of being right even if they havent studied at all. Teachers like them because theyre easy to correct. Tonight, I thought we'd have a little true-or-false test of our own, just for fun.

1. First question: "President Reagan was never nominated for an Academy Award." True or false? True, he never was. He's probably a better President than he was an actor.

2. "Theres no business like show business." True or false? True, but theres no business like the insurance business or the used car business, either.

3. "Hamlet is the name of a small town in Iowa." False.

4. "Things will probably get worse." True.

5. "Houston, Texas, is bigger than Dallas." True, although a lot of people dont think so because theres never been a television show called *Houston*.

6. "There are 5,280 yards in a mile." False. There are 5,280 yards in three miles.

7. "The average Russian lives longer than the average American." True or false? False. Living in Russia, it just seems longer.

8. "The square root of the hypotenuse seldom comes up in real life." True, it seldom does.

9. "Abortion, gun control, nuclear energy and school prayer are three subjects to stay away from when talking with friends." False. Theyre four subjects to stay away from when talking with anyone.

10. "A penny post card now costs 10¢." True or false? False. A penny post card used to cost 10¢. Now who knows what one costs.

11. "Students dont write English sentences as well as they once did because of television." True or false? False. Students dont write as well as they used to because of true-or-false tests.

So thats our little true-or-false test. If you got all the answers correct, youve got a warped mind.

Cookbooks

Do you know the two biggest best-sellers in bookstores year after year?

Number one is cookbooks. Cookbooks outsell everything else in a bookstore.

Number two best-seller year after year? Diet books. How not to eat what youve just learned how to cook.

We picked up a collection in bookstores. I brought in some from home. But these are just a few of the books that are available. *Fanny Farmer* and *The Joy of Cooking* are the American favorites.

Americans arent really very good cooks, considering that they have the best ingredients to start with. We spend millions of dollars a year on cookbooks, and then we go home and open a jar of Aunt Millie's spaghetti sauce for dinner. I think we always have the idea that someone else's cookbook will save us: Italian, Japanese, Chinese, German. The Germans cook about as well as the British.

Take *Betty Crocker's International Cookbook*. Betty is one of those non-existent people.

Its hard to make things look the way they make them look in the cookbooks, isnt it? The pictures always look so great.

Then there are the all-time classics: *Larousse Gastronomique* and *Escoffier*. You really have to know how to cook to use these.

Julia Child couldnt get everything she knows in one book. Hers comes in two volumes. Good book, though. I like Julia. She assumes you arent an idiot in the kitchen, even though you may be.

I also have a theory that the only people who should use cookbooks are people who already know how to cook. If you have to have a cookbook, youre in big trouble.

The best way to use a cookbook, I think, is just for incidental reading. Dont read it in the kitchen, when youre cooking; read it in the living room, in front of the television set, something like that.

Space Shuttle

I love the idea of space exploration. I guess I'd rather see the Government waste money on space exploration than on just about anything else there is. I suppose all of you watched the spaceship Columbia land Tuesday. Its always exciting. Makes us proud to be Americans.

There is a problem, though. Pretty soon I think theyve got to let us in on exactly what it is theyre looking for out there. We all knew what they were doing thirteen years ago when they went to the moon. They were trying to find out what the moon was made of.

NEIL ARMSTRONG (stepping onto the moon):
One small step for a man, one giant leap for mankind.

ROONEY:
That landing on the moon in 1969 was one of the single most exciting events in the whole history of the world.

PRESIDENT RICHARD NIXON (on phone to astronauts on moon):
For every American, this has to be the proudest day of our lives. And for people all over the world . . .

ROONEY:
Its as if we had pictures of Christopher Columbus discovering America. The moon, of course, turned out to be one big dull rock. Cost us $25 billion to get there, and no one's been back in ten years. Most of us would rather see them go back to the moon, I think, than do what theyre doing now. Maybe build something up there that we could see from down here. McDonald's, something like that—anything American.

We're beginning to look for practical results from our space shots. Tell us we'll be able to spy on the Russians—look right through the Kremlin windows. Thats what we want to hear. We want someone up there looking down who can catch the guy breaking into our house. Maybe they could find some wonderful new place out there for us to go on summer vacation. We wouldnt even mind if they figured a way to get some of that speed into the trip to Chicago.

Americans are practical people. They dont care what effect orbiting the Earth has on a ballpoint pen. This last trip they said they wanted to find out what effect the sun would have on the tail end of a spaceship. That isnt good enough, NASA. For this kind of money, we expect you to find out things like how many miles outer space goes; and if it ever ends, what's just beyond there. The space program's been getting a little vague since Walter Cronkite dropped out of it.

Credits

At the end of every television broadcast, the names of the people who worked on it are listed. Why, you may ask yourself sometimes, would so many people want to take credit for such a bad show? Well, its just like what's happened to the dollar. Credits in television suffer from inflation. There are more of them and they arent worth what they used to be, even on the good shows. It used to be a television broadcast had a producer, a writer and a director. Now a show can have something like this:

SENIOR EXECUTIVE PRODUCER He doesnt do anything. If the show is being done in New York, he flies to Los Angeles a lot. And if the show is being done in L.A., he's always having to go to New York.

SENIOR PRODUCER He's worked for the company a long time, and they gave him the title instead of a raise.

ASSOCIATE PRODUCER The Associate Producer is important usually but none of the other producers will associate with him because they all make a lot more money than he does.

Then maybe theres:

a COORDINATING PRODUCER This is often a woman named Linda.

an ASSISTANT TO THE PRODUCER

and a PRODUCTION ASSISTANT This is the vice president's son or daughter getting a start in business after flunking out of college.

DIRECTOR The director's in charge of the cameras, of course, so youll notice that his name usually stands alone and stands there longer than anyone else's.

the ASSOCIATE DIRECTOR

ASSISTANT DIRECTOR

ART DIRECTOR He directs anyone named Art.

CONSULTANT He or she is often a friend of the executive producer's wife from a former marriage.

There are a lot more special credits, of course.

HAIR DESIGNED BY

HOTEL ACCOMMODATIONS PROVIDED BY This means the show was too cheap to pay its own hotel bill.

And of course:

MR. ROONEY'S WARDROBE BY This means someone gave the star a suit with square shoulders.

But even the credits on *60 Minutes* have changed. On the second show fourteen years ago there were thirty-five names. On January 24 of this year there were sixty names. And of course, *60 Minutes* is still the same length it always was—fifty-two minutes.

You may think credits go by too fast to read but you arent supposed to be able to read them. Credits are only meant to be read by the person's agent and his mother.

And if all of us in television had to choose between credit and money, we'd do the right thing.

Weather

President Reagan must be happy over how bad the weather's been this winter, because its the one thing no one's blaming on him. Theres nothing television news likes better than bad weather, and we sure get a lot of it in the United States.

Several times a year one part of the Country or another provides cameras with great flood pictures. President Reagan himself had his picture taken putting his finger in the dike in Fort Wayne, Indiana, recently.

The Gulf Coast of Florida is often hit with a photogenic hurricane for television. Its called a hurricane when the winds reach seventy-three miles an hour; sixty-nine miles an hour is just a strong wind. Parts of Colorado got forty feet of snow this winter, and New England had a lot. A lot of snow isnt like a lot of rain, and the places that get the snow dont usually mind. They know how to work in it—and to play in it. They know what to do with snow. They like snow.

The Midwest and the Southwest often get a tornado or a cyclone. My dictionary doesnt make it crystal clear what the difference is between a cyclone and a tornado.

In the California desert, they have some of the worst heat in the world. It often goes as high as 130 degrees in the summer. Heat may be the worst weather we have, but it doesnt make as good pictures for television as floods or snow.

Because the weather's been so bad this winter, I was trying to think which city in the United States has the worst weather. You cant count out Bismarck, North Dakota. It goes down to 40 below in Bismarck in the winter, and it has been as high as 114 in summer.

Omaha, Nebraska, is no bargain. Neither is Louisville, Kentucky.

Los Angeles would win the worst weather award, if you were talking about what people have done to ruin naturally good weather.

Washington, D.C., does the worst job with what weather it gets. Washington keeps thinking its a

Southern city, and it isnt. Three or four times a year, it gets snow, and everyone goes around talking about how unusual it is for them to have snow. It isnt unusual. Three feet doesnt bother Vermont or Minnesota; an inch and a half brings Washington, D.C., to a standstill. The Government shuts down.

Two candidates for worst weather are New York and Chicago. Chicago probably has the edge. Ive taken a little survey among CBS News people who travel a lot. Their vote for the city with the worst weather was a tie. Those cities are Houston, Texas, and—

Sorry about that, Buffalo, but people are best where weather is worst.

Twofers

I wish people who sell things would stop trying to guess how many of something we want to buy. I want to buy things one at a time.

Saturday, I went to the supermarket to buy the ingredients for a Chinese beef dish. I wanted one green pepper. They came in packages of six. I didnt want six green peppers.

Every once in a while I have a desire to eat an apple. I dont have a desire to eat six apples.

Theyre packaging everything in groups now.

Ive got a package of four shoelaces. I know when one shoelace breaks, I should change them both, but I dont. My life just isnt that well-organized. I use shoelaces one at a time. I dont want four shoelaces.

Hangers come in packages of four. How do they know I dont want three hangers or five hangers or nine hangers? Why do socks and jockey shorts come in packs of three and hangers in packs of four? Batteries now always come in packages of two or four. It just so

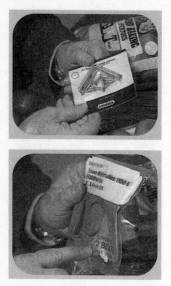

happens I have a flashlight that takes three batteries. What do I do with the odd one?

Hardware stores are packaging a lot of things now because its neater and more convenient for them. Angle irons, for instance, in packages of two. You need one angle iron, so you buy a package of two. You dont need another for three years, but by that time of course you cant find the one you had left over from the last package, so you buy two new ones—for a job that only calls for one. It isnt the cost, its the waste.

Vacuum cleaner drive belts come in packages of two. We've had our vacuum cleaner for fourteen years now, and it still has its original drive belt. Say that breaks tomorrow. I go buy this package of two. We use one. That'll take us another fourteen years, until 1996. If I can find this second drive belt by then, I'll put it on. The second belt should take us another fourteen years. That'll be the year 2010. Well, in twenty-eight years the vacuum cleaner will be forty-two, I'll be eighty-nine—and frankly, if I live to be eighty-nine, I wont care whether theres dust under the bed or not!

Tanks

President Reagan wants to spend $216 billion on defense and war equipment next year. He's going to spend a lot of it on tanks. The Army's released a film it made with pictures of the new M–1 tank and an armored bulldozer that goes with it.

I think they have the same writer they had when I was in the Army. You notice that over the years when the Army shows us a new tank, the tank is always doing its fanciest stuff, but its doing it in an open field somewhere. I want to see the tank go into those woods there. Thats where the enemy is. But see, tanks dont work in the woods. Tanks have been a problem everywhere. The Russians always show their tanks rolling through Red Square. I hope Russia spends a lot of money on tanks because tanks are at their best in parades. But wars arent fought in Red Square or in open fields. Today's battlefield is not usually a field at all. Its a small city, or a town with narrow streets. Its woods, or beaches, or water. Tanks dont work in places like that.

Army films about tanks always have very shallow water. They dont talk much about Omaha Beach on D-Day when a great many of the tanks were unloaded in twelve feet of water, where their crews drowned.

I dont want to be negative about all this, though, and I do have a positive idea. The new M–1 tanks are going to cost $2.7 million each. That means for every tank you could buy more than 300 Chrysler Le-Barons. From my experience in Germany with the Second Armored Division, I can tell you that 300 Chryslers would have been more help than one tank. The Army's going to spend $19 billion for 7,000 new tanks. Chrysler LeBarons cost about $8,000. So for $19 billion you could buy 2,375,000 Chrysler LeBarons. That means that every soldier in our Army could have three brand new cars all his own. I'd just like to see what that could do for reenlistment. They dont put an estimated mileage sticker on the new tanks, of course, because the tanks need four gallons of gas to go one mile. If I were President Reagan, I'd forget those tanks, buy 2,375,000 LeBarons, make Lee Iacocca their commanding general, and solve this whole budget crisis with a healthy rebate from Chrysler.

Maps

I tend to get lost a lot when I drive anywhere. Ive been lost in just about every State in the Union.

When it comes to getting lost, there are two kinds of drivers. The first kind hardly ever gets lost, but when he does he stops and asks directions.

The other driver, my kind, gets lost a lot but never stops to ask anything of anyone. He just keeps going no matter how lost he is and no matter how mad the person sitting next to him gets.

The alternative to stopping to ask directions, of course, is the road map. I dont use maps much when Im lost, either. Very often, a map is the reason why Im lost. I dont know why it is, but where I am on the road never looks like where I ought to be on the map. On the map, the road definitely goes this way; in the car, the road sort of goes this way.

Exxon is the only oil company that still gives away free road maps. They have about twenty-three maps that cover forty-one states. I talked with their map maker, and he's got his problems too. The little states with a lot of roads and cities are the tough ones for him—New Jersey or Rhode Island, for instance. Rhode Island has 6,500 miles of roads, and its tiny compared to a State like Montana. California and Tennessee are tough for map-makers too. They have to fit on basically the same size sheet of paper, but Tennessee is long and narrow and runs east and west; and California isnt very wide, but its long up and down. And they have to go on the same size sheet of paper. What the map makers love are the square states without much in them, like Wyoming.

Most drivers arent satisfied having a passenger tell them which way to turn, even if the passenger has a map. The driver wants to see the map himself. That means pulling over and stopping—and then comes the hard part. First, you have to find out which side of the paper its on, the map you want; then you have to fold it so you can handle it, see where you are; then you try to locate your position. Now, none of these problems is the worst thing about a car map, though. The worst thing about a car map is trying to fold it back the way you found it, and get it back in the glove compartment.

To tell you the truth, I'd rather get lost. Sometimes getting lost is the most fun I have on a long drive.

Gloves

The way I can tell when winter's about over is by my gloves. You can tell its been a long winter already, because I have ten gloves here without mates, six lefts and four rights. And of course, that doesnt include the pairs Ive lost both of. If I had my choice, I'd rather lose a whole pair than just one. One good glove is so sad. If you lose both of them, you forget it. The wound heals quickly. But it breaks my heart every time I look at some of these I only have one of. I cant stand to throw them away either. I keep hoping the mate will come home.

I dont know where gloves go. I lose so many and find so few. I dont buy expensive gloves anymore. I buy work gloves, even to play in. My daughter gave me the only really good gloves I own. Everyone said I'd lose them. Every time I go out of the house now, someone says, "Dont lose those good gloves Ellen gave you!" Well, I havent lost them. I havent lost them because Im so scared of losing them that I havent worn them.

I dont think Ive ever had a pair of gloves that were too short in the fingers. I must have stubby hands. I always have a little part left over.

Ive had one pair of mittens for years now. It says, "Genuine deerskin, full lamb-lined." Youd think the deer would have thought of that, wouldnt you? These are nice and warm, but name one thing you could do well if youre wearing mittens. Nothing!

Gloves always seem like a good idea when I leave the house on a cold morning, but I never leave them on my hands for long. I take them off to do something and end up carrying them in my hands, stuffing them in my pocket or losing them.

I guess I can make out with these work gloves for the rest of the winter. I just hope I dont have to go anywhere fancy.

Fast / Slow

There are fast people and there are slow people in the world. The same things keep happening to the same people all their lives, because they do things either too fast or too slow. Theres no in-between.

Eating, for instance.

A fast person is getting finished while everyone else at the table is just getting started.

The slow eater often puts down his knife and his fork as if he was done and talks for a while. In a restaurant, the waiter will come along and ask if he's finished. He isnt.

Fast eaters ask for a check, quick.

Getting off an airplane separates the fast people from the slow people.

Fast people unfasten their seat belts as soon as the plane touches down. Before the plane gets to the gate, they stand up. The pilot tells them to sit down.

Slow people on an airplane dont unfasten their seatbelts until the plane comes to a full stop, like the pilot says. Then they start getting their things together.

If youre a fast person trapped in a window seat, slow people drive you crazy.

At the movies, the fast person is out on the street before the credits are over.

The slow person is looking for his or her gloves on the theater floor.

Fast people get driven crazy more than slow people, because theyre always getting trapped inside or behind them.

Fast people dress in a hurry and get out of the house.Theyre waiting in the car in the driveway, for the slow people to come out.

Slow people are upstairs. Theyre making sure that all the windows are closed.

Fast people watch the traffic light like a hawk and take off the instant it turns green.

Slow people comb their hair in the rear-view mirror and wait until some-one behind them blows the horn.

Fast people drive sixty-five in a fifty-five-miles-per-hour zone.

The slow people drive thirty-five, forty miles per hour in a fifty-five-miles-per-hour zone.

Fast people get where theyre going late.

The slow people get there early.

Fast people get up and switch all the channels looking for a better television show all the time.

Slow people set the channel once, early in the evening, and never really touch it again until its time for bed.

Im not going to tell you which kind I am, but if you see me coming—

I'd appreciate it if youd get out of my way.

Dumb Letters

My friend Reed Alvord says he's always been suspicious of a person who writes a lot of letters and ends them all with "Sincerely." I agree. And furthermore, Im not sure all letters should begin with "Dear." I often get letters at home that start out, "Dear Sir or Madam." Isnt that nice? This fellow calls me "dear" and he doesnt know whether Im a man or a woman. I wonder what that makes him?

I get a lot of mail here, and most of its very nice. Its fun to read. I do get some dumb letters, though. Here's a fellow from Hobson, Montana. Three pages. He wants me to do something about Poland. I would do something about Poland, sir, but I promised myself I'd get a haircut this afternoon. I mean, do I strike you as someone who could do something about Poland? Here's one from a school kid. "Dear Mr. Rooney: My teacher has assigned me interviewing a famous person. Please answer these questions and mail it back to me. I have to have it Thursday." Theyre always in a hurry. This kid not only wants me to do his homework for him, he wants me to be quick about it.

A lot of them ask God to bless me. If they ask God to bless me, the letter is usually at least three or four pages long. I dont know why that is.

I received a lot of mail about the piece I did on gloves a while back. I lose gloves. Jean Watson of Kalamazoo, Michigan, says, "Regarding your story on lost gloves, why dont you have your mommy sew a cord on them so you can run them through your sleeves?" No one likes a wise guy, Jean. Here's a funny one about gloves from someone in Saint Helens, Oregon. She says, "A woman looked out the train window—it was pulling away from the station—and saw one of her good new gloves on the platform. The woman quickly stood on the seat, opened the train window, and threw her other glove out." Now thats what I call a nice person. Someone found a *pair* of good gloves.

Here's one from someone named John Rappel of Chicago. "Dear Andy: What are Mike Wallace, Morley Safer, Ed Bradley and Harry Reasoner really like? Are they as nice as they seem?" Well, Mr. Rappel, as Ive said before, two of them are and two of them arent.

Car Names

I wish I was more confident our auto makers in Detroit knew what they were doing. They arent doing very good, we all know that. We're all worried about it too, I think. We wish their business would get better. Even Americans who drive Volkswagens and Toyotas are worried about it. People who drive Mercedes are worried because they own General Motors stock. One place I think Detroit's wrong is with the names theyre giving their cars.

When I was young, the time passed quickly on long rides because kids in the back seat would make a game out of counting cars. "I got a Packard!" "I got two Oldsmobiles!" "I got four Buicks!" "I got a Pierce Arrow!" Well, kids dont play that game any more, because even kids cant tell a Cavalier from a Citation or a Malibu from a Mirada. For years, the biggest-selling American car was called just plain Chevrolet. Do you realize theres no longer a car called just plain Chevrolet? Why would they throw away a great old car name like that? The name Chevrolet doesnt even appear on the car in some models. If you want a Chevy now, you have to buy one of these—Camaro, Citation, Chevette. Looks as if they started to give them all names beginning with "C," and couldnt think of any more when they got to Monte Carlo. Of course, they could have called that a Carlo Monte.

Ford still puts the Ford name on all its cars, but the cars are all called something else. Car companies tend to follow each other around with an idea like this. If one does it, they all do it sooner or later. Fords are all Mustangs, Granadas, Thunderbirds or Fairmont Futuras. Fairmont was a model of a Ford, and Futura was a model of a Fairmont last year. This year, theyre all Fairmont Futuras, and there are different models of those. Now, how do they expect us to keep track and be proud of the name of our car?

Already you can see the wave of the future in car names. I was at a car show last week. We've already got the letters—the K-car and the J-car—and now theyre going to numbers. You know, they'll be the XKD–6000 or the DKX–8000. The DKX will be a convertible, and if it starts raining while you have the top down, youll just be able to press a button on the dashboard and, presto, it'll stop raining.

My idea for how Detroit could improve business would be for them to spend less time naming their cars and more time making them.

1983

You're Fired!

No one ever gets fired any more. If you're an auto worker in Detroit, you get "laid off." Some companies give office workers "early retirement." If you have a big job in Government in Washington and get the axe, you "resign."

Cabinet members like Al Haig or Richard Schweiker "resign" because of "policy differences."

Even if you get caught with your hand in the till in Washington, you don't get fired. Congressman Fred Richmond was found guilty of income tax evasion, drug possession and bribery. He "resigned" from Congress so he could serve a year in jail. I guess it'll look better on his resume.

Senator Harrison Williams, who was caught with his hand in the till in the Abscam caper, resigned too; probably quit so he could spend more time with his family.

Anne Gorsuch Burford has just resigned. She was President Reagan's environmental protection administrator. It was the same familiar dance. Several congressmen accused her of wrongdoing. She denied it. The President kept saying he had complete confidence in her.

Last Wednesday, someone released a resignation statement.

BILL PLANTE (CBS News):
She offered her resignation, for reasons that we are told were entirely personal. It was accepted. President Reagan called her resignation "an act of unselfishness and personal courage." He said that she had faithfully carried out her mission.

ROONEY:
Come on, Mr. President! Why is it so difficult to get the truth about anything anymore? President Reagan's an honorable man. Why would he act as if there wasn't a chance in the world he was about to fire the woman? Why would he try to con us? The President always made it sound as if the reporters had invented the whole thing, just to cause trouble.

PLANTE (at news conference):
Is there a scandal brewing over at EPA?

PRESIDENT RONALD REAGAN:

No. Theres one viewing at—brewing in the media thats talking about it.

ROONEY:

She did the same thing. You wouldnt have dreamed she knew she was about to get fired.

ANNE GORSUCH BURFORD:

Im trying to do a good job. Im trying to protect the environment. Im trying to run an agency.

ROONEY:

I dont know. We're so used to hearing things we know arent true in our lives—in advertising, in political speeches, everywhere. We're even used to friends saying theyre just fine when we know theyre sick. We're used to everyone not saying quite what they mean. But wouldnt it be nice if just once the President of the United States caught someone doing something wrong and said, "You! Out! Pick up and leave, and dont give my name as a reference. Youre fired!"

Travel Folders

Ive got a batch of travel brochures here. Its never been absolutely clear to me why people like to go away as much as they do, but theres no doubt about it: Americans love to travel. The only thing better than taking a trip for me is coming home from one.

The people who write these travel folders live in a world of their own. They make every foreign country in the world look beautiful and exotic. Scenery's always magnificent. Water's always crystal clear and blue—never any polluted water in these travel brochures. And theyre filled with scenes of natural wonders, too. Apparently it never rains in any of these foreign countries. Ive been looking at travel pictures in brochures and magazines since I was a kid. I dont think I ever saw a rainy day in one.

The travel agents and airlines all have special plans. Tahiti Holidays, seven days, from $699; Bora-Bora Holidays, seven days, from $911; New Zealand Holiday, fourteen days, from $1,741. Its that "from" you have to watch out for. If you believe thats all its going to cost you, you could easily decide it was cheaper to go away than to stay home.

The natives are always dressed in colorful costumes, according to the pictures in these brochures. The Guard is always just changing at Buckingham Palace. Youd think everyone in these faraway places went around looking like this all day. When you actually get to these places, everyone is dressed just like you are. They all look like they come from St. Louis.

My favorite travel advertising is for Hawaii and those exotic islands in the Caribbean. The girls in the pictures are all built like Bo Derek, wearing tiny bikinis. Ive been to some of these places. I dont know where they all go when I get there. Ive waded in Waikiki. I never saw a girl like that there. And none of the guys look like him, either.

I guess the travel business hasnt been very good lately. I say that because you never see any crowds in these pictures. The beaches are almost always empty, just you and a girl in a bikini.

Teethbrushes

You never get over worrying about brushing your teeth, I dont think. I bought a new toothbrush the other day. I didnt realize there were so many different kinds. And Im not sure why they call them toothbrushes either. Its as though you were only brushing one tooth. Why not teethbrushes?

You have to decide whether you want one soft, medium or hard, too. I avoid the hard ones because Im afraid of wearing away the enamel on my teeth. For six months a year, I treat my teeth with kid gloves. Then I go to the dentist and he cleans them with sandpaper, a chisel, a wire brush and a quarter-inch drill.

The people who make teethbrushes always talk as if their brush was the only one a dentist would use. "The head dentists prefer . . . " "Recommended by dentists." Obviously, they are trying to get in good with dentists. "See your dentist twice a year." ". . . when used as directed by your dentist." Did your dentist ever direct you how to brush your teeth? All he ever says to me is, "Spit out, please." This label says, "Theres a Butler toothbrush for every member of the family." Well, I certainly hope so. I dont want anyone else using my toothbrush.

I think I know why they make some toothbrushes in such terrible colors. Compared to these, anyone's teeth would look good. Colgate's box says "new color." Come on, Colgate, you can do better than that. This toothbrush is red. Red isnt a new color. We've had red for years. I had a friend named Red when I was twelve years old.

They keep making the handles in different shapes, as if that was going to put an end to false teeth. Some brushes have those rubber things on the end. Dentists may like these, but I hate them because they wont fit down through the hole in the toothbrush holder.

Theres a class toothbrush with real bristles. The instructions are written in English and French. You can tell anything's expensive when the instructions are written in two languages.

One brush from Squibb says it has hundreds of bristles. I thought I'd do a hard-hitting, investigative piece for *60 Minutes*, so we cut off all the bristles and counted them. Here are the results of that investigation. There were more than hundreds. There were 1,260 bristles. Now you know why Im not one of the investigative reporters on *60 Minutes*.

Theres an automatic electric toothbrush. It says it goes up and down 3,600 times a minute. What if you want to go sideways a few times?

I dont know, I think I'll stick to brushing my teeth by hand. Some days brushing my teeth is the only exercise I get.

Report Card

In the past couple of months, Ive stayed at several hotels and flown with a couple of airlines that give you one of those report cards to fill out. They want to know how theyre doing with you.

American Airlines, for instance. They said that they were delighted to have me on board and would I answer these twenty-four questions. Well, American's a good airline, but theyre asking for trouble with something like this. "What did you do with your baggage today?" is question number nine. Let me ask you some questions, American Airlines! What did *you* do with my baggage?

There are a lot of questions I'd like to ask. How come the seats are so small and close together now?

How come it costs $377 to fly to Los Angeles from New York one day, and only $99 the next?

Here's one. They want you to tell them what you think of the flight attendants. When you finish answering the questions, youre supposed to turn this in to your flight attendant. If I said the flight attendant was poor and turned this in to her, what chance do you think there'd be of anyone else ever seeing it, or of me getting a life jacket if we went down in the water?

Howard Johnson wants to know how I like their hotel. How was the room? How were the services? Excellent, satisfactory or unsatisfactory?

I'd like to ask you some questions, too, Howard. How come I cant get the windows open in half the hotel rooms I stay in?

Here's one from the Century Plaza Hotel in Los Angeles. Question number five: "Is there something about your room youd like to see changed?" Well, yes, as a matter of fact there is. Your average room costs about $125. You could change that to half if you wanted to.

I got this one in a Hertz Rent-A-Car. "How do we rate?" Hertz only asks eight questions. The last one says, "Are there any additional comments you may have about this car-rental experience?"

Well, something does come to my mind, Hertz. How come the place where your cars were parked at the airport was two miles farther away than my hotel in town?

Hertz values my patronage, it says.

I think the best report card a company can have is the business theyre doing. If business is good, they dont need answers from me.

Reagan's Budget

Tonight I'd like to go over the federal budget with you. President Reagan goes over the budget every year, of course.

The first thing to do, if youre going to take a good look at something, is to write it down. Our national debt is one trillion dollars. This is what a trillion dollars looks like: $1,000,000,000,000. Its a lot of zeroes. Last year the Government borrowed another $100-billion. Not million; *billion* dollars! You think it borrowed $100 billion so it could give us all something nice, like a new highway? No. The Government used that $100 billion it borrowed to pay interest on the trillion dollars it already owes. Next year it'll have to borrow even more because it'll have to pay interest on one trillion one-hundred billion dollars. That'll look like this: $1,100,000,000,000. You only have to change one number. We make it too easy for them.

When President Reagan was a candidate, he said he was going to balance the budget. Let's let him explain what happened.

PRESIDENT RONALD REAGAN:
Since there have been, in spite of all the talk and the term budget cuts, there have been no budget cuts. Each year, spending has gone up.

Well, I dont think I have to say anything more, except to say I think I know why President Reagan and all the other Presidents have never been able to balance the budget. Its because once a President gets into office, he gets out of touch with money. Do you think President Reagan takes his money out of his pants pocket every night and puts it on top of his dresser? Or in his dresser drawer, so Nancy wont pick at it? Of course not. A President doesnt carry money, because he never needs any. What's he going to do with it? He cant spend it. Does he go to the store? Does he buy lunch when the king of some place comes to Washington? Does he take the White House limousine to the gas station and say, "Fill 'er up" or "$15 worth of regular, please"? He does not. I'll bet the President doesnt have a nickel in his pants pocket this very minute.

Its not that President Reagan's cheap. Its just that no one ever lets a President pay for anything.

I'll tell you what I'd like to see. I'd like to see him have to write $1 trillion on the blackboard a hundred times every day. And it wouldnt hurt if he had to go out every morning and buy his own newspaper with cash, either.

Age Limits

We have some funny ideas about what age its okay to do things in this Country. Sometimes it seems as though the age limits are set because of our brains, sometimes because of our bodies.

For instance, you can join the Army when youre seventeen, but after youre thirty-five they dont want you anymore. On the other hand, if you want to be President, you cant run for the office until you are thirty-five. Obviously, the Army thinks the body's shot at thirty-five, and the writers of the Constitution didnt think anyone was smart enough to be President until they were thirty-five.

Youre supposed to be smart enough to be a senator when youre thirty. To be a congressman, you dont have to be very smart at all: twenty-five.

In fourteen states you can get a driver's license when youre fourteen.

Marriage laws vary wildly. In Texas, Utah, Alabama and New Hampshire you can get married when youre fourteen, if your parents approve. In Utah you have to be sixteen, if youre a boy. In Alabama the law says you dont have to have your parents' permission to get married at fourteen—if youve already been married before.

You couldnt drive to your own wedding in any of these states, because their driving age is sixteen. In most states you can get married before you can get in to see a dirty movie without your parents' permission. Seems funny! In other words, if a fourteen-year-old girl in Utah got married to a sixteen-year-old boy and they had a baby and then some night they wanted to go out and see an R-rated movie, theyd have to bring the baby's grandmother along.

The states are most divided about drinking laws. They keep changing. Theyve just raised the drinking age in my State, Connecticut, and I approve of that. Drinking's a bad habit, and I dont care how high they raise the drinking age, just as long as they keep it under my age.

Catalogues

I think we've got to do something about Christmas catalogues. Ive already got dozens this year. A lot of them are beautifully done and obviously expensive, but I throw most of them out without even looking at them. Ive never liked buying anything from a catalogue.

I have two ideas about what to do with these. First, maybe someone ought to put out a catalogue catalogue. In September, we'd each get a catalogue that had the covers of every other catalogue being put out. We could mark what we wanted to receive and what we didnt want to receive. That way, we'd only get what we wanted.

I have an even better idea, though. Make every company that sends out one of these Christmas catalogues put two names and addresses on each one of them. If it was for me, for instance, it would have my name up in the corner, and when I was finished with the catalogue, I'd peel off the label. Underneath would be the name and address of a Russian citizen, someone living in the Soviet Union. All we'd do is peel this off and put the catalogue back in the mail, headed for Russia. A man I met in Russia several years ago told me I could send him one letter and the authorities would let that go through.

How would that be for propaganda? Flood Russia with Christmas catalogues from Saks Fifth Avenue, Bloomingdale's, Tiffany's, Macy's, Garfinkel's, L. L. Bean, I. Magnin.

Our Christmas catalogues are really beautiful. But if you dont want them, theyre junk. I dont want most of mine, but I feel terrible throwing them out. I'd just love to let a few million Russians see what's available here for Christmas this year.

Dairy Subsidies

President Reagan signed a bill this week that will pay dairy farmers not to produce milk. It means higher milk prices for the rest of us, but the dairy farmers are happy about it. This follows President Reagan's program last year that paid wheat farmers not to grow wheat.

Its the kind of program I'd like to get in on. Im a writer. Thats what Im producing, writing.

Milk producers are producing milk faster than the rest of us are drinking it. Writers are doing the same thing. Writers are writing it faster than you readers are reading it. We need some government help, too. The bookstores are filled with books people arent buying.

Which do you spend most on in a year? Milk or books? Milk, I bet. So, why isnt the Government buying surplus books? It could make powdered books and stockpile them against a rainy day.

Why isnt the Government paying writers not to write so much? If I were paid not to write on *60 Minutes*, not to write my newspaper column, not to write books, it would cut down on surplus writing and at the same time provide me with a good living at government expense.

How much would the Government have to pay writers not to write? Make us an offer, Mr. President.

What do you produce? Write your congressman. Write the President. Get yourself a government subsidy for not doing something. Dont be the last sucker on your block working for a living.

1984

Dog Show

I went to the Westminster Dog Show again this year. Going to the dog show somehow eliminates the need I have to own a dog. I met some great dogs there.

I like big dogs better than small dogs. If you can carry a dog, its too small. I want a dog, not another baby.

Some of these dogs must watch a lot of television. They seem to recognize me.

My favorite's the bulldog. We used to own a bulldog. I'd get another dog if it wasnt so sad when they die.

Ive never cared much for poodles. I think its because of what people do to them. No one likes a dog with a fancy haircut. No wonder poodles are dropping in popularity.

The big news in the dog show world is that, for the first time in sixteen years, the poodle is not the most popular dog in America. The American Kennel Club's made a list of fifty different breeds, in order of their popularity.

Number one in 1983 was the cocker spaniel. The Labrador is three, and thats good, but look at this! In fourth place is the Doberman pinscher. Now, how come a nasty dog like the Doberman is ahead of a sweet dog like the golden retriever, in sixth place? The collie is way down at seventeenth place this year, and the boxer has dropped to twenty-two. Here's the Lhasa apso—thats a new dog—way up to thirteenth.

I always like the dogs better than the dog show. Professional dog handlers and dog show judges have a funny idea about how to judge a good dog. They keep making them stand the way the judge thinks they ought to stand—not the way the dogs think they ought to stand. Leave him alone, for gosh sakes!

If I were a judge, I'd have different standards. I'd take points away from any dog whose hair had been blow-dried, or combed by a person, or fussed over too much.

I'd give the most points for friendliness. They dont seem to count friendliness at all at a dog show.

And personality would be a big factor with me.

I'd give dogs points if they could relax.

If I were judging dogs, I'd sit down and talk it over with them. The winners would not only be good with young children; theyd also like old writers.

Famous People

We're getting awfully short of famous people in America. Just a few years back, we were short of oil. Now its famous people. Famous people are an important part of our economy. Unless we have plenty of them, a lot of Americans who depend on them for their livelihood will be going out of business.

Theres a growing need for them, too. Take a good gossip column in a newspaper. It can go through twenty or thirty names in a day. Magazines need them, especially the magazines that specialize in famous people. Some of those come out every week. They need a new famous person on the cover every time. Thats fifty-two a year. Where are they all going to come from?

Sports Illustrated has had to use Muhammad Ali on its cover twenty-nine times. theyre even short of famous sports people.

I mean, how many really famous people are there? President Reagan, Jacqueline Kennedy, Henry Kissinger, Paul McCartney—I dont know, probably no more than twenty or thirty all together.

Take Michael Jackson, for instance. He's one of the best known Americans, to some people, but he's not a genuinely famous person, because a lot of other Americans never heard of him.

John Kenneth Galbraith is like Michael Jackson. Genuinely famous people should have heard of each other, and I doubt if Michael Jackson and John Kenneth Galbraith ever heard of each other.

Television shows use up a lot of famous people, shows like Johnny Carson, Merv Griffin, and local news shows, too. They grab any famous person who comes to town. Usually that famous person is selling a book, a television show or a movie. You can tell by the introduction whether the guest is really famous or not. If they have to keep superimposing his or her name on the screen, the guest is only semi-famous.

I can tell Im not a genuinely famous person, because half the people who stop me on the street think Im either Art Rooney, Charles Kuralt or someone they knew in high school.

Hiding Places

We're running out of places to hide things. No one puts anything under the mattress or in the sugar bowl anymore.

President Reagan has the whole Country. He cant even find a place to hide the MX missile.

There used to be places in the middle of our Country that hardly anyone knew about. Not any more! The Russians probably dont even have as many spies here as they once did because we dont have as many things hidden that they cant find.

Kids used to be able to hide in tree houses they built in vacant lots. There arent any vacant lots left, hardly any tree houses, no place at all for a kid to hide.

Houses are built differently. In old houses, there were some corners no one knew about, but not in new houses. No corners to hide in, no basement, no attic.

In a lot of the banks around the Country theyve even run out of safe deposit boxes. People want safe deposit boxes so they can hide the jewelry they dont dare wear because they have no place to hide it in their homes when they arent wearing it.

One of the most common things we all try to hide is the key to the house. Everyone used to hide the key under the doormat. We all knew where the key was hidden. It was an unwritten American agreement. You cant do that anymore.

They used to make men's pants with a little watch pocket. No one used it for a watch. You used it to hide a few bills folded up there for an emergency. They dont put the watch pocket in pants anymore.

Im always running out of money in the office, so I like to keep a ten--or twenty--dollar bill hidden somewhere for an emergency. I usually keep it in the dictionary under "M," on the page with the definition of money. Everyone on the floor knows where it is. I might as well leave it right here on my desk.

We're just terribly short of good hiding places in America.

Good Statistics

I keep meeting people who are tired of me because I never say anything good about things, and Im tired of them. Many of you feel that everyone in television news looks at the negative side of everything. Tonight we're going to look on the brighter side of some statistics.

We're always reporting crimes. Did you realize that 99 percent of all Americans are not now, and never have been, in prison? There are 235 million of us and only 1,955,500 people have ever been in jail or prison.

Divorce. From news reports, youd think everyone gets divorced. Not true. Ninety-nine million married Americans have never been divorced. Only 12 percent of the population is divorced; and, of course, each divorce counts for two people.

In the past ten years, 50 million American cars have *not* had to be recalled because of manufacturing defects. They were perfect.

Ninety-five percent of all the farmers are not in danger of bankruptcy. Eighty percent of them arent even in any trouble.

You worried about murder? Forget it. Last year 99.98 percent of all the people in this Country didnt murder anyone.

And here's an even better statistic. The average baby born in the United States this year will still be alive in the year 2057.

Drop-outs. Everyone talks about kids dropping out of school. Eighty-five percent of all the high school students we have do not drop out: they graduate. Pretty good!

Sixty-three percent of all adults dont smoke cigarettes. Eighty-seven percent of all teenagers dont smoke, or at least they say the dont; they may sneak one once in a while.

Drugs. Youd think everyone took them, if you read the papers and listened to television. The fact is, there are only seven million hard-drug users and thirty million marijuana smokers; so, two hundred million Americans dont take any drugs at all.

In addition to that, Americans are kind to animals.

So, dont say I never say anything good about us.

Be Kind
to Politicians

Tonight, I want to speak to my colleagues, the newspapermen and women and the television reporters in this Country. The American public is tired of bad news and tired of all the bad things we're all saying about politicians. We've got to start being nicer to politicians. How would news-people like it if they had someone like Roger Mudd on their backs all the time? Every week, reporters pick on a different politician, it seems. Recently, its been President Reagan's Secretary of Labor Raymond Donovan. Just because Donovan was indicted on charges that could put him in jail for 551 years, newspeople thought it was a story. Big deal. They had to go blab it to everyone. Reporters are always giving the bad news about politicians.

LARRY KANE (Anchorman, WCAU, Philadelphia):
They were once political powerhouses in the Philadelphia area, tonight they are behind bars—six former Philadelphia-area politicians caught in the Abscam net.

ROONEY:
Arent there any good, honest politicians you could report on? Sure there are, probably. Who knows whether all these politicians did anything wrong or not, anyway? You say they did. They say they didnt.

REPRESENTATIVE DANIEL J. FLOOD (Democrat—Pennsylvania):
I deny, with all my heart, that I have committed any criminal offense.

SENATOR HARRISON A. WILLIAMS (Democrat—New Jersey):
In my heart, I know I did no wrong.

REPRESENTATIVE JOHN M. MURPHY (Democrat—New York):
I am not guilty of, and categorically deny—

VICE PRESIDENT SPIRO T. AGNEW:
. . . categorically and flatly deny the assertions . . .

PRESIDENT RICHARD M. NIXON:

. . . because people have got to know whether or not their President's a crook. Well, Im not a crook.

Why do reporters expect politicians to be perfect, when none of the reporters are? Is Mike Wallace perfect? Well, Mike may be an exception, but most reporters are not perfect. I hope President Reagan and Walter Mondale are nice to each other in these debates starting tonight, because the only people who say worse things about politicians than reporters say are other politicians.

The Debate

The big game last week was the debate. People are still arguing about who won. Let's look at some reruns of last week's game.

President Reagan clearly won the handshake. You see them both come out and shake hands.

Now let's watch that again. Here's the middle of the field, about there, and here are the two podiums. Watch who gets across midfield first. See Reagan coming on. There he is, in good field position, over in Mondale's territory.

Now they start back for their podiums. Each starts to draw. We'll see that in slow motion, and you can decide which man has the fastest draw with his speech. Youll notice President Reagan draws from the hip, Mondale from the chest.

I thought Mondale won neckties. They both wore good-looking ties. Reagan's was striped. Mondale's was spotted. Dotted, I guess, would be better to say. Mondale tied his necktie in the familiar four-in-hand knot. Reagan used the fancier Windsor, a Republican kind of a knot for an expensive tie.

Reagan won makeup hands down. Reagan is seventy-three and, with makeup, he looked sixty-three. Mondale is fifty-six. With makeup, he looked sixty-six.

Reagan won points with his joke, but Mondale struck right back. Let's take a look at that.

PRESIDENT RONALD REAGAN:

But I am not going to exploit for political purposes my opponent's youth and inexperience. (Crowd laughter)

ROONEY:

Reagan delivered his punchline; Mondale intercepted and came up with a very genuine and winning smile. It got him almost as many points as the joke got Reagan.

Theres always a big question about who you should look at when youre on camera. The candidates were divided on this, too. President Reagan always faced his questioner and answer him or her. Walter Mondale would start to answer the questioner, but then he'd remember he was told to look into the camera.

The experts have complained that most of us didnt pay close enough attention to the issues. Thats probably true. On the other hand, you can tell a lot about a man from the way he combs his hair.

Politics

Its always hard to believe the summer's really over. These are the days when you realize that time doesnt last as long as people think it does. The politicians certainly never gave us much vacation. Theyre still at it, just the way they were last spring. I have an idea that newspapers and television and politicians are more interested in politics than people are. This contest for who's going to be President has gone on for too long. If someone doesnt know who theyre going to vote for by now, they'll never know. The candidates fly someplace, theyre met by a cheering crowd, they give a speech. Does anyone come out to hear Geraldine Ferraro who isnt already going to vote for her? Would you cross the street to hear George Bush if you were a Mondale supporter?

Who are they trying to convince with their campaign speeches? Theyre talking to voters theyve already got. I figure once both candidates have made fools of themselves by putting on the American Legion hats, they ought to quit. Mondale wants to have six debates with the President. Six debates! There isnt a politician alive who couldnt tell us all we want to know about him- or herself in twenty minutes. In high school our debating team used to take one side of an issue one week and the opposite side of the same issue the next week. Thats what the candidates ought to do. They ought to switch positions once in a while.

VOICE OF WALTER MONDALE (over footage of President Reagan):
And theres not one party that believes in God and one that does not. (Applause)

VOICE OF PRESIDENT REAGAN (over footage of Walter Mondale):
First, we must rid ourselves of liberal superstition that crime is somehow the fault of society and not the wrongdoer who preys on innocent people. (Applause)

ROONEY:
This way, we get to know which one of them thinks best, and they get to know what to do after the election. Theres no doubt the election's taking too long. If it were a television show, it would have been canceled after four weeks. We could save everyone time and money by having the presidential election tomorrow and the inauguration a week from Wednesday.

Recipes

It seems to me that newspapers, magazines and television are pushing more recipes at us than anyone has time to eat, let alone cook. I read them, but I hardly ever try one because they always call for some ingredient we dont have in the house, you know—"Take two ripe pomegranates."

Here's something from the *Los Angeles Times* I dont plan to make for breakfast—French Tofu Toast. It starts—one half teaspoon of sweet basil seeds. Now, for me, thats a bad start. I hate trying to measure half a teaspoon of anything, and we dont happen to keep sweet basil seeds around the house all the time. Three tablespoons of water—we have that. Two tablespoons plus two teaspoons of lime juice. Would three full tablespoons of lime juice really ruin your Tofu Toast?

The pictures are always great. I love them. But if I made something that fancy and someone cut into it, I wouldnt like it. It ought to be framed, not eaten. Pictures in magazines dont look like the food they serve in the CBS cafeteria.

I guess if you wrote recipes for a living, after a couple of years youd get tired of the same old stuff. But they do some crazy things. Look at this—Peach Soup? I only eat ten peaches a year and I like them fine the way they are. I dont want peach soup.

Good Housekeeping has two pages of pineapple recipes, things to do with pineapple. You cant help wondering if *Good Housekeeping*'s enthusiasm for Pineapple Chicken has anything to do with this full-page ad for Dole pineapple on the next page.

McCall's has a recipe for pot roast. First, you take an eight-pound pot roast and you add all these things to the pot. Way down here, you add two sprigs of parsley. Will someone tell me what effect two sprigs of parsley is going to have on a big, tough piece of meat?

Family Circle has a bunch of diet menus. Here's one. For dessert, you get one persimmon. I suppose if you want to lose weight twice as fast, youd eat two persimmons.

Every once in a while, I'll pick up a recipe when Im cooking weekends and maybe forty-five minutes before dinner time, I'll decide to make it. I get started, and invariably, half way into the recipe it says set aside and marinate overnight.

We eat a lot of macaroni and cheese.

Telephone Books

Something's got to be done about phone books. These are the books for New York City alone in this pile, including the Yellow Pages.

Here's one for Louisville, Kentucky. Thats all right. Greater Baltimore, thats too big. Here's Detroit. Now why is Detroit so much smaller than Denver when Detroit is so much bigger than Denver? I guess the people in Detroit just drive over instead of calling.

This is the phone book for a little town I live in summers in upstate New York. Thats about the size a phone book ought to be. But I keep all these New York phone books in my office. I ought to charge the phone company for storage space. I hate them, too, because they wont stand up on edge. Theyre too floppy. You have to lay a phone book flat and it takes up too much space flat.

I just called the operator to find out how much it cost to call information for a number instead of looking it up yourself in the book. The operator said, "May I help you?" I said, "Yes, how much does it cost to call information?" She said, "What number do you want, sir?" I said, "I dont want any number. I want information. How much does it cost to call information?" She said, "Just a minute, sir. I'll give you my supervisor." Well, the supervisor told me it costs 40 cents in New York after the first two calls every time you call information for a number.

To tell you the truth, theres no one whose number I dont already know that I want to talk to that bad. I checked around a little. It costs 35 cents to call information in Dallas, 30 cents in Chicago and a quarter in Atlanta.

I always find the phone book hard to use. For instance, nothing in the Yellow Pages is ever listed where I look for it first. I want a doctor. Under *D*? Its under *P* for physician. No listing at all under eyeglasses. You have to go to optometrist or optician. I want to rent a car. Thats different. C-A-R, nothing. See automobile. Hertz, Avis, National, Budget are all under Automobile Rental. You want to buy a new car. You look under automobile dealers, new cars. You want a used car. You look under automobile dealers, used cars. Why dont they just call them new and used cars in the first place?

Here's my idea for all these. Put the telephone company back together and break up the phone books.

1985

Jaywalking

Last year in Los Angeles, there were 818 murders and 313 of the murderers got away with it without being caught. During that same time, the Los Angeles police issued 40,747 tickets to people who were caught crossing the street illegally.

Police in Chicago and Boston didnt give out any tickets for jaywalking. New York police gave out 517 in 1983. Drivers and walkers are at war with each other in America. Pedestrians hate drivers; drivers hate pedestrians.

Some cities dont have many pedestrians. In those cities, there are more drivers than walkers. A big city like Dallas, for example, doesnt have many pedestrians. Los Angeles doesnt have many either.

If youve ever crossed the street in both New York City and Los Angeles, you know how different an experience it can be. In New York City, anything goes. In Los Angeles, you wait on the curb. The nearest car may be in Beverly Hills, but you wait on the curb. Even drivers are more respectful of pedestrians in Los Angeles. The incredible fact is, the per capita death rate for pedestrians in Los Angeles is higher than in New York City.

In New York, a pedestrian's on his own. Its sink or swim. Crossing the street in New York keeps old people young—if they make it. The best street-crossers are graceful as a matador. In New York, the pedestrians move faster than the cars, usually. New York has spent millions installing "Walk" and "Dont Walk" traffic lights. New Yorkers find them attractive as street decorations. Then dont pay any attention to them.

This is just a bit of friendly advice. If youre crossing a street in New York, watch out for the cars. If youre in Los Angeles, watch out for the cops.

Super Bowl XIX

The Super Bowl game is next Sunday, and this year its being broadcast by ABC, opposite *60 Minutes*. So, its sort of nice of me to mention it at all. But because a lot of Americans who arent real fans watch the game, I thought it might be a good idea for me to explain some of the phrases youll be hearing from the game announcers.

When you hear one of them say, "This is a passing situation," he means its third down.

When he says, "This is a kicking situation," its fourth down.

"He was really hammered." "Hammered" is this year's word. It means that someone was blocked or tackled.

"Shaken up." When they say someone was shaken up, it means the man lying on the field probably has a broken leg or a dislocated shoulder.

When a player is hammered, he's often shaken up.

"Thats a smart move by the coach." Here, the announcer is either a former player or a former coach, and he wants you to know he understands the game better than you do.

"He lost his concentration." The receiver dropped the ball.

"He's an underrated player." This doesnt really mean anything; the announcer's just filling time.

"He has great hands" means he can catch the football.

"This game is far from over." This means that the game really is over. Its in the fourth quarter, theres still nine minutes to play, but the score is 37 to 3 and the trouble is they have fourteen commercials they want to show you; so, they dont want you to leave. Thats why they say "This game is far from over."

"What a year this young man has had." This doesnt mean much, either. Dont forget, theyre going to be on for six hours next Sunday, and they have to keep talking.

"Thats a ball that never should have been thrown." They say that when theres an interception.

"I'll bet he'd like to have that one back" is another way of saying the ball was intercepted.

"The clock continues to run" means, of course, that the clock is running.

And "Flags are down all over the field." The officials have seen one of the players violating the rules.

So, there you have it. I hope this little explanation makes it more enjoyable for you to watch San Francisco beat Miami next Sunday, but dont go away. The clock continues to run and this show is far from over.

Shopping Carts

With the exception of the automobile, a shopping cart's America's favorite four-wheel vehicle. Since the supermarket replaced the neighborhood grocery store, people have been buying more food less often, and it takes a shopping cart to carry it all.

There are some terrible drivers. Unlike automobile drivers, shopping cart drivers dont have to pass a test to get a license. Some drive as though they were the only ones in the aisle.

There arent any "no parking" signs in a supermarket. Shoppers park anywhere. The ones who leave carts in the middle of the aisle are the worst, although anyone who doesnt parallel park obstructs traffic too.

You often have to push someone else's cart out of the way to get through. Others leave their carts in one place and bring their purchases back to it.

Very few people pack a cart neatly. They just throw things in. Some try to make it easy by putting everything in the small upper part of the cart. Others fill the whole cart. His shopping cart runneth over.

Kids love shopping carts. Some people fill their carts with kids so theres no room for groceries.

If the shopper comes without a car, he or she has to bring a personal shopping cart to get the groceries home in. This means that, while at the store, the cart is in the cart.

The worst crush is at the checkout counter. Some people push their carts right through. Others simply abandon them on the grocery side.

Often youll see a full cart standing in the checkout line, with no person. That means the shopper's run back to get the can of coffee he or she forgot.

On those days when nothing goes right, you always get the cart with the wobbly wheel. If its really a bad day, you get one wobbly wheel and one that doesnt turn at all.

I suppose the next thing will be a motorized shopping cart, and we'll all have to wear seat belts in the grocery store.

Valentine's Day

Valentine's Day cards are a lot cheaper the day after Valentine's Day than they were the day before, so I bought a stack.

A valentine should be sweet and simple, I think—and red. "For the one I love." "Remembering you on Valentine's Day."

I like the ones with a cutout of a heart on them. You open them up and theres a message inside, "A Valentine For You."

I cant get over how much valentines cost. One was two dollars.

The poetry is always bad in a valentine, and thats the way it ought to be.

A Valentine to keep in touch

With someone I think about so much.

Now, thats bad poetry.

There are a lot of dirty valentines this year. A valentine should be more about love than sex. I can understand why one left over the day after Valentine's Day said "To a fine person!" I mean, I dont want a sexy valentine, but "To a fine person" is going too far the other way.

Theres one that just says, "Have a nice day." "Have a nice day" isnt a Valentine message.

And one says "To Someone Special." The special thing about it is it costs $ 4.95 and plays a song.

None of us is agreed on what we call our mother and father. Mom and Pop, Mom and Dad, Mother and Father, and Mother and Dad.

This seems like sort of a cheap trick—"From Both of Us." I mean, if you really love someone, it doesnt seem as though you ought to chip in with someone else and buy one card from the two of you.

And I question this one: "For Dad and His Wife". You get it? These card companies are touching every base. Dear old dad has been divorced and remarried, and this is for the kid who wants to send him a card. My question is this: How does dear old mom, wherever she is, feel about it? Well, here's the answer to that: "For Mom and Her Husband". Thats where dear old mom is. She's got herself another guy.

We've come a long way. Used to be you only sent a valentine when you really meant it. You didnt send one to every Tom, Dick and Mary. Sometimes youd slip one in a girl's desk at school and not even put your name on it. All it said was "Will you be my Valentine?"

I like Valentine's Day. The trouble is the florists and the candy-makers and the card people are all advertising so much, you dont dare let the day go by without making an offering, whether you mean it or not.

Money exceeds affection.

Army Inc.

A group of experts that has been studying the Defense Department announced recently that our whole military system is a wasteful mess and should be reorganized. President Reagan's trying to solve other budget problems by turning them over to the individual states and to private enterprise. He wants the states to handle their own welfare, for example. So, why doesnt he do the same with our armed services? Let Alabama, California, Illinois, Wyoming, all the states, pay for their own army, buy their own battleships, their own MX missiles, their own nuclear warheads.

If Texas wants to get into Star Wars, let it. If the Russians wanted to declare war on us, theyd have to decide which states to declare it on. They probably dont even know the names of all of our states.

The alternative would be private enterprise. Sell the Defense Department, the Army, Navy and Air Force, lock, stock and barrel to private corporations. Turn the Pentagon over to Big Business. Let General Motors run it.

You can bet there'd be some changes made if Big Business was paying to have weapons made, instead of being paid to make them.

The first thing a businessman would do if he was president of the Army would be to cut costs. He'd start firing some people. Look at the officers we have in the armed forces now. We have thirty-five four-star generals, almost 100,000 captains, and we have 14,671 colonels or their equivalent in the Navy. And there are 32,884 lieutenant colonels. The lieutenant colonels are just standing around waiting to be made colonels. A lieutenant colonel's pay is $39,758.40 a year. The only people who know the difference between a colonel and a lieutenant colonel are the colonels and the lieutenant colonels. Any hard-headed businessman running the Army's going to eliminate one of them. By laying off all the lieutenant colonels, the corporation would save $1,307,402,072 a year.

Big business is smart in America. Take the General Dynamics Corporation. The General Dynamics Corporation has made $2 billion in profit in the last twelve years, selling weapons to our armed forces. During that time, it hasnt paid one penny in taxes. This is the kind of know-how we need at the Pentagon.

Thank Yous

Im not considered a real friendly person and I resent it. The reason Im not considered friendly is that I only smile when I feel amused, pleased or affectionate. I only say "thank you" when I want to thank someone. I only say "thank you very much" when I want to thank someone very much.

We're diminishing the importance of a lot of good things, like smiles and thank you's, by using them when we dont mean them. We're using them too often as a sales tool.

Theres a gas station I pass all the time that has a sign that says, "Your purchase free if we fail to say thank you." Now, what kind of a thank you is that? Some poor guy making $3.35 an hour pumping gas is told by the boss that, if he doesnt say thank you, he'll be fired. Is this from the heart? Of course not! Its from the pit of his stomach, where fear lies.

If you make a long-distance call now, you get a recorded message that says, "Thank you for using AT&T."

Theres no machine ever invented that can say thank you and mean it. Have you ever called an airline ticket office and been put on hold?

AIRLINE PHONE RECORDING:
Thank you for calling Delta Air Lines. Our reservations and sales agents are all busy at this time. Thank you.

ROONEY:
I dont want them thanking me. Im not doing business with the airline as a favor to them. Im calling because they have a flight that goes where I have to get to. Dont thank me; just get the plane there on time.

They say "all" their sales agents are busy—they probably have only one.

When the flight's two hours late, the pilot, on instructions from management, Im sure, always says, "We're sorry for the delay. Thank you very much for your patience." I dont want to be thanked for my patience; Im mad. I havent been patient at all, and I'll thank the pilot not to thank me for it.

Well, thank you very much from all of us here at *60 Minutes*, and have a nice day.

Funerals

I didnt go to Konstantin Chernenko's funeral in Moscow Wednesday. I thought about going, but I had a dentist's appointment Tuesday; Wednesday, I went to see the man who helps me with my taxes. Thats all the grief I can take in one week.

None of us in America got to know much about Mr. Chernenko. He may be the least famous world leader of the last fifty years. Still, if he got to the top in the Soviet Union, we have to respect him and assume he was an outstanding person. Its difficult to believe he was a year younger than our President, Ronald Reagan. I like having a President older than I am. President Reagan still leaves me hope that I might get to be President when I grow up.

Theyre talking about how young the new Soviet leader, Mikhail Gorbachev, is. He may be only fifty-four, but if the differences between Russia and the United States could be decided with a footrace between Reagan and Gorbachev, I'd put my money on our man. Gorbachev is not what you call agile.

The Russians seem to like big state funerals. Maybe it reminds them of the good old days when they had a czar.

There've been a lot of great state funerals in my lifetime. The first and most moving was Franklin Delano Roosevelt's—so many people, so sad. Winston Churchill had a funeral with the pomp and circumstance befitting a truly great man. I felt great personal sadness when Dwight Eisenhower died; he'd been so important in my life. The death of a young man is always sadder; John F. Kennedy's funeral had the air of tragedy about it.

I dont know why we have parades for important funerals. People have never known what to do about a funeral. I guess thats it. Nothing's really any good to do but we feel the need to do something—to have a ceremony.

Im often suspicious of myself when I go to the funeral of someone I didnt know very well or, even worse, didnt like very much. President Reagan was right not going to Konstantin Chernenko's funeral. He didnt know him, didnt like him. You shouldnt go to a funeral because you think you should.

Driveways

There are 60 million private homes in the United States. Some of them are simple and some of them are fancy. Some homes have a basement; some dont. Some have a swimming pool; most dont. One thing almost all the 60 million homes have is a driveway. Americans want their cars nearby where they can get at them in a hurry. They want them as close to the door of their homes as they can be. If the cars arent by the front door, theyre by the side door. I hope this door opens in.

Many houses have two-car garages but almost no one puts a car in either one of them. When the garage door is left open, it become obvious from the street why the car is not put in the garage each night. Theres so much junk in the garage, theres no room for even one car.

Ninety percent of all U.S. families own a car. More than half of them own at least two cars. Almost 20 percent own three. A few even own four. Like the garage, the driveway is never quite big enough. There never has been a driveway big enough in the whole history of driveways. Our driveways runneth over.

The camper is the new driveway hazard. Often its not only too big for the driveway, its bigger than the house its parked outside of.

The difficult driveway is a constant source of trouble to the people in the house it leads to.

Some driveways are long. If you cant see the house from the driveway, rich people live there. Other driveways are so short theres hardly room to park the car if you dont put it in the garage.

Cement driveways crack eventually. You cant make grass grow on your lawn and you cant keep it from growing between the cracks in your driveway.

There are some expensive driveways made of brick. You wouldnt dare drive on this in a cheap car.

The driveway is an indispensable part of the American home. Where else would the paper boy throw the newspaper each day?

You may not think driveways are important, but let me give you one figure. A car parked behind another car in the driveway, with the keys removed and temporarily misplaced, is the third biggest cause of divorce in America today.

Ice Cream Cones

Almost everyone's good at something. I, for example, am one of the outstanding experts in the world on eating ice-cream cones. One important rule of ice-cream-cone eating is this: Dont get involved with anyone else. You cant talk and eat ice cream at the same time. If you trade bites, you should be related or, at the very least, good friends. Dont try to buy a cone and bring it to anyone. Dont try to handle two cones at the same time.

No one with a beard should ever eat an ice-cream cone.

Make it a practice to pay for your ice-cream cone before the person dipping it gives the cone to you. Once you have an ice-cream cone in your hand, its very difficult to make change.

The most common mistake inept ice-cream eaters make is to start at the top, licking. Anyone who knows anything at all about ice-cream eating knows you start at the sides and work up. Too many people twist themselves out of shape eating ice-cream cones. They cock their heads this way and that. They strain their necks getting into position. Dont turn your head or twist your neck. Make your wrists do the work by turning the ice-cream cone itself.

Eating ice cream is nothing you should dawdle over. The quicker the better. Get right at it. Being a licker is wrong. You bite an ice cream cone with your front teeth.

Double-decker cones are twice as good as single-dip cones, but they arent for amateurs.

Walking and eating an ice cream cone at the same time is something you should only try if youre an experienced ice-cream-cone eater. Many people find walking and eating difficult.

Some fancy ice cream parlors have recently started the disgusting habit of wrapping paper around the cone itself. Unwrap it and discard that immediately. Once youve eaten the top and forced the rest of the ice cream down into the cone, it makes a delicious combination. No one wants paper in the way.

There are a great many people who make the mistake of getting a cone with rainbow sprinkles on it. No real ice-cream eater takes rainbow sprinkles. Chocolate sprinkles are somewhat more acceptable.

The flavor a person likes and the way that person eats an ice cream cone say a great deal about his or her personality. Vanilla people are a lot different from either chocolate or maple-walnut people, and I, personally, have never trusted the tutti-frutti few.

Geneva Peace Plan

The United States and the Soviet Union are having peace talks in Geneva, Switzerland. We dont know what theyre talking about, but they say theyre talking. I have a proposal. I'd like to see them issue a joint statement that would read like this:

We, the representatives of the people of the United States and the Soviet Union, being of sound mind, do hereby suspend all military expenditures for one year. Its agreed that, whereas we already have enough weapons to kill everyone in the world, we dont need any more.

Between us we spend $500 billion a year on arms. Because theres so much that needs to be done in the world, we hereby agree to spend that same amount on things that'll do some good for a change. This is our budget: to clean up toxic waste dumps, $75 billion; to clean up the lakes, rivers and oceans we've ruined, $50 billion; for education of every kind, for schools, for colleges and for the education of more teachers, more scientists, more ordinary people, $100 billion; for highway and road repair, $100 billion—thats our highways, their roads; for the poor and hungry of the world, $25 billion—the money will be spent not to feed them but to help them find ways they can feed themselves; on new and old libraries, $25 billion; on museums,

$15 billion; on medical research, to find a cure for cancer perhaps, $20 billion; to bail out the farmers in both the United States and Russia who seem to be in such sad shape, $10 billion; for joint space research so we can find out whether what's out there is any good for us here on Earth, $75 billion.

In the event the people of our two countries dont agree that this is a better way to spend $500 billion than on weapons, with $500 billion we could give every man, woman and child alive on Earth a hundred dollars to have a good time with. That includes all one billion Chinese.

Youll notice this figure only comes to $495 billion. Because we all know how things work in the world we've allowed $5 billion for graft and corruption.

Thats my Geneva peace plan.

Geography

Most people arent much better at geography than they are at mathematics. Ive been to every State in the Union, but I still have to look at a map to find things. You know, for instance, I never know where Kentucky is in relation to Tennessee.

The average American moves once every five years. We get restless. Its too bad we cant move the states instead of the people.

For instance, how about moving California east? Look how big California is. It would take up most of New York, part of Pennsylvania, Delaware, New Jersey, Maryland, parts of Virginia and a little bit of both North and South Carolina.

Im tired of Florida being where it is, too. Its a nice State, but its attracting too much of a crowd and its been getting a lot of bad publicity. We'll put Florida up where Montana is. That ought to kill the fruit tree canker and stop the drug traffic from South America, too.

Maine. I'll exchange Maine with Nevada. Let's see if Frank Sinatra can sing in the cold.

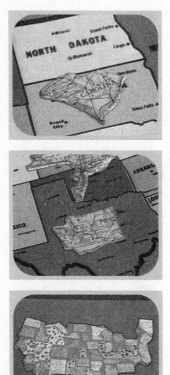

Iowa. Iowa ought to stay where it is. The people of Iowa like it there and I think most of us like having Iowa right where it is.

North and South Carolina, I'd separate. Theyve been together too long. Theyre sort of inbred. I tell you, we'll put South Carolina right under North Dakota.

Texas ought to change its image. The State of Washington gets a lot of rain. Texas is too dry. Let's move Washington right into the middle of Texas. That still leaves plenty of room around the borders for cowboys. Now, Texas? Let's put Texas out where Hawaii is.

We still have this void where California was. Its nice out there—the weather. Goodness knows Chicago deserves better weather than its been getting. Let's move all of Illinois to southern California.

Now, Virginia has always had sort of a superior attitude to the rest of the states. We'll put Virginia where Wyoming is, just to teach it a lesson.

Mississippi, Alabama and Georgia have been the Deep South all their lives. We'll move them and make them the Deep North. We'll put them in Alaska.

This is all dreaming, of course, but it would make the Country a better shape without Florida and Texas sticking way down. The truth is, no matter what its faults are, people like having the State they live in right where it is. They also love having the weather different someplace else. It gives them an excuse for going somewhere.

Moving the Office

I want to begin this new year by being honest with you. This isnt the way my office normally looks. Usually when Im working in here, its neat as a pin, but when we start to take the pictures, we spend hours setting it up so it looks this way. You know, its just part of my public image.

Well, things are going to be different next year. For one thing, CBS is moving me into a new office. And to tell you the truth, I hate to go. I dont know what's wrong with me, but I take inanimate objects like offices and old cars very seriously. I get to love the cup I drink out of. I love the chair Im sitting in. I like this desk. Its not much, but I like it.

And Ive been happy in this office. Ive been sad. Ive been worried. Ive succeeded. Ive failed. Ive been everything in here. This office is a piece of my life, and this is the end of it. They'll move someone else in here. That person wont know or care that Ive lived twelve great years of my life in here. To them it'll just be four walls, four freshly painted walls.

But how would you like to have to get out of here? I mean, you cant take all these things and put them in a new office. Ive hung things on the walls. Ive got all this stuff in boxes. Where am I gonna put it? Ive acquired them over the years, and they seem right in here, but you cant hang old junk in a new office.

How long do you think it'll take before I get my new office looking like the old one? Look at the drawers in the desk. Just perfect! Not even a paper clip floating around in there.

Nothing's ever right when you move. For one thing, I hated the desk. So, I got myself a new desk. Well, I didnt actually get it; I made it. This is a piece of walnut from an old tree that came down in upstate New York. I think its a beauty. I love it. I put these ebony dovetails in here to keep it from splitting any more. But this is it. Next week they ought to have my new bookshelves in and this place will begin to look more like home.

Any place any one of us spends a lot of time gets to look like us after a while. Then all I have to do is think of something to say.

Professional Products

For the last twenty years, its been getting so expensive to pay a professional to do a job for you that the do-it-yourself movement has gotten very big in this Country. People are trying to do everything for themselves, even if they dont know how. The salesmen have tried to get in on this by calling a lot of things that any amateur can buy "professional." Professional tape measure. Professional hammer. Here's a professional paint brush. You can

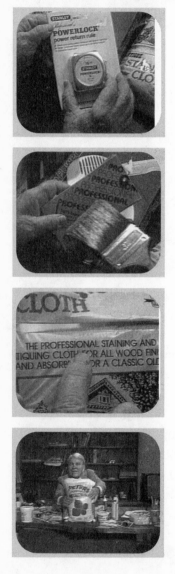

tell its professional because it has "professional" written all over it. Elmer's Professional Carpenter's Glue. This is a professional staining cloth. Look! Its just a cloth; thats all it is. I have a feeling that a professional stainer would use an old rag.

Products having to do with women's hair are often called professional. There is a professional hair dryer. Professional hair spray. A professional hair brush. Something called Professional Conditioning and Styling Mousse. M-O-U-S-S-E. I looked up the word "mousse." My dictionary says, "a sweet, frozen dessert made with whipped cream and egg whites." I think Ive seen some women with that in their hair.

"Professional repair for steel-belted radials." I dont know. I dont think I'd ever feel comfortable tooling down the highway at the speed limit if I'd fixed my own flat with this.

Take a bag of Peter's Professional Potting Soil. Peter's Professional Potting Soil! Professional dirt is what it is. If you dont like the amateur dirt you have in your back yard, you can buy this. Professional dirt! They have this little container of professional plant food to go with it. You wouldnt want to give amateur food to professional dirt, would you?

Water plug—stops leaks instantly. The label reads: "The product professionals prefer." If I call a professional to stop a leak, I want him to find out what's leaking and why. I dont want him just plugging it up with this stuff temporarily.

As a matter of fact, I personally think the do-it-yourself movement's gone too far. What we need is a national dont-do-it-yourself movement. I dont care how professional they say all this stuff is. My advice is: If you want a professional job done, call a professional—if you can find one.

E. B. White

(ON THE OCCASION OF THE DEATH OF E. B. WHITE.)

E. B. White may have written the English language more gracefully than any American who ever lived.

Each of us wants everyone else to know what we know, to like what we like. E. B. White was my literary hero, so give me this. Andy—he was known as Andy to his friends—was not as widely known as those movie stars, or even as well known as a lot of writers who arent as good as he was. Seems terribly wrong, but Im probably better known than he was. As the phrase goes in the newspaper business, I couldnt carry his typewriter.

It was partly Andy White's own fault, although "fault" isnt the right word. He wanted no part of celebrity. All the people he cared about already knew how good he was, and thats all that mattered to him. He didnt care whether his picture was ever taken, and he refused to be interviewed for television.

Several times over the past twenty years, I told him he owed it to the world to submit to an interview on camera so everyone would know what he looked like and how he was. He just laughed. He said that people would be disappointed because he didnt talk as well as he wrote, and theyd think he was a fake.

For the past few years Andy has been ill with all the things that can go wrong with an eighty-six-year-old body, and he'd lost interest, too, after his wife died eight years ago. "Life without Katharine," he said, "is no good for me."

I talked to a mutual friend who had seen him only last week. He said Andy's eyesight was failing and the thing he most liked was to be read to from one of his own books. Strange, in a way, but I suppose for a writer it was like looking at old photographs of yourself when things were good.

I got to know Andy White when I adapted this little masterpiece of his called *Here is New York* for television, years ago. When we were finished, we were nervous about showing it to him, but he liked it. He had only one complaint: the director filmed the actor, playing the part of E. B. White as a young writer, lying on a bed in the Algonquin Hotel with his shoes on. Andy told us he'd never lie on a bed with his shoes on. His prose is like that, too.

Heroes are hard to find. He's been my hero for fifty years. Life without E. B. White is not as good as it was for me.

Helmets

We all worry about where our Defense Department spends the $300 billion we give it. They dont spend it all on "Star Wars" equipment and nuclear submarines. For one thing, our Army's always spending money trying to develop new equipment that will protect our soldiers. Some of these inventions are successful. Some, of course, are not.

The U.S. Army Research and Development Center in Natick, Massachussetts, has just come up with a new helmet for our soldiers. We went there to look at it.

This is the old World War One pie-plate helmet. Our soldiers wore this until about 1940. The helmet was the same as the one the British wore.

This is the helmet we're all familiar with. I suppose we made 20 million of these in the last forty years. Its the helmet our GI's wore through World War Two, Korea and Vietnam.

And this is the new helmet. It took more than ten years and cost $6 million. Two engineers who work for the Army designed it, and theyre very proud of their work—Philip Durand and Lawrence McManus. But $6 million for a hat?

LAWRENCE McMANUS:
That—that presents a—more target area, because it stands up on the head.

DURAND:
The—the area of this helmet here is 1.3 square feet. If you take the area of this larger—largest helmet, it is 1.3 square feet. However, this helmet provides—covers 11 percent more area of the helmet—of the head, simply because it rides lower on the head. Thereby, you provide more ballistic protection, because it covers 11 percent more area of the head.

ROONEY (trying on new helmet):
I like it.
Its going to be hard for us to get used to seeing our soldiers wearing that new helmet. We've become so accustomed to seeing them in the old one.

By the way, this isnt our new $6 million American helmet. This is the German World War II helmet. This is our new design that they came up with. The Germans abandoned this one in 1956. The German army now wears a version of our old World War II helmet. It costs the Germans the equivalent of about $34. Our new one costs $87.

We just like to keep you up to date on where some of that $300 billion goes.

Traffic

This has been a special week in New York City. It was the fortieth anniversary of the United Nations. I know a lot of you dont care a fig about New York or the United Nations, but you do care about cars, and cars were the most interesting thing about New York this week.

Its possible that there have never been so many cars in so little space in one place, in the whole history of the world. There were reported to have been 20,000 big long black limousines in New York alone. Those were to carry the diplomats to and fro, and then back to fro again.

It doesnt have to be a special week in New York, though, for there to be a lot of trucks and cars here. On an average day 832,000 vehicles come into New York City every morning. There are 200,000 cars that are registered and live here. There are 10,000 resident limousines and 8,000 taxis in Manhattan on any given day. So, thats a total of 1,050,000 vehicles.

Just for a round number, say there are one million cars in New York. There are more than that but call it a million. Do you know how long a car is, bumper to bumper?

Your normal, average, everyday Pontiac is about fifteen feet, six inches, but some cars are as long as twenty-one feet. So, call the average car eighteen feet long.

The New York you all know, the island of Manhattan, is twelve miles long. One million vehicles times eighteen feet comes to 3,409 miles.

There are 504 miles of streets in New York City. Thats 504 miles of streets with 3,409 miles of cars in them.

No wonder we have traffic jams.

Magazine Covers

Years ago, I used to make my living writing for magazines, and I still read magazines, but I dont understand some of them anymore.

How come they all look the same? You stand in front of a newsstand, your eye moves along a row of magazines, and all you see is the blank stare of a  pretty woman, one pretty woman after another looking out at you, wearing very little. If theres a man at all on the cover, its usually because he's married to Princess Diana.

Look at a pile of some of the most popular women's magazines. You can hardly tell *Glamour* from *Mademoiselle, Redbook* from *Vogue.* And it isnt just one month. Look at a pile of old copies of *Vogue*. Each month looks like a Xerox copy of last month. You wouldnt know which one to throw out at the end of the month.

It isnt only American magazines, either. Even the women's magazines from Europe look like that.

Sometimes the women on magazine covers look you straight in the eye. You wonder who these women are and what theyre thinking and what language theyre thinking it in—or, of course, whether theyre thinking anything at all. Lately, Ive been noticing a lot of them look as though they were around the corner or something. Theyre turning their heads and looking at us sideways.

Of course, when a magazine is mailed, some terrible things can happen to those pretty women. The people who slap the address stickers on dont know or care anything about makeup. This attractive woman probably spent hours getting ready for this picture, but when the mailers got through with her, you cant even tell who she is. The sticker covers half her face.

I have some questions for magazine editors. Do women buy most of your magazines? Do women always want pictures of other women on the cover? Men dont seem to want pictures of men. I can understand having a picture of a woman on a dirty magazine like *Playboy* or *Penthouse* every month, but why always a woman on *Ladies' Home Journal?* I think it might be more interesting if they occasionally had a man on the cover.

We'd get to know how to cock our heads, to pose in the manner that was right for a cover. We're willing to learn to be cover boys.

Worn Out

More work has to be done on the parts of things that wear out first. Why should one part of something always give out before the rest of it does? Look at this shirt Im wearing. Its a good cotton shirt. You see anything wrong with it? The front looks okay, pockets okay. The buttons are fine. But look at this. The collar's gone, starting to get frayed, and I wont be able to wear it much longer; and I have six shirts just like this at home. Theyre perfectly good except for the collar. My shirttails never wear out! Cant they make a shirt thats strong in the collar and weak in the shirttail? Something's wrong here.

Theres a winter coat Ive always liked. Its light and warm, made of really good wool. I admit Ive had it for twenty years, but look at this: the button-holes are worn out. If the buttonholes werent worn out, I could wear it for another twenty years—unless I wear out first.

I have a raincoat I wear a lot when it isnt raining—perfectly good, except the sleeves are gone. And a jacket, a sweater, or a wool shirt always goes first at the elbow. Cant they make these with stronger elbows?

The heels of shoes: Did you ever have a pair of shoes that wore out first at the toes? Look at mine, look at the heels. And the right one always wears down before my left one. (I must come down on it harder when I walk.) I ought to be able to go into a store and ask for a pair of shoes with a very strong right heel.

Im also the kind of person who worries about rugs. We always walk on the same part of rugs. Other parts of rugs never get walked on. Its not the rug's fault. This carpet in my new office; its very nice now, but I know Im wearing a path under my feet here, because I keep rolling my chair between my desk and my typewriter.

There are a thousand things like this. Car mufflers. Cant they make car mufflers last as long as car engines? If we could get all those things to wear out evenly at the same time, we'd be able to save enough money to waste more of it on nuclear weapons, and President Reagan wouldnt have to be nice to Mr. Gorbachev at all.

Football Uniform

Unlike other games that people enjoy watching on television like baseball, tennis or golf, most have never actually played football. I played a lot of football in school and I never get over dreaming Im back out there on the field. The game's changed, of course. I dont even recognize the names of some of the positions anymore. We didnt have anything called a tight end, for instance. We just had an end. He wasnt tight or loose. And, of course, the uniforms have changed.

Just in case my team, the New York Giants, needs me for one of the last games of the season, and it looks as though they might, I got myself equipped with a uniform this week. Ive got one of just about everything.

We weighed all this stuff down in the nurse's office. When a player runs out in the field carrying all this, he's got about twenty-six pounds of dead weight on him: shoes, socks, a little cast-iron underwear, the pants, along with the thigh guards, the knee pads and the shin guards, and a hinged knee stabilizer. Hip pads add another couple of pounds and so does a flak jacket. Shoulder pads, of course; anybody'd look like a football player in that. A jersey, for over everything else. Now I'll need elbow pads and these forearm pads and a wristband. I'll need a neck collar too.

Gloves. A lot of players are wearing gloves these days, even when its warm. Some are actually scuba-diver's gloves. The pass catchers wear these, or the pass droppers. And there are the padded gloves that the linemen wear.

And I'll need a little eye-black to cut down on the glare of the sun or the lights. And the helmet; four pounds, four ounces of helmet. Can you imagine how much the injury and death rate would go down if everyone dressed like this, in a football uniform, when they drove a car or flew in an airplane? Or even just crossing the street?

1986

Sports Fans

Like a lot of Americans, Im a sports fan. Ive made a list of things I'd like to see done to make sports even more enjoyable.

First, newspapers should stop listing game broadcasts as beginning at 12:30 when the game doesnt actually start until 1:00. I dont care what time the pre-game show starts.

Second, the game should be played by the athletes, not by the coaches. Football coaches shouldnt be allowed to send in the plays. Quarterbacks should call all the signals. If they have a dumb quarterback, a lineman should call the plays.

Sign language from the coaches on the sideline should be prohibited in any sport.

Basketball coaches are so objectionable they should be made to stay home and watch the game on television.

Next, throw the jerks out of the stadium. If the jerks are in the stadium, dont encourage them by showing their pictures on television.

Theyve tried to eliminate drugs from sports. Now they ought to eliminate chewing tobacco from baseball. If baseball players insist on this disgusting habit, they ought to have to swallow, not spit.

Im not through yet, either. There are now fifty thirty-second commercials in a televised football game. Cut the number to thirty.

After the final game of the World Series, please spare us the pictures of players pouring champagne over each other's heads. We've seen this picture too often.

Brent Musburger's good, but dont keep cutting back to New York with scores of other games when we're interested in the one we're watching. And dont cover up the field with scores on the screen either. What makes you think we dont enjoy watching our team line up?

My last request is to all sports announcers. Will you please, for goodness sake, stop talking? We like you, but you dont have to fill every second with the sound of your voice. You dont seem to understand that we savor pauses. The pauses in the game are when we enjoy thinking about what just happened and about what's going to happen next. John Madden, Joe Garagiola, Pat [Summerall], Al [Michaels], Vince [Scully], Frank Gifford, youre all great, but stop talking as though you were paid by the word.

Any of these ideas used without my written permission would be greatly appreciated.

Spies

Ive never been able to take spying seriously. I have this theory that when a spy's caught, he ought to be spanked and put to bed without his supper, and not allowed to go out and play with the other spies again for two weeks. Its my opinion that very little would be lost to any country if they quit spying altogether. The most important information a spy gets about another country is a list of that country's spies.

Just recently, we caught a Soviet spy named Zakharov. A week later, the Russians arrested an American reporter named Daniloff. They said he was a spy. President Reagan says Daniloff is not a spy.

REAGAN:
The continuing Soviet detention of an innocent American is an outrage.

ROONEY:
But then, so, why did we agree to make an even trade? It sure makes Daniloff look like a spy to the rest of the world. Keep in mind that by Russian standards, half the journalists in Washington would be in prison as spies.

"Spy" is a strange word. There are good spies and there are bad spies. Our spies are good. Their spies are bad. James Bond is a good spy.

Last year a spy gave the Russians our Navy's communication code. We said it was serious because it would allow the Russians to listen in to what our Navy at sea was saying to our Pentagon in Washington. So, what was the Navy saying that was so secret? Are they planning to attack Moscow?

I like to think my Country is doing all good and honorable things, nothing sneaky. If thats true, what do we care whether the Russians are listening or not?

I sat at a dinner the other night in Washington with William Casey, head of our Central Intelligence Agency. I was surprised that he'd never even heard of the tennis champion Ivan Lendl. Now, what kind of intelligence is that? Maybe Mr. Casey ought to fire his spies and just read the newspaper.

Presidents

I dont know what's wrong with me anyhow, but Im soft on Presidents. President Reagan's been busy trying to talk himself out of this arms deal he made with the Iranians. These are the same Iranians who held fifty-two Americans captive for 444 days five years ago. Almost everyone but the President thinks he made a mistake.

PRESIDENT REAGAN:
I dont think a mistake was made. It was—(coughing)—it was a high-risk gamble, and it was a gamble that, as Ive said, I believe the circumstances warranted.

ROONEY:
Even though President Reagan makes a lot of mistakes, like this one, and even though he believes in a lot of things I dont believe in, it doesnt make me think he's a bad person. I like President Reagan.

Now, before you decide Im your kind of guy, I have to tell you I also liked Jimmy Carter when he was President. I almost always like our President, no matter who he is.

Im old enough now to have an opinion on nine Presidents, beginning with Franklin D. Roosevelt, and Ive only really hated one of them.

One of the good things about our Country is that who the President is doesnt really matter most of the time. The President doesnt have anything to do with what time we go to bed, what time we get up or whether we have cereal or toast for breakfast.

The President doesnt control Christmas, bowling, business, colleges, museums, libraries, newspapers, television. All of those things have more effect on our lives than the President does. Thats why I laugh at people who go crazy when someone they dont like gets elected.

A lot of patriotism, I think, is dumb, but I never forget a patriotic lesson I got in a farmhouse in Iowa twelve years ago. The farmer had this picture of President Nixon hanging in his kitchen. It was just at the time Nixon was in all his trouble. "I guess you like Nixon," I said to the farmer. "I see you have his picture hanging there." "No," the farmer said, "I have a picture of the President of the United States."

And thats why I dont name the only President I ever hated.

Pill-Bottle Cotton

Do you realize Ive been doing these comments on *60 Minutes* for nine years now and havent once mentioned the cotton they put in pill bottles? I

 dont know anything offhand that mystifies Americans more than the cotton in pill bottles. Why do they do it? Are you supposed to put the cotton back in once youve taken a pill out?

Here's a bottle of vitamins I bought. Look at all the cotton they got in here. I bought another bottle just like it. Take the cotton out of that one, too. I'll bet I can get all the pills in this bottle into the other bottle now that it doesnt have any cotton in it.

This is a bottle of Eli Lilly bicarbonate of soda. Is that much cotton really necessary? I called the Eli Lilly Company in Indianapolis. They seem like a good, responsible company as far as I know. I wanted to talk to the person in charge of deciding how much cotton to put in a bottle of pills. I learned, among other things, that they dont even use cotton at Eli Lilly. Their cotton is rayon.

This is Maalox for upset stomach. The bottle comes in this box. You take the bottle out of the box, take the cotton out of the bottle, and, if theyd just used the box and not used the bottle, look at this! All these pills would have fit into the box and theyd have had room for three times as much cotton. Its enough to give you an upset stomach, isnt it?

This is a bottle of Rolaids. It has cotton in it. And this is a giant bottle of

Tums. Look! No cotton. Why do you think they decided to go without cotton for Tums? The only thing I can think of is that cotton is more expensive than Tums.

I bought this box of Johnson & Johnson cotton, just to see how they were selling cotton, and look at this! The box is stuffed with paper. You dont run into the cotton till way down here.

Thats my report on the cotton in pill bottles.

No Fault

Have you noticed that nothing is anyone's fault anymore? Everything is someone else's fault. No one's ever to blame.

No young person has done anything wrong in the United States in the last twenty-five years. He's a youth. The parents of the boy who holds up the corner grocery store say he's a good boy who got in with the wrong crowd. Its the wrong crowd's fault—although, you notice, the wrong crowd didnt hold up the grocery store; the good boy did.

Alcoholics are no longer to be blamed for drinking too much. They have a disease.

The murderer isnt responsible because he was legally insane at the time. He's sane enough now not to want to go to prison.

Big business blames its problems on big government, foreign imports and the economy. The labor unions blame their problems on Big Business. It isnt even a little bit the fault of U.S. auto makers and American workers that theyve lost 25 percent of their market to Japan.

President Reagan is concerned about the increased use of drugs, but neither the President or anyone else blames the people who actually buy and use drugs. It isnt their fault. Its the fault of the dealers, the smugglers or the farmers back in Colombia. God forbid we should blame the innocent people actually taking the drugs. Theyre victims.

Schoolchildren are using drugs, but they arent to blame, and neither are their parents. Its the fault of the dealers selling it to the kids.

President Reagan says we're going to increase our efforts to enforce our drug laws, but there arent enough people in the whole United States Army, Navy and Marine Corps to prevent smugglers from bringing drugs into this Country.

How come it never occurs to anyone that the best way to end the drug problem would be for individuals to stop using them? We're becoming a nation of people who dont feel responsible for anything.

I suppose these comments may not be very popular, but dont blame me. The devil made me do it.

Magazine Page Numbers

I have fourteen magazines and newspapers here. One, two, three, five, seven, eight, eleven, twelve, fourteen, right? Thats the way these publications count their pages. Do you ever wonder where some of the pages go in magazines?

Take *Time* magazine, for instance. Now, I like *Time* magazine, but I dont understand how they number their pages. Here's page fifty-seven. I understand that. On the next page is an ad. Do they number that? If it is, its fifty-eight, fifty-nine. Right? Thats page sixty. So, they oo number their pages. Now, this is page sixty, then sixty-one, sixty-two, sixty-three. Presto! Page sixty-one. Do they or dont they number their advertising pages?

Take *New York* magazine. Page sixteen, seventeen. Wait a minute. Page twenty. They must count this thing as two pages. This is page seventeen and this is page eighteen. This is a page?

People magazine. The editor who numbers the pages must be out to lunch when they put this issue out. Here's page seventy. Nothing, nothing, nothing, no numbers. Pretty soon you come to an insert thats F1, A1, A2, and then you go all the way back here to page 119 before you hit another page number. Nothing between page 70 and page 119.

Here's America's biggest newspaper, the New York *Daily News.* You want page ten? Here's a page ten here. Here's a regular news page ten. Here's an insert "M"—page 10M. And here's an insert within the insert called "Extra" page ten. So, you got three page ten's for the price of one.

The world's champion worst-numbered publication is *TV Guide. TV*

Guide sends me a free copy every week and I dont want to sound ungrateful, but if I get my copy Friday for the following week, its usually Wednesday before Ive figured out where anything is in there.

Iran/Iraq

First, I want to show you where Iran and Iraq are. Here's Iran, right here on the blackboard, and here's Iraq, smaller, as you can see, and it fits right in there.

To give you an idea how big Iran is, this is France here. And if you dont know how big France is, its about the same size as Texas.

The war between Iran and Iraq began on August 23, as far as anyone knows, back in the year 600 A.D. Theyve been fighting ever since.

There are 45 million people in Iran and a million and a half cars. But fewer than half the people can read, so you have to be very careful when you come to a four-way stop sign.

Iran has two million television sets. The Iranians who cant read watch television, just like here.

Iran also has more than a million telephones. But, of course, so does Detroit.

Now, Iran, the big one, is close to Russia, and Iraq, the little one, is close to Israel. This accounts for why Israel helps Iran instead of Iraq. If Iran is attacking Iraq, Iraq has to fight back instead of attacking Israel.

Iraq used to be called Mesopotamia. Iran used to be called Persia. Persia is a better name for a country than Iran. Youve all heard of Persian rugs. How many of you have ever heard of an Iranian rug?

The capital of Iraq is Baghdad. You remember Baghdad from *Ali Baba and the Forty Thieves.*

The *World Almanac* says that attacks by Iran and Iraq on each other's oil tankers have caused insurance rates to go up. This is nonsense. As we all know, *everything* causes insurance rates to go up, *everywhere.*

Both the Iranians and the Iraqis are Moslems, which is the same as being Muslim but spelled differently.

Iran and Iraq hate each other for the same reason Catholics and Protestants in Northern Ireland hate each other, the same reason the Sikhs and the Hindus in India hate each other. Its because people everywhere take a great deal of satisfaction out of hating each other.

Thats the story on Iran and Iraq. Remember, you heard it here first.

Drug and Truth Tests

President Reagan's Commission on Organized Crime announced recently that, in its opinion, all working Americans should have to submit to regular drug tests. Last December, President Reagan himself said that all government workers should submit to lie detector tests.

As the great leader of this great nation, President Reagan should lead us in this test taking. I call on him to do that. A great leader doesnt ask his followers to do anything he wouldnt do himself. I call on President Reagan to set an example for all of us by being the first to take these tests. Let an impartial jury of physicians take a sample of whatever it is they take samples of from the President and test it.

Now, I in no way mean to suggest the President is on any controlled substance. Of course, he isnt, and I dont want a lot of letters saying Im disrespectful of the President, either, because Im not. But even if he's only hooked on jelly beans, the nation has a right to know, and that should become part of his permanent record with the FBI.

Now, lie detectors. President Reagan obviously puts a lot of faith in these machines. In the six years Mr. Reagan has been President, he has held thirty-four televised press conferences. I propose that at his next press conference, Mr. Reagan have himself attached to one of these lie detector machines. If a reporter asked a question and, God forbid, our President told an untruth, a red light would go on, bells would ring and a sign over his head would read "Tilt!"

Again, Im not suggesting the President has ever lied or would ever lie, except in the national interest, of course. Im just saying that if he expects us to submit to lie detector tests, he should submit to one himself. Perhaps the three network anchormen—Peter Jennings, Dan Rather and Tom Brokaw—would agree to have themselves hooked up to lie detectors if the President set the precedent. Someone asked if I was kidding about this suggestion. Im not. Im telling you the truth.

Datebooks

Nothing irritates me more than people who remember my birthday. Theyre organized people who keep little datebooks. They can tell you where they were and what they did three weeks ago Wednesday. They can tell you where theyre going to have lunch next Tuesday. These are the kind of people who buy little books.

One book I found has a place where you can write down the numbers of your insurance policies and the make of your car. I guess thats in case you forget whether you own a Ford or a Cadillac.

Another "Week at a Glance" diary has a place where you can enter the numbers to call if you lose your credit cards. If you want to know the major national holidays in Australia or Brazil, just turn to the next page. Its right there. How many people need to know that February 11 is a national holiday in Brazil?

Another one is called a Tax Organizer. You write in your business expenses every single day. Theres a place for capital gains or losses, estates, trusts, partnership and Subchapter S corporations. Wouldnt a wheeler-dealer who had all those things have someone who kept his books for him? He wouldnt be scratching stuff in a notebook. Alimony, moving, and political expenses—all on one page! You can see what kind of perverted minds put these books together.

The big craze this year is these big fat diaries with everything in them. Men carry them like women carry pocketbooks. Its got a pen for you, and up front, its got a calculator and a place to put your checkbooks. You can organize your whole life in one of those books if youre an organized person, I guess. Theres a place, for instance, where you can write down your goals. What kind of people have to write down their goals to remember them?

One book divides the day between 7 A.M. and 7:30 P.M. into fifteen-minute intervals. I suppose its for a doctor. You know, you call the nurse, the nurse gives you an appointment for 9:15, and the doctor sees you at 10:45.

The notion that our lives can be kept in order by keeping notes in a little book is a persistent and recurring disease we suffer from. People who really believe life can be organized by a book called an organizer needs more help than a little book can give them.

How-To Books

Do I look any better to you tonight? Thinner, healthier, richer, better adjusted? Do you think Im remembering things any better than I did last week? Ive been reading up on how to improve myself. The other day, I went out and bought $184 worth of How-To Books.

I dont think anyone has ever gotten thinner, happier, sexier or more successful in business by studying How To. *How To Take Charge of Your Life.* Youve been making a mess of your life for thirty years. One day you read a book and suddenly everything gets better? I doubt it.

How To Be Happy. You know the first thing the author says in here? Chapter One begins, "There is no such thing as happiness as it is popularly understood and pined for."

So, why does he call his book *How To Be Happy?* Why isnt the title *There Is No Such Thing As Happiness?*

Because suckers like us would never buy it if he called it that, thats why.

How To Be An Assertive (Not Aggressive) Woman, in Life, in Love and on the Job. Here's a woman who couldnt even decide what the title of her book should be, and she's giving advice on being assertive!

How To Get What You Really Want. Obviously, Barbara Sher wanted her name to be bigger on the cover of her book than her co-author Annie Gottlieb's name, and she got what she really wanted.

How To Make Documentaries, How To Produce an Effective TV Commercial. A lot of times, the authors of these How-To Books have failed at the thing theyre writing about. They cant find work in their field, so they write a book about how to do it.

Theres lots of advice on love, too. *How To Start a Conversation and Make Friends.* This is a book for losers.

How To Find a Husband in 30 Days. How To Have a Perfect Marriage with Your Present Mate. I'd like to know the divorce rate among the authors of books like this.

Doctors write a lot of these diet books, real doctors and fake doctors. *Dr. Abravanel's Body Type Diet and Lifetime Nutrition Plan.* That title could lose a little weight, Doc.

How To Be a Really Nice Person. If theres anyone I cant stand being around, its someone you know is trying to be a really nice person. Youre either nice or you arent nice, and theres nothing any one of us can do about it by trying. I am not a nice person. I could memorize this book. It wouldnt help.

I dont want to be negative about all this. I guess we have to keep trying, but the fact of the matter is we are what we are, and the same things keep happening to the same people, no matter which How-To Books they read.

The Moon

What I'd like to know is whatever happened to the moon? Remember all the talk about how important it was for us to get to the moon? It was sixteen years ago that Neil Armstrong and Edwin Aldrin landed there. It seemed like one of the most important events of all time. The moon was going to be a space station, maybe even have colonies there with regular bus service to Earth.

Remember when the astronauts brought these rocks back? They said it might be weeks before the scientists could analyze them and give us their results.

Do you ever remember hearing that rock report? I think the scientists are embarrassed to tell us those rocks are just like the ones we have on Earth.

Its been ten years since anyone's even mentioned the moon. NASA's doing a good job with the space shuttle, but we spent $25 billion getting to the moon, and for what? One television show?

The moon's been ruined as a place to sing about. When songwriters used to write about the moon, the moon was mysterious and romantic, because we didnt know anything about it. It was just a nice, warm glow in the sky. Now we know its a pile of rocks.

NASA's talking about Halley's comet and landing on Mars now. To be honest with you, Im not very interested in Halley's comet. Ive been out there looking for it. Even I have trouble finding the Big Dipper some nights.

Someone in charge ought to say to NASA, "Hey, wait a minute, fellas. Whatever happened to the moon?" Never mind sending the first poet or the first heart-transplant patient into space.

Maybe the moon could even become our fifty-first state, with a zip code, food stamps, air pollution and a seat in Congress. Congressmen would get money to build roads all over the moon, put up a lot of new government buildings, lots of expensive bridges to get from one crater to another, and, of course, dams—we'd put dams on the moon. I know theres no water on the moon, but that never stopped a congressman from getting money for a dam in his district.

It just seems to me that the moon is being wasted.

Muscles

The only consolation most of us can take when we look at ourselves in the mirror is that everyone looks funny but in a different way. Its hard to improve how we look. Cosmetic surgery, dying your hair—nothing works.

Last summer, I was driving along at about fifty miles an hour, with my arm out the car window, when I noticed flabby little waves on my arm from the wind. When I got back to the office, I brought this ten-pound dumbbell with me. The first day, I had a hard time doing twenty lifts. Now I can do about a hundred, and this arm muscle's a lot firmer; but next time I was in the car, I stopped for gas at one of those self-service places, and I noticed I had a hard time getting the cap off the gas tank. My hands werent very strong; so, I bought one of those hand exercisers.

Now I can get the top off the peanut butter jar a lot easier. But one thing led to another and I decided I wasnt getting enough exercise; so, I bought an exercise bicycle. I used it for a while, but it seemed so silly, peddling away and not going anywhere, and I dont use it anymore.

I got a thing to strengthen my forearm and make my tennis game better. Nothing.

I'd like to look more muscular, but some of the muscles that look best in a bathing suit are the ones used the least in real life. I hardly ever use this muscle anymore. The heaviest thing I pick up with it is the Sunday paper.

The people who spend full time developing their muscles look silly. Its a full-time job and they end up looking like side show freaks.

The big question is this: How much time do you really want to spend on your body? The body seems to do best if we just go about our business without paying a lot of special attention to it.

I admire people who exercise to build up their muscles, but Im not one of them. We've got 600 muscles in our bodies and there just isnt time to work on all of them, not if we're going to get any work done.

Pennies

Tonight I want to talk to you about pennies. There are 91 billion pennies in circulation, according to the U.S. Mint. Stores dont think thats enough. I think its too many. Trouble is, those pennies are not in circulation. Stores run out of pennies because the pennies are all home in jars in our kitchens or in boxes in our bedrooms. Every night we empty our pockets of pennies. Next day we come home with more.

Pennies are produced by sales taxes and by stores that charge a dollar ninety-nine for things.

Tuesday we made a test around Grand Central Terminal. We wanted to see whether Americans care about pennies or not.

First, I put a penny on the marble floor of Grand Central. In more than half an hour, no one picked it up.

Then I put a penny at the top of the escalator coming out of the station at rush hour. Five thousand people went by that one penny. No one touched the penny until a cleaning man from the Pan Am Building came along with a broom. Did he bend over and pick it up to keep, a little bonus from his job? He did not. He swept it into his bin with the cigarette butts.

Next, we went to one of the exits. After no success with a penny, I added a dime and a quarter. They lasted less than ten seconds.

I decided to see if anyone would bother with four pennies. No one wanted four, either, so I added a dime and a quarter to them. A few people passed them; then someone kicked the dime; in a flash, another man scooped up the dime, returned for the quarter, and took the thirty-five cents. He left the four pennies right where I'd put them.

Thats what America thinks of pennies. I say get rid of them. A penny saved is a waste of time.

Walking

Except for all the time we spend sitting and sleeping, there are very few things we spend as much time doing as we spend walking.

Like so many other things human beings do, walking begins to look funny if you watch someone do it for long. People do odd things with their feet. As a matter of fact, feet themselves are odd.

If you get staring at feet, you realize its a wonder we get around on them as well as we do. Most people's feet dont seem to fit on the end of their legs quite right. As a result, most of us dont walk with our toes pointed straight ahead the way they should be.

A lot of people walking north have their toes pointed east and west. Others of us walk with our toes pointed towards each other on a collision course.

There are all kinds of ways of walking. You can saunter. You can stroll. Strolling is just a little faster than sauntering.

Then theres the purposeful walk of people who know where theyre going and want to get there in a hurry, even if theres nothing for them to do when they arrive.

Strutting is a special way of walking. You can strut on the beach.

Do you think she doesnt want anyone to notice her, by any chance?

You know the bouncy walker. Bouncers take more moves than they have to when they walk, and, when they stop for a light, they leave their engines running.

Walking is something best done alone at your own pace. Sometimes, though, you dont want to be alone when youre walking. You walk together the best you can—cancan.

Walking hand in hand or arm in arm is difficult because no two people walk at exactly the same pace. One of them has to adjust.

When you walk a dog, theres no compromise. You walk at the dog's pace. You go when the dog wants to go, stop when the dog wants to stop. Walking with a child is not far off walking with a dog.

Walking and talking dont mix. If you really want to make a point, you have to stop and make it.

The only thing as hard as walking and talking is walking and eating or walking and drinking.

If walking and doing something with your hands is difficult, youd think walking with your hands in your pockets doing nothing would be easy but it isnt. If your hands are trapped in your pockets, it interrupts the natural rhythm of your gait.

Its depressingly easy to guess the age of a person by how he or she walks. Walking is one of the things in life you dont appreciate being able to do until you cant do it well anymore.

Armies have created a walking style of their own called marching. The official U.S. Army manual calls for every soldier to take 120 steps, thirty inches long, every minute. This will carry an army about three and a half miles in an hour.

Walking is the only inexpensive thing an army does.

1987

Drinks

Life magazine has a feature this month in which they ask twelve presidential candidates seven questions. For example, *Life* asked them to name their favorite drink and here's how they answered.

George Bush and Richard Gephardt said milk.

Paul Simon and Jack Kemp said Pepsi-Cola.

Pete DuPont and Pat Robertson said tea.

Al Haig, orange juice.

Bruce Babbitt said Tecate beer.

Al Gore, Gatorade.

Bob Dole, Michael Dukakis and Jesse Jackson didnt answer the question.

Let's analyze this poll and see what it tells us. First it tells us all these men are politicians and they gave the answers they thought people wanted to hear. But how honest were they? The two most popular drinks . . . water and coffee . . . arent even mentioned.

Milk is great but would you want a President who drinks milk all the time? *Life* didnt ask but I wonder if these two still suck their thumbs.

Pepsi must have seemed like a good answer but politically, its dumb. The world is divided between Coca-Cola and Pepsi-Cola drinkers. No Coke drinker is going to vote for a Pepsi drinker or vice versa. A Coke drinker thinks of Pepsi as an imitation.

Haig tried to play it safe with orange juice.

But do they mean to say that not one of these guys enjoys a shot of scotch or a martini before dinner? Dont any of them like wine? Dont any of them trust us?

You have to give Bruce Babbitt credit for saying his favorite drink is a Mexican beer.

Pete DuPont, who used to be called Pierre before he was a candidate, and Pat Robertson said tea. Do they think theyre running for Parliament or something? Americans think of tea as a namby-pamby drink.

Al Gore said Gatorade . . . which tastes like 6-Up to me.

Dole, Dukakis and Jackson win this contest because they were too smart to name a favorite drink.

The trouble with all this is, no one can honestly name his or her favorite because what you feel like drinking depends on the time of day. The chances are they all drink orange juice and coffee for breakfast, water with their pills, milk with their cereal, an occasional beer, Coke or Pepsi with lunch and a little whiskey before dinner . . . but Gatorade?

Gatorade is the favorite drink for pouring over the coaches' heads when their team wins.

Baseball versus Football

Professional sports keep moving in on each other's territory. At this time of year theres a collision of interests between football and baseball and between the fans who prefer one game over the other.

Theres a big difference between football fans and baseball fans.

Football fans are Republicans who voted for Ronald Reagan. Baseball fans are Democrats . . . who voted for Ronald Reagan.

The baseball fan's idea of a good time is to sit out in the hot sun, drinking warm beer from a paper cup . . . while watching grown men in baggy pants try to hit a ball with a stick. On cold days football fans drink hot coffee from thermos bottles.

Baseball fans wear T-shirts with what they consider to be clever things written on them . . . or they use their jackets to announce their business affiliation.

Football fans are more conservatively dressed . . . and women football fans are a lot better looking than women baseball fans.

The single best thing about baseball is, teams dont have cheerleaders.

At halftime on a cold day, football fans talk about what happened, ignore the marching band on the field, perhaps have a little something to eat . . . and pour a little more hot coffee.

Baseball is all halftime. Baseball fans observe a custom known as "the seventh inning stretch." This is to keep themselves from falling asleep during the game.

Baseball is a game for people who like statistics better than action.

A player who hits the ball three out of ten times is said to be "hitting .300." Three hundred what? I suppose it just sounds better than saying he's only hitting the ball 30 percent of the time.

I dont know why they need a World Series. Baseball teams have played 162 games among themselves this season and if they dont know which team is best by now, they'll never know.

New Products

Ive always enjoyed keeping track of trends in the advertising business. There are certain words advertisers love.

The word this year seems to be NEW. About half of all the products in the stores these days have labels on them that say NEW . . . very often with an exclamation mark after the word.

They still use FREE quite a bit and SAVE is still very popular but the big word now is NEW. Never mind whether its any good or not, just tell everyone its NEW.

Look at these Ive picked up . . . not an old product in this lot.

Spic and Span has a "NEW! NO RINSE FORMULA."

Cheer has a "NEW FORMULA."

Joy is "NEW!" with an exclamation mark.

Comet is "NEW!" It says "SAFER FOR SURFACES" too. Apparently Comet didnt used to be very safe for surfaces but I dont ever recall them telling us that on the label.

Head & Shoulders shampoo is "NEW!"

Ivory Liquid is "NEW." Or wait a minute. Im not sure about this. I guess just the price is new with Ivory Liquid.

And the toothpaste. This is "Refreshing Blue NEW." I think just the color is NEW there. You wouldnt want to put New Blue toothpaste on an old toothbrush, would you? Well, here's a "NEW! Toothbrush."

Bounty paper towels says "NEW" on it but I

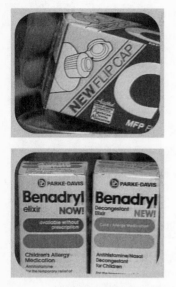

think, again, thats just the color and the pattern thats new. The paper is probably the same. It doesnt matter what it is, as long as they can put NEW on the package.

Colgate toothpaste has a "NEW CAP" on it.

Here's a sort of a mystery to me. One of the big drug companies puts out this cold medicine called Benadryl. This one says "NEW!" on it. But look at this one. It doesnt say "NEW." It says "NOW!" Do you think thats a misprint?

Kleenex. They says Kleenex is "NEW!" I dont know. I certainly wouldnt want a box of "*OLD*" Kleenex.

Advertisers have given a whole different meaning to the word NEW recently. When you see a product called NEW now, it means its smaller and more expensive.

Supreme Court

In anticipation of the possibility that I might have been asked by President Reagan to be a justice of the Supreme Court, Ive been reviewing my life to see what there is in it that anyone would object to.

First, theres my politics. Politically, Im middle-of-the-road Independent and, sometimes, Im all-over-the-road Independent.

As far as I know, Im the only one in my political party. I disagree with everyone on something.

Where do I stand on bussing? I stand on the corner . . . unless its payday or raining, in which case I take a taxi.

You ask if Im prejudiced. Yes, Im prejudiced. There isnt time not to be. I call it experience. Everyone is prejudiced about something. It has a bad reputation but it makes sense. I know I dont like Jell-O.

On the other hand, I was arrested in St. Augustine, Florida, in 1942 for insisting on sitting with black soldiers returning with me to Camp Blanding because I was outraged that they were forced to sit in the back of the bus.

I think women should be paid the same wage for the same job as men . . . although I dont think they can lift as much.

Some of my best friends are Jewish . . . but so are some of the people I like the least . . . to name just a few.

I am opposed to abortion but I like the people who are for it better than the people who are against it.

I dont believe in flying saucers or the Loch Ness monster and I am not on drugs or religion. I dont know my astrological sign.

I am against school prayer for the same reason Im against church arithmetic. I think its wrong to encourage children to think they can get what they want by asking God for it.

I like animals . . . although Im not a vegetarian.

I am against the death penalty but if I could get my hands on some of the people I read about in the paper, I'd like to kill them.

I love my Country but Im dissatisfied with it right now because I think we're selling things better than we're making them.

I believe that if all the truth were known by everyone about everything, it would be a better world.

Do you think I'd be a good Supreme Court justice?

Season Slip

Youve probably heard this is the beginning of the twentieth season for *60 Minutes*. It hardly seems possible that anything twenty years old is twenty years old.

People are always talking about the passage of time. They say they dont know where it goes or "Can you believe its almost October already?"

One of the reasons time seems to go by so fast is our own fault, I think. We're always hurrying time along by looking forward to what's next instead of enjoying what we have today.

This is September 20 and the October issues of a lot of magazines have been around so long theyre old already. What's their hurry? Why is tomorrow or next week or next month so much better than this month, this week or even today?

We keep rushing everything. Thats why time goes by so fast . . . although there may be another reason, too. When you work eight hours a day or you have a headache or youre driving 400 miles, time often seems to drag, but I think the real problem is time doesnt last as long as we think it does.

When I was a small boy, my family had a cottage on a great lake in northern New York State. I loved my summer vacation there but I could never believe how quickly the summer went by. I remember lying in my bed in late August, dreading the thought of having to put on my shoes to go back to school in a few days.

We own a nice summer place now, too. I loved my vacation this year but I cant believe how quickly the summer went by . . . lost and gone forever.

If I didnt have the football season to look forward to, I'd be depressed over the loss.

Medicine Cabinets

I dont know of a door that I open more often that has nothing in it that I really need than the door to the medicine cabinet. One of the things theres almost none of in our medicine cabinet . . . is medicine. Why do we keep calling these little closets in the bathroom "medicine cabinets" when theres no medicine in them?

I say none, but actually there is a little medicine in mine. Two bottles of aspirin. I dont know why two.

And there is some real medicine. I know you arent supposed to do this, but I kept a prescription after I got over whatever it was I had about five years ago. I hated to throw it away. Even though I forget what I had, I'll have the medicine for it if I ever get it again.

I also have adhesive tape. Band-Aids . . . vintage 1950.

Two cans of Johnson's Baby Powder. The youngest person in our house these days voted for Harry Truman but we still have two cans of baby powder.

Vicks VapoRub. An old eye cup back there. We have tincture of merthiolate for cuts. We used to have iodine. I felt as though it worked because iodine stung. Tincture of merthiolate doesnt hurt so I dont trust it.

And there are a few old standbys. Calamine lotion for poison ivy. Unguentine . . . this is an old-timer . . . for burns.

There are always a couple of brushes of some kind in the medicine cabinet that I dont understand. A comb with broken teeth. And this is what I hate. Who puts old toothbrushes in there anyway? No one ever admits theyre theirs. No one wants someone else's toothbrush in the medicine cabinet.

Sloan's Liniment . . . makes me feel athletic.

Bits of soap. I confess I do this. Im not really cheap but I can never bring myself to throw away soap after its too small to use in the shower.

There are always razors and razor blades floating around in there . . . along with shaving cream and even a shaving brush . . . even though Ive been using an electric razor now for twelve years.

I brush my teeth with baking soda.

This is an old lipstick, probably a color thats out of date. This is an empty toothbrush holder.

But then, see . . . there are a lot of things in here I dont dare mention because Im not sure what they are.

One thing is clear. Unisex medicine cabinets dont work. Every man and every woman should have his or her *own* medicine cabinet even if it doesnt have any medicine in it.

Treaty

This has been a big week in Washington. In between parties, the Soviet Union and the United States agreed to destroy all their medium-range nuclear weapons.

A group in Washington has estimated that it will cost the United States taxpayers $8 billion for the weapons we're destroying. It seems like such a waste. Think of all the people we could have killed with those missiles.

This is typical of one of the weapons they have to throw away . . . a U.S. Pershing missile. It can travel

1,000 miles carrying the nuclear equivalent of 50,000 tons of TNT.

Just to give you some idea what 50,000 tons of TNT would do . . . it took only 100 pounds of TNT to take down this Atlantic City hotel.

This is a picture of what the Russians say is one of their missiles. David Martin, the CBS correspondent, points out that this isnt a missile. Its the container for a missile and we dont know whether theres a missile in there or not.

I wasnt asked to participate in these disarmament talks but Ive had quite a bit of personal experience with disarmament.

We were heavily armed back on Partridge Street when I was eight or ten years old. My favorite weapon was a water pistol. A water pistol is a good weapon because you use it on your friends, not your enemies. I'd sneak up on Bobby Reidy or Bud Duffie and try to get them in the back of the neck with it.

We used bean-blowers, too. We shot dried peas with them. And sling shots. Sling shots were good weapons because you couldnt really hit anything.

My first experience with disarmament came when I was 11 and it was a bitter one. My second cousin was allowed to have a .22 so he sold me his old BB gun for a dollar. It was a terrible time in my life. My mother took the gun away from me and thats why I feel so bad about all our generals. I understand how terrible they must feel about losing all their weapons like I did.

My mother actually threw that BB gun away. I dont know where she threw it but away somewhere. She didnt approve of any gun.

It isnt going to be so easy throwing away billions of dollars worth of nuclear missiles.

I wish my mother was around. She'd get rid of them in a hurry.

Photography

When you go on vacation, you ought to decide in advance whether youre going to take pictures or have a good time. You cant do both.

Kodak says that Americans took a total of 13 billion pictures last year. And Kodak didnt say so but I can tell you about 12 billion 999 million of those pictures were bad.

On vacation, everyone's got a camera hanging around his or her neck.

They say the cameras are all automatic now but people sure dont make taking pictures look easy.

Everyone with a camera knows those little numbers mean something but forget exactly what it is they mean.

Photographers go through all sorts of motions just to take one snapshot.

They dream of being artists with the lens.

Wherever the photographer is, he wants to be someplace else. Wherever the subject is, the photographer wants it to move over or back just a little.

Why do so many people seem to think that squatting down with a camera makes better pictures?

People with cameras are always squatting.

Or twisting themselves out of shape.

Squinting seems to be important. They never tell you anything about squinting in the book of instructions that comes with a camera, but apparently you have to know how to squint to take pictures.

Photographers can never decide which way to hold the camera either. Youd think it made a big difference whether the camera was horizontal or vertical.

When the cameraman has everything just right, he's usually forgotten to cock the shutter.

Or the photographer spends ten minutes getting set and at the crucial moment . . . someone walks in front of the lens.

No matter how many pictures photographers take, they always want just one more . . . as if just one more would make it perfect.

No one wants to look at your pictures when you get home and you only want to look at them once yourself. Three years later you look at the pictures. Your clothes look ridiculous. You look ridiculous. Youre depressed for the rest of the day because you looked so young then and so old now. Why put yourself through it?

We're all trying to save our lives forever by taking pictures of it . . . and it doesnt work.

Super Bowl XXI

At this time of year, a lot of poor sports start saying theres too much in the paper about the Super Bowl game. Well, these people dont know what theyre talking about. There isnt *enough* in the papers about the game.

I dont want to hear a lot of complaints this year from those of you who arent interested. Just leave us alone. Accept the fact that this game between the Denver Broncos and the New York Giants is bigger than both of you.

There are people who make fun of us for watching a football game every Sunday. They say things like, "You arent going to sit there in front of a television set on a beautiful day like this, are you?" You know, real superior-like. People who dont watch football on television pretend to be nice people, but theyre really vicious. Theyre like defensive backs. They take cheap shots. They'll spear you if they get the chance. They'll say, "How come you sit around all day watching someone else play a game instead of going out and playing one yourself?"

Well, I can tell them why I watch football instead of playing it myself. Its because Im too old and fat, thats why.

Non-watchers always suggest that fans are wasting their time. You'd think they were always doing real cultural stuff like going to the opera or reading Shakespeare. Ive seen what some of them do instead of watching football on Sunday. It isnt much, I'll tell you that. It isnt like theyre getting to be President or something while we're wasting our time. I dont even notice any of them baking a cake or knitting a sweater. What do *you* do? You go out and wash the car in the driveway? Big deal!

If those of you who arent football fans and dont care who wins the Super Bowl want to do the right thing, dont be smug. Just smile at us nicely and let us have our fun. And most of all, try to be kind when the game is over. Remember, when the football season ends, for us its like a death in the family.

I want to tell you a little story. Next week, *60 Minutes* was to be on after the Super Bowl game. I talked them into letting me do a comment after the game was over from out there. I wangled myself a ticket to the game, I made my hotel and plane reservations, and then they decided there wouldnt be any *60 Minutes* next week because of the game. So, here I am, stuck with a plane reservation, a good hotel room, and this Super Bowl ticket. I dont know whether to go anyway or stay home and wash my car in the driveway.

Talkers

We do a lot of talking at this time of year, what with family around and Christmas and New Year's parties. There are eight or ten basic types of talkers you run into. You must've met all of them. You probably are one of them.

For example, people say I talk too loud. I personally dislike loud talkers. So, Im sorry if I am one.

I'd rather be a loud talker, though, than a real quiet talker. Quiet talkers are the worst. I dont know why it is, but I always think that someone who speaks softly is saying something important. I lean forward trying to catch what the soft talker is saying. "What?" "What'd you say?" "Pardon me?"

Then there are the mumblers. Pipesmokers are mumblers because they talk with their teeth clinched. Mumblers have a reputation for being smart, but I think thats only because you cant hear what theyre saying.

Then there are the talkers who keep repeating themselves. They dont believe you heard them the first time, so, they say it again. "This is a mess in Washington, isnt it? A big mess. We never should have got ourselves into this mess. What a mess!" You understood this guy the first time. You dont want to hear it again, but he keeps telling you. "A real mess!"

Then theres the person who never finishes talking. He pauses in the middle of a sentence, at the commas instead of at the periods, so you cant break in and say what you want to say.

Another type of talker is the person who demands that you answer questions all the time. He'll keep saying, "Isnt that right?" or "Dont you think so?" "You agree with me on that?" This talker seems to want constant confirmation that youre listening. "You know what I mean? You know, dont you?"

The person I least like to talk to is the one who stands too close. He comes right up to your face. I always find it embarrassing. Nose to nose. I normally look a person in the eye when we're talking, but if the person is only eight inches away, my eyes tend to wander when Im talking to him.

Last are the talkers who gesture. They use their hands a lot. They illustrate everything in sign language. They can talk about the whole world or just about some tiny little thing . . . all with their hands.

The gesturers are at their worst giving you directions on how to get somewhere. "You go down here to the third light, take a right, then come back around in—and the thing—its right in here somewhere." I nod but I dont understand.

Conversations can be difficult everywhere, though. For one thing, most of us listen faster than we talk. If everyone had to write out what he or she was trying to say, it'd be a lot more accurate and save listeners a lot of time.

U.S. Embassy

The building constructed in Moscow as a new home for the United States Embassy there has been found to be filled with Soviet listening devices. Theyre built right into the walls by the Russian workers.

Its so bad that even though this building cost us $190 million, we're thinking of tearing it down and starting over again. Its such a waste. Ive been thinking of some other things we might do with that building.

It could be turned into a Holiday Inn, for instance . . . the Holiday Inn Moscow. Divide the building into a couple of hundred bedrooms and rent them out to American tourists. Everyone could listen in on everyone else. Most American tourists dont actually enjoy being in Russia anyway. They just want to tell their friends theyve been there.

If Holiday Inn isnt interested, make the U.S. Embassy in Moscow into a McDonald's, opened to Russian citizens. They could get themselves a Caviar McMuffin. The Embassy McDonald's should have a drive-thru pickup.

Most Russians dont own cars, of course. It would be just a subtle little propaganda device, for us.

Another idea. We'd pretend to use the building as our embassy but all the personnel in it would be actors. Maybe we could get Jimmy Stewart to play the part of our ambassador.

Even the Marine Guards would be actors. I dont think a Russian lady spy would fool around with Mr. T.

Knowing that the Russians would hear everything they said, the actors' lines would be written for them. Every morning theyd get a new script. The script would be full of misinformation . . . false lists of our spies, things like that. It could list the head of the KGB as one of our spies.

Our real ambassador, meanwhile, would work out of a Winnebago in the backyard of the Embassy building.

Another thought. Turn the building into a retreat for our President. Wherever our President goes now, whether its his home in Santa Barbara or Camp David, he's hounded by reporters. The Russians watch U.S. reporters so carefully they dont go anywhere. Moscow is one place the President could go without being followed by reporters.

My last idea may be the best. The building could be used as a prison. It costs $35,000 a year now to keep a prisoner in the United States. Send some of our dangerous criminals to Moscow. Let the Russians watch them the way they watch every other American who goes there.

Appliances

When you buy an electrical appliance for your home, the first thing you have to do is learn to ignore the settings they have printed on the thing and find out how it really works.

Here's a Waring Blender, for example. I call them Waring Blenders but this was actually made by Hamilton Beach. This claims to have fourteen settings. WHIP, STIR, AERATE, PUREE, CRUMB, CHOP, MIX, GRATE, GRIND, BEAT, PULVERIZE, BLEND, FRAPPE and LIQUIFY.

Come on, Hamilton Beach, who are you trying to kid? And what sales executive decided WHIP should come ahead of STIR? Shouldnt STIR be the slowest? And what's with this FRAPPE here? What happened? You run out of English words to use?

Ive been looking around the appliance stores and theres a lot of this sort of thing going on.

Take a new washing machine. You notice its HEAVY DUTY. Youve never seen a LIGHT DUTY piece of equipment of any kind, have you? And it also has three settings: LIGHT SOIL, NORMAL SOIL or HEAVY SOIL. Now I have a dirty shirt. What do I want? LIGHT SOIL, NORMAL SOIL or HEAVY SOIL?

Irons have a lot of settings. One has seven settings for different kinds of material. They could have had just two: CHEAP and EXPENSIVE. And I like this. This is PERMANENT PRESS. Thats where you set the iron for ironing things that the manufacturer says dont need to be ironed.

Toaster Ovens. I never know whether Im baking a potato or toasting a slice of bread. One has DEFROST, BAKE and BROIL. And it also has LIGHT, TOP BROWN and DARK. It doesnt have a BURNED setting for toast. It does that by itself. Why doesnt it turn off automatically when it starts to burn? They should make a toaster that smells smoke.

Vacuum cleaners havent changed much except for the writing on them. This has HIGH, NORMAL and LOW and it also has LOW SHAG, MEDIUM SHAG and DEEP SHAG. Then it has something called EDGE CLEANER and VIBRA-GROOMER II . . . if you want to groom your vibras.

This drier has DAMP DRY, LESS DRY, NORMAL DRY, MORE DRY and VERY DRY. If youre drying your underwear, how do you want it? You want it DAMP DRY, LESS DRY, GENTLE DRY or VERY DRY? I just damn well want my shorts dry!

I'd like to say this to you appliance makers. Some of your products are very good but dont try to kid us with a lot of buttons when all we really need is an ON/OFF switch.

How to Carry Money

There never was so much talk about money as there is these days. IRAs, money market accounts, mutual funds, home equity loans. Money's gotten more complicated. You have to be smart with money. I hate trying to be smart with money. Its hard enough just making it without having to do something else with it once you make it.

The only money Im any good with at all is the cash I carry on me. Here's the way I carry my money around. In a lump. Whatever bills I have I just stuff in my pocket along with the elastic bands, paper clips, Kleenex and whatever else happens to be in there.

Ive got quite a bit today because I just cashed a check. I normally carry $35 or $40. It may look messy but its very efficient. Nothing between me and my money . . . no wallet, no billfold, no money clip.

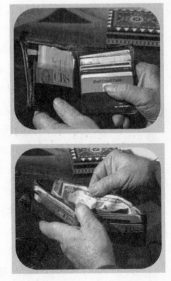

Most men carry a wallet. They keep it in their hip pocket with all this stuff in it. This is the wallet of Bobby Clemens, the cameraman. To tell you the truth, I dont have the ideal build for keeping a lump like this in my hip pocket.

This is Bob Forte's. He's got all his bills lined up . . . twenties, tens, fives. He's even got a two in here.

I think men's wallets tend to look like their garages. If their garage is a mess, their wallet's a mess.

My garage is a mess.

Women keep their money in their purse. When a woman wants to pay for something, she has to mine for her money. She opens up her purse, starts unsnapping things, unzips the side here, goes in and gets the bills. Then she fishes down in here . . . gets this out . . . opens this up. She takes this out, opens this up, and then goes down in here for the quarters. It can take a woman eight minutes to pay for an item that costs $1.29. And then once theyve paid for something, they have to repack. They put everything down and they start back in, putting everything back in, zipping and snapping away for five or ten minutes. Men hate to get in a line at the checkout counter behind a woman.

Some men carry little purses too . . . little change purses. When I see a guy with one of these things with the two balls on top that he twists to open, I know Im behind a guy who is very careful with his money. He's usually . . . well . . . he's cheap, is what he is.

I dont care what the financial experts say you should do with your money, though. You cant beat the good feeling of carrying some of what youve made around with you.

The real problem with the money we carry around is that you cant tell how much the bills are worth by the feeling of them in your pocket. I cant figure why they decided to make each coin a different size when they made the twenty-dollar bill the same size as the one-dollar bill.

The richest friend I ever had, Steve Slesinger, never had any money with him. I'd like to be that rich. Steve would go into a restaurant, for instance, and just say, "Send me the bill," and theyd always do it. I'd like to see him try that in the CBS cafeteria.

Arms Control

Ive never understood disarmament conferences. No one ever seems to get disarmed at one of them. If a country has 100 nuclear weapons and agrees to give up three, does this make the world safe?

Soviet and American negotiators are back in Geneva again arguing about how many long-range missiles one country gets, how many short-range ones the other one gets. Big deal.

Each country in the world should get a weapons allowance . . . a specific amount it could spend on arms . . . and the country could spend that allowance any way it wanted to.

If Russia wanted to spend all of its money on missiles, thats Russia's business. Maybe we'd spend all of ours on Star Wars or on nuclear submarines. If Russia had nothing but tanks and we had nothing but submarines, it would make a very interesting war.

I have some information on how much the world spends on weapons. These figures are for 1985.

The United States spent $204 billion. Russia spent $146 billion. The Russian workers are probably paid less than our workers so the Russians get more bang for the buck. Great Britain spent $30 billion; thats about the same as what China spent. And all the smaller countries spent a lot of money considering what they have.

The whole world will spend about $1 trillion for arms in 1987.

If the world spent all the money on food that it now spends on weapons, no one would ever be hungry. For the smartest animals on Earth, humans are sure dumb sometimes.

Theres one missing figure here. I left it out intentionally. Japan spent only $11 billion for weapons in 1985, compared to our $204 billion.

After World War II we foolishly limited the amount that Japan can spend on weapons. Its one of the reasons Japan is doing so well. Theyre making all the good things, television sets, computers, toasters, cars for the whole world, because $300 billion worth of our production goes into nuclear warheads, fighting airplanes that none of us can fly in and tanks we cant ride in. The Japanese dont have a single nuclear submarine or one atomic bomb. Shame on you, Japan.

According to my plan, to keep the Japanese from taking over the whole world peacefully, we'd insist that they waste at least as much money on weapons as we do.

1988

Too Much

I dont know about where you are, but where I am, theres too much to read, too much to watch.

Every day theres another newspaper coming out with all sorts of interesting stuff to read in it. There are movies I ought to see and dont get time for. I havent even seen *Kramer vs. Kramer* yet. Its got so I hate to go past a book store because there are so many good books I feel bad about not reading.

When I come into Grand Central Terminal every morning and head for the office, I pass a newsstand. Its got every magazine known to man and quite a few most men never heard of. I'd like to read all of them.

And you can talk about how bad a lot of programs are on television but it isnt the bad ones that bother me. I love the bad television shows because I dont feel guilty about not watching them. The more bad television shows there are, the more free time I have.

I look through the television guides in the magazines and newspapers hoping to find something I dont want to watch. Here's one: DELIVERYMAN FROM CHINESE RESTAURANT FINDS HIS LIFE CHANGED WHEN HE ACCIDENTALLY UNCOVERS AN INTERNATIONAL SPY RING.

Thats what I love to find because I know I dont want to waste my time watching it. *David Letterman* is one of my favorite television shows and Ive never even seen that because its on too late. I dont know who stays up watching television after midnight.

We have cable television in our house because we get better reception with it. There are fifty-three channels, not counting the dirty ones. Now, when does anyone watch fifty-three television channels?

I paid $500 for a videotape recorder. In the past three years Ive recorded forty-seven television shows to watch later. Ive never had the time to watch one of them. I still mean to watch *Roots*.

I read *The New York Times* every Sunday. Its very good but you know what's happened? There are so many ads in it now that my newspaper deliverer cant carry the whole thing. He brings half of it on Saturday and the other half Sunday. If he cant carry it, how am I supposed to read it?

There were 834 pages in the *Times* last Sunday . . . that would take me five days to read. The deliveryman would be coming with next week's paper.

Theres simply too much to read, too much to watch. When do we get to sit down and just worry?

Warning Labels

We're always being warned. Had you noticed how often we're being warned? I feel sorry for people who make some products. They spend millions of dollars on advertising, telling us how great their stuff is, and then in little black and white letters on the bottom of label, the Government makes them say things like "YOU BETTER WATCH OUT FOR THIS STUFF BECAUSE IF YOU ARENT CAREFUL, IT COULD KILL YOU."

Every package, no matter what it is, has a warning on it saying "CAUTION," "DANGER" or "SEE YOUR PHYSICIAN."

If you read the labels on half the products you buy, youd be too scared to use them. You buy medicine and the label tells you not to take it.

This is some kind of a decongestant. The label says, "DO NOT USE THIS PREPARATION IF YOU HAVE HIGH BLOOD PRESSURE, HEART DISEASE, DIABETES, THYROID DISEASE, ASTHMA, OR GLAUCOMA. DO NOT TAKE THIS PRODUCT IF YOU ARE PRESENTLY TAKING A PRESCRIPTIVE ANTI-HYPERTENSIVE DRUG CONTAINING A MONOAMINE OXIDASE INHIBITOR . . . "

Well I have no idea whether Im taking a "monoamine oxidase inhibitor" or not. Is there any in Shredded Wheat? Everybody over thirty has a disease of one kind or another.

Here's a box of washing machine detergent. "IF SWALLOWED CALL PHYSICIAN IMMEDIATELY." Thats what it says on this little can of wood finish, too. "IF SWALLOWED CALL PHYSICIAN IMMEDIATELY." If I swallowed either of these I wouldnt be able to get to the phone.

Everything dangerous should be kept where kids cant get at it but is any adult really going to eat this detergent accidentally . . . and then wash it down with a can of varnish?

I find it strange that we have a law forcing manufacturers to put a label on a box of soap telling people not to eat it.

Here's a bottle of good bourbon. Its interesting to note that theres no warning at all on this. If you swallow a little of this, dont call your doctor . . . he's probably swallowing a little of it himself.

This bottle of glue I keep on my desk. I like to live dangerously. "DO NOT USE NEAR FLAME" it says, and "IF SWALLOWED CALL PHYSICIAN IMMEDIATELY."

"Hello, Doctor? I just drank a quart of glue by mistake. What should I do? Should I stick around?"

Our Government treats us as though we were idiots who dont know how to take care of ourselves. Are people really as dumb as the Government thinks?

Please . . . dont answer that question.

Money for Sale

The one thing all presidential candidates seem to agree on is, we've got to do something about the National Debt. They call it the National Debt . . . it should be called the Government Debt but the Government doesnt want to take the blame.

ROBERT DOLE:
The National Debt is about $2.4 trillion. We're paying $150 billion a year interest on the debt.

RICHARD GEPHARDT:
Ronald Reagan's created more debt in the last seven years than all the presidents between Washington and Carter.

PAT ROBERTSON:
We cannot continue to run up these enormous debts. We are mortgaging the future of our kids.

Here's my idea. We're advertising-crazy in this Country. We've got it everywhere. Why doesnt the

Government sell space on our money? I'll bet a lot of people would pay plenty to advertise on a dollar bill. Take George Washington off it. He doesnt need the publicity.

Chrysler might go for a picture of Lee Iacocco on one side of a ten-dollar bill and a Chrysler Le Baron on the other.

It would be a great opportunity for presidential candidates to push themselves on us. Pat Robertson might become better known if he had his picture on a five.

Business tycoon Donald Trump would certainly go for $10 million to have his picture on the face of a twenty and his gambling casino in Atlantic City on the back.

NBC might want to promote Tom Brokaw.

The only other way I can think of to reduce the National Debt is silly, I guess . . . that would be to stop spending so much on weapons.

Paint

I dont want to abuse my position here . . . I know CBS gets a lot of money for a commercial on *60 Minutes* . . . but Ive got some stuff I'd like to sell. Does anyone need paint? I was down in my basement the other night and I can offer you a very good deal on used paint.

Here's a can of grey, circa 1968. Its for "terior" use. All I can read is "t-e-r-i-o-r" because of dripped paint, so I dont know if its for INterior or EXterior.

I want to be honest with you, too. I cant hear the paint sloshing around in here so it may not be any good . . . in which case youd get your money back, of course. Thats how you tell whether to keep an old can of paint or not. If you can hear it sloshing around in there when you shake it, you keep it.

This is a good can of paint . . . or was anyway. PITTSBURGH SPEED-HIDE ALKYD. I dont know what "ALKYD" is . . . I dont know whether its water or oil base. Its different from "ACRYLIC," I do know that. This is "ACRYLIC." I dont know what that means, either.

Dont believe everything you read on a can of paint, even if you buy it from me. This one says ONE COAT—NO DRIP. You want to bet? When I paint with something that says ONE COAT—NO DRIP, it takes three coats and the only thing that gets covered with paint is me . . . from the drips.

Look at this picture on this can. Do you believe this guy really painted anything in that turtleneck sweater? He's an actor, not a painter. And these three women. Theyve painted their faces, you can see that. Theyre models.

I can give you a good buy on this if you like it. This is turquoise. You can see the color chart here on the back.

The directions on these cans are all the same. It says "THE SURFACE TO BE PAINTED MUST BE CLEAN AND FREE OF GREASE OR DIRT." It goes on. Well, if the surface is that good, who wants to paint it anyway?

This can of shellac looks almost new. This should bring a top price. This one says its varnish. I dont know what the white paint is doing there, dripping down the side, if its varnish. You can look inside and make sure before you buy it.

You know the thing about varnish and shellac, dont you? You can put varnish on over shellac but you cannot put shellac on over varnish. Or is it vice versa?

Well, anyway, here's an old can of spray paint. Ive got a lot more of these where this one came from. You can hear theres still plenty in here. It sloshes. I'll mark this one down though because it doesnt spray any more. The little hole is all clogged up. I'll throw in a hairpin at no additional cost.

By the way, with each can of paint I sell Im going to give away a free paint brush. The brushes have been used and theyre hard . . . you cant paint with them . . . but other than that, theyre good as new.

Free

Theres a four-letter word that Americans love more than any other word in the English language . . . and the word is FREE. Free has two meanings and both meanings are good. Americans like the idea of *being* free . . . and they love the idea of *getting something* free.

Wouldnt you just know that the advertisers would try to get in on this great word and ruin it for us? Look at these clippings from magazines and newspapers and you can see the same thing on television. Everything's FREE.

"FREE MILK." "FREE COOKBOOK." Reach out and you can get a "FREE LONG DISTANCE PHONE CALL."

How many people think theyre really going to get something free?

I bought a package of four bars of soap that cost $2.37. It says "BUY THREE GET ONE FREE." If youre buying four, youre paying 59 cents each for the bars of soap. Now, if you figure youre only buying three, each bar of soap costs 79 cents and one free. Why are they trying to kid us?

Here's another FREE ad from Ritz Crackers, made by Nabisco. This is all you have to do to get a free box of Ritz Crackers. "Buy two boxes of Ritz Crackers and two boxes of Ritz Bits. Send four brand seals (whatever a brand seal is), two Ritz Crackers brand seals and two Ritz Bits brand seals." Send them to El Paso, Texas. "Allow eight weeks for handling" and you get a FREE box of crackers. Thats all there is to it.

First you buy a lifetime supply of their crackers. Tear the boxes into small pieces. Send the pieces to Texas and presto! Eight weeks later you got another box of crackers. Meanwhile, of course, the kids have decided they dont like Ritz Crackers.

Here's a bag of cat food that says it has a "FREE COLLECTIBLE COIN INSIDE." The bag cost $3.99. "One of these genuine coins is inside FREE" it says. A $5 gold coin, a Lincoln penny, a silver dollar, a Kennedy half dollar.

Which do you think will be in here? A gold coin, silver dollar or a penny? Anyone like to make a bet?

Well, Im going to cut it open and see. Let's see what this is going to be. A gold coin, do you think? I'll just see what this is.

Well, what do you know, a Lincoln penny . . . surprise . . . which means this bag cost only $3.98, not $3.99.

None of these ads saying things are free represent what any of us think when we think how much we like the word FREE.

History Unknown

For every well-known person or event in history, there are a thousand that are lost. Tonight we thought we'd tell you about a few that never made the history books.

In 1776 George Washington crossed the Delaware River. You recall the picture of him standing in the bow of the boat. Shortly after this picture was painted, the man rowing the boat yelled at General Washington to sit down so he could see where he was going.

In 1876 Alexander Graham Bell invented the telephone. As we all know, the first sound transmitted was Bell's voice saying, "Mr. Watson, come here, I want you." We never knew what Bell heard back on that first phone call and tonight we have that message.

WATSON:

I cant come to the phone right now but if youll leave a message, I'll get back to you as soon as possible. Please wait for the beep.

You recall Benjamin Franklin proved that there was electricity in lightning when he attracted it to a key at the end of a kite string during a storm. Well, this was the key that Franklin didnt use because it was to the back door of his house and he didnt want to lose it.

Every school child hears about that famous early day American Buffalo Bill. Well, there were other great buffalo hunters and no one ever hears of them anymore because somehow their names never caught on . . . Buffalo Ralph . . . Buffalo Clarence . . . and Buffalo Bruce.

In 1863 Abraham Lincoln delivered his famous Gettysburg Address after writing it on the back of an envelope that he had in his pocket during the train ride from Washington. This is another envelope that Lincoln had with him, but he didnt use it because it had one of those little windows in it, and if he'd tried to write his Gettysburg Address on this, he wouldnt have had enough room.

Someday we'll show you the pilot film made for *60 Minutes* that failed to get on the air. Executives at CBS News blamed it on the title. It was called simply *One Hour.*

The IRS

Im planning on doing my income tax in the next two or three weeks now.

They give you a booklet, *INSTRUCTIONS FOR PREPARING.*

On the cover, theres a letter from the commissioner, Lawrence B. Gibbs,

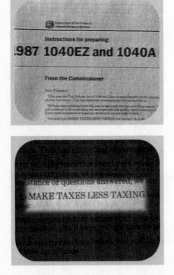

and its the kind of thing that makes you wonder about the IRS.

"Dear Taxpayer," he begins. He calls us "Dear." I guess he likes us.

"This year the Tax Reform Act of 1986 will have a major impact on the preparation of your tax return."

"Major impact." Thats the way they say "change" in Washington. "Impact" is Government talk meaning "change."

Next paragraph. "We have been working hard this year to get ready for the next filing season."

Now, is this any place for him to be telling me how hard he's been working? Do we care? Is there any place on the tax form for me to tell him how hard *Ive* been working?

How about this? "Our goal is to MAKE TAXES LESS TAXING." He puts that in capital letters. Very clever, Larry. Have you ever thought of going into advertising? Maybe you could invent slogans. You know, WE MAKE MONEY THE OLD-FASHION WAY. WE TAKE IT FROM YOU.

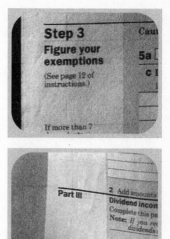

Then he says he has a few suggestions.

"Start preparing your return earlier than ever before."

They always tell you it will make it easier if you do your tax return early. What they dont tell you is who it'll be easier for. It will be easier for them, thats who it'll be easier for. It wont be any easier for you.

Here's the so-called simplified tax form, 1040 EZ. On the first page of this form, they have Step One, Step Two, Step Three, Step Four and Five. On the next page they dont feel like doing the Step thing anymore. They call them Parts. Part One, Part Two, Part Three and you notice they decide to use Roman numerals over here, too. Roman numerals give a number more class.

I think Lawrence Gibbs, our tax commissioner, knows Im just kidding about all this. Just a little joke, Larry. Youre doing a great job. I'll have my tax return in early this year because I want to make it easy for you fellows.

Maybe I could take you and the Missus out to dinner some night . . . Could I deduct that as a business expense?

Escalators

My Aunt Anna took me to New York and gave me my first ride on an escalator in Macy's when I was six years old. I'll never forget it.

Theres something magic about an escalator. The idea of stairs that move up or down, carrying anyone standing on them, and then, folding into the floor when they get to the top or the bottom is one of the craziest, most orig-

inal, most work-saving inventions of all time. What brilliant nut thought of that?

We all love anything free and escalators seem like a free ride. They dont move as fast as elevators but you dont have to wait for an escalator to come, either.

The classic stance going up is to put one foot on the next step. Its comfortable and it leaves the rider ready to get off. And there are all kinds of variations to that.

Conservative riders grip the moving rails for safety even though its not a dangerous ride. Coming down, some people hold both rails . . . like standing on a diving board ready to jump.

Those who use escalators all the time are casual on them. They ride easily. Its a piece of cake . . . or a cup of coffee. Some riders are impatient with the slow rumbling pace of the staircase. They double the speed by walking . . . or triple it by running.

On crowded escalators the riders trying to get somewhere in a hurry make their way past the tourists.

Kids never cease to be fascinated by these steps that move. If they had their choice in a store, they wouldnt do anything but ride the escalators up and down all day long. Theyre always fooling around on them. They love running up the down staircase.

Escalators keep doing their thing relentlessly whether theyre crowded or empty.

For some riders an escalator provides a brief interlude for quiet looking around . . . a miniature plane ride . . . a pause in the day's occupation. The world around them is a moving picture and their tangential movement provides them a second dimension within it.

Aunt Anna's gone now. She was awfully good to me. She'd be pleased I think of her every time I ride on an escalator.

Cigarette Smoking

I never smoked cigarettes. There wasnt anything virtuous about it, I just never did. I tried them a few times but they made me cough and made my mouth taste bad so I never smoked.

Those of us who dont smoke dont like to have smokers in the room with us but I think the time has come for us to be more tolerant of smokers. We've been awfully mean to them and theyve got a problem.

You can see how people get hooked on smoking. We all like to do the things we know how to do best and smokers get very familiar with all the little moves they make with cigarettes.

They have this solid little pack of goodies in their hands that makes them feel secure. They unwrap it carefully and they take out a cigarette and they tap the first one out. You know the way they do it. And then they hit it on something solid. They put it in their mouth and they light it.

Lighting a cigarette must be a big part of the fun. I can understand that. Ive always loved to play with fire. Theres something magic about a match. One flip of the wrist . . . two flips of the wrist . . . and you have flame enough to burn down all of Chicago. Its pretty, its dangerous and it lights the cigarette.

I always envied the guys who could light their girls' cigarettes . . . sort of romantic, you know, particularly when theyd light one for themselves and hold it. Or else theyd light the match and then theyd cup their hands and it would light up the girl's face as they did it.

I traveled with a lot of newspapermen and some of them never took the cigarette out of their mouth. Theyd ask questions without ever removing the cigarette. Theyd talk all the time that way. A friend of mine named Homer Bigart used to get ashes all over his necktie.

Some serious smokers hold their whole hand over their mouth when they smoke. The cigarette stuck out between their second and third finger. And women do it just the opposite sometimes . . . women with red nail polish, particularly. They hold a cigarette way out at the end between their thumb and forefinger, as if they were trying to get away from it.

The English are terrible smokers. They smoke cigarettes right down to the last nub. They want to get the last gasp out of them. Their fingers turn yellow.

The Russians and some Europeans have this crazy way of holding a cigarette. They do it upside down and backwards.

But no matter how they smoke them . . . COUGH . . . no kidding . . . you have to remember that cigarette smokers are people, too. We all hope they'll stop but whether they stop or not, let's all be nice to a cigarette smoker today . . . after all, we may not have them with us for long. COUGH.

Astrology

Ive always been interested in astrology . . . the same way Im interested in a lot of other things . . . things like flying saucers, weeping statues of the Virgin Mary, the Loch Ness monster, poltergeists, fortune tellers, faith heelers . . . Im interested because theyre all nonsense.

Several years ago I interviewed Jeane Dixon, who is reported to have been the first astrologist whom Nancy Reagan relied on for guidance.

ROONEY:
Isnt it almost un-American of you not to give the State Department your best advice?

JEANE DIXON:
Oh, would I love to have the State Department ask me for advice. If they did, Mr. Rooney, I can tell you that this Country would not be in the trouble it is today. I can tell you that because if you knew the things I have told the State Department . . . that I have written to the Presidents of the United States. Sometimes they take the advice and sometimes they do not.

ROONEY:
The other day I asked Lynne Palmer, an astrologist in New York City, what she thinks is coming up for President Reagan in the immediate future.

LYNNE PALMER:
Starting the fifteenth of this month, he's got some upsets in, you know, with astrology and the whole thing.

ROONEY:

What kind of thing do you think is apt to happen?

PALMER:

Well, you know, he's got a lot of shocks and surprises and he may not be as charming as normal. He may be a little erratic coming up from the fifteenth of this month to the fifteenth of next month.

ROONEY:

But youre comfortable having the United States guided by a man who takes advice from astrologists?

PALMER:

Well, I think he's a wonderful President.

ROONEY:

Whatever we think of the President's politics, most of us like Ronald and Nancy Reagan. We like their love affair with each other. She really cares for him. He cares for her more than for the Presidency. Its nice.

Why are so many people disturbed then by the report that the President and Mrs. Reagan have relied on astrology?

I'll tell you why. Because it means theyve turned the governing of our Country over to something other than the best thing we have going for us, our brains.

If everything we are and everything we're going to become depends on the stars and on hoping and praying and betting on the lottery, then the brains we have dont matter. Logical thinking doesnt matter. Education doesnt matter. The experience of history doesnt matter. Being a good parent doesnt matter. None of these things matters because our destiny isnt in our own hands. It all depends on luck. Why knock ourselves out? If its in the stars?

Good Things

Im as patriotic as the next person but I dont think being United States citizens makes us wonderful people . . . it makes us *lucky* people.

With all the negative talk we've had during the campaign about what's wrong, I thought this would be a good night to talk about what's right with America. What's right with America?

Well, we have more good food in our grocery stores than any other country in the world . . . our shopping carts runneth over . . . and if Macy's opened a department store in Moscow, the Russians would pay money just to come in and look.

We're the only Country on Earth that has more cars and trucks, 181 million of them, than we have people over 18 years old—179 million, who are old enough to drive them. If all the drivers in California got out of their cars at the same time, there wouldnt be room enough for them to open their car doors.

Theres less snobbery in the United States. It doesnt matter who you are. You can make it on your own even if your parents are rich.

We're Number One in toilet paper. Our toilet paper is better than the paper money in most countries. In some countries, you cant tear the toilet paper and the money falls apart in your hands. Charles Kuralt said that.

A lot of us hate each other but our laws are on the side of equal rights for everyone. Theres racism, theres sexism, but the star of the most popular show on television is a black American, Bill Cosby, who's made so much money that last week he gave $20 million to a college that has only one white student and no men at all.

You may not like the news you get in your newspapers or from television but none of it is controlled by the Government.

We have laws that protect us from each other. No one can make a medicine and sell it before the Government tests it. And a can of something has to say what's in it.

Our handicapped people are not all hidden away in back rooms.

Our telephones work.

There are thousands more things right with America. We have thirty-seven flavors of ice cream, 3,406 colleges, three oceans. We have freedom of religion and freedom from it if we dont want it.

We have the World Series, the Super Bowl and Disneyland and you can turn right on red in all fifty states. And the one thing that makes us all like America better than any other country . . . there are more Americans living here than any place else.

Pockets

What I am about to say, I say in the friendliest possible way. I offer it in the form of advice, not criticism. In my opinion, the only thing holding back women in their quest for equality with men is the fact that they dont have enough pockets in their clothes. Lots of dresses dont have any pockets at all.

When a man is dressed in a suit, he's apt to have as many as ten pockets. Look at this. I have this outside pocket where I keep my glasses. I have these

two side pockets at the sides in this jacket. I dont even use this one. This one has another pocket over here. And look, this one has a little pocket inside the pocket where I keep my change. Its very handy.

Then I have my two pants pockets. I keep my keys in here . . . and my money and my comb over here. Then I have two back pockets in my pants. Four pants pockets. In one back pocket I keep a handkerchief usually or a Kleenex.

Then I have these inside here. I keep odds and ends in this side. I dont carry a wallet so I keep my credit cards in this pocket. Ten pockets all together for a well-dressed man. None for women. The more expensive a woman's clothes are—the fewer pockets. Twelve are in them.

The trouble is women put fashion in front of convenience by not having pockets. Some dresses, of course, arent big enough for pockets.

Even when women wear pants, the pants are often made without pockets. Women dont want men looking at them when they have something in their pockets and thinking thats the shape *they* are.

Carrying stuff in a pocket does tend to make a person lumpy. Thats the price you have to pay for having something where you can find it.

Because women often dont have pockets, they carry a lot of bags to put their things in. This may account for how the custom of a man opening a door for a woman got started. She has only one hand free because her purse is in the other one.

Its why a man is expected to pay when a man and woman go out to eat together. It takes too long for a woman to find her money.

No pockets may account for why we've never had a woman President.

1989

Please Cover Up

Fashion Is Spinach (Thurber Said)

I dont offhand recall any history lesson that told me when men and women started covering their bodies for some reason other than modesty and warmth.

Obviously, at some point thousands of years ago, our ancient ancestors realized they could make themselves look better by hiding some of their body parts behind cloth.

We make things beautiful because beauty enriches our lives in some way we cant explain.

We grow gardens because we like pretty flowers.

We hang pictures that improve the appearance of bare walls.

We cover the walls of our houses with decorative paper.

We put fountains in public places.

I understand all that . . . but I dont understand women's fashions. A woman can look her best but she cant look any better than her best by hanging expensive cloth over her body.

The best most of us can do with clothes is hide how funny we look naked. The strange thing is, the women they use as models to sell clothes by posing in them, are among the few who wouldnt look bad without any.

The fashion industry, the people who design, make and sell women's clothes, play cruel tricks on the average woman. They try to make her think . . . and often succeed in making her think . . . that she can look just like the model in the picture if she will spend enough money on clothes.

The average woman will never look like the model in the picture. The clothes were made for perfectly shaped models and bought by average, imperfectly shaped women. The average woman, like the average man, is seriously less than perfectly shaped.

Dress designers have perpetrated the hemline hoax on women for a hundred years. A good piece of cloth is a work of art. I hate to think of all the good pieces of cloth that are thrown out, discarded with the trash because it has been decreed that the bottom of the dress is closer to the floor than fashion dictates it should be this year.

Why am I the only one who knows for certain where a dress should come on a woman's leg? A dress or skirt should come just below the knee.

Some things are better left covered and knees are two of them.

No woman's knee is so good-looking that it should be featured by the dress the woman has on. A knee is about as good-looking as an elbow and that isnt saying much for it.

The only reason designers make dresses that show the knee is because of the promise of more that the knee and a short skirt offer.

A great many women wear pants that cover not only the knee but the calf. Fifty years ago no one would have thought theyd be making fashionable pants for women but pants have opened up a whole new world for designers.

They say women dress for men but its not certain that this is true. If women dressed for men, theyd never wear pants because men dont like pants on women.

You can complain and say this is a sexist attitude men have, which may be true . . . but saying so wont make it go away.

The advertising of women's underwear is even more outrageous than the advertising of outerwear.

When they began advertising women's underwear, it was to show how warm, practical and functional it was. Somewhere along the line, something went wrong. Instead of covering women, the ads began to show how much underwear could uncover.

In these ads, youd think women went around all day with nothing on but their underwear.

Are women really fooled into buying underwear because they think theyll look like the models in the ads?

Its funny all the underwear theyre trying to sell because when they show women wearing dresses in advertisements, half the time it doesnt look as though the women are wearing any underwear at all.

The less the underwear covers, the more it costs.

Theres something wrong with magazine ads. Just like some of the offensive commercials on television, I dont want to be stared in the face by a woman in her underwear when I open a magazine.

Ive actually been to a fashion show in Paris. Its a terrible experience everyone should do once . . . like staying up all night at the senior prom.

The models on the ramp at the show didnt walk the way I thought they were going to. They must be teaching models a new way to walk. They moved more like construction workers carrying lunch pails . . . although these girls obviously dont eat lunch.

If I'd been looking for something to wear as a Halloween costume, I was in the right place.

At the show, I kept noticing I was the only one who was laughing. People who go to fashion shows take fashion shows seriously.

Too many of the clothes I saw here and in pictures of other fashion shows, were trying to be different for no reason.

Women's fashions are change for the sake of change and I dont really mind them . . . its just that sometimes it seems as though there must be something better to do with money.

What's in the Package

Youve probably had this happen. You have a friend or a relative who's sick. You mean to call or visit and the person dies before you do it. Makes you feel terrible.

A couple of years ago I got a phone call. A woman's voice said, "Mr Rooney?" I said, "Yes," because thats my name and she said, "Would you talk to Cary Grant?"

Would you like to talk to Cary Grant? Would I talk to Cary Grant? Would I talk to the President if he called?

You know why Cary Grant called? He wanted to suggest I do something about packages that are hard to open. I didnt have the heart to tell him, but three out of five people who call me want me to do something about how hard packages are to open and every once in a while, I do it.

The fact is, the people who figure out how to wrap things are probably smarter than the rest of us who have to open them.

Here's a good example. A little package of crackers. You get these with soup at a lunch counter. Its tidy. Its attractive. It keep the crackers fresh . . . but you cant get at them. Theres supposed to be a little tab here but you can never find it.

They also give you little containers of butter. Theyre supposed to have a tab you pull but even if you find the tab, you cant pull it.

Theres only one way to get into something like that. Use your teeth. I know that isnt what the inventor had in mind.

The same with the little bag of nuts airlines give you to make you forget how jammed in you are and how long you had to wait at the ticket counter.

Cardboard boxes of food. A lot of things come in this kind of package. You know, it says, PUSH IN AND PULL UP.

Sounds good but you cant push it in and if you do get it pushed in, you cant pull it up.

This is a box of Minute Rice. It may cook in a minute but it takes three minutes to open the box.

If theyre going to keep packaging things like this, we're all going to have to develop stronger fingernails. Short of having a sharp knife in your pocket, how do you get into this?

We get five packages a day in the office that say things like PULL HERE TO OPEN. Pull WHERE to open?

Cary Grant spoke specifically about the new tape you cant tear. Here's a good example of that. This is a book in here. You cant tear the tape . . . and look . . . they dont want you to cut it with a knife.

I bought a roll of stamps at the post office. Beautiful little package but I need a can opener to get at the stamps.

I hate a package thats smarter than I am and harder to open than a bank vault.

Thanks for calling, Cary. I loved you in *To Catch a Thief* with Grace Kelly.

Do It Yourself

Theres been a big Do-It-Yourself movement in this Country. Everything's Do-It-Yourself.

The latest Do-It-Yourself thing is at the gas pump. Theyre making us pump gas ourselves now. Seventy-nine percent of the pumps are Do-It-Yourself now.

The first thing you have to learn, if youre going to fill your own gas tank is which side your tank is on.

If you pull in on the wrong side, its hard to get the hose to reach. Sometimes its not only hard, its impossible or illegal.

Both men and women often have trouble pumping their own gas. Something isnt right. Fewer women than men like to Do It Themselves. Its hard to do it without getting the smelly stuff on your hands and women dont want to spend the rest of the day smelling like garage mechanics.

Some women are very good at it though.

What to do with the gas cap is a problem with some cars . . . once you have it off, you have to find a place to put it while you pump.

With the new safety hoses, its harder to get the nozzle into the gas tank.

It takes about two minutes to pump fifteen gallons of gas and it seems like a long wait.

There isnt much to do while the gas is flowing. Customers try to get comfortable. Some are relaxed . . . they take it easy.

They lean on their cars . . . they look for someplace to put their feet.

Other gas pumpers are tense . . . they check the meter like a hawk . . . watching the money go down the drain

People in the gas business say its quicker, cheaper and just as safe to Do-It-Yourself.

Well, I like saving the money but I still dont want to do a lot of things myself. I want to pay someone to do them for me. Im not a plumber and I dont want to do my own plumbing. Im not a gas station attendant and I dont want to pump gas.

What we need in this Country is a new movement: DONT DO IT YOURSELF!

The Fine Print

Tonight . . . I want to take a look at the fine print.

For years theyve warned us about the fine print in legal documents but you have to watch out for the fine print everywhere these days.

All the good stuff is easy to read in normal-size type . . . then you get down to the bottom, where you need a magnifying glass . . . and you get the real story in small print. The type is smaller than the smallest an eye doctor has on that chart he nakes you try to read.

Every offer in small print is "SUBJECT TO CHANGE WITHOUT NOTICE."

Or it says, "PRICE SUBJECT TO CHANGE."

"Handling charges" are big in small print. They always mention handling charges where you dont notice them.

This says, "PLUS SHIPPING AND HANDLING."

I understand shipping . . . you have to expect youll pay for the stamps or the freight company . . . but what's this "handling" they always mention? How much does "handling" cost them? I dont want a lot of people "handling" something Im buying.

My question to these companies is this: "How much would it cost if you didnt handle it before you sent it to me?

The travel ads are filled with small print from airlines and hotels.

The biggest small print item in the hotel ads is "DOUBLE OCCUPANCY." Watch out for double occupancy. One says $49, "double occupancy." I called the number and you pay $114 for this hotel room for one night. Prices are per person and they wont rent it to just one person.

Here's an offer for video tape cassettes. Shipping and handling are extra, of course. But look at this:

"PLEASE ALLOW UP TO EIGHT WEEKS FOR FIRST SHIPMENT."

Two months? To get some video tapes you probably wont want by then? They must wait until you order the tapes before they start making them.

Some of these phrases I dont even understand.

"RETURNS SUBJECT TO RESTOCKING FEE."

Ive been doing a little survey and here are some of the most-used phrases:

"CERTAIN RESTRICTIONS APPLY."

". . . NOT INCLUDED." It doesnt matter what it is, you can bet its not included.

"OFFER NOT GOOD IN NEBRASKA." I dont know what it is about some states like Nebraska but offers are never any good there.

"QUANTITIES ARE LIMITED."

"WE RESERVE THE RIGHT TO . . ."

"OFFER NOT GOOD AFTER . . . "

"NOT ALL MODELS AVAILABLE AT ALL STORES."

"VOID WHERE PROHIBITED." Nebraska, probably.

The one thing you can be certain of: Nothing in fine print is good news.

Food for Thought

We all eat out in a restaurant once in a while. It can be a good or bad experience and it doesnt all depend on the food. All the little things are important.

Youre in a restaurant, you sit down, start looking at the menu. The waiter or waitress comes up.

"My name is Bob. What will we have tonight? We have several specials that are not on the menu."

"Hmm . . . let me see . . . "

"I'll give you a minute."

He's gone. Thats the last you see of him for twenty minutes.

Or another situation: I was in an expensive restaurant that had a menu with 237 items on it.

The waiter said, "In addition to what you see on the menu we have several specials tonight I'd like to tell you about. The chef has prepared a filet des escargot la ripaille finished with flaming calvados. We have a nice rognon de canard fettucini al fresco au jus, tournedos de turbot en mille feuille, a lagnappe of sauted grenouille on a bed of endive, poularde au citron, finished with a raspberry moutarde aux chanterelle."

I havent read the menu . . . I didnt understand half the dishes he read off but I know we're going to lose the waiter if I dont decide. "I'll have a cheeseburger."

Maybe Im the only one this bothers but I dont like a restaurant that has someone who does nothing but fill the water glasses every time you take a sip. Its usually a bus boy trying to make waiter. He doesnt have anything else to do and he's spilling water on the rolls.

I dislike a restaurant where the table comes up to my chin.

Either the table is too high or the chair is too short. I feel like a midget sitting there.

And why do tables in restaurants rock so often?

Where do they buy these tables with four legs that arent the same length? They used to put a matchbook under the short leg but restaurants dont have matchbooks anymore.

And what's the big deal about pepper?"

"Would you like fresh pepper?" the waiter asks, poised above your food, threatening it with a pepper mill.

"No, thank you," I always say. "Do you have any aged pepper?"

If the dish needs pepper, why didnt the chef put it in when he was cooking it? Did he leave out the salt?

Now, the waiter brings you your dinner. You take the first mouthful and there he is standing next to you.

"How is everything?"

How do I know how everything is? I havent even swallowed yet.

Finally, youre finished. Its time to pay the check. The busboy is still filling your water glass.

The waiter must be in the kitchen having dinner . . . or he's gone home . . . maybe I'll just get up and start to leave and see if that gets his attention.

Where's the Elevator?

Almost every time I get on an elevator, someone says to me:

"Hey, why dont you do a piece about elevators?"

Well, here are my comments about elevators. Almost all of us have an elevator or two in our lives somewhere. We wait for them, we ride on them. We're annoyed by the wait but pleased with the lift.

My survey shows that the average person spends six minutes waiting for an elevator for every minute he or she spends riding one.

People waiting for an elevator dont know what to do, standing with strangers. There is nothing to do. Its an uneasy time. Some press the button repeatedly as though it would help . . . or hit it hard. Sometimes they screw things up by pressing both the UP and DOWN button.

They seem to think it will bring the elevator faster.

Theyre thinking of the days when every elevator had an operator who heard a buzzer when the button was pressed.

Being an elevator operator is a dying profession.

Elevators are focal points and show places in big buildings . . . often ornately lined with panels of figured wood.

Where they are attached to the outside of a building, theyre a tourist attraction, like one out in San Francisco. Getting up or down is secondary to the sights to be seen.

Just missing an elevator . . . arriving as the door closes . . . is a bad way to start the day. Riders develop fast hands . . . or feet. If you stick in a body part, the closing door reopens. You hope.

Some people who just miss head for the stairs if its only one or two flights.

The etiquette of elevator riding has changed. Women used to be allowed to enter and leave first. Now some women are offended by such courtesy.

Theres still some occasional gallantry.

Once on an elevator, even a crowded one, people ride in close proximity without speaking. Your nose can be six inches from the hairdo of the woman in front of you . . . you do not know her name . . . you do not speak . . . yet, theres no other place to put your eyes.

The changing floor numbers on some elevators provide riders with the only place to look other than at each other.

Most elevator rides are accomplished in silence. If it were a dance floor, there wouldnt be room for the compact little crowd to waltz or tango.

And, if youre alone, you never know who's going to join you.

Crime on elevators has led to the television monitor. Big Daddy's watching from overhead.

An elevator can be a frightening place. Its being lifted or dropped by a series of cables and pulleys . . . youre in this little box moving up or down inside solid walls . . . trapped in a modern cave. You shouldnt start thinking about it because it can induce panic or claustrophobia.

We're on the seventh floor of our building at CBS. If I had as much time on this broadcast as I spend waiting for the elevator to get me here, theyd have to call this broadcast *80 Minutes.*

How to Play Baseball

It was good to see President Bush throw out the first ball on opening day of the baseball season Tuesday. He looked pretty good. He should have, of course. He was captain of the Yale baseball team.

President Bush invited Egyptian President Hosni Mubarak to sit with him at the game.

They dont play baseball in Egypt and Mr. Bush had to explain the game. You couldnt hear what they were saying but here's the way I imagine it went:

BUSH:
There are nine players on each side. The pitcher throws the ball over the plate . . .

MUBARAK:
They eat while they play?

BUSH:
No. It isnt really a plate. They just call it a plate.

MUBARAK:
If they dont eat while they play, what does he have in his mouth?

BUSH:
Thats tobacco. Let's watch the game, shall we. See, each man gets three swings trying to hit the ball.

MUBARAK:
That was five swings he just took.

BUSH:
He was warmng up. The swings dont count until the pitcher throws the ball. When a player connects his bat with the ball, you know, strikes it, its called a hit.

VOICE:
What happens if he misses?

BUSH:
If he doesnt strike it, its called a strike.

MUBARAK:
You say the Middle East is confusing to Americans?

BUSH:
Let's just enjoy the game, shall we, Hosni? May I call you Hosni ?

MUBARAK:
May I call you George, Mr. President?

BUSH:
That was a ball. If the pitcher doesnt throw the ball over the plate, its a ball.

VOICE:
They never throw a rock?

BUSH:
Every time a team comes to bat, it gets three outs before the other team comes in.

MUBARAK:
Theyre in until theyre out?

BUSH:
When a man gets a hit, he runs for first base and if he gets there before the ball does, he's safe.

MUBARAK:
What if the ball gets there first? Is he unsafe?

BUSH:
No, he's out.

VOICE:
Out of the game?

BUSH:
No, Hosni, not out of the game, just out. He's, you know. Out. When three men are out, thats the end of the inning.

MUBARAK:
When you asked me to the game, you said we'd have an outing. Is an inning the same as an outing?

BUSH:
Let's just enjoy the game, Hosni.

MUBARAK:
What was that? He hit the ball over the fence. The ball went too far. Does he have to pay for a new ball?

BUSH:
No. Thats what we call a home run.

MUBARAK:
Good . . . so we can run home now?

BUSH:
Say, Hosni. Why dont you go get us some peanuts and Cracker Jacks, I dont care if you never get back.

Well, I dont really know how it went when President Bush took Hosni Mubarak to opening day of the baseball season. Maybe Mubarak can get back at President Bush if he goes to Cairo by taking him to a camel race.

The Right Tool

Every time anyone gives you advice about doing a job, they tell you to be sure to have the right tool.

What they dont tell you, is how to do the job if you DONT have the right tool, which is more apt to be the case. Let's face it, no one ever has all the right tools for a job.

If you do have the right tool, you cant find it.

What happens is, a lot of us use the wrong tool. Right here where I sit, I regularly use things for jobs they werent meant to do.

Here's a simple example. I can never find a letter opener because its buried under a pile of papers. I look in a drawer and maybe find a nail file . . . if not, I use a pencil to open letters if I cant get in with my finger.

Say I want to find out what's on the top shelf up there. Do I get a ladder or do I do what most Americans do? I do what most Americans do . . . I stand on a chair.

We're always taking things apart. You take the backs off things to fix them or to put new batteries in. How often do you have a screwdriver handy?

You use a knife for a screwdriver which is a perfect way to ruin a knife, or a better solution . . . you use a dime. A dime is worth more as a screwdriver these days than it is as ten cents.

One of the most versatile tools known to man is the simple wire clothes hanger. The first thing you do with a hanger to use it as a tool is bend it into some other shape. You never need the hook.

Say you get locked out of your car. You bend the hanger in two, then bend the end of it into a small hook and try to catch your door handle. Car thieves are very good with clothes hangers. They can get into a car quicker with a coat hanger than the owner can with the key.

If your muffler falls off and starts dragging on the road, you can use a coat hanger to hold it up until you get enough money to have the muffler fixed.

How often have you been thirsty and set out to open a bottle of Coke or beer and found you didnt have a bottle opener. It can happen in a hotel room.

The best tool for opening a bottle is the catch on a door. Some people can open a bottle on the sharp edge of something by hitting it.

The single thing I use most often for something it wasnt designed for is a checkbook or an envelope. Im always writing notes to myself on the back of a check or on an envelope because I dont have a note pad with me.

Credit cards are also used by both thieves and honest people to open locked doors. You slide them in and push the catch back.

In the summer, when there are flies, and you dont have a fly swatter, a rolled up newspaper makes a good tool.

A tool chest is anywhere you find it.

Get Healthy

This is the time of year when people start thinking about what theyre going to look like in bathing suits this summer. They decide they ought to lose some weight and get in shape.

Thats why you see so many ads for what they call "health" clubs. The business of health clubs isnt really health, its what people look like in bathing suits . . . thats the business health clubs are in. They dont care if you drop dead as long as you look good in a bathing suit.

And thats okay but why do they try to kid us?

Have you ever, once in your life, seen a picture of an unhealthy person in a health club ad?

Why do they always have pictures of people who dont need to go to health clubs?

If you looked great like this, would you bother to go to a health club?

Cher poses in ads for the Jack LaLanne Fitness Center. Cher looks as though she's in good shape but if Jack really wants to do something for her he ought to cut her hair. Cher's hair covers more of her than her shirt does.

Beautiful and shapely young women are always emerging from the health club pool, dripping wet, in the ads. When I go to a pool, the women are never this good-looking and they hardly ever get wet.

When you actually get to a health club or a gym, theres never anyone around who looks like the ones in the ad.

The place usually smells a little sweaty and the women arent undressed the way they are in the ads . . . half of them are wearing baggy sweat suits.

Another thing that strikes me as strange about health clubs is why, with all the hard work to be done in the world, people have to find some kind of artificial work to get tired. Able-bodied men will hire someone to mow their lawn . . . and then go to a health club for two hours and pay to get some exercise.

They have walking and running machines in these places. People walk or run on a treadmill so they dont go anywhere. They run on these things for half an hour without getting anywhere and then take a cab or drive their car to the office.

They have rowing machines without a boat. You pretend youre rowing a boat in the water just for the exercise.

A stationary bicycle is ridiculous. If people want the exercise bicycles provide, why dont they get on their bicycles and go somewhere. Why fake it?

Im in favor of health. Im in favor of exercise and Ive always liked the atmosphere in a locker room but I dont like anyone trying to kid me into thinking that if I pay my money and join the Acme Gym Club . . . Im going to end up looking like Arnold Schwarzenegger.

The Price of Gas

Its hard to understand where our Government spends one trillion 55 billion dollars a year.

I thought it might be interesting to zero in on just one item, gas. We all understand about buying gas. How much diesel fuel do you think an M–1 tank burns?

If you picked up your brand new $2.5 million M–1 in Detroit, fully loaded with sun roof, you could drive it to Chicago before stopping for gas again. The M–1 tank holds 500 gallons. The tank burns one gallon going three fifths of a mile.

The F16 fighter plane holds 1,000 gallons of gas and burns 500 gallons an hour . . . so dont go too far from home if youre driving.

We have 1,700 F16s and 2,000 pilots who know how to fly them. Each pilot flies eighteen hours a month . . . thats 216 hours a year. At 500 gallons an hour, each pilot burns 108,000 gallons of fuel. There are 2,000 pilots so we pay for 216 million gallons of fuel a year for the F16s, according to my calculations. That'd take you back and forth between home and work quite a few times, wouldnt it?

The B–1 bomber's the baby that really burns fuel . . . 2,000 gallons an hour. It would take 30,000 gallons to get from Kansas City to Moscow and back. No wonder we want peace with the Soviet Union.

The Navy spends one billion 700 million a year on fuel. An aircraft carrier cruising at normal speed burns about 200,000 gallons of fuel a day. I wonder if they ever thought of sailboats?

The original World War II Jeep was too good and too cheap so the Pentagon replaced it with something called the Hummer. The Army ordered 54,000 of these at $20,000 apiece.

Doesnt anyone in the Army walk anymore?

We know candidates dont walk if they can get their picture taken riding in something. These Hummers get fourteen miles a gallon . . . without the windshield wipers going.

I thought youd be interested to know, the Government has money to burn.

On Your Vacation

Its all over now. The summer of 1989 is dead and gone.

I had a great vacation.

For one thing, we didnt travel. Thats my idea of a good vacation . . . not going anywhere.

I just hung around in my workshop all day getting sawdust in my hair.

There ought to be travel agents who specialize in arranging vacations for people who want to stay home and be alone.

I feel sort of bad about President Bush's vacation. It was so public. The reporters and the cameramen were always after him.

They had their long lenses on him and if the President played golf . . . they took pictures of how far he hit the ball.

If he went fishing, they took pictures of him not catching a fish.

Half the time he might as well have been working because most of his White House staff was there in Maine with him.

Foreign visitors came there to see him. No one wants visitors when theyre on vacation . . . especially foreign ones.

When someone important came to see him at his vacation home, you could tell he'd just thrown a coat on over the sport shirt he was playing in before they arrived.

All his relatives came. There are just so many relatives you want visiting you on vacation, too.

President Bush spent a lot of time out on a boat. And of course, he had trouble. Its a mystery why cars work and boats always have trouble.

Boats and having to go somewhere are the most trouble anyone has on vacation.

I think the President ought to make a deal with reporters.

He'd promise not to make any news, if theyd promise not to follow him around waiting for him to make some.

Of course, theres one way to avoid the kind of attention George Bush gets. Lose the election.

We called a television station in Boston and asked if they had any pictures of Michael Dukakis on vacation.

They said he went to the Berkshire Mountains . . . but they didnt have anyone follow along to take pictures of him.

Without

It has recently come to my attention that when you dont want something in something, it costs extra.

Why is that?

In the grocery store, things cost more if they dont have something you dont want in it.

For example, when they dont put sugar in food, it almost always cost extra. A regular box of fake strawberry Jell-O costs $1.05 . . . and a smaller box of fake strawberry Jell-O . . . "without sugar" . . . costs $1.19. How come?

Now, you could say that whatever they put in instead of sugar costs more than the sugar in Jell-O but what about cans of Hunt's tomato sauce? Both are the same size but one costs ten cents more than the other because they didnt put any salt in it. How much does it cost them not to put salt in tomato sauce? Whatever it is, they hand the cost of not putting it in on to you.

Same with cheese. If they put salt in its $1.89. If they dont, its $1.95. You wonder how expensive it is for them not to put salt in cheese.

A box of salt costs 49 cents. How much would they charge for a box if they didnt put salt in it? Fifty-nine cents?

The same with coffee without caffeine. Decaffeinated coffee costs as much as a dollar a pound more than regular coffee. Yet if you go to a drugstore and ask for something to keep you awake, they sell you caffeine. . . . A little box of caffeine costs $2.93 . . . and they probably took it out of YOUR coffee.

If they dont put in any artificial colors, flavors or preservatives things often cost more.

A regular quart of milk costs 79 cents . . . skim milk, with no cream in it, costs 89 cents.

At the gas pump, if you have a car or a lawn mower that takes regular gas with lead in it, its cheaper. The unleaded gas, gas they dont put lead in, is ten cents a gallon more.

I first ran across this strange phenomenon several years ago when a friend told me he didnt want his name listed in the New York telephone book. He wanted an unlisted number so he called the telephone company and guess what?

They told him there would be an initial charge of $9.90 for not being listed in the phone book and then a monthly charge of $1.88 for not having his name in it.

In Chicago, Illinois Bell charges customers $11.50 not to be listed and then $1.45 a month after that.

Can you imagine how much the telephone company would charge if you didnt even want a telephone ?

Lock It Up

Maybe you think crime is all bad . . . but look at it this way, if we didnt have thieves, a lot of people would be out of work.

There are 600,000 policemen in this Country, not counting the FBI, and more than a million more in the security business. All those people would be out on the street, looking for your job, if everyone was honest.

The security industry had a convention and we went.

All these people can thank God for criminals. If there were no criminals none of them would be making a living selling burglar alarms. The sellers of locks and keys wouldnt have any income. There'd be no television surveillance business. No one would prosper by making bulletproof vests.

We walked around the displays at the show to see what theyre selling to make us safe.

It turns out that there are thieves who'll steal absolutely anything . . . manhole covers, for example. The metal in a manhole is valuable.

We stopped and had a nice chat with two bulletproof-vest salesmen.

Its a mystery where the criminals get their equipment because everyone at this show said they wouldnt sell anything to them. Guns, for example.

At the convention, they had a listening device that goes down under the corner of a rug and picks up conversation in a room. I wouldnt mind having one of those to put under a couple of rugs I know.

You can install one of their listening devices in a wall behind an electrical outlet.

If you want to bug someone around your office, they even have a microphone and tiny transmitter that fits into this stapler.

They had everything a spy would need but they assured us they didnt sell to spies . . . just to people trying to catch spies.

They had a briefcase with a motion picture camera inside. The lens is just a little hole.

They had a car antenna. It rotates and the lens of the camera looks out a little hole. You could drive around taking pictures of anything.

It would be nice if we could all leave home without locking our doors . . . or without taking the keys out of our car. Every time we lock something, the bad guys have beaten us just a little. They made us do it. Just by making us feel we have to lock something, the thieves have put us under their power.

The security industry is one of the fastest growing business in the Country. Its nice to know someone's making an honest living off stealing.

Cant Eat It

Americans have become a lot more health-conscious in the last few years. We all want to eat the right things so we'll live forever.

They make it so hard for us though, to know what's right and what's wrong. Theyre always warning us about something and then deciding its okay after all.

The other day this report warned that alcohol is apt to produce heart disease in men but then, further down in the report, it says that alcohol lowers the cholesterol level.

The first time I remember we were all warned not to eat something under threat of death was the great cranberry scare of Thanksgiving 1959. They told us some cranberries were found to be bad for mice because of something the cranberries had been sprayed with. *Life* magazine did a whole layout on it and people avoided cranberries that Thanksgiving. It killed the cranberry business that year. Whatever it was about cranberries that was bad, the mice disappeared almost immediately.

In our house, we used to have swordfish for dinner about twice a year because thats how often we could afford it . . . then we were warned not to eat swordfish because it contained mercury.

I always thought mercury was found only in thermometers.

I dont know what happened to the mercury but we have more money now and we're having swordfish once a month these days.

According to a report a few weeks ago, mushrooms from China may be dangerous.

The cattle industry had to buy high-priced ads because doctors have convinced all of us that meat has a lot of saturated fat . . . fat that doesnt melt at room temperature. That was good news for cows but bad news for cowboys.

Lately there have been reports that the fat in meat can lower your cholesterol level. I mean, who knows?

Remember the cyclamate story? The soft drink companies making diet sodas were told not to sweeten their drinks anymore with cyclamates. It cost them a fortune to switch to something else . . . now the Food and Drug Administration says it made a mistake. Cyclamates are okay after all.

Back in March, we were warned not to eat grapes from Chile. I wouldnt recognize a Chilean if I met one on the street, let alone a Chilean grape.

Theyd found two grapes with something wrong with them and it almost ruined Chile's economy for a few months.

The warning that still bothers me the most was about coffee.

According to a 1981 report from medical researchers at Harvard, people who drank three cups of coffee a day were three times as likely to get cancer of the pancreas as people who dont drink coffee at all.

Where does that leave me? I drink eight or ten cups a day.

Because of all these stories, a lot of Americans are eating what they call "health" foods now.

Im waiting for a report that health foods should be avoided because theyve been found to be bad for mice.

1990

Good and Bad Shapes

There are good shapes and bad shapes. This old Underwood of mine has a classic shape. I suppose it looks good because it is good. I use this computer a lot now but its shape will never be a classic.

This original small Coke bottle was one of the great shapes of all time . . . certainly a better shape than the cans the stuff comes in now.

This old Hamilton pocket watch of mine is a great shape. A baseball cap is a good shape. Remember how homely those old fedoras used to be? All men wore one of them fifty years ago.

A book is a good shape. Books fit so nicely together on a shelf. Publishers should get together on size though.

Almost anything round is a good shape. An orange, for instance, could hardly be improved on. A football isnt round even though its called a ball. Its an ellipse. The word "ellipse" comes from a Greek word meaning "falling short." But you probably knew that. A football falls short of being round.

Let's go to the blackboard for an instant.

Circles are good but one of the first things kids learn about how tough life can be is how hard it is to draw a circle freehand with your first box of crayons.

The basic difference between a square and a circle is that a circle rolls and a square does not.

Triangles are interesting but not very useful. The most famous triangles are the pyramids, which are a dead loss except as tourist attractions. Triangles, like squares, dont roll but, unlike squares, cannot be sat on comfortably.

One of the best names of any shape is the isosceles triangle. Unfortunately, while isosceles triangles are big in high school, they very seldom come up in real life.

The word "square," of course, is also used to describe someone who doesnt get it.

Pocket Full of Papers

Im always ending up with a pocket full of tickets, slips, receipts and odd pieces of paper with writing on them that I cant read and numbers that dont add up.

I know its partly my own fault but it would be a big help if there were a general agreement that all receipts were the same size and shape . . . you know, like dollar bills.

This is for a pair of pants that I left to be cleaned and pressed.

This is a receipt for a dinner I had that I hope to be able to deduct from my income tax. You can bet the restaurant can read their copy okay but I certainly cant read mine.

This is a parking ticket I got in New York. I havent paid it yet. I will if I can figure out how much I owe from these numbers theyve got on it.

The worst pieces of paper I get are the airline tickets. Would it really be impossible for airlines to design a sensible airline ticket thats easy to read and easy to handle? What is all this stuff, anyway?

Every time they handle it, they put it in another envelope. I never know which is the ticket and which is my receipt . . . or which is my return trip ticket . . . or which is the receipt for the return trip ticket . . . or which the baggage claim ticket.

When I go up to the gate, I just hand the whole mess over to whoever's standing at the door, envelope and all. I let them sort it out. They always look at it as if its the first time theyve ever seen one too. They fool around with it for awhile, tear some pieces off of it, and then stuff it back in a new envelope and give it back to me.

I always end up with a lot of pieces of paper I dont dare throw away when I buy an airline ticket. I save them for my tax too but the tax people dont seem to want them either.

My idea of a ticket is the one for a Giants football game. Why cant an airline ticket be like that? You can read where you sit, how much it cost and what time youre supposed to be there. Thats all you need on a ticket. Unlike an airline flight, the game starts on time too.

Problem Sleeping

Last week I went to a restaurant in New York for dinner with some friends and drank too much white wine. That night I woke up about 3 A.M. and couldnt get back to sleep. You think of some plenty strange things when you cant sleep and I got thinking about why I couldnt sleep.

When you come right down to it, the body isnt very well shaped for sleeping in a bed . . . or mine isnt, anyway.

The most sensible way to relax all your muscles, it seems to me, is to lie on your back. I dont know about you but when I lie on my back and go to sleep, I dream about all sorts of terrible things . . . like death and paying my income tax and letters I havent written to people.

Even if Im lying on my back and Im awake, I get thinking about how much time I have left in life. This is no way to get a night's sleep.

Also, if Im on my back, my palate seems to drop down into my throat sometimes and Im more apt to snore. So, I turn on my side and curl up a little. My pajamas stick to the sheets when I turn over so only half of my pajamas go with me and theyre all twisted up for the rest of the night. We obviously need slippier sheets.

But here I am on my side. Now being on my side is okay except for my shoulder. Where do I put my shoulder? This is what happens when you cant sleep. You get analyzing things.

And what do I do with my arm? Its stuck there between me and the mattress too. Sometimes a pillow can help. Theres a gap where your shoulder goes before it sticks down into the mattress. But what do you do with your arm then?

The experts always say its better for your back if you sleep on a firm mattress but I dont like a firm mattress. I like a mattress thats really mushy.

I often put my arm up under the pillow when Im on my side like that. It takes a long bed though because with your arm up over your head, even a short person needs about seven feet of bed. Its comfortable for a while this way but then your arm goes to sleep and you wake up with a tingling sensation in your fingers and you have to turn over and take your head off your arm.

Turning over in bed in the winter is very difficult. What I do is I flip the blankets up and get some air under them and then I try to turn over myself quickly, before the blankets settle down.

The good thing is that when I havent had too much white wine to drink, I dont think of any of these problems. I get into bed, take a book off the stand next to me, open the book and fall fast asleep until morning.

The Return

NOTE TO READERS: Writers all have an idea of what their best work has been but their opinion doesnt always agree with what others think. It has always bothered me that I became best known for my short essays at the end of 60 Minutes *when the best work I ever did was a dozen long documentaries I wrote and produced.*

Every December around Christmas, CBS News used to broadcast an hour long review of the past year. They were fun and satisfying to make because there was so much material available. I was assigned to do the year 1989 and it led to one of the most unpleasant incidents of my long career in television. It'll end up in my obituary and I hate the thought almost as much as the thought of dying.

In one short paragraph in the broadcast, I said, "There was some recognition in 1989 of the fact that many of the ills that kill us are self-induced; too much alcohol, too much food, drugs, homosexual unions, cigarettes. They were all known to lead quite often to premature death."

Homosexuals everywhere were furious with my insensitive remark. Their argument was that I should have said that it was "unsafe sex," not "homosexual unions," that led to AIDS. In retrospect I agreed that I shouldnt have put it that way but it was too late.

A reporter for a gay magazine called The Advocate *called and I talked to him at length. When his article appeared he quoted me as saying "blacks have watered down their genes." It isnt anything I would have said and doesnt sound like anything I would have said but there it was in print. What I had said, which was probably inadvisable, was that I thought we might be in danger of diminishing our collective I.Q. in this Country because the dumbest*

Americans were having the most babies. I did not say or mean that they were necessarily black.

The president of CBS News, David Burke, took the word of the reporter for the magazine over mine and suspended me for three months. While I never really believed my absence caused the decline, 60 Minutes *ratings sunk. It was a lucky coincidence for me and my suspension was suspended after three weeks.*

I wrote this on my return to the show:

Last Wednesday I was sitting at the kitchen table, having a third cup of coffee I didnt want. I was just staring because I couldnt work.

I remembered a strange old poem I liked in high school. The words were spoken, I think, by a young woman whose true love had died.

Mother, I cannot mind my wheel,
My fingers ache, my lips are dry,
Oh! if you felt the pain I feel!
But oh, who ever felt as I!

Thats how I felt. I couldnt mind my wheel. I couldnt write. I'd lost my true love. I didnt feel like doing anything—including nothing.

There never was a writer who didnt hope that in some small way he was doing good with the words he put down on paper and, while I know its presumptuous, Ive always had in the back of my mind that I was doing some little bit of good.

Now, I was to be known for having done, not good, but bad. I'd be known for the rest of my life as a racist bigot and as someone who had made life a little more difficult for homosexuals. I felt terrible about that and Ive learned a lot.

As much as I love my work here, I could get out of the Andy Rooney business tomorrow and have a great time . . . if I could leave here with my reputation.

What do I say to defend myself? Do I say "I am not a racist." That sounds like Nixon saying "I am not a crook."

How do I apologize to homosexuals for hurting them with a remark I made that I didnt realize would hurt them?

Its demeaning to have to sit here and defend myself. In the Army in World

War II, I was infuriated to find that black soldiers had to sit in the back of the bus. I got on a bus in St. Augustine one day to go back to Camp Blanding and I insisted on sitting in the back with the black guys. I was arrested.

In 1970 I set out, with a camera crew, to find out what happened to the man who was twice tried for the murder of that great civil rights leader, Medgar Evers. I was arrested and dragged into court in Jackson, Mississippi, by two redneck sheriffs who didnt like what we were doing.

I wrote a broadcast called *Of Black America* for Bill Cosby in 1968 that Im proud of. In 1970 I wrote the show called *Harry and Lena* for Harry Belafonte and Lena Horne. I liked Lena better than Harry. Does that make me a feminist?

My son says that one of the worst experiences of his young life was the night I asked a guest to leave our house because he kept using the word "nigger."

I'd feel the same today if anyone used an insulting word about homosexuals.

Dr. Benjamin Hooks, the director of the NAACP, said earlier in the week that he knew I was not a racist. I liked that a whole lot.

I have had good letters from just about everyone Ive ever known. I hope, on the day of my funeral, these people dont say "I already gave."

The other morning I was wishing I'd heard from Eric Sevareid and Garry Moore. Half an hour later the mail came with letters from Eric Sevareid and Garry Moore.

And now comes the hard part. What do I do to justify the action David Burke, the president of CBS News, has taken in putting me back on the air? What do I do about the kind words heaped on me by friends and strangers? Its overwhelming. How do I live up to such praise? Let's face it, even on the nights when Im good, Im not that good.

Do I have any opinions that might irritate some people? Youre damn right I do. Thats what Im here for.

The Pitchman

Fifteen or twenty times a year some advertising agency approaches me asking if I'll do a commercial. I dont do commercials but I am curious about how I'd be as a pitchman.

IS YOUR HANDWRITING HARD TO READ? DO YOU NEED TO WRITE THINGS DOWN QUICKLY AND ACCURATELY? DO WHAT I DO. USE A TYPEWRITER.

NOT JUST ANY TYPEWRITER. FOR LASTING VALUE, GET YOURSELF ONE OF THESE UNDERWOOD #55'S. NOTHING TO PLUG IN. THERE ARE NO BATTERIES. YOU DONT HAVE TO WIND IT AND THEY WONT BE COMING UP WITH A NEW MODEL THAT MAKES YOUR OLD MODEL OBSOLETE NEXT YEAR.

IF YOU MAKE A MISTAKE, YOU CAN AUTOMATICALLY CORRECT IT. OFFER VOID WHERE PROHIBITED.

ARE YOU IN THE MARKET FOR A GOOD USED CAR? WELL, Ive GOT A CAR HERE THATS GOOD AND USED . . . A REAL CREAMPUFF! I CAN GIVE YOU A GREAT DEAL ON THIS CAR. $1,500 REBATE. YOU GIVE ME $3,500. I'LL GIVE YOU BACK $1,500 CASH. WHERE ELSE ARE YOU GOING TO MAKE $1,500 THAT EASY? THE CAR STARTS IN THE COLDEST WEATHER . . . USUALLY. AND IF IT DOESNT, IT COMES WITH JUMPER CABLES.

ARE YOU BROKE EVERY WEEK BECAUSE BY THE TIME YOU GET YOUR PAYCHECK, YOUVE ALREADY SPENT IT?

ARE YOU A SLAVE TO YOUR CREDIT CARD?

DO YOU LIVE IN FEAR OF BEING ROBBED IN A FOREIGN COUNTRY BECAUSE YOUVE WATCHED TOO MANY AMERICAN EXPRESS COMMERCIALS?

DO WHAT THE RICH PEOPLE DO. PAY CASH.

THESE GREEN PAPER DOLLARS ARE GOOD ANYWHERE IN THE WORLD. YOU DONT HAVE TO SIGN YOUR NAME WHEN YOU PAY WITH DOLLARS. NO ONE HAS TO MAKE AN EMBARRASSING PHONE CALL TO CHECK YOUR CREDIT.

CUT THE TIME YOU SPEND BUYING IN HALF BY PAYING IN CASH. WHEN YOU PAY WITH ONE OF THESE $20 BILLS, THE CLERK IN THE STORE DOESNT WASTE YOUR TIME WRITING DOWN ALL THE NUMBERS ON THESE BILLS. WHEN ITS MONEY, ITS GOT TO BE GOOD. CASH . . . THE EASY WAY TO PAY FOR ANYTHING.

DONT LEAVE HOME WITHOUT IT.

High Prices

Government officials in Washington are always announcing that the rate of inflation is low . . . something like 5 percent a year. Why is it then that every time you go to buy something, its not 5 percent more, its 20 percent more than it was the last time you bought it?

You get used to the prices of most things, I think, but there are certain prices I never get used to.

You know what I mean. I know a Mercedes or a Cadillac costs $50,000 or something like that and it doesnt surprise me. I dont plan to buy one but it doesnt surprise me.

But now, what about a pair of glasses? I swear that a pair of glasses has gone up a lot more than most things in the last five years. I paid $85 for these two months ago and I know for sure I bought a pair almost exactly like them two years ago for $45. Why should a simple pair of glasses cost so much more now?

I dont get used to the price of a good pair of shoes. Women's shoes, for example. Look at this pair of nothing with all these holes in them . . . $255.

Women get stuck with higher prices for a lot of things. Women's haircuts, for instance, are a lot more than a man's haircut. And all kinds of clothes cost women more.

Here's a Macy's ad. The linen jacket is $320. The skirt is $120. I dont know whether you can see the skirt or not. Imagine what it would cost if it came to her knees.

And the price of a good hotel room never ceases to amaze me. I stayed at the Palmer House in Chicago in 1975 and it cost me $39. We called this morning. The same room now costs $109.

Here's a 1973 bill from a Ramada Inn . . . $21. Today the room is $84 . . . four times as much.

Books seem expensive. Here's a book I bought by a friend of mine, Ernie Pyle . . . $21.95. Ernie probably didnt make that much a week when he was writing it.

The price of a nickel candy bar now is incredible.

And have you seen a movie lately? You go to a lot of them? If you do, you must be rich. In New York City a movie now costs $7.50. You think thats special?

Look what a movie costs in Hollywood . . . $7. Wouldnt you think a movie would be cheaper right there where they make them? I guess they dont have factory outlet movie theaters.

Census Bureau Forms

By now I hope youve all filled out and returned your Census forms.

This is what they call the short form . . . which isnt very short at all . . . and this is the long form that some of you got.

I know the Census Bureau is important but Im nervous about all the questions the Government is asking. I dont think the Government is out to get me. Im just afraid its out to sell me something. Or maybe help someone else sell me something. Thats what a lot of these questions look like. Why else would the Census Bureau want to know how much I make? Doesnt the IRS already have that figure? How many Government agencies do I have to tell?

And Im suspicious of any form thats folded cleverly. What's all that folding for anyway?

The Census Bureau gets in trouble right away at the start of this thing. Look at this. PERSON ONE it says. It wants you to put down who is PERSON ONE in the family.

Now is that a way to start trouble in a family or isnt it?

I'll be darned if Im going to say Im PERSON ONE. Let someone else be PERSON ONE.

I suppose they think that in the average family the man will put himself down as PERSON ONE. Well, I think American men are too smart for that these days.

Can you imagine what would happen to the man who puts himself down as PERSON ONE? The guy comes down to breakfast in the morning and his wife says "Good morning, PERSON ONE. Can PERSON TWO get PERSON ONE a cup of coffee?"

There are a lot of things I dont understand on this form. For instance, it says RACE. And then it says WHITE, BLACK or NEGRO, INDIAN, ESKIMO, ALEUTIAN, CHINESE, JAPANESE. Who at the Census Bureau decided the Chinese and the Japanese are a different race? Or the Koreans and the Vietnamese, for that matter?

Where does that leave me? I dont see Scotch/Irish or English listed as a race anywhere. You talk about racist. What about Italian, French, German? Nowhere here. Never mind did I come from the Aleutian Islands.

Here's a question. WHAT WERE THIS PERSON'S MOST IMPORTANT ACTIVITIES? What do they mean IMPORTANT? IMPORTANT to whom? IMPORTANT to the Government? IMPORTANT to world peace or international trade? Does everyone have to be doing something important? What about the nap I take Saturdays?

HOW MANY HOURS DID THIS PERSON WORK LAST WEEK? Okay, eight hours for five days. Say you worked 40 hours last week. Next question.

HOW MANY MINUTES DID IT USUALLY TAKE THIS PERSON TO GET FROM HOME TO WORK LAST WEEK? Last week? Well, it takes half an hour a day, five days. The answer for the week is two and a half hours. I dont think thats what they meant though.

I hope the Census Bureau does well but PERSON THREE is not confident.

The *World Almanac* says India's population is 833,422,000.

You look at our relatively good census takers and the mistakes theyre making and you wonder how in the world anyone has any wild idea how many people there are in India or China or anywhere else on Earth.

Lithuania

I keep wishing the United States would do what's right in the world instead of what seems smart.

We keep supporting the bad guys because we think its good for us. It usually involves money or oil or a military base. It happened with Marcos in the Philippines. It happened with Noriega in Panama. We supported these two bad guys.

Back in the bad old days when big countries had colonies . . . the Spanish sailed to Mexico and South America, for instance, took all the gold and went back home with it.

The British had Canada, Australia, New Zealand, South Africa, India.

The French still have the island of Tahiti. Its a nice warm place but it costs the French a bundle.

A big country cant move in and take all the good stuff out of a smaller country anymore. Now, if a big country gets involved with a small country, it costs them.

The Philippines cost U.S. taxpayers millions just so we can have a naval base there and the people hate us. Who needs it?

Japan doesnt have an empire and its doing pretty good with nothing but its little island.

Right now the Soviet Union is making a dumb mistake with Lithuania. Here's Lithuania on a map. There are about four million people here . . . our Census Bureau misses more people than that.

Lithuania's had a terrible time trying to be its own country for centuries. They had a king once who married the queen of Poland and he got to be king of both Lithuania and Poland.

But what does the Soviet Union want Lithuania for?

Didnt the Russians learn anything in Afghanistan?

I'll bet Lithuania costs Russia money just the way Cuba does. The Soviets pay Cuba about seven times what Cuba's sugar's worth to support them.

Gorbachev has now cut off Soviet oil going to Lithuania. You know what's going to happen? A bunch of Russians in the oil business are going to say: "Hey, Mikhail. These Lithuanians are paying us big rubles for that oil, you know. Youre killing us."

I think President Bush ought to stop talking about talking and say to

Gorbachev: "Look. Read my lips. Do yourself a favor. These people want to be free. Let them be free."

The days of empire are over, fellows.

Joggers

People who jog are special. They have more self-discipline than the rest of us. They may even be better people . . . not that theyre perfect. There are a lot of nuts who jog . . . and they often get off to an early start.

Some joggers are athletes. You can see it in the way they stride. They have coordination, power and grace. They cover a lot of ground.

A lot of women run with style. Theres something about effort that lends beauty to a woman in action. Even their hair is in good shape.

Running comes easily for some. Its a social occasion. They can join a friend and laugh and talk and run for miles.

The day of the plain old grey sweatsuit's about over . . . often replaced now by the kind of neon colors used to warn motorists away from obstructions in the road. Togetherness on the run.

It appears as though a lot of joggers went to college . . . although a sweatshirt is not the same thing as a diploma, of course.

Some joggers dont have time to suit up, run, go home, change, shower and dress for work. They dress . . . and jog to work.

And as if running on a flat surface were not difficult enough, they love a flight of steps. They dont walk up them . . . they run up them . . . and when they get to the top . . . they run back down the steps.

Joggers are often masochists. They enjoy pain. They inflict it on themselves in a variety of ways. Some of them carry weights to make their trip more difficult and painful. They feel pain is good for them so they set out to hurt themselves. Theyre grim, determined.

Joggers are fascinated with their bodies. This man couldnt wait to see a doctor. He's taking his own pulse to see if he's still alive and well.

Some joggers exercise themselves and their dogs at the same time. People enjoy jogging more than dogs do. Dogs seem to find it pointless. They lag behind.

This woman jogger has everything . . . her newspaper, her dog, her coat and in her ears Mozart . . . or perhaps Bruce Springseen.

Joggers have a lot in common with cigarette smokers. Joggers pretend theyre doing it for their health but if sweatsuits came with a warning from the Surgeon General that read JOGGING CAN BE DANGEROUS TO YOUR HEALTH, theyd still do it. Joggers are addicted.

Crime Stories

Theres been some great news lately . . . the release of two American hostages and putting that big telescope in space . . . really good news. Most news is terrible though . . . so much crime and we're fascinated by it.

Ive collected about fifty newspapers, at random. Theyre filled with theft, arson, kidnap, rape and murder.

In local papers theres usually a dramatic crime the rest of the Country never hears about. If you dont live in Tennessee, you wouldnt have heard that over in Meigs County, they charged Jerry Underdown with killing his rich father and his stepmother.

Walter Nixon of Hattiesburg, Mississippi, a Federal judge who was run out of office for lying a few years back, was arrested in Pascagoula for using bait to hunt birds. If you dont read the *Arkansas Gazette*, you wouldnt know that.

In Dallas, FACTS RIVAL FICTION IN GRISLY CASE. Nothing like a grisly murder over a second cup of coffee. Perhaps you think that nothing much ever happens in Laconia, New Hampshire.

Usually its fun when they catch a murderer. Some people even like it when we murder the murderer.

And we enjoy it when they catch a stockbroker or a banker who's been caught stealing. They caught Michael Milken. He makes Billy the Kid look like a piggybank thief.

The dishonest public official who gets caught with his hand in the till makes good reading.

The *Albuquerque Journal* has a little story . . . 7TH CABBIE KILLED in New York. Local papers love a bad story if its about someplace else . . . especially if its about New York City.

Newspapers run feature stories all the time about the big picture in crime:

CITY GANGS BLAMED . . .

CRIMINALS WHO HIT THE AGED . . .

CRIME RISING IN LOWER GRADES . . .

WEAPONS IN HANDS OF CHILDREN SPAWN A CULTURE OF FEAR.

We read all these newspaper stories about crime as though crime was entertainment . . . just as long as it doesnt happen to us.

Iraq

I read a story the other day about how much this Middle East thing is going to cost us in the United States. Theres even a lot of talk about the possibility of a recession because of Iraq's invasion of Kuwait.

A single aircraft carrier costs a million and a half dollars a day to run. You pull up to the pump with one of these babies and it costs you real money. It costs $4,000 an hour to fly one of these F–15 fighter planes so it costs about $250,000 in gas just to get four of them to Saudi Arabia.

Its strange though—all of a sudden, when theres a chance of a lot of people being killed . . . American soldiers . . . money doesnt seem important.

When a war comes along and the Country's in trouble, something happens. We get revved up. We get going.

PRESIDENT GEORGE BUSH:

Over the past ten days you have launched what history will judge as one of the most important deployments of allied military power since the Second World War.

ROONEY:

Saddam Hussein—not to be confused with the King of Jordan with the same last name—talks about all Arabs uniting against outside intruders. He means the United States. Baloney. All Arabs ought to unite against the handful of leaders in their own countries who live in palaces, own fleets of Rolls

Royces and vacation on their own yachts while the average Arab doesnt have a tent to sleep in.

BOB SIMON:
"All Arabs may be brothers," they say, "but some struck it rich and treated the rest of the family like dirt."

ROONEY:
I think Americans have probably taken too much money out of those oil countries but we havent begun to steal from them the way their own leaders have.

If President Bush can lead the world out of this mess in the Middle East and force Iraq out of Kuwait without getting a lot of people killed, Im willing to excuse him for his false promise not to raise taxes. This is more important than campaign promises.

Iraq Experts

With all the Mideast experts on television these days, youd think theyd have all our problems solved by now. They tell us what happened, what's going to happen and how to prevent it. Tonight we've invited three Middle East experts to talk to us.

ROONEY:
Our first guest is a man who once lived near Henry Kissinger. Good to have you with us, sir. Tell us what you know about the Middle East.

MAN:
Perhaps it would be best if we went to the map here. Here's the South here. Here's the Middle West around Chicago. And here's the East, New York. Down East, thats Maine. And here's the Middle East here, Pennsylvania, Ohio and West Virginia. Are there any questions?

ROONEY:
Our next guest expert is a former Assistant Secretary to the Assistant Sec-

retary of the Navy under Jimmy Carter. Admiral Yelvington. Good Evening, Admiral. Could you give us a military assessment of our position in the Middle East from your unique point of view?

ADMIRAL YELVINGTON:
Bush has no business playing golf when our boys are in the Gulf. President Carter stayed in the White House during a crisis.

ROONEY:
Hardly a military assessment, Admiral. Now, do you think we can handle this Iraqi aggression?

ADMIRAL YELVINGTON:
Bush has a boat that uses two gallons a mile. Jimmy didnt even have a rowboat.

ROONEY:
We didnt invite you here to criticize our President in times like these, sir. What we want to know from an old Navy man is this: Can our tanks do the job?

ADMIRAL YELVINGTON:
They'll get sand in their wheels. Jimmy never even took a vacation.

ROONEY:
Come back real soon, Admiral.

ROONEY:
Our final guest is a professor of old rocks and stones at Princeton, Laidlaw Waddington. We understand you spent a weekend in Cairo years ago. Tell us what you know about the complex situation in the Middle East.

PROFESSOR WADDINGTON:
Sand. Lots of sand. Everywhere you go, sand.

ROONEY:
What kind of sand can our boys expect to find in Saudi Arabia?

PROFESSOR WADDINGTON:
Dry. Very dry. Just like our sand at the beach but no beach.

ROONEY:
How do you account for the fact that so much of our sand here is at the seashore when Iraq has all sand and no seashore?

PROFESSOR WADDINGTON:
Youll have to ask my wife that question.

ROONEY:
She's an expert on sand?

PROFESSOR WADDINGTON:
Yes. She sells seashells by the seashore.

When you hear the experts talk, you realize how little we understand about what's going on in the Middle East.

Time Goes By

A lot of you think I have a good deal here because *60 Minutes* uses reruns all summer and I get to go on vacation.

Well, Im not denying I have a good deal but how would you like to spend the summer looking at pictures of yourself when you were a lot younger? Its no fun being reminded every week that you used to be thinner and better looking. Youre sitting in your living room with friends. You come on the television screen and everyone starts laughing—not at what youre saying but at what you look like.

For instance, in 1979 I did an essay on "Fences." Fine, but they reran it this summer and I didnt recognize myself.

Funny thing about age, some people are lucky. They look better than they used to. Walter Cronkite, for instance, is better looking and more distinguished looking now than he was in 1953.

Frank Sinatra is better looking at seventy-four than he was at twenty-eight.

Some people are permanently one age in our memory: Albert Einstein . . . Winston Churchill . . . Marilyn Monroe.

Some women hold up very well. Barbara Bush, the First Lady, was eighteen here. Now she's grey-haired and overweight and a little wrinkled but she's more interesting looking now at sixty-five.

Its hard to put your finger on what makes someone look old. It isnt just grey hair and wrinkles. The whole body gradually assumes a different attitude.

Babe Ruth showed his age from the back as he said goodbye to his fans in Yankee Stadium years ago.

Im amused by people who dye their hair or have cosmetic surgery to make themselves look younger. They dont look any younger. They look different. They look just as old but they look as though theyve dyed their hair and had plastic surgery.

The actress Jessica Tandy has never had anything done to herself as far as I know. She's eighty-one. She looks her age but she looks great.

We didnt look any different to ourselves in the mirror this morning than we did yesterday morning but its surprising how different all of us look from month to month and from year to year.

If I had known, eleven years ago when I did that essay on "Fences," that it would be rerun this summer, I think I'd have dyed my hair grey so it wouldnt have hurt so much when I watched it in July.

Arab Dress

We've all learned a lot we didnt know about the Middle East in the past few months.

For one thing, the clothes people wear in many of those desert countries look strange to us. We've been seeing lots of pictures of women in Saudi Arabia. Women have to be completely covered when they go out, including their faces.

In the Pacific Islands women go bare-breasted without giving it a second thought. And you wouldnt say that Saudi Arabian women who cover everything are any more modest or moral than those Polynesian women who dont cover much of anything.

It depends on the situation. American women think its pretty strange that African women hang ornaments from their noses but American women dont think its funny when they decorate their ears like Christmas trees.

People everywhere have their own customs of dress and anything else seems funny to them.

Its beginning to look as though the American Army uniform is what's strange in the desert. American soldiers are all complaining that theyre too hot.

The natives know how to dress for 120-degree temperatures. This is typical dress for a Saudi Arabian man. This is called a djellaba . . . Im probably not pronouncing it right. It has this long undershirt that goes underneath it . . . and you put the djellaba on . . . so you have several layers of clothing. All this stuff is hung from your shoulders . . . nothing tight around your waist . . . no belt or anything and no pants.

As you move, the air flows around your body . . . sort of a convection process that cools you a little bit. Its why women in skirts in this Country are cold in the same room where men are hot.

This is the hat or head covering. Its just a piece of cloth. Its called a kaffiyeh. You put the cloth over your head and then you hold it on with this thing called an egal. I never knew why this stayed on but it seems to.

I'll bet that if our guys are there for a year, the Army is going to come up with a uniform that looks more like this than the uniform we have now.

Getting Started

The hard part of any job is always getting started. What do you do first? Sometimes you can sit around thinking about it for days before you get at it. It doesnt matter what the job is.

Where would you start if you had to erect a bridge across the Hudson River?

Maybe you know how to sew. If youre going to make a jacket, for example, what's the first thing you do? Where do you take the first stitch?

Thats the problem I often have doing these essays for *60 Minutes*. Getting started.

Ive been watching baseball and football games and theyve got a great way to start. Each player comes running out . . . the announcer tells you who it is . . . what he does . . . where he's from and everything. The crowd yells. The players get all revved up.

Now, thats how to start something and we decided to borrow that idea. MUSIC. CROWD CHEERING.

Soundman, video technician, and loose end, out of Philadelphia . . . Lincoln Warner!

On camera, from Rosemont, Pennsylvania, picked up as a free agent this year . . . Walter Dombrow!

At stopwatch, home—Long Island, Mount Holyoke College, a twenty-year veteran at CBS . . . Jane Bradford!

At the video console, at 5 feet 7 inches, 271¼ pounds, out of the Bronx, New York, editor and director, Bob Forte!

And, behind the desk tonight, from a lot of different places, not too tall and weighing quite a bit, the designated talker, Andy Rooney!

CHEERING. APPLAUSE.

And now that Im started, let's take a time out for a few commercial messages . . . while I think of something to say.

Ballgame Food

A lot of Americans have been sitting home watching World Series games this week but if anyone says to you, "Take Me Out to the Ballgame," watch out. Theyre talking big numbers. A ticket to a World Series game in the third deck is $40. A ticket in the first or second deck is $50.

And that isnt all either . . . not if you want something to eat.

Here are some of the prices at the concession stands in the Oakland Coliseum.

The large hot dog, "Colossal" they call it, is $2.75. The small one, called "Jumbo," is $2. A large beer is $4. A small beer is $2.75.

They got you where they want you at the ballpark. Its like the movies. You can spend as much on popcorn as on the ticket. And dont think youre missing the commercials if you actually go to the stadium either. Theres as much advertising in the ballpark as there is on television.

Theyre a lot more careful handling food than they used to be at the concession stands. Theres a young man wearing sanitary plastic gloves . . . and just to make sure there arent any germs left in there, he blows in the bag.

At the ballpark in Anaheim, you can get a frozen margarita, a gourmet hamburger for $4. A baked potato goes for $3.75. Maybe they have to buy tickets for those potatoes to get in.

At the great American game you can also get fajitas, Polish sausage, sukiyaki, sushi.

Usually one person sitting with you in the stands is the designated getter. Never send the fat kid who's more interested in food than baseball though. If you do, the food's apt to be gone before he gets back with it.

No matter who goes for food, make sure he has money. My bill for a snack for a small group was $26.75.

The price of ballpark food could easily triple in a few years too. Wait until those three-million-dollar ballplayers' agents realize they ought to have a clause in their contracts that give them a percentage of every hot dog sold.

Beauty Parlor Names

Its difficult for a man to make any kind of general statement about women these days without getting in trouble with at least one of them. I want to be fair and careful in what Im going to say.

It is my opinion that a great many women have one thing in common—they spend too much time and money fooling around with their hair—or having someone else fool around with it. Torturing it to death is what theyre doing to it.

You know theres something wrong with any group of businesses that call themselves "beauty parlors" . . . or "beauty salons." The average woman is no more beautiful than the average man is handsome . . . and they wouldnt call a barbershop a "handsome salon."

I dont know what the word "salon" means anyway. I suspect a place that calls itself a salon feels it can charge more.

One of the things that makes me suspicious of women's barbershops is their names. There is no single group of businesses on Earth that suffers more from the cute name syndrome.

Someone going into the beauty parlor business must sit up nights for weeks before they open up, trying to think of a cuter name than the last place.

CURL UP AND DYE / TRESSES / THE CLIP JOINT / BLADES / SCISSORS / SHEAR FANTASY / THE SHEARING STATION / JUST CUTTING UP / THE SMART SET / HEADQUARTERZ / MAKIN' WAVES / SHEAR PERFECTION / THE MANE ATTRACTION / SCISSORS OF OZ / HAIR WIZARDS / HAIRLINES / HAIRWAYS / HAIR TODAY / HAIRPORT / HAIRSMITHS / HAIR WE ARE / HAIR I AM / HAIR IT IS.

This may be the winner of the worst name contest: BEST LITTLE HAIR HOUSE.

Some places cut both men's and women's hair. They have names like ROMEO AND JULIET or BONNIE AND CLYDE. And some of them dont just fix hair, they do coiffures. I imagine a coiffure is twice as expensive as a haircut. JILIE'S SALON DE COIFFURES.

I just cant understand why a man goes to the barber and has his hair cut when a woman has to go to a beauty parlor and have her hair done for three times the price.

The Cost of Ingredients

I keep looking at things I buy and thinking about how they got to cost that much. A lot of things you buy look to me as if they cost more to package and to sell than they cost to make.

This bottle of Canada Dry club soda was eighty-nine cents. What is it? You know, they take some water, put bubbles in it, and put it in a bottle. For eighty-nine cents? Which costs the most . . . the water, the bottle or the bubbles? I'll bet the bottle costs the most.

This bottle of Listerine was $3.99. A fancy package. Theres a bottle in there somewhere.

If you buy a new car, a pair of shoes or a chicken for dinner, you at least feel you got something for your money, even if it costs too much. Its a lot of other things I worry about.

Here's a tube of Crest toothpaste, for example. Its the biggest-selling toothpaste by far. It has the American Dental Association stamp of approval and, as far as I know, its good toothpaste.

We paid $1.99 for one family-sized tube and $2.39 for the same tube in another drugstore.

I asked a company called Industrial Testing Laboratories to analyze the contents of a tube of Crest and give us some idea how much the ingredients would cost.

Im sure we could have done the same thing with Colgate, Aqua-Fresh or any other brand of toothpaste.

Here's the breakdown they gave us. The twelve ingredients, based on published prices, came to a total of twelve cents.

Now, I know a figure like that can be unfair. Its like saying I only work three minutes a week because thats about how long Im on the air. They have to pay the factory workers, salesmen, scientists who develop their formulas, executives. They have real estate to pay for . . . all sorts of things. I know that.

But still, twelve cents worth of stuff for $1.99 seems like a lot.

Crest sold about 200 million tubes of toothpaste last year. 200 million tubes times twelve cents each would mean they spend a total of $24 million on the ingredients in the Crest.

Packaging experts told me that the tube and the box probably cost somewhere around a nickel. A nickel each for 200 million tubes comes to $10 million. The advertising budget for Crest last year was $41 million. Add the cost of the package. Thats $51 million.

So I figure the ingredients cost less than half as much as the package and the advertising . . . not to mention the salesmen's salaries.

If they sold 200 million—let's round it off—for $2—they took in $400 million.

I just wish that packaging and selling products in the United States didnt so often cost more than what's in them.

Uniforms

Ive always hated uniforms. I never joined the Boy Scouts because even at twelve, I couldnt stand the thought of wearing the same clothes as the other boys.

During four years in the Army, I took every opportunity to get out of my uniform and into civilian clothes even if you werent supposed to.

People are divided about uniforms. A lot of people love them . . . they take any opportunity to get into one. They feel uniforms carry with them a great deal of authority and prestige.

On the occasion of a parade, there are always people who dig out their old uniforms and put them on . . . often trying to recapture the glory of days past.

I dont think people who dislike uniforms are better people than those who love them . . . but theyre different.

There are all kinds of jobs that call for people to wear special uniforms. Often a business will decide its employees should wear uniforms . . . although a uniform doesnt seem very important to a drive-in dry cleaning establishment or to the kid who gets your parked car.

And restaurants like their waiters in uniform so that one customer doesnt ask for a menu by mistake from another passing by. Uniforms are very big with hotel doormen. Thats probably because the doorman should be immediately identifiable in the crowd waiting for a cab.

City policemen and women all wear uniforms . . . except for the sneaky undercover cops, of course. The ordinary cop's dress carries a lot of respect and authority in most communities. I dont know why it is but city cops' uniforms are always blue. Some state troopers, on the other hand, are distinguished not by the color of their uniforms but by their hats.

In the past twenty years, theres been an explosion of the number of private security police who are not police at all. They wear uniforms, trying to look like police, hoping that will ward off crime. They have no gun, no authority, and very little at all going for them except their uniforms . . . and they arent much either.

The Army puts a lot of emphasis on conformity and the uniform is a big part of that although its not the best uniformed soldiers who make the best fighters.

Its a funny thing about uniforms. Sometimes you find them in unexpected places. If the word "uniform" means the same, then often young rebels fighting the system are so persistently unconventional and non-conformist that their uniform of rebellion is as identifiable as the hotel doorman's. That was certainly true of the hippies of the 1960s. They all dressed alike.

I still have my old Army uniform. Maybe I'll wear it into the office someday to show you how I looked in it . . . just as soon as I lose thirty pounds.

The Sound of Silence

One of the things thats disappearing from Earth, along with big trees, elephants and certain species of butterflies, is silence.

If someone wants to work on an invention the world needs, he might come up with a silent jackhammer. One that wouldnt rattle your teeth from two blocks away.

The garbage truck at 4 A.M. is a city noise.

In shopping malls, you can no longer be alone with your thoughts because theyve begun extensive in-store advertising over their public address systems.

Noise is sound you dont want to hear. And, of course, one person's sound is another person's noise. For me, rock music is noise.

A lot of people seem unaware that the noise theyre making is an intrusion on someone else's peace and quiet.

Somehow we've come to associate noise with gaiety. On New Year's Eve, people have those little noisemakers. When things are loud, we arent lonesome.

This accounts for another phenomenon.

There are millions of homes in America where the radio or television set is turned on in the morning and never turned off until everyone goes to bed at night.

I suspect I know why we've replaced the quiet in our lives with sound. Its because when theres no sound, we're forced to turn inward to our own thoughts, and almost always we prefer to have those driven out by noise. Its easier to listen than it is to think.

Over Population

Is there anyone who can explain to me why growth, getting bigger, is always considered good while staying the same size or getting smaller is considered bad?

A front-page news item in *The New York Times* says, "ECONOMIC GROWTH NEAR A STANDSTILL, U.S. FIGURES SHOW."

The story goes on to say, "the meager growth is far worse than previously thought." What does the reporter mean, "meager growth is far worse"? I'd have said, "the meager growth is far BETTER than expected."

The worst problem we have in this Country . . . in the whole world for that matter . . . is growth. We dont need bigger. We need better.

Everything is already too big. There are too many people, too many buildings, too many cars, too much Government and too many big companies.

The roads are too crowded and when you get where youre going, theres no place to park. They have to build playgrounds for kids because there arent any vacant lots left.

I get fund-raising letters from a good small college I went to. They tell me they have to have money for new buildings to take care of more students. Why dont they just stop taking more students?

The Bible says, "Be fruitful and multiply," but the Bible was written several thousand years ago when there were fewer than one million people on Earth. Today there are five billion people. There are more people in Houston alone than there used to be on Earth. There are more people alive today than have ever died in the entire history of the world.

I have an idea that if God were to rewrite the Bible, he'd change that "Be fruitful and multiply" to "Enough already."

1991

Ready for War

When you get up in the morning, are you ready for work? All organized? Ready to go? When you take a trip, are you sure you have everything youre going to need?

Of course, you arent. Not being ready is part of life. No one has ever been absolutely, positively ready for anything.

The day after tomorrow is the deadline thats been set for Iraq to get out of Kuwait. President Bush has threatened to stop talking and drive the Iraqis out if they dont get out. Are we ready to do that?

A couple of weeks ago, General Calvin Waller, second in command in Saudi Arabia, said we arent ready and that we wont be ready by the January 15 deadline.

What does the general mean we arent ready? Not being ready is part of every war ever fought.

Lincoln fired General George McClellan during the Civil War because McClellan procrastinated instead of attacking. Eisenhower could have used another month before invading Europe in 1944 but he did it June 6 because that was the day he had to do it. Day after tomorrow is D-Day in the Middle East.

If we arent ready, how come? Since 1970, Americans have paid out something like 4 trillion dollars for the weapons and the people it takes to fight a war.

We gave up fixing our roads, our bridges, our cities so we could crank out the bombers, battleships, submarines, fighter planes, tanks, guns and missiles, those things it takes to fight a war . . . and we're not ready?

What was the money spent on if we're not ready?

For forty years we were getting ready to fight the Soviet Union, 300 million people and an army of 3 million soldiers . . . now we arent ready for war with an Arab country of 18 million people? We arent ready to fight a country about the size of North and South Dakota thats in financial trouble because it fought an eight-year war with Iran without ever winning it.

Americans dont want a war in the Middle East. No question about that. But if the United States isnt ready for war now, someone ought to give us our money back. They ought to return that 4 trillion dollars. That would be $16,000 for every man, woman and baby in the United States.

War

Even though we all say we want peace, the stories and pictures of war are more interesting than those about peace. War is exciting.

This is so true that we're often caught up with the action of war to the exclusion of the ideas about it. Even so, theres an assumption by those of us alive today that we're more civilized than people were in the days of Attila the Hun or even more recently in American history when early settlers were wiping out colonies of Indians.

We're convinced that civilized countries no longer go to war to take something away from one another as Iraq did with Kuwait. We like to think that we're so civilized that we only go to war to defend some ethical principle like freedom or democracy.

If its true, though, that hardly anyone wants war, it certainly is strange that in the twentieth century, our century, we have killed more than 80 million of our fellow human beings . . . on purpose . . . at war with each other.

Since 1900, a date some people think modern civilization began, more people have intentionally killed more other people than in any other ninety years in history.

Probably the reason we're able to do both—believe on one hand that we're more civilized and, on the other hand, wage war to kill—is that killing isnt as personal an affair in war as it once was.

The enemy is invisible. We dont hear him scream. We no longer look another man in the eye and run him through with a sword. He's killed by remote control . . . a loud noise . . . a distant puff of smoke . . . and then . . . silence.

We dont see the pictures of the dead soldier's wife and children that he carried in his breast pocket. They are destroyed with him.

The question of pity, compassion or remorse doesnt enter into it. The enemy isnt a man, he's a statistic.

More people are killed in modern wars now because we're better at doing it than we were when we did it with swords or bows and arrows. We have spent more money on weapons designed to kill people than on our education or on our health.

One man with a modern weapon can push a button and kill hundreds of thousands.

The world's record for killing was set by us at Hiroshima on August 6, 1945.

Let's hope no one's about to set a new world's record.

The End of the War

The 1991 Gulf War is over, and we feel together.

This has been the fourth war in my life, the fourth in the lives of many of us. Just when it seems as though we may not have another, we have another.

We all agree when we talk about war, that war is bad and yet its not really certain that all wars are all bad. There are some good things about war sometimes. Everyone accomplishes more in times of war, our hearts beat faster, our senses are sharper.

Theres no way to quantify some things . . . no measurement like feet or inches by which to judge beauty or love, and no statistic you can apply to war to determine whether totally its good or bad.

This War in the Gulf has been, by all odds, the best war in modern history . . . not only for America but for the whole world, including Iraq, probably. It was short and the objectives of victory were honorable. In spite of all the placards, the blood was not for oil. It was for Freedom. We did the right thing.

This war has made it clear that the news stories of young Americans with too little education, too little muscle, on drugs and committing crimes, werent about all of them. Young Americans can still do what we've always been so proud they can do.

If this war saved a million lives that might have been lost to Saddam Hussein in the year 1997, does that make it a good war? Youre darn right it does. If the war established the power of the United Nations as a force that can make the whole world better and safer, does that make it worthwhile? Youre darn right it does. What if the spirit of togetherness and pride that this war has produced among us all gets America up off its tail and starts us going again? What if fewer people are cold, hungry and homeless next winter because we're working better? Is that worth 10,000 lives? A hundred lives? One life?

Probably . . . although not if its yours, or the only life of someone you love.

Gulf War Ads

You must have noticed how many people who didnt have anything to do with the great success our troops had in the Middle East are trying now to get in on that success. Theres nothing illegal about people associating themselves with the War in the Gulf when they had nothing to do with it. Its just irritating.

I saw a tacky advertisement for sable coats from a place called Christie Brothers. "Please join us in celebrating the triumph of Peace," the ad says.

By buying a sable coat for $50,000? What's killing fuzzy little animals in Russia to make coats in the United States got to do with peace?

A store window on Broadway is trying to sell women's dresses by out-American-flagging and out-yellow-ribboning their competitors.

The telephone company, AT&T, is in the middle of a takeover of a company called NCR that doesnt want to be taken over, so AT&T is very conscious of its public image these days.

NCR ran an ad explaining its opposition to the takeover.

AT&T didnt get into the argument. It posed as Mr. Nice Patriotic Guy with an ad for the USO Gulf Support Fund.

Its for a very good cause but do you think theres any wild chance that AT&T thought it might be a good public relations move to get its name associated with the War and the USO instead of with the takeover in order to make the company seem more lovable and less greedy?

Last week the New York State Conservative Party paid $45,000 for a full-page ad in *The New York Times*. It was knocking Senator Moynihan for voting against going to war in the Gulf.

Senator Moynihan is a bright, responsible senator with whom I disagree about half the time and his opposition to the war was part of the democratic process we're all so proud of. The politicians who supported the President deserve to have their support on the record and to their credit but having been against our entry into that War doesnt make anyone a bad American.

The interesting thing about all this is that while the War was actually going on, many advertisers didnt want to have anything to do with it. Several sponsors actually took their commercials off *60 Minutes* if there was a piece that night about the War. That was before we won the War.

Senator Alan Simpson

You probably read where Senator Alan Simpson of Wyoming accused the CNN reporter Peter Arnett of being a sympathizer of Saddam Hussein because Arnett continued to report from Baghdad all during the Middle East war.

Senator Simpson also suggested that Arnett, a Pulitzer Prize winner for his work in Vietnam, might have been in sympathy with the Communist Vietcong during that war because Arnett married a Vietnamese woman.

Well, Senator Simpson wrote a letter to *The New York Times* this week, apologizing to Peter Arnett. In his letter, Senator Simpson said he was wrong repeating the rumors about Mr. Arnett's family connection to the Vietcong because he couldnt prove them.

"I said from the outset," Senator Simpson wrote, "that if it couldnt be proven, I would apologize."

In that same spirit, I'd like to apologize to the Senator tonight. For some time now, at our dinner table and when Im among friends, I have referred to Senator Simpson as "Saddam Hussein's friend."

Senator Simpson did go to Baghdad to see Hussein last April 13, and at that time he comforted Hussein for things being written about him in our newspapers by saying that American reporters were pampered and haughty.

Thats why Ive been calling Senator Simpson "Saddam Hussein's friend."

Well, now I feel sort of bad about it. I shouldnt have done that.

Senator Simpson says *The Wall Street Journal* has suggested he's a racist, too. I certainly wouldnt suggest he's a racist because I simply dont know.

Ive heard rumors that if he could, he'd repeal the First Amendment guaranteeing Freedom of the Press. Ive heard rumors that he's one of our dumbest Senators.

It would be unfair of me to repeat those rumors because Im not sure theyre true. Ive never even met him.

Neither can I prove that Senator Simpson is a friend of Saddam Hussein. It is not certain that theyre friends and, unless the facts prove otherwise, I apologize to him for having said they are friends.

I hope you take this apology in the spirit in which its intended, Senator . . . unless you can prove otherwise.

U.S. Postal Service

There are few small pleasures in life that exceed the pleasure of getting a good, personal letter from a friend . . . and the experience has almost disappeared. One first-class stamp costs 29 cents now and people think twice before mailing a simple, friendly letter.

The Postal Service handles 160 billion pieces of mail a year and only 6 percent of that mail is real letters. Eighty-three percent is business mail. Eleven percent is mail from people writing back to businesses. You know, sending in their checks for the phone bill . . . things like that.

Almost half of all the mail they handle is what you call junk mail. The Postal Service doesnt mind it though because its easy to deliver and it brings in a lot of money.

Here's the way the price of a first-class stamp has gone up.

From 1919 to 1932, it was 2 cents.

From 1932 until 1958, a stamp cost 3 cents.

In 1958, it went to 4 cents.

And then, 5 cents . . . 6 cents.

In 1971, it went to 8 cents. Thats the year the Post Office went out on its own and became the Postal Service.

1974, 1975, 1978 . . . all 10 cents.

In 1981 there were two raises. First it went to 18 cents and then to 20 cents. Thats because the following year, 1982, they got their last tax subsidy money.

In 1985, 22 cents. 1988, 25 cents

And finally 1991 . . . 29 cents. . . . Stay Tuned.

There are about 740,000 full-time postal workers and 30,000 part-time workers.

The average postal worker makes about $42,000 in salary and benefits. I suppose the part-time workers make less and the full-time ones make more than that.

The average teacher in the United States makes $31,000.

Everyone likes his mailman but complains about the Postal Service and I have a suggestion about how it could improve its public image.

My idea is this. Let people mail letters to soldiers in Saudi Arabia free. It wouldnt cost the Postal Service much because they dont have mailmen over there anyway.

And here's a suggestion about what to do with the junk mail. Once a week, load it on to a B–52, fly it to Iraq and drop all of it on Baghdad. Junk mail might bring Saddam Hussein to his knees.

Church Architecture

There are more than 350,000 churches in the United States . . . one church for every 400 Americans who go to church occasionally.

There are wooden churches . . . stone churches . . . brick churches. There are churches that are tall . . . churches that are short . . . round churches, square churches . . . churches in every imaginable shape. God must be impressed by the ingenuity of the architects.

The greatest contribution religion has made to what America looks like is the simple white New England church with its graceful steeple. These lovely buildings are pure American.

In their own way these churches dominated our early villages just as certainly but a lot more simply than the cathedrals of Europe dominated their communities.

Generations of French citizens of Reims, France, devoted their lives to their cathedral, a monument to their belief in God.

There are cathedrals in America. Many of them are much-loved but they are modern reproductions of those great cathedrals of Europe.

Most churches, no matter what the religion, are empty six days a week and less than a quarter filled on Sunday. Hundreds of thousands of churches, with a total capacity in the millions, are sparsely attended except on Easter. There may be more seats available in church pews than there are people in the United States to sit in them!

Because of their tax-free status, the biggest churches in the busiest, most valuable sections of a city make religion an expensive freedom that Americans are willing to pay for.

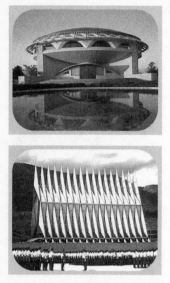

St. Patrick's Cathedral occupies a site comparable to the one across the street for which Saks Fifth Avenue pays millions of dollars in taxes every year. The cathedral pays nothing.

Another church, St. Bartholomew's, has recently been denied the right to build a skyscraper over itself as a money-making venture.

The old Trinity Church on Wall Street seems about to be engulfed by commerce but dont worry for Trinity. The church owns many of those skyscrapers that surround it.

The church attended by more Americans than any other is Robert Schuller's Crystal Cathedral with its adjacent drive-in church in Garden Grove, California. The Crystal Cathedral is evidence that even in religion, Californians are not exactly like the rest of us.

If the believers of marginally different faiths knew how much the tax-exempt status of other churches in town was costing them, they might find a way to be friendlier and meet to pray under fewer roofs.

Minorities

Every time you turn around, some minority is complaining because it thinks its being discriminated against . . . and often it is.

When they had the St. Patrick's Day parade in New York, there was a big flap because the Irish minority didnt want two sub-minorities, the Irish homosexuals and the Irish handicapped, to march in their parade. The black Mayor walked with the homosexuals. The Italian Governor marched with the handicapped. The Catholic Bishop snubbed the Irish homosexuals and the black Mayor.

During the Gulf War, there was a great cry about the large number of black soldiers who'd been sent there. A lot of good black kids had signed up for the Army as a way out of poverty. What are you going to do, not let them join up because theyre black?

The fear was that a disproportionate number of blacks would be killed. Of the 210 Americans who died in the Persian Gulf, twenty-seven were black. The Pentagon either does not know or will not tell me how many were killed in action.

The Italians complain about movies like *The Godfather* that have stories involving the Mafia.

We all used to tell Polish jokes but the Poles complained so now you cant touch a Polish joke with a ten-foot Pole.

Jews have an Anti-Defamation League.

Downstairs here at CBS on the bulletin board, they announce women's meetings. If CBS men put up notices announcing men's meetings, there'd be hell to pay.

Lots of times the minorities are in the majority.

Here are some numbers:

There are 122 million men, 128 million women in the United States. Some minority!

There are 200 million whites, 30 million blacks, 22 million Hispanics, 7 million Asians. There are 10 million Other.

Thats what I'd like to be . . . Other.

There are 145 million Christians, 6 million Jews, 6 million Muslims.

Minorities divide up to make themselves even more minor. There are Orthodox and Reform Jews, Shiite and Sunni Muslims, Protestant and Catholic Christians. Christians further split into minorities like Baptists, Presbyterians, Methodists and Episcopalians.

We like being in the minority and then we complain about it.

Its the great American majority that isnt organized and doesnt protect itself. It gets defamed, taxed, scorned, made to look like idiots in the movies and theres nothing the majority can do because its scared to death of what one of the minorities will say if it does anything.

The diversity that used to be America's strength has become its weakness. I wish all of us would start thinking of ourselves, and of each other, less often as black, white, Irish, Italian, gay, Southern, veteran, Jewish, Hispanic, male or female, and more often as Americans . . . or maybe just Human Beings.

TV Rules

You probably read where the news broadcasts of the television networks are in financial trouble. I wouldnt be surprised if they decided to save money this summer by going to reruns. We could win the War in the Persian Gulf all over again.

I like news on television and watch a lot of it but there are some changes I wish theyd make.

The first thing I'd do is throw out those unpleasant commercials for embarrassingly personal problems, for products like Attends, Anusol, Polident, Kaopectate.

We all know a lot of people have problems you cant talk about. Why talk about them? Do we have to be subjected to them every night while we're watching the news? The networks need money but we dont need it that bad.

Rule #2. I'd prohibit any anchorman or woman, local or network, from thanking any other reporter on their broadcasts. The correspondent doesnt do the report as a favor to the anchorman. They both work for the same company. Their pay checks are signed by the same person. "Thank you" doesnt enter in to their relationship.

Rule #3. I'd make sure no Washington correspondent ever again quoted "a usually reliable source" or "a high government official." If the correspondent cant name the person, he shouldnt use the statement. I always have the funny feeling that the reporter may have written the quotation himself.

#4. If any show on television had a telephone ringing any time during the broadcast, no matter how much the situation called for it, I'd take away the station's license. Three times on the average night I get up to answer the telephone and it turns out to be a phone ringing in a television commercial.

The Last Rule. I'd make it illegal for anyone on an interview show to say to a guest: "In the few seconds we have left, please tell us briefly how youd deal with the recession, the Middle East problem, drugs, poverty and homelessness."

SHOW HOST:

In the few seconds we have left, Joan, what are your constituents saying? What are they telling you they want to see happen?

ROONEY:

I mean if there isnt time for a guest to answer a question, dont ask the question.

In conclusion, I'd like to thank Mike, Morley, Ed, Steve, Lesley, Don, Phil, Merri, Esther, Joe . . .

Baseball Analyst

The big news in baseball, the great American pastime, isnt how they play the game, its how much money the players are making. 233 baseball players make more than a million dollars a year. 32 make $3 million. And they arent all potential Hall of Famers either.

Tony Phillips must be the clean-up hitter. Youd think they could get someone to do this for less than $1,556,000.

Just for example, three Detroit Tigers, Deer, Fielder and Tettleton, struck out 489 times last year . . . but they were paid $5,316,000. I understand theyve been offered an incentive bonus. If they can raise their strikeout total to 500 this year, they'll be paid $6 million.

When they broadcast the games on television, they have a play-by-play announcer and what they call a color man. Theres no sport on Earth so obsessed with statistics as baseball is. Its a numbers game. Money has become so important that they ought to add a financial analyst to the broadcast booth. And here's the way it would go. Jack Buck and Tim McCarver are doing a Detroit Tigers–Chicago White Sox game. I'll be the financial analyst.

FINANCIAL ANALYST:

I'll take it from there, Jack. Deer is making $1,966,667 this year. He has a diversified portfolio with an emphasis on pork belly futures.

JACK BUCK:

. . . will be a tough customer for the Tigers to handle today, 2 and 0.

FINANCIAL ANALYST:

You can say that again, Jack.

JACK BUCK:

. . . will be a tough customer for the Tigers to handle today, 2 and 0.

FINANCIAL ANALYST:

Right you are, Jack. The White Sox pitcher, Greg Hibbard, is one of the lowest paid players in the League. He makes a piddling $150,000. He started 33 games last year but only finished 3. He has never come up to bat and hit the ball even once in his whole Major League career.

SPORTS ANNOUNCER:

Rob Deer.

FINANCIAL ANALYST:

Last year Deer had the second highest DPH on the team. He got 92 hits but struck out 147 times. His DPH . . . that means "dollars per hit" . . . was $21,374.64 which he put in tax-exempt municipals paying 9 percent for a yield of 11 percent.

ROONEY:

Baseball is the only game in which some of the players are paid more money than they know how to count.

Harry Reasoner

Harry Reasoner was one of the original correspondents on 60 Minutes *when it first aired in 1968. He decided to retire in 1991.*

In 1961 CBS asked me to write a show for Harry. We'd never met so I called him and suggested we talk first. He put me off. He wasnt unfriendly, he just wasnt interested in talking about it. Harry's like that.

Writing for other people on television, I learned something. I learned that its hard to write for someone who couldnt do it without you and easy to write for someone who doesnt need you. Harry was always easy to write for.

And you could ask Harry. There are people who know things and people who dont know anything. Harry knows things. He's an omnivorous reader with a great memory. He's got a lot in his head . . . some of which he'd be better off without, of course.

Once I saw someone come to him with a blank map of Africa . . . just the outline of the countries. Harry sat down, looked at it and filled in the names of all fifty-two African countries.

Harry Reasoner's my best friend. Of the ten people I say that about, Harry's the most complicated and the hardest to be best friends with. He's worth the trouble.

People wonder why he's leaving. Harry's leaving CBS because he never really liked to work. It made him mad when anyone suggested he was lazy. He's not lazy but of all the people doing this kind of work, Harry enjoyed actually doing it the least. Mike Wallace loves to work. Harry hates it.

In 1979 I questioned the overuse of the word "superstar." I tried to say who was and who was not a real superstar.

A superstar is always a person who has something more than skill and talent that attracts the rest of us to him. In this business, Walter Cronkite's a superstar. Ten years ago, I said that of the four correspondents on *60 Minutes*, two of them were and two of them were not.

For months after that people asked me who I thought the two superstars were. I never said, of course, but I can tell you now. Harry Reasoner was one.

Clarence Thomas

You probably watched some of the Senate confirmation hearings for Judge Clarence Thomas. You should have. It was more fun than *Monday Night Football*. You sat there cheering the good guys and booing the bad guys . . . whoever you thought they were.

I couldnt decide who irritated me most, the senators who were predictably conservative or the senators who were predictably liberal.

I was thinking what it would be like if I had to sit in front of a panel of senators to be questioned on what I thought about those hearings.

SENATOR:
Mr. Rooney, do you think Judge Thomas is the best qualified judge for one of the most important jobs in the United States?

MR. ROONEY:
No, obviously there are better qualified people. But its a good idea to have a black judge on the Supreme Court anyway.

SENATOR:
Do you think Clarence Thomas is a smart enough man for the job?

MR. ROONEY:
Marginal. Probably he is. The other Supreme Court justices arent all geniuses either, you know. He has an averageness about him. That may be good.

SENATOR:
Did he give honest answers or was he trying not to lose any votes?

MR. ROONEY:
He was semi-honest. He didnt lie but he was trying not to lose any votes. He weaseled on abortion. What would you have done?

SENATOR:
Do you think Clarence Thomas will vote with the conservative majority on the Supreme Court if he gets on it?

MR. ROONEY:

He may fool some people . . . including President Bush.

SENATOR:

How did you feel about Judge Thomas when the hearings were over?

MR. ROONEY:

I liked him.

SENATOR:

Could you tell the American people whether youd vote for or against Judge Thomas's confirmation?

MR. ROONEY:

Senator, I believe the United States is the greatest nation on Earth. I believe in freedom of speech, homes for the homeless, Arnold Schwarzenegger, Norman Schwarzkopf, women's rights, civil rights, rightists' rights and leftists' rights. Thank you.

SENATOR:

Thank you, Mr. Rooney. You are a great American and a fine human being and we are honored to have you here with us today.

Well, I shouldnt say how I'd vote but I will say this. If Clarence Thomas isnt approved by Congress, I'll buy dinner for Orrin Hatch and Teddy Kennedy . . . just the three of us.

Soviet Disunion

Who would have thought a year ago that the fifteen States in the Soviet Union would decide to split up?

What would the newspaper headlines look like if that happened here in the United States?

"PRESIDENT BUSH PLEADS BUT BREAKAWAY STATES DEFY HIM, PUTTING FATE OF U.S. IN DOUBT."

"BUSH THREATENS TO QUIT UNLESS NATION FINDS A WAY TO PRESERVE UNITED STATES."

"U.S. LEADERS PRESS A REBELLIOUS OHIO TO REMAIN IN UNION."

You have to consider the possibility it could happen here. Let's face it, our fifty states aren't that friendly. Florida is jealous of California, Colorado and Arizona fight over water and, as far as Mississippi is concerned, New York could drop dead. Never mind Russia . . . we've got our own problems.

There are a lot of reasons why a State might want to get out. Some States think their citizens pay more than their share of taxes to the Federal Government. Here are the top five tax-paying States:

Californians pay the most . . . $127 billion dollars. New York is next with $109 billion.

These are the States that pay the least:

Wyoming . . . just $1.2 billion. That wouldn't pay the Congressional travel allowance.

What if California says, "Hey, listen, Wyoming. Go get your own Army. We're tired of paying for all this stuff for you deadbeats."

And there's going to be a war between the young and the old in the United States, too. The old folks in Florida might decide they don't want to pay for the education of the young anymore. They'd vote to leave the Union. This happens in towns all across the Country.

Texas might get tired of supporting little States like Rhode Island. What does Texas need Rhode Island for?

Imagine what the continental United States would look like without California, New York, Texas and Florida.

Well, it won't happen, of course. Every kid dreams about running away but if they do, 99 percent of them decide it was a bad idea and come home.

My bet is that in a few years, half those Soviet states that left the union will come home.

The Homeless

They say a million or two, but no one knows how many homeless there are in the United States. Theyre harder to count than grains of sand or snowflakes.

You see them everywhere, in the nooks and crannies of New York City. We call them homeless, but all of us make a nest wherever we are, and even the homeless make homes for themselves. They make them out of the raw materials of the city: discarded scraps of plywood, sheets of abandoned plastic, old rubber tires, and the favorite building material of all, big old cardboard boxes.

The simpler homes for the homeless are just a box and a park bench. Some look as though they might have a guest room for visitors.

Somehow you can ignore a million different characters on the streets of New York, but the look of one homeless person in the morning can intrude on your thoughts for the rest of the day.

The street people are often social misfits who dont want to be cogs in society's wheels. Whose fault? Your fault? My fault? Their fault?

I spoke with several:

FIRST MAN:
Well, in a way it is my fault. In a way it is society's. Society is a bad word.

SECOND MAN:
Mostly my fault, but it just happened to be the wrong circumstance at the wrong time, you know. The timing was wrong.

FIRST WOMAN:
The only reason why Im homeless is because I was with the wrong people, and because of drugs.

THIRD MAN:
I dont know, drugs did it to me.

ROONEY:
Do you mind being homeless?

FOURTH MAN:
No.

ROONEY:
You dont mind it?

FOURTH MAN:
Well, I do mind it, but like the way things are these days—

ROONEY:
Youre not unhappy?

FOURTH MAN:
Very unhappy.

ROONEY:
It seems likely that the homeless we see on the streets in New York are not the saddest cases. The saddest cases are hidden away, unseen, the mother with children, the elderly poor, the mentally sick.

Most of us are torn between sympathy and impatience with the homeless. Thats probably because some of them deserve our sympathy, others our impatience. Many of the homeless are simply inept at living. Life gets away from them. They cant cope, and theyre sentenced to long-term unhappiness because of that. Like each of us, to some extent the homeless are victims of their own incompetence. When we feel sorry for them, we see in them a little of ourselves.

Sexual Harassment

This is an example of something I did on television that doesnt mean much without the pictures. We're printing it anyway with a few examples.

Ever since the Clarence Thomas hearings and the charges made by Anita Hill, there have been a lot of stories in the newspapers about sexual harassment. There are new stories every day about the problems women are having being sexually annoyed by men.

Men have been slow to learn that women dont want the kind of attention that has anything to do with sex. Its especially annoying to women who work in offices. They say men are always staring at them at the fax machine. Men make uncalled-for remarks all the time.

Women want to be looked at by men the same way men look at other men in the office. All a woman wants is to be able to do her job, without being treated like a sex object. They want to be one of the boys. They want to stand on their own two feet.

Day after day, there are new stories about sexual harassment. Women who never dared speak up before are coming forward with facts about unwanted attention that they get. Women want to relate to men as business associates, not as potential dates after work. If this episode with Clarence Thomas doesnt do anything else, it should make it clear to men that women are sick and tired of being treated as playthings. I dont know why men cant leave women alone.

Theres no doubt we've all become more aware that there is sexual harassment in the workplace and elsewhere. Women have begun to make men aware of how unpleasant this incessant suggestion of sex is to them. Theres no question it has to stop.

Im more aware of it than I was just a few weeks ago, but I do want to say one thing to women, in men's defense. Give us a break, will you?

LESLEY STAHL:
You dont have to be one of the *60 Minutes* old-timers to know we're going to get a lot of mail about that one—and you answer it, Andy.

Sexual Harassment Response

Well, I did get a lot of angry mail about that and made a piece out of it the following week.

Being a critic is hard work these days, because there arent many things you can be critical of without getting in trouble. I got in big trouble last week when I pointed out the irony of newspapers running stories about sexual harassment on the same page with ads that featured attractive, half-dressed women. I was snowed under with complaints.

"Im never going to watch *60 Minutes* again."

"Im writing Laurence Tisch, the chairman of CBS."

"Youd get a break if you lived in my house—a broken nose."

"Lesley Stahl should refuse to introduce you."

"The producer of *60 Minutes* ought to be ashamed of himself for having you on the show."

"Im writing all your sponsors to tell them Im not buying their product if they advertise on *60 Minutes*."

I dont know why people associate advertisers with what's said on this broadcast. Advertisers arent buying what any of us say. They buy time thats left open in a broadcast that attracts a lot of people to watch it. Theyre buying viewers, not opinions. Advertisers dont see this show before its broadcast. They dont approve or disapprove of anything on it.

Last Monday, after the show, I spent the day answering the telephone. I told one woman I didnt think she had any sense of humor. Big mistake. Never tell anyone that he or she has no sense of humor. People would rather be accused of shoplifting than be accused of not having a sense of humor, especially people without a sense of humor.

But putting aside the question of whether my remarks were fair or unfair, Im disappointed at how little I can say thats honest and direct—even when Im wrong—without getting in trouble. Does anyone really believe that what I did last week means that Im in favor of sexual harassment?

There are only a few safe targets left, just a few groups of people you can say anything negative about without getting in trouble for it. Ive made a list of safe targets and I probably ought to stick to those. Politicians, for instance. You can say anything you want about them, and it doesnt matter how unfair you are. People seem to like it and they dont complain.

Other safe targets are insurance companies, doctors, television, rich people, the telephone company. You can criticize any of those without getting in trouble. But if you want to be safe, dont say anything about women, blacks, Jews, Catholics, the poor, homosexuals, American Indians, the Mafia, abortion, Scientologists, the Eskimos, Moslems or Greeks.

WALLACE:
As Andy fades out, let me fade in with the mail, and none better to start with than the letter we got from Andy's daughter Emily Rooney, news director of station WCVB-TV in Boston. She wrote:

"... Nothing [my father] says about women surprises me. But I was shocked to learn he doesnt know how to pronounce harass ... "—Emily Rooney, Boston, Massachusetts.

Or is it harass?

Labels

Ive had quite a few complaints lately from people who like it when I complain about things. They say I havent complained about anything lately. So tonight, for you complaint fans, I have a complaint.

My problem is with the labels they stick on things you buy. You could spend ten minutes soaking off labels on something in hot water, or scraping it with a knife. These plastic refrigerator boxes have labels that are too hard to remove. Who wants to live with Rubbermaid's advertising on their leftover stew in the refrigerator? You cant get these little suckers off.

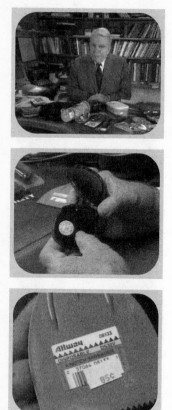

They have directions on this thermos bottle for everything except how to get the label off. "For hot or cold beverages," it says. I wonder how it knows which to keep them?

This is one of those pans thats supposed to be no-stick. I never had much luck with no-stick pans, even when I spray them with that no-stick stuff. And if its no-stick, how come the label they stuck to it doesnt come off easily?

Did you buy a pair of sunglasses during the summer? This is the most idiotic stick-on of all: right on the lens. The sticker doesnt soak off, and if you try to get it off with a knife, you scratch the glass.

This broad knife has one of those bar-code tags on it. I never trust bar codes. If a store has a machine that reads these and gives the machine the price, why cant they make a bar code we can all read with our eyes? What's the secret? Something sneaky going on with bar codes.

And look what they did with this. The store planted its own price right over the bar code price. Would you think this price was higher or lower than the price they pasted over?

And these things are a delight, arent they? Youre trying to get dressed in the morning, in a hurry. You find one of these on a new shirt, and you have to stop and find a pair of scissors to cut it off.

Too many of these gimmicks are better for the store than they are for the customer. These little plastic bubbles they use to encase products, look at these. Theyre attractive, but how do you get in?

This is a knife inside this one. Fine. Trouble is, you need the knife to open the package that its trapped inside of.

I just wish manufacturers would spend more time making their products and less time packaging them and gluing labels on them.

Bills

It may come as a surprise to some of you to learn that I havent always had enough money to pay my bills.

Now I have the money but a lot of times I dont pay them right away because I dont understand them. Do they really need all these numbers they put on bills?

Here's a Visa bill. "Reference numbers," it says. There are eleven reference numbers and each one of them has twenty-three digits in it. A solid page of numbers there.

Here's a beauty from All State Insurance. Look at the size of this bill. It goes through all the details. It says, "$250,000 each person, each accident." "Income continuation . . . $100 per week."

Over here it tells you how much each thing costs you. "Bodily injury $165. Auto collision $150." It comes to a total of $462.60.

Then, after all this, go down into the corner and they have this PAYMENT NOTICE. Youre really fuming by now. But look what it says: "YOUR POLICY IS PAID IN FULL. PLEASE DISREGARD THIS NOTICE."

These people who send out bills dont seem to understand either that no one wants to read a lot of cute advertising on their bills.

Here's a bill from the Public Service Electric and Gas Company in New Jersey. It says, "With old man winter on the way, get control of your heating bills today."

Just stick to your long numbers, Public Service Electric and Gas. Dont try to be funny. No one wants a funny gas company bill. Just tell us how much we owe and when we have to pay.

Here's a personal account number with Con Edison in New York. Its fifteen digits . . . a billion is ten digits. There are only 5 billion people in the world. Why would a company have to give out a personal number higher than the number of people there are in the whole world? Does anyone have the number one or twenty-seven or 1,027? Why not?

Cable television bills are always an experience. They get you four or five different ways.

BASIC CABLE SERVICE $14.95.

STANDARD CABLE SERVICE $4.00.

STANDARD PLUS SERVICE is an extra $1.00.

Some companies know their bills are confusing so instead of making them simple, they send you a brochure explaining them. Here's a brochure from Macy's. I cant tell whether this is a bill or directions for installing a storm window.

Here's one: UNDERSTANDING YOUR BILL FOR ELECTRIC/GAS SERVICE. This is a sample statement they have to explain how simple it is. It says here: "A charge or credit will be made when the estimated twelve-month average cost per kilowatthour to Public Service of energy produced, purchased and interchanged is 0.001 mills per kilowatthour above or below 35.000 mills per kilowatthour."

I guess that explains that bill.

Letter to the President

Dear President Bush:

How are you? I hope you had a nice weekend in Kennebunkport. Its nice up there. Do you leave the heat on all winter even when youre not using the house?

Ive been thinking a lot about this mess we're in.

One thing everyone says, when this war's over we ought to stop using so much oil from the Middle East. I read where we burn 130 billion gallons of gas a year just traveling. What about asking Americans not to use so much gas, Mr. President? They like you. I bet if you asked, theyd do it.

You travel a lot yourself. Just since youve been President, youve traveled to Japan, China, Belgium, Poland, Burlington, Vermont. You probably cant even remember all the places youve been.

You must have been to 100 cities where all you know is a hotel room and the main road to the airport. How much gas does one of those motorcades use? Just for one person? You.

I was talking to a woman a few weeks ago who said she'd been in every state of the Union except Tennessee. She and her husband were going to drive to Chattanooga next summer so she could say she's been in all fifty. Youll pardon me for saying so, Sir, but half the traveling you do is as pointless as that.

Why not suggest that people stay home more? Set an example yourself. Youve got yourself a nice place there in Washington . . . a big White House. Room for the whole family.

If you asked Americans to stay put and enjoy their hometowns, theyd do it and we could cut our oil bill by 25 percent without building one more atomic energy plant.

The airlines arent going to like this idea, I know that. But theyve got it coming the way theyve treated us. We should all join an Infrequent Flyer Club.

Just a respectful suggestion, Mr. President. But I know what I'd like to do. I'd like to spend more time home and less time getting someplace else that isnt as good. If you write back, dont forget you need a 29 cent stamp now.

Sincerely,
Andrew A. Rooney

1992

Progress

Why is it that nothing helps? I keep buying things that seem like the answer to all my problems, but Im never any better off with them than I was without them. And this is universal. Edison invented the light bulb, but people dont read any more than our grandparents did by candlelight.

Is dinner any better since we got microwave ovens?

With television, we learn all about our politicians before Election Day. Do we get better politicians? I dont think so.

You may have noticed that, for the past few years, Ive had this computer here, next to my trusty old Underwood. Im embarrassed to tell you I write on the computer more now than I write on the typewriter. The computer makes writing easier, makes editing what Ive written easier. Youd assume that it would make me a better writer, wouldnt you? Why else would I have spent a lot of money for it? Well, it doesnt make me a better writer. The fact is, I'd be the same writer if I used a quill pen.

When I played football, everyone wore a leather helmet with felt padding inside. Now, the helmets are plastic and hard as steel. Are there fewer injuries since helmets got harder? I havent noticed that there are.

Theyre advertising a new television set. You can see two programs at once on it. The question is this. Is watching two bad programs a big improvement over watching one bad program on television?

The post office started using this great new zip-code system in 1963, going to make everything better and faster. Have you noticed your mail arriving sooner than it did a long while ago? They used to deliver it twice a day. Are you getting your mail delivered three times a day now, since they have zip codes? I dont think so.

For years, I carried a big old Hamilton railroad watch. Keeps good time, not great time. It gains or loses maybe twenty seconds a month. When I carried it, I was often a few minutes late getting someplace. Now I have a quartz wristwatch that keeps perfect time. Do I get to places on time now that I have a better watch? I do not. Im just as late as I always was.

Im a shopper. I buy one of almost everything new that comes along, but nothing makes my life any different. The fact is, if you cant do it by hand, you wont be able to do it with a new tool, either. If you cant do it without the piece of new equipment, you wont be able to do it with it. Nothing helps but us.

Education

(NOTE: This evoked a large amount of angry mail.)

We spend more than any country in the world on education, a lot more. We've raised teachers' salaries, we've built new schools, we've introduced new systems. And yet, a lot of kids arent getting much education.

If I get in a taxi in New York City and the driver is Haitian and went to school in Haiti, one of the poorest countries on Earth, he's always better educated than a driver who grew up and was educated in New York City. Now, how does that happen?

Here's what President Bush said about improving education:

"We must be the world's leader in education. And we must revolutionize America's schools. My plan will give parents more choice, give teachers more flexibility and help communities create new American schools."

Well, I dont think we need new American schools. I dont think teachers need more flexibility, whatever that means. I think I know what the problem is and politicians dont dare say it: The problem is we got a lot of dumb kids.

Dumb kids are hard to teach. The best teachers in the world cant teach a fence post.

These kids werent born dumb. They were brought up dumb. Their mothers and fathers—if they had a father around—never made it clear how important an education is. The parents dont care so the kids dont care.

Maybe we ought to encourage some mothers and fathers to go to school at night instead of watching television.

This isnt two or three kids at the bottom of the class we're talking about. This is about 50 percent of all the kids in the Country.

For better schools what we need isnt a better educational system. It isnt better teachers. What we need is better students.

And to get better students, we'll have to start with better parents because thats where the problem lies.

Drug Companies

Every day is Christmas in a doctor's office and the drug companies are Santa Claus bringing presents. I have here a collection of stuff that was sent to just two doctors by drug companies trying to get them to prescribe their brands of medicine.

They got all sorts of sample pills, and nostrums of various kinds. Doctors get a lot of nice leather notebooks, calendars. They get pens, pencils. A doctor got a pen he is supposed to hang around his neck. Would you go to a doctor who had something hanging around his neck that said "Real Orange Taste"?

Or would a doctor keep a paperweight on his desk all day that said "Zantac 300"? Or a coffee warmer pushing "Seldane"?

One doctor got a tube of something called "Lotrisome." Its really a flashlight. They get lots of flashlights. He also got a little light that you put on your bed post.

In Washington Senator David Pryor claims that drug companies spend ten billion dollars a year to sell their drugs and only nine billion on research.

We dont know if thats true but we do know that you shouldnt invite Senator Pryor and the president of any drug company to the same dinner party.

I know a doctor who works in an office with five other doctors and a staff of about fourteen people. He told me that a different drug company comes in twice a week to those offices and caters a complete sitdown lunch for everyone in the office. This would not be acceptable in the news business.

Drug companies sometimes offer doctors money for every patient they can switch to their brand of pills. The drug companies, of course, claim its research, not bribery.

These pharmaceutical companies, trying to get doctors to prescribe their medicine, will fly a group of them to a fancy resort for the weekend, give them a lecture for an hour or so, and the rest of the time the doctors can go out and play. They call it "Continuing Education."

Drug companies are making big bucks in this Country and the price of medicine is going up so fast that a lot of people who need it cant pay for it. Maybe they ought to stop spending a fortune on junk and reduce their prices.

President Bush gave his health speech the other day and he talked about the kind of health care people want. Well, I can tell him what we want. We all want the kind of health care a President gets. If the President faints, there are two doctors taking his pulse before he hits the floor. Thats the kind of health care we'd all like to have.

Presidential Families

A President of the United States shouldnt have any relatives. Wives, children, brothers and sisters—theyve never been anything but a problem for a President. Even nephews havent been much help.

You never heard of any problem involving James Buchanan's wife or children, did you? Of course you didnt. Thats because he was never married and didnt have any children.

Relatives were nothing but trouble for Ronald Reagan. First it was Nancy spending all that money redecorating the place, then she freeloaded on a lot of designers for expensive clothes. She had that dizzy astrologist. And if that wasnt bad enough for Reagan, he had all those children. I never knew for sure which of his kids were whose. It would have been a lot easier for President Reagan if he'd never been married at all, except in the movies.

President Nixon had a brother who brought him nothing but grief. So did Jimmy Carter. Poor Jimmy was trying to do his best in the White House and on the next page of the paper youd see a picture of his good-old-boy brother Billy, guzzling beer.

In 1990, President Bush's son Neal got in that Silverado bank scandal. Its embarrassing for a President to have his son involved in a bank mess like that. Barbara Bush seems like a nice lady, but theres always been the rumor that she's in favor of a woman's right to have an abortion. We know George is against it. Barbara may not talk about it in public, but you cant tell me it doesnt come up at night when theyre home alone.

Its hard enough being President without having to be a husband, a father and a brother, too. Can you imagine what we're going to do with a husband of the first woman President? I mean, suppose he wants to redecorate the White House? What if he wants to fix his car in the driveway?

Let's look for a bachelor or an unmarried woman president. If priests and nuns can do without husbands and wives, why cant Presidents?

Movie Critics

You can tell the Oscar awards are getting close because of all the ads for movies.

If you want to be a movie reviewer who gets quoted in the newspaper, here are some words to use: powerful, compelling, spectacle, extravaganza, impassioned, hilarious, absorbing, sweeping and profoundly poignant—whatever that means—breathtaking. I have never had my breath taken by a movie. Movie reviewers apparently have the kind of breaths that are easily taken, because it seems to happen to them all the time.

Reviewers often find a movie mesmerizing. "Ray Liotta is mesmerizing." The movie is "wonderfully acted." I dont want a lot of good acting in the movies I go to. If you notice how good the acting is, the acting wasnt very good. When a review talks about the acting, its probably because the movie itself wasnt worth talking about.

"Dazzling special effects"—that means the movie isnt much, either. "Sensuous, erotic"—that means that what you have here is a dirty movie.

"Enormous" or "enormously" are favorite words with reviewers—"enormously witty," "enormously charming," "entertains enormously." Im waiting for a reviewer who says, "Its an enormous little film." Reviewers call them films, too, not movies. A film sounds more important than a movie, so it makes the reviewer sound more important. "Cinema" is most important.

Im skeptical about whether some of the ads will attract viewers, though, for instance, "The funniest movie since *Home Alone*." Well, fine, but I never saw *Home Alone* and have no idea whether it was funny or not.

You can always tell when a movie's a real turkey. One sign is if the ad quotes reviewers you never heard of, who work for a publication you never heard of. "Jim Whaley, Cinema Showcase." "Joanna Langfield, of the Movie Minute." They were plugging a bomb called *Radio Flyer*.

Theres a movie called *The Mambo Kings* thats apparently pretty good.

The ad quotes Janet Maslin of *The New York Times* as calling it, "Jubilant, upbeat, fiery, impassioned." What the ad doesnt quote is another *Times* reviewer who said, "There are times when the director doesnt even seem to know where to put the camera."

Hollywood movies are probably our best art form in this Country. We still make movies better than the Japanese. I have to say, as a matter of fact that, with a few exceptions, the movies are better than the critics who review them.

Political Platform

It sure seems as though we need some different candidates in this Presidential race. Right now, there are only two choices. You can vote FOR George Bush or you can vote AGAINST George Bush. There really isnt anyone else.

Ive outlined my own position on some of the main issues here.

TAXES—Poor people dont buy expensive cars. They dont buy big houses and they dont travel. They dont need a lot of money. Its rich people who help the economy by spending. Politicians have attacked the rich for too long now.

BUSINESS—For every dollar a big company saved by firing blue-collar workers, it would be required to save an equal amount by firing executives. If General Motors laid off 100 workers who each made $600 a week, thats a savings of $3 million a year. General Motors would also be required to fire one vice president, making $3 million dollars a year.

RACISM—Its unrealistic to think we can like everyone. Each of us would be allowed to hate just one other group of people or race. Anyone who hated more than that would be called a racist.

HEALTH—Anyone caught smoking would be required to wear a smoke detector. It would be surgically implanted like a pacemaker. Whenever that person sneaked off and lit a cigarette, their alarm would go off.

HOUSING—We'd save federal money by turning Camp David into a vacation retreat for all the imprisoned murderers that *60 Minutes* says didnt do it.

EDUCATION—Close all law schools. We have some good lawyers and we have some bad ones. We dont need any more of either. In the future law schools should train the specialists we need . . . plumbers, carpenters, electricians, garage mechanics. Let me point out too that 244 of our Congressmen are lawyers. We could use more plumbers and fewer lawyers in Congress.

Neighbors

When it comes to a neighborhood, there are two kinds of people. There are the responsible people who feel some kind of obligation to keep their places looking halfway decent and then there are the slobs. Im sure you have one or two of them down the street from you.

The trouble is, for every ten people who try to make things look good by taking care of their place or even by just putting a flower pot on the windowsill, theres a lazy inconsiderate one who ruins the whole neighborhood by letting the place go to hell.

Theres always somebody who leaves junk everywhere. Its hard to tell his yard from the local dump.

If you have visitors coming, there are places near yours you hope they never see. What is it with these people anyway? Someone plants shrubbery. The next morning theres a beer can in the bushes.

If theres a pretty body of water, you can bet somebody will throw their garbage in it.

Why would somebody think he can leave a boat in his driveway so that it dominates the whole look of the street? Is this a house or a boatyard?

And how can people park ugly campers in the front yard eleven months of the year? If theyre campers, why dont they get out of there and go somewhere and camp?

People cover their front lawns with everything but grass.

Theres always somebody who ruins what little nature we've left on the face of the Earth too. Along every country road, someone has ruined the pristine look of an open field by leaving a rusting piece of

farm equipment. Its discouraging to see how they destroy the good things responsible people have done.

The owners and architects of great buildings spend time and money trying to make the city look a little better . . . and the destroyers of beauty come along and trash that.

And then there are public-spirited citizens with more ambition than most of us who spend their own time and their own money making public places look better . . . and what happens to those places?

We're all more aware of everything around us in the spring. We get outside for the first time, look around, and one thing seems certain. Its a war between the good guys and the bad guys and, as usual, the bad guys are winning.

Rodney King

It seems strange at my age . . . Ive lived more than 26,000 days . . . that if I had to pick one of the saddest days for my Country, I'd pick the day the jury came in with a NOT GUILTY verdict for the cops who beat Rodney King.

I assume it'll be okay with you if I dont take this opportunity to show you that tape again for the 10,000th time. You know what it looks like.

There are some things I would like to say, though. First, anyone who says he or she doesnt believe there are differences in the races probably isnt telling the truth. Do I think there are differences in the races and ethnic groups . . . blacks, whites, Jews, Turks, the Irish? Youre darn right I think there are differences.

Does this make me a racist? Listen, if Im a racist, so are 98 percent of the American people including blacks and we have to find another word to call what we are.

There has always been one thing, though, that the good people of America believed in—even the people who didnt really believe that all men are created equal. They conceded that we should all be equal before the law.

In the 1960s when blacks were still sitting in the back of the bus, the overwhelming majority of American men and women were in favor of every anti-discrimination law that was passed by Congress. They believed in equality before the law even if they privately felt superior to the guy over on the other side of town. Even people who were prejudiced and discriminatory in their personal lives . . . you know, belonged to clubs that didnt accept blacks or preferred to live in all-white neighborhoods . . . even these people were fair enough and good enough to understand that before the Law in our Country, everyone should be treated the same.

And thats the tragedy of this Rodney King case. This one black man didnt get fair and equal treatment under our Law.

Its depressing and sad for all of us. I feel worst for the majority of black people in America, the ones the television cameras didnt see, the ones who when the decision was announced, didnt riot. They put their black faces in their black hands and wept.

Campaign 1992

Theres still a long way to go in this Presidential campaign before the Election and Im not sure I can take much more of it. These two men, George Bush and Bill Clinton, are a couple of the smartest people in the Country. Why is it then when theyre campaigning, they look so dumb?

When the candidates talk the way they do, I dislike both of them. I dont want to hear my President, who I like and respect, talking like a vacuum cleaner salesman.

I dont want to hear a bright young public servant like Bill Clinton trying to fudge his way into the job of being my President. I dont think either of these two men is doing himself much good in this campaign.

If I were President Bush, I'd go back to the White House and go about my business of being the best President I could. I wouldnt be out there saying what someone else wrote for me that the writer thinks will get me reelected. I wouldnt attack my opponent either because I dont think people like that. I'd just act superior . . . above the battle.

If I were Bill Clinton, theres one thing I'd keep saying over and over. "Mr. President," I'd always be respectful. I'd say, "Mr. President, you keep telling us what youre going to do if youre reelected. How come you didnt do in the last four years what youre promising to do in the next four years?"

And if I were Bill Clinton, I know what I'd say about the draft.

I'd say, "Look. Im tired of trying to kid you. I thought the war in Vietnam was wrong. I didnt want to go and get killed for something I didnt believe in. I did everything I could to get out of the draft."

Part of this whole mess we call a Presidential campaign is our own fault, of course—those of us who vote. We almost demand that candidates lie to us or we wont vote for them. Then, we're smart enough to realize theyre lying, so we dislike them for it.

There must be a better way.

The Rodney King Tape

Everyone has seen the pictures of the Los Angeles police beating Rodney King more times than is necessary. Television news has used almost any excuse to repeat it. I know that.

Within the past month, Ive had several letters accusing television news— and me as an incidental part of it—of not letting the public see all of that tape. They say we hid the first part of the tape that provoked the cops into beating King.

On September 15, an organization known as Accuracy In Media ran a full page ad in a New York newspaper. The ad said, "WE'RE FED UP WITH NEGATIVE, ONE-SIDED, DECEPTIVE TV NEWS."

There are several things I agree with in this ad. I agree that, generally speaking, network news people are liberal. I guess I'd say I have a liberal bias myself most of the time.

Further down the ad said, "We're DISGUSTED at the way you repeatedly showed us a video tape of Los Angeles police officers beating Rodney King but EDITED OUT the first part where Rodney King attacks the police."

Ive been in this business for long enough to know that there isnt any way you could get ABC, NBC, CBS and CNN to agree on a conspiracy to keep anything away from the public.

Last week I got hold of the complete Rodney King tape . . . all of it. I'd never seen it myself. It runs nine minutes and twenty-five seconds. What most of us saw runs for forty or fifty seconds. We're going to show you the beginning of that tape, the part you never saw. You can believe it is the beginning because it starts with a few pictures that the cameraman took of two people sitting on a couch in his own apartment.

. . . Rodney King on the ground. He gets up . . . either falls or lunges. It goes out of focus. Then the part youve seen begins. Here it is one more time in slow motion. Rodney King being beaten by the police.

We're not going to show you the part that youve seen over and over again. The rest of the tape, about seven and a half minutes, shows Rodney King on the ground, hog-tied, and the police milling around, getting ready to leave.

You can decide for yourself if you think we've been part of a conspiracy to hide something from you.

Medical Bills

After my experience, I understand better all the talk about health costs. My kidney stone cost a total of $11,360.83.

I was in the hospital for two days and three nights. The hospital was absolutely first class and the doctor who took out the kidney stone—I'd rather not go into a lot of detail about how he did that—was great.

The doctor's bill was $2,000 for what he called "the procedure." Again, youll pardon me if I dont describe "the procedure." Compared to some things Ive paid for, that doctor's bill was a bargain.

More than a month later, I got a statement from Blue Cross. They were letting me know that they had paid my hospital bill of $8,324. Here it is. It says just "Hospital services."

It seemed wrong that they didnt tell me specifically what the charges were for so I called and asked for a detailed bill.

My room cost $1,611 for two days and three nights. In addition to my hospital room, I had the emergency room for $104 . . . the operating room for

$1,257 . . . and the recovery room was $256. Thats a total of $3,228 for four rooms.

Medical surgical central was expensive . . . $2004.47. Ive tried and I cant find out exactly what medical central is. Thats the trouble, really. None of us know what this stuff is.

Radiology diagnostic, x-rays, that is, $1,636. Theres a laboratory fee of $778. And, keep in mind, this is a good honest hospital.

I was showing this bill to my friend Bob Forte. His wife, Sheena, had a gallstone at the same time so he brought in her bill.

Her doctor tried that new way they have of removing a gallbladder without surgery. Thats it here: $2,000 for what they call a laparoscopy.

Well, that didnt work so he did it the old-fashioned way by making an incision. Cholecystectomy, its called. He charged her $2,000 for the one that didnt work and another $2,500 for the second one that did. Youd think he might at least have given her the first one for half off.

As far as my hospital bill goes, I suppose they gave me a little extra attention. They figured if I died in there, theyd have to watch me complain about it the following Sunday on *60 Minutes*.

Baseball and the Debates

Im sure most of you have been watching the debates. There was a problem with the first debate last week because it was on opposite the baseball playoff games.

I was interested in both baseball and the debate so I did what any red-blooded American would do, I switched back and forth.

Let's face it. In both a baseball game and a political debate, theres plenty of time when nothing's happening.

For instance, the pitcher gets the ball but does he throw it right away? He does not. He fools around with it. He tugs at his cap. He pulls his sleeves. He licks his fingers. Sometimes a pitcher wastes so much time that it looks as if he's afraid to throw the ball. I know that so I switch to the debate.

Okay, so Im at the debate. I hear the beginning of a question. I know its going to be long and I wont miss anything if I dont hear it so I go back to the baseball game. You know when the manager leaves the dugout and walks out on the field to tell the pitcher he's finished that its going to take a long while. He tries to break it to the pitcher gently.

We timed this. It took three minutes and twenty-one seconds to get the pitcher off the field. Plenty of time to see some of the debate. Back to the debate.

Ive heard the candidates say almost everything theyre ever going to say. When one of them starts an old familiar theme, I go back to baseball.

You have time to go to the refrigerator between the third out for one team and when the batter for the other team comes to the plate. Instead of the refrigerator, go to the debate.

I know I can leave the debate permanently when the moderator asks the candidates for their final statement. Ive never heard anything new in one of those canned wrapup speeches. They were written yesterday—by someone else.

Sometimes the arguments on the field are more interesting than the arguments at the debate. Zap, I cut back to the game for good.

CBS didnt show any of the first debate because the playoff games ran late that night. I dont want to tell my bosses here at CBS how to run their network but they missed a bet not showing a baseball game and the debate at the same time. It would have improved both.

Election Quiz

If you havent decided who to vote for yet or if youve decided but arent sure youre right, dont worry. You arent alone. Maybe your problem is, you dont know enough. Well, tonight we're going to give you a little election quiz to see how much you do know.

— George Bush says Bill Clinton cant be trusted. Bill Clinton says George Bush cant be trusted. Indicate who you think is right.

BUSH   CLINTON   BOTH RIGHT

— No matter who is elected, do you think taxes will go:

A. UP   or   B. WAY UP

— The National Debt is four trillion dollars. How many zeroes are there in one trillion?

— Which two of these five men are not running for President? If you said "Larry King" and me, youre right.

— President Bush ends every speech the same way: "And may God bless the United States of America."
Because of Mr. Bush's request, do you think God will be:
A. More apt to bless America.
B. Less apt to bless America.
C. Wont want to get involved.

— This is a different kind of question. We're asking you to fill in the one word in the following sentence that best describes how both George Bush and Bill Clinton feel about Ross Perot. Here's the sentence:

"ROSS PEROT IS AS —— AS A FRUITCAKE."

Fill in the blank with one word.

— If you were getting a haircut, whose barber would you choose? Bill Clinton's barber? George Bush's barber? Ross Perot's barber?

— This is a trick question. At ten minutes past noon on Wednesday, January 20, 1993, how many living ex-Presidents will there be? Name them. I'll help. Richard Nixon, Gerald Ford, Jimmy Carter, Ronald Reagan. Anyone else next year who used to be President? Hmmm?

The Plum Book

One of the first things a President-Elect has to do is get his own people in key jobs in Washington so they do things his way—once he decides what his way is, of course.

This is the list of the jobs that the President and his people can appoint. They arent competitive like Civil Service jobs, and for that reason this is known as the Plum Book. Every one of the jobs in here is a political plum. There are about 9,000 of them.

Six pages of White House jobs alone. Here's one: Deputy assistant to President for Presidential Messages and Correspondence. A person doing that job probably gets to send those telegrams they read from the President at parties congratulating someone for being 100 years old or for winning their company bowling trophy.

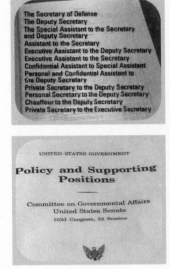

There are six speechwriter openings here. The President makes speeches all day long and you cant expect him to think of something new to say himself all the time. You know, he needs new material when he meets the Olympic volleyball team or speaks to a bunch of Boy Scouts in the Rose Garden.

But 211 pages of jobs here! Do you know this many people youd want to give jobs to? Once youve taken care of a few friends and everyone in your family, where would you go to fill these?

Here's the Defense Department. Clinton has said he's going to make some cuts there. It should be possible.

— THE SECRETARY OF DEFENSE
— THE DEPUTY SECRETARY
— THE SPECIAL ASSISTANT TO THE SECRETARY AND DEPUTY SECRETARY
— ASSISTANT TO THE SECRETARY
— EXECUTIVE ASSISTANT TO THE DEPUTY SECRETARY
— EXECUTIVE ASSISTANT TO THE SECRETARY

— CONFIDENTIAL ASSISTANT TO THE SPECIAL ASSISTANT
— PERSONAL AND CONFIDENTIAL ASSISTANT TO THE DEPUTY
  SECRETARY
— PRIVATE SECRETARY TO THE DEPUTY SECRETARY
— PERSONAL SECRETARY TO THE DEPUTY SECRETARY
— CHAUFFEUR TO THE DEPUTY SECRETARY
— PRIVATE SECRETARY TO THE EXECUTIVE SECRETARY

You notice the chauffeur doesnt have a deputy or a secretary.

Cant you imagine the new kid from Little Rock coming to school in Washington next fall? The teacher asks him what his father does and he says: "He's deputy assistant secretary to the assistant deputy secretary."

I know one thing. When Bill Clinton crawls into bed at night and wants to relax with a good mystery before he falls asleep, this is the book for him. The mystery is why all these jobs are necessary.

The Election

Ive always thought the smartest person in the United States should be President. The only time in our history when that might have happened was when Thomas Jefferson got the job in 1801.

Bill Clinton would probably agree it didnt happen this time either. Not that he's dumb.

One reason it doesnt happen is, the smartest person doesnt *run* for office because he doesnt *want* to be President. He's too smart.

All of you who didnt vote for Clinton can take some comfort from the fact that no matter who's President, this Country always survives. Our system dominates the person in charge of it.

I wish we werent so nasty to our President when its someone we didnt vote for. It would be nice, for instance, if all his supporters were as gracious about his defeat as President Bush was. As a matter of fact, if Mr. Bush had been as nice a guy during his campaign as he was when he made his concession speech, he probably wouldnt have had to make it.

There are several things we learn from this election.

1. We learned that an election with Ross Perot is more fun than an election without him.

2. There should be a three-month limit on the length of time a campaign lasts.

3. Companies should be prohibited from buying influence by giving large amounts to political campaigns. If a company wants to buy votes, it should pay the voters themselves directly, not the politicians.

4. Anyone who conducts a poll should be prohibited from announcing the results until after the election. Im tired of polls.

5. The winning candidate should be made to post a list of his election promises in large type on the wall in the Oval Office.

Something else I'd like to say because no one else is going to say it for the people in the news business. I think reporters and columnists did a remarkably good job of digging out stories and explaining things. They were, for the most part, fair and accurate and they did it in an interesting way that attracted a huge number of voters.

President Bush thought the press was unfair. A President always thinks that. But you know what I think? I think that after four years during which we all read a lot of good and bad, accurate and inaccurate stuff about the President, we all know George Bush better than he knows himself. And we dont dislike him either. I hope he knows that.

Somalia

Americans have an instinctive desire to be honest and decent. We are not full-time harassers of women in the workplace, S&L bank manipulators or dishonest politicians. The idea of doing the right thing appeals to us. Its why we went into Vietnam. We thought we were doing the right thing. It turned out to be wrong but that doesnt change the goodness of our intention.

Most Americans approve of going into Somalia.

You hear some people say, "Let's take care of the hungry and homeless right here in our own Country."

Well, thats right but we can do both. We could save everyone starving to death in Somalia without denying our own homeless anything. Bags of food isnt the problem in America.

The homeless in America would starve to death using a bag of Pillsbury flour for a pillow. They wouldnt know what to do if they could open it. If I was hungry, I wouldnt know what to do if someone gave me a gunnysack of soybeans.

Perfectly sensible people say that getting involved in Somalia is a mistake.

A *New York Times* critic says the reason we're helping Somalia and ignoring other countries with starving children is because our television cameras have been in Somalia.

The New York Times Magazine had a picture of Somalia on its cover last week. It was okay, though, for *Times* readers. A flip of the page and they were back in their own world. (Attractive woman in bikini.)

Theres no doubt that television and press coverage have turned a serious event into a circus. But we have to ignore that, too. The operation in Somalia may be harder than we thought. There will certainly be all sorts of things wrong with it. Forget all that. Its still worth it. None of us wants to see more pictures of eight-year-old Somali children weighing thirty-five pounds with flies at their eyes and looking like walking cadavers.

If we see a child who's been hurt, we stop what we're doing. We go to help. We dont think about right or wrong. We dont worry about failing or looking foolish. We dont say to ourselves, "There must be a lot of kids who need help. I cant help all of them so Im not going to help this one."

What Americans do is, they stop and help.

The Royal Family

I usually enjoy what Im doing but tonight it is with some reluctance that Im going to say something to the people of Great Britain. The statement I wish to make is in regard to your Royal Family. What I want to say, quite simply, is this: Give it up, will you?

Having a king and queen has been fun for you since 1016 but the joke's over. Grownup countries in the twentieth century dont go around having Royal Families.

Queen Elizabeth is one of the ten richest people in the world and never worked a day in her life. What kind of an example does that set? There are eleven other people in her family who get paid millions of dollars just for being royal. What duties do they perform? We have a Vice President who does about the same thing for somewhere around $160,000, a bargain!

Queen Elizabeth has five official castles or palaces. She's got Buckingham Palace, St. James, Hampton Court Palace, Kensington Palace, Windsor Castle and several more castles of her own.

Dont get me wrong. Queen Elizabeth seems like a classy lady. If you have to have a queen, she's perfect for the job. Imagine having to sit on a chair called a throne. I wonder if she ever sat there on it, watching television?

And the family! Philip's a nice looking guy, seems decent, but the kids and their wives and husbands! Where did they come from? Without the Royal Family, half of London's newspapers would go out of business . . . which wouldnt be a bad idea.

Princess Diana is the popular one. Beautiful, really, but she's flaky and a little sad. She seems to be laughing with tears in her eyes.

Andrew's wife, Fergie, got caught topless on a beach with a guy who wasnt her husband. Do we really care? Is this woman someone you want to see topless?

The monarchy is an anachronism and you British ought to get rid of it. What's all this curtsying nonsense? Demeaning!

I'd like to have the British people say to Queen Elizabeth: "Look, Queen, youve played this dollhouse game just great for a long time but thats it. Its all over. No more kings, no more queens, no more princes, dukes or lords. From now on, youre just one of us. And that goes for your kids and your cat, too."

1993

Matisse

For several months now crowds have been showing up at the exhibit of the paintings of the great French artist Henri Matisse at the Museum of Modern Art in New York. I think "modern art" means it doesnt look exactly like what its supposed to be. Im more apt to go to a football game than to a museum but I did go to the Matisse exhibit and even I could see Matisse was a genius.

I liked so many of them. I never think of myself as being alive while any of the great artists were still painting their pictures but Matisse didnt die until I was thirty-five. Either he was younger than I thought or Im older than I think.

You got the feeling Henri didnt get out much. He painted a lot of stuff sitting on tables . . . bottles, books, bowls, flowers. Anything at hand. Even when he shows some outside, its usually through a window or out a door. In "Open Door, Brittany," he's inside looking out. Get some air, Henri!

They didnt say how long it took Matisse to run up some of these things. I wonder how long one painting took. An hour? A day? A month? I dont know.

Matisse did make a lot of money before he died. Its good to know that not all artists starve waiting to be discovered. It always seems wrong when I read about a painting that sells for, you know, ten million dollars after the artist is dead. He doesnt get a nickel.

Matisse painted a lot of nude women . . . not many nude men. Its strange theres never been a great woman artist who painted men without any clothes on. I think its because men nudes are more naked than women nudes.

I dont ever recall seeing a self portrait of a nude artist either. They know what they look like and they dont want any part of it.

There were 412 of Matisse's works in the exhibit. They were great but it was like listening to all nine of Beethoven's symphonies at one sitting.

I dont know whether any of these paintings are bad or not . . . could have been eliminated. They dont say. I suppose a museum wouldnt. Someone must know.

I would like to say just one thing, though, in defense of football fans. I think we're more broadminded than art lovers. Ive been to a lot of museums in my life but I never see any art lovers at a football game.

The Clinton Inauguration

I watched the Inauguration of President Bill Clinton in my office. I leaned back, put my feet up on the desk and enjoyed it.

The television set belongs to CBS so I thought it would be only fair to watch it on CBS. Dan did the commentary along with the great Charles Kuralt. They were nicer than I was.

I did my own commentary . . . you know, just talking to myself here.

Holy Mackerel! Where'd you get the hat, Hillary? Did Bill really say he liked it? A guy'll do that to you, you know.

DAN RATHER:
The new President is a Southern Baptist as is the new Vice President.

ROONEY:
Is there a difference between a Southern Baptist and a Northern Baptist?

JUSTICE BYRON WHITE:
Senator, if you will raise your right hand and repeat after me.

ROONEY:
Whoops, you blew it, Al . . . raised your hand before he told you to. Maybe he's left-handed.

MARILYN HORNE:
"Oh, Say, can you see by the dawn's early light . . . "

ROONEY:
Boy, she is good. Its been a long time since I heard anyone sing that song the way they wrote it.

No yawning during the National Anthem, Chelsea. We saw you.

CHIEF JUSTICE WILLIAM REHNQUIST:
Governor, are you ready to take the oath?

ROONEY:
Thats the last time anyone will call him "Governor."

BILL CLINTON:
I am.

ROONEY:
This is some dramatic moment . . . not the World Series . . . not the Super Bowl or a movie. Boy, this is for real . . . a new President taking over.

BILL CLINTON:
On behalf of our nation, I salute my predecessor, President Bush, for his half-century of service to America.

ROONEY:
I like this. I dont know whether he means it or not but its nice. I mean, the guy did his best. Bush should have come up and shaken hands there. He'd have brought down the house.

CLINTON:
Instead we have drifted, and that drifting has eroded our resources, fractured our economy, and shaken our confidence.

ROONEY:
Now he's sticking it to Bush, though. No more Mr. Nice Guy.

CLINTON:
It is time to break the bad habit of expecting something for nothing from our Government or from each other.

ROONEY:
Okay, thats good stuff, Bill. Why do politicians all use so many of the same hot air words, though? Theyre in every speech.

CLINTON:
George Washington . . . Thomas Jefferson . . . Franklin Roosevelt. Let us resolve . . . Let us put aside . . . Let us give . . . Let us begin anew. And so I say to all of you here . . .

ROONEY:

This isnt a great speech—good maybe. Not great. He's trying too hard to write quotations for the paper tomorrow morning.

CLINTON:

This is our time. Let us embrace it. (APPLAUSE)

ROONEY:

It was a great event . . . a great day. And for all the bad stuff we've got going in this Country, we can be proud to be Americans on this one day anyway.

We voted. Clinton won. President Bush didnt call out the Marines to take over the Government and the people who voted for Bush accept Clinton as their President.

When everything seems to be going to Hell in America, its good to know we still have a civilized way of governing ourselves. What a good idea democracy is.

Clinton's Plan

I suppose you watched President Clinton give us the bad news the other night. When he passed ten o'clock, I started thinking of Fidel Castro. I wish we could have had a faster version of the speech without the applause. It was like having root canal work done by a happy, talkative dentist.

I dont want a lot of angry letters but I like President Clinton. There is one question I cant get out of my head, though . . . about him and every other politician. Why do they lie to get elected? They do lie to us, dont they?

GEORGE BUSH:
Read my lips! No new taxes!

BILL CLINTON:
You know what my plan is. Im going to raise taxes on people whose incomes are above $200,000, whose taxes went down in the 1980s while their income went up. Im not going to raise taxes on the middle class.

Maybe its our own fault, not their fault. We wont vote for them if they do tell us the truth. President Clinton claims he has to raise taxes because Bush hid the facts about how bad the economy was. Well, of course Bush hid the facts. Bill Clinton's a smart guy. What did he think Bush was telling us during his campaign . . . the truth? Dont be silly. Clinton knew better than that because he wasnt telling the truth either.

But Im not blaming Bush or Clinton. Politicians arent bad guys. Theyre public-spirited people trying to help the rest of us who are incapable of governing anyone including ourselves. Candidates know we're so dumb they have to lie to us. Its for our own good.

I got thinking of my own taxes. Between this job, my newspaper column, my books and a few speeches, I make a lot of money. With Clinton's new 40 percent federal tax, two state taxes, Connecticut and New York, sales taxes, real estate taxes, school taxes, gas taxes, I'll be paying out more than half my income in taxes. Half!

I work hard for what I make and naturally, I think people who work the hardest make the most. I suppose its right to tax hard-working people the most. By working hard, they cause unemployment because they take jobs away from people who dont work hard.

Hillary Rodham Clinton

As you all know by now, President Clinton's wife, the First Lady, wants to be known by her first name, her maiden name and her married name— Hillary Rodham Clinton. Something about this bothers a lot of people. I dont like the people it bothers, but it bothers me too.

The custom has always been for a woman to abandon her own name and take her husband's name. This is a lousy deal for women . . . no question about it. It doesnt seem right but I dont know what we should do about it. Using two names is clumsy. Maybe the wedding ceremony should include a flip of the coin to see whose name the couple will take, the man's or the woman's.

"If its heads, do you, Bill Clinton, solemnly swear to take the name of this woman, Hillary Rodham?"

People are proud of their names. It accounts for why so many kids are called "junior." I always thought it was unnecessarily confusing to give a kid the same name as his father. I guess fathers feel it gives them some kind of immortality if they pass on the name. Not so many girls are given their mothers' first name.

Im suspicious of politicians, too, who insist on being called by affectionate nicknames. For instance, Im not pleased calling the President "Bill" when his name is "William."

A lot of politicians list themselves officially by a nickname as if they were lovable. I mean, "Bob" Packwood? Congressman "Sonny" Callahan? Congressman "Buck" McKeon?

President Theodore Roosevelt didnt call himself Teddy. People called him Teddy because they liked him.

Its all Jimmy Carter's fault. He started it, and I'll bet he regrets it. President James Carter might have been reelected.

Politicians should tell us what their names are and let us decide whether or not we feel like calling them by a friendly nickname.

You can see why Mrs. Clinton wants to keep the name "Rodham." Its a good name and its distinctive. It comes from a part of England known as Northumberland and it means "homestead at a cross"—whatever that means.

I called telephone information in Northumberland and there are six Rodhams listed there. I looked through all the big city telephone books they keep on film in our CBS library and found forty-seven Rodhams in the United States, including Hillary's father and mother.

I know how Im going to handle the problem with the First Lady if Im ever invited to the White House. I'll just put out my hand with a big smile and I'll say, "Hey . . . love your dress." Maybe Hillary wont notice I didnt call her by name.

Base Closings

President Clinton is trying to pay off on his promise to cut the deficit. Politicians agree costs should be cut . . . but not in their area.

CONGRESSWOMAN BARBARA KENNELLY:

The point is that we have to fight for our State because we know everybody else is fighting for their State.

ROONEY:

The purpose of a military base or a defense plant is not to provide jobs. Its wrong to keep a base open because if its closed it will be bad for the candy store down the road.

We shouldnt be building submarines we dont need merely to provide jobs in New London . . . or aircraft we dont need for jobs in Seattle.

The people working in defense plants are capable people. They know how to do things and theres a shortage of people who know how to do things in this Country. They ought to be doing work that needs to be done.

If you dont think theres a shortage, try to get a plumber to do some work around your house. Look for a good carpenter, an electrician. Try to get an expert mechanic to fix your car the day it breaks down.

Anyone who knows how to do anything is too busy.

Most Americans never see all the make-work stuff theyve paid for in the recent past. There are warehouses full of military equipment . . . nothing we need, just things they were making because no one told them to stop.

LESLEY STAHL:

If the Pentagon stopped buying supplies today, there would still be enough machine tools in stock to meet the Navy's needs for 1,000 years.

ROONEY:

The biggest Navy in the world, ours, is mostly stored away in mothballs . . . a flotilla of battleships, cruisers, destroyers, aircraft carriers that your parents or grandparents bought to fight World War II.

There are a few billion dollars worth of airplanes left over from the war we were going to fight with Russia . . . sitting on the desert floor near Tucson, Arizona, now. We already have plenty of weapons we dont need.

Why do we talk as if there arent going to be enough jobs if we stop making more of them? There are more jobs, more work to be done for the good of us all than we'll ever accomplish.

How about building more city rail systems to cut down on car traffic?

I'd like to see more medical research. Maybe they could delay my demise. Which do we need most right now, more schools or more tanks at two and a half million dollars a tank?

What about fixing up the housing thats fallen apart in America?

The trick will be to find a way to get the people who need work together with the work that needs doing.

There may be people out of work in America but theres no shortage of work that needs to be done.

School Books

On three separate occasions recently Ive been in a grade school, talking to some of the kids and teachers. Ive looked at dozens of the books theyre using and Ive come to one conclusion. Schools are treating nine-year-olds like four-year-olds. Textbooks are over-simplified.

Theyre teaching kids that life is a coloring book.

Textbooks are a big business . . . lots of money . . . and the publishers who put them together dont dare offend anyone or they'll lose business.

This one isnt called just *Mathematics*, its called *The Mathematics Experience*. No book ever written by a committee is much good. This one has three senior authors, one senior consulting author, thirteen plain authors (they must be junior authors), twenty-three critical readers, three multicultural reviewers and twenty-eight field test teachers.

They probably make the kids wear rubber gloves so they wont catch an idea in here.

This is called *Invitation to Mathematics*. I dont know what ever happened to arithmetic. Two times three equals six. Well, thats true but one whole page of a picture of a muffin pan to prove it?

Here's a book for very young children called *How Did Numbers Begin?* I was interested in how they were going to explain how numbers began. I looked through here and this is what I found. "When did people start using numbers? No one really knows." So how come you called your book *How Did Numbers Begin?* if no one really knows.

Some of these books are attractive. They look good but its as if the schools were afraid to tell the kids that some of the things they should learn are hard and might even take some effort.

I went to one class of fourth graders. They were supposed to be learning mathematics from a game they were playing. They each put down a series of numbers on a pad, depending on which square of the game they landed on after they threw some dice. When the game was over, I asked one of the kids to add up her numbers and she said, "Well, I have to wait until one of the other kids finishes using the calculator."

No one should be allowed to use a calculator until he or she can add and subtract without one.

Years ago educators decided that just memorizing things wasnt a good idea. Well, maybe, but I dont know anything I ever got out of school thats been more help in my life than memorizing the multiplication tables up to 12 times 12.

If I have to go to 12 times 13, I keep a calculator handy.

Snow

I was disappointed to miss the big snowstorm in the East last week. I was in San Francisco. They called it "The Storm of The Century" . . . its the third "Storm of The Century" in eight years.

Im sorry I missed it because theres nothing as good as a bad snowstorm.

Snow is one of the most glorious gifts of nature . . . so clean, so white, falling so fluffily, coating everything with an even layer of beauty.

They say there have never been two snowflakes alike. Maybe. Hard to prove, though.

Theres nothing in life better for a young boy or girl than to play in slippery snow. After wallowing in it all day, kids go home chilled but glowing, and if they have a good mother, she makes them a cup of hot cocoa. Fathers of kids with cocoa-making mothers get out their skis and drag young ones on sleds.

Any hill is valuable real estate when it snows. Big plastic dishes have replaced Flexible Flyers now, but the fun's the same. If theres a living thing that loves snow more than kids its dogs. Dogs, kids and snow are a great mix.

If youve never skied, you dont know what youre missing.

You experience a thousand sensations coming down a hill . . . freedom, exhilaration, fear—most of the best things to do in life are a little dangerous.

Snow is in such demand at ski resorts that when they dont get it, they make it. Seems presumptuous . . . preempting nature's decision not to snow.

Shoveling your sidewalk is a satisfying thing to do, too. Everyone gets their toys out of the garage. Its usually harder to move snow with the toys than with a shovel.

I like the disruptive influence of a heavy snow. Its a force for disorganization . . . and yet, the common problem of dealing with it brings us all together.

People in San Francisco kept telling me how lucky I was to be there during the storm in the East in their warm, sunny, dull climate. Theyve never even made a snowman.

News Stories

Ive been looking for something to talk about tonight . . . so many unpleasant stories in the news.

—For instance, its hard to tell what's going to happen to Boris Yeltsin. I cant even decide whether I care or not. He's a little wacky . . . looks as if he belts down a few vodkas before lunch or maybe before breakfast . . . but he's smart and seems to understand democracy and free enterprise.

He's got parts of Russia actually looking like a real country again. Ten years ago everything was state-owned there. Now theres private initiative, advertising all over the place.

—The Clinton Administration says the airlines are in trouble and wants to help them. If you ask me, its the passengers who are in trouble. We're the ones who need help.

I have some suggestions for the airlines. Stop all this nonsense with fares. Figure out how much it costs to fly a passenger from here to there, add a little for profit and charge us that. Dont flimflam us with fifty different fares for the same trip.

—Woody Allen and Mia Farrow. What a sad, tawdry story that is. Its sad because Woody's one of the funniest and most talented people in the world.

He was a fool for getting involved with Mia's adopted daughter thirty-six years younger than he is but Mia got back at him. If you want to destroy a guy, accuse him of molesting a seven-year-old child. Apparently the doctors say he did nothing but Woody Allen's always going to be the guy accused of molesting a child. And theres nothing funny about that.

—Those people in Waco, Texas, call themselves the Branch Davidians. Everyone else calls them religious fanatics. A religious fanatic is someone who believes in a religion you dont believe in.

Theyre talking about raising the tax on cigarettes to two dollars a pack. Its called a "sin tax." Ive never smoked but a two dollar tax isnt the way to make smokers quit and it isnt the way to pay off the national debt either.

If theyre going to tax sin, put a tax on sex. Too many people are having more kids than they can take care of so the rest of us end up taking care of the kids for them. A tax on sex might help there. And youre talking big tax dollars here.

—A lot of basketball on television this week. I used to like watching my high school team but I really dont care whether Southwestern Louisiana Tech beats St. Xavier of Loyola or not. The best colleges usually have the worst basketball teams.

Ive watched a lot of this NCAA Tournament. Theyre sure wearing baggy pants this year. If my mother had sent me out to play in pants that looked like this, I'd have run away from home.

Theres big money in basketball. I was thinking I might make a little extra money myself doing commercials. I bet I could get Nike to pay me *not* to wear their sneakers.

Cigarettes

Its illegal to advertise cigarettes on television so this wont be a commercial but I bought a carton of Marlboros for $21. A few minutes ago I cut open all 200 cigarettes because I was curious about how much tobacco there is in a carton. The cigarette manufacturers pay about $1.75 a pound to tobacco farmers.

Of every dollar spent on cigarettes, the manufacturer gets 50 cents . . . the tobacco farmer 3 cents.

I put all that tobacco I took out of those 200 cigarettes on a scale . . . it weighs 5¼ ounces. The packaging, the carton, the pack itself, I even threw in the cigarette papers, weighs a little less . . . 4¾ ounces.

It costs them about 11 cents to make the 20 cigarettes in a pack. I dont think many smokers roll their own anymore. Then they have to wrap them and ship them and a pack ends up costing about a quarter to get to the store.

Manufacturers have gotten so good at making cigarettes that its cheaper than it used to be. They sold 500 billion packs of cigarettes last year and made about 55 cents on every pack. Thats even more than a baseball player makes catching balls.

Smokers are having a tough time. Theyve been driven outdoors by the holier-than-thou non-smokers and everyone hates them. If smokers were a race, the rest of us would be racists.

People are sympathetic to alcoholics and AIDS victims but theyre mean to smokers. Maybe they should start calling themselves "tobacco victims."

I dont know how people who make a living selling cigarettes go to sleep at night, knowing that theyre contributing to the miserable death of 1,000 people a day in this Country.

The tobacco people are divided into three groups:

— The first group says it hasnt been proven that cigarettes are bad for anyone.

— The second group knows theyre bad but figures if they dont sell them, someone else will. They also say that if they stopped selling cigarettes, it would cause unemployment.

— The third group doesnt give a damn what happens to anyone as long as they make money.

The tobacco industry spends more on advertising and promoting cigarettes, 16 cents a pack, than it does on making them in the first place. Advertising agencies make more than tobacco farmers, too.

The trick is to catch kids young and hook them so they'll be customers until they cough to death in later life.

Its surprising that cigarette companies have to advertise at all because there arent any ads for cocaine or heroin but drug dealers cant keep the stuff in stock.

Philip Morris just announced its cutting the price of a pack of Marlboros by 40 cents because theyre losing business to the cut-rate brands like Bronson.

Would you like to guess who makes Bronson? Why, the Philip Morris Company makes them.

Waco, Texas

We like to find a place to put the blame and our Government is our favorite place to put the blame for anything . . . as though what our Government does is not our fault, too. Ive been irritated all week by the stories questioning which Government agency is at fault for the deaths of the eighty-six people in that religious cult compound in Waco, Texas.

Theres a question about who set the place on fire. But you know something? Most people dont care who started it. They can only think of the children who burned.

Seven weeks before, the Bureau of Alcohol, Tobacco and Firearms sent 100 men to open up that compound because they knew they had bought at least $44,000 worth of illegal weapons in 1992 alone. Semi-automatic rifles, grenades, gunpowder. Four of those law officers were killed. You know, four normal guys with normal lives and families.

Was it their fault? Was it the fault of the Texas Rangers? People were blaming the FBI. Was it the FBI's fault? Janet Reno, the new Attorney General, had to defend herself on television as if she was guilty of something.

Now theyre calling for a Congressional investigation. Of what? Whose fault was it that those cult members died? It was their own damn fault, thats whose fault it was.

The blame belongs to those religious nuts in the compound with their leader, David Koresh. Theres no nut like a religious nut and the world is filled with them. The tragedy none of us can get over is that they took twenty-four children with them. How could they have done that?

The idea that any part of our Government or any police force was at fault is nonsense. Someone asked Koresh's lawyer if he was considering any lawsuits. Listen, if anyone gets sued, it ought to be the nine members of the cult who got out alive. And if the cult has a nickel left in any bank account, it ought to go to the families of the four officers who were killed.

I have a hard time feeling much of anything for those Branch Davidians. There are too many unfortunate people in the world to waste time feeling sorry for the Waco whackos.

Mike Wallace's Birthday

Today is Mike Wallace's seventy-fifth birthday. Its too late to wish Mike a Happy Birthday because its almost eight o'clock. His birthday is just about over. He either had a happy birthday by now or he didnt and nothing we wish him will help. He's probably had his cookies and warm milk and gone to bed. Mike usually goes to bed Sunday night as soon as his own piece is over.

As a young man, Mike dreamed of being a concert violinist but fortunately he awoke from the dream and realized he was terrible at it. Instead, Mike became a reporter and the best interviewer there has ever been on television.

Even as a young man, Mike was going after the newsmakers with hard-hitting investigative journalism. Over the years Mike has interviewed a great many of the world's best-known people. One bad thing now is, Mike is better known than most of the well-known people he interviews. This shouldnt happen to a reporter.

Sometimes the subject of his interview will play up to Mike, you know, trying to soften him up to get easy questions. Well, Mike wont have any part of that.

He's known every President of his time. He interviewed Richard Nixon many times. He knew Ronald Reagan when they were both doing commercials.

Mike never approaches an interview casually. He evokes good answers because he always gets close to the people he's interviewing.

He usually knows the answer to a question before he asks it. That helps.

One reason I like having Mike around is, he's older than I am. Its a comforting feeling . . . sort of a buffer between me and eternity. I hate Steve Kroft because he went to school with my son.

Mike and I are different in many ways but theres one thing we have in common. We both say we dont dye our hair.

If youre still awake, Mike, Happy Birthday, what's left of it. Youre a good guy. Old but good.

The Rich

Tonight I call on every man, woman and child in America making more than a hundred thousand dollars to go on strike. Let the politicians know we're tired of being kicked around, and we're not going to take it anymore. We'll bring the economy of this nation to a screeching halt. Politicians are always after the rich, and they cant even decide who is rich.

PRESIDENT BILL CLINTON:
For the wealthiest, those earning more than $180,000 per year . . .

GEORGE STEPHANOPOULOS (Senior Adviser to the President):
The income tax increases will only fall on families with taxable income of about—over $140,000 a year.

VICE PRESIDENT ALBERT GORE:
Eighty percent of all the revenue comes from people with incomes above $180- to 200,000 per year.

PRESIDENT CLINTON:
Seventy percent will be paid by those who make more than $100,000 a year.

ROONEY:
Politicians attack people with money because voters who dont have as much of it love to hear it. People hate anyone with more money than they have. Even rich people hate that. Listening to politicians, youd think rich

people got that way by stealing. The fact is, most people who have money got it by knowing how to do something and working hard at it. This year, those people are going to be paying almost 60 cents of every dollar they earn in taxes—federal taxes, state taxes, school taxes, real estate taxes, excise taxes, sales taxes—thats why Im calling for a strike. All of big business will close down.

There arent any corporate executives who make less than $100,000. There wont be a World Series. The lowest-paid major-league baseball player gets $109,000. Dont get sick during the strike. The average doctor makes $179,000 a year.

So let me say something to you, President Clinton. You get paid $250,000, plus room and board and all you can eat. You deserve it. Its the working rich like you who make the wheels go round. If the United States didnt have some rich people, you might as well be president of Somalia. And one more thing: When everyone making more than $100,000 goes out on strike, dont look for a *60 Minutes* show that week.

Health Care Plan

The President and his wife and a lot of other people in Washington spent last week trying to work out some kind of a health plan. They want to make it so no one ever gets sick and dies again.

PRESIDENT CLINTON:
If you get sick or a member of your family gets sick, even if its a life-threatening illness, youre covered.

You cant complain about a President who's trying to do the right thing for us. The trouble is theres no way that every American is going to get all the medical attention that he or she would like to have because there isnt enough of it to go around. Thats true of all the good things in the world, not just health care and not just in the United States.

I mean everything . . . land, food, water, houses, cars, fine wine, lawyers, doctors.

Even here in our great United States, theres a limited supply of the good things. The Government doesnt dole out diamond rings or Rolex watches to people who dont have them. Health is more serious than that, of course, but we dont have enough money to pay for first-class health care for everyone.

Theres a second thing that makes any medical plan difficult and maybe the Clintons can do something about that. Theres no business in the world where so much cheating is going on. Everyone is taking a little something ... hospitals, doctors, insurance companies, drug companies, health groups. Even patients are cheating. A normally honest person who wouldnt think of taking an extra paper bag in a supermarket doesnt consider cheating an insurance company to be dishonest.

And, of course, insurance companies dont consider ... But why should I get them mad at me?

I admire both Clintons for trying to do something about this health mess. Im just afraid theyre dreaming. If the plan doesnt work, it will be because like everything else, we all want more health care than we have money enough to pay for.

So, I have a little advice for everyone. Dont get sick. There never was a health plan yet that cured anyone of anything.

Octane

If you drive say 10,000 miles a year, you probably buy about 500 gallons of gas. Thats what I do. And I never drive into a gas station without wondering which octane I should buy.

You know the oil companies want you to buy the premium gas because thats what they advertise. You never see them pushing their 87 octane. Thats because they make the most money off premium. It costs them a few pennies more a gallon to make and they charge ten pennies more.

Experts I talked to said very few cars need premium gas and theres no more energy in 93 octane gas than there is in 87 octane. I dont care what the experts say. I always think Im being good to my car when I buy premium gas. Im the all-American idiot the oil companies love because I pay more for gas than I need to.

Lately Ive been buying mostly 89 octane. Looking at the prices the other day, I suddenly realized that 89 octane is the worst buy—you get least octane for your money—and I think Ive figured out a better deal.

Here's what I do. I buy five gallons of 87 octane gas. So five gallons of 87 octane gas cost me $5.93.

And then I get five gallons of 93 octane. That costs me $6.97.

So here's the deal. I bought five gallons of 87 octane for $5.93. I bought five gallons of 93 octane for $6.97. Ive got now ten gallons of 90 octane gas for $12.90.

If I had bought ten gallons of 89 octane gas, at $1.34, it would have cost me $13.40. Thats a difference between $12.90 and $13.40. I have one extra octane, mixing 93 and 87, 90 octane, and it costs me 50 cents less.

Im sure gas stations all across the Country are going to be very pleased that Ive pointed this out. And one more thing. If youre going to fool around moving from one pump to the other, please dont do it when Im waiting in line behind you.

Camp David

We've all heard a lot about Camp David, the Presidential retreat in Maryland but we dont know what it looks like. President Bush often went to Camp David but President Clinton has only been there twice, once with his Cabinet members.

President Clinton doesnt want to get *away* from it all on vacation . . . he wants to get *into* it all.

I thought that as long as we're paying for Camp David, we deserve a look at it so I tried to get in the compound and take some pictures.

Well, I had an awful time. Camp David is in the Catoctin National Park so I called the National Park Service. The Park Service said its actually run by the Navy.

I called the Navy. The Navy said yes, it was a Navy installation but that its actually run by the White House. I'd have to get permission from the White House.

I called the White House and three days later I got my answer back. No, I could not take pictures of Camp David to show you.

I was getting very curious by now so I tried to find out how much it costs to maintain Camp David. Again, the Park Service said it was on the Navy's budget, the Navy said it was on the White House budget, and a nice woman in the White House Press Office said she couldnt find out whose budget it was on or how much it costs.

So, I decided to go to Catoctin Mountain myself to see how close I could get to Camp David. It was a lovely drive up the mountain. Too bad the President misses it going by helicopter.

We turned in off the main road and kept going a few hundred yards to the guard house at the gate. We got what youd call a very cool reception from some of the company of Marines guarding the place.

ROONEY: (TO GUARD)
We wondered if we could get permission to take pictures?

GUARD:
No, Sir, Im terribly sorry but you cannot.

ROONEY:
Right. We screwed up the detail there?

GUARD:
Yes, Sir, Youre going to have to wait here for just a couple of minutes.

ROONEY:
Sure.

GUARD:
Youre going to need to fill out a form, all right?

ROONEY:
Sure.

GUARD:
Would you turn that camera off, please.

ROONEY:

The Marines frisked our car, had us fill out intruder forms and asked Bob Peterson, the cameraman, to turn over the tape in his camera. We have those pictures you saw because, by mistake, Bob gave them a blank tape.

We were allowed to leave after the Park Police gave me a $25 ticket for ignoring the sign out by the main road.

So, here's the story. We've got this great Presidential vacation spot on our hands. No one knows who runs it, no one knows how much it costs, they wont let us see what it looks like, and the President hardly ever goes there.

Thats all I can tell you about Camp David.

Cigarette Taxes

Politicians keep raising the taxes on cigarettes because they say it will bring in more money and discourage people from smoking. Now theyre talking about raising the tax on a pack to more than one dollar. Its called a sin tax.

Im not a smoker but raising taxes on cigarettes is an unfair way to try and get people to quit smoking. How come everyone feels sorry for alcoholics but not for cigarette smokers? These people are addicted. Non-smokers act smug and superior.

Smokers are hounded out of their workplace. They have to sneak puffs outdoors as though they were committing a crime.

Outside office buildings everywhere, all day long, there are little clusters of furtive smokers. They left the office and said they were going to the men's room . . . to the ladies room. They didnt fool anyone.

They steal a few puffs, search for cover, then hurry back, hoping to get there before anyone notices theyre gone.

Even the people in charge of our health cant stop. They gather outside the Health and Human Services building in Washington—for what else? For a smoke.

Here's a sneaky smoker in the shadow of the Capitol where Congress voted for non-smoking taxpayers to pay farmers to grow tobacco. The subsidy makes tobacco the single most profitable crop in the United States.

If its good to raise the tax on things that are bad for us, why dont they raise taxes on French fries, bacon, lettuce and tomato sandwiches and chocolate ice cream?

Why dont they raise the tax on handguns? In New York State, for example, the State and Federal tax on cigarettes is about 40 percent on a pack. The Federal and State tax on a gun is about 19 percent. Why is the tax on cigarettes higher than the tax on guns?

Cigarettes dont kill people. Smoking them does.

Warren Buffett

The other day I was looking at *Forbes* magazine. It cost five dollars so I didnt buy it, I just looked at it.

This is the issue with the 400 richest people in America. *Forbes* says Warren Buffett is the richest. He has $8 billion. *Forbes* also says Warren Buffett is a nice guy. I'd be a nice guy too if I had $8 billion.

My boss, Larry Tisch, head of CBS, is one of the poorest of the 400 richest. He only has one billion three hundred million. No wonder he's grumpy.

This list gives me an idea, though. The biggest problem we have in this Country is the budget deficit. Make a special cabinet position for Warren Buffett . . . call him Secretary of Money. He'd control all government spending.

The national debt is 4 trillion dollars. Any company run that way would go out of business. You can bet Warren Buffett wouldnt run the Country that way.

Here's the deal, Warren:

The Government spent one trillion 496 billion dollars last year. It collected one trillion 241 billion in taxes. You can see, theres a gap there, a deficit, of 255 billion dollars.

If you could run this Country more like one of your companies, cut the waste and the stealing and spend only, say, one trillion 141 billion dollars, we wouldnt have a deficit. One trillion 241 billion dollars, what we take in in taxes, minus only one trillion 141 billion, what youd spend . . . that would leave us a surplus of 100 billion dollars.

We'll use half of that to start paying off the national debt, know we have to make this worth your while so youd get to keep half of that . . . 50 billion dollars for yourself, Warren. Its still a good deal for us.

We'd raise money the way your companies do—by putting the United States on the stock exchange. Any American would be able to buy stock . . . actually own a piece of this Country.

If we had trouble with some small country like Haiti or Somalia, we wouldnt send troops, we'd do what one of your corporations does . . . buy the country and take it over.

The United States would be out of trouble and we'd erect a new memorial alongside the Washington Monument . . . in honor of Warren Buffett, the Father of our Company.

Ghostwriters

Theres been a revolution in the bookstore business recently. A lot of good small bookstores run by people who like books better than money are having a hard time because of all the big cut-rate places that are opening up.

Those places are selling a lot of books, which is good, but a lot of the books theyre selling are bad—which isnt good.

They sell a lot of "as told to" or "written with" books. I never read those. Some famous person puts his or her name on a book and a professional writer does most of the work.

General Colin Powell has just signed a book contract for $6 million. General Powell is going to have a ghostwriter although they never call them ghostwriters, of course. I dont know. General Powell is one of the capable people in this Country. For $6 million, dont you think he ought to write the book himself?

He's just following a precedent, I guess. General Norman Schwarzkopf's book was called an autobiography. The definition of autobiography is "the biography of a person written by himself." They shouldnt call it "an autobiography" when its written by someone else. I notice this says "written with Peter Petre."

Every President's wife does it. Betty Ford. Nancy Reagan. Nancy did it twice. This was sickening: the story of their dog, Millie, "as dictated to Barbara Bush."

Larry Speakes was President Reagan's spokesman, but apparently Speakes, the spokesman, had to get Robert Pack to be his writesman.

Books by superstar athletes are almost always "with" someone. Mickey Mantle. And how much of this book do you think Magic Johnson wrote?

William Novak is the biggest name in the "with" writing business. "With Magic Johnson," "With Nancy Reagan," "With Oliver North," "With Tip O'Neill," "With Lee Iacocca," "With the Mayflower Madam."

In the introduction of his book, Iacocca calls himself the author. But on the cover of the *Mayflower Madam* book it says, "With William Novak, writer of *Iacocca*." So, who did write *Iacocca*, Fellas?

As-told-to-books go back a long way in history. After all, a big part of the Bible, one of the greatest books ever written, is the story of Jesus Christ as told to Matthew, Mark, Luke and John . . . and they never even met the guy.

Letters

I get a lot of complaints from people who write to say they'll never watch *60 Minutes* again.

A few weeks ago I talked about how much smaller and more expensive rolls of towels and toilet paper had become in recent years. Sue Tanner, who works for Procter & Gamble, a company that makes many of those products, complained that I should have taken inflation into consideration. People could easily have drawn the conclusion that they were being taken for an expensive ride, she says.

Ms. Tanner goes on to say that if we'd done this research, *60 Minutes* probably wouldnt have used the piece.

Well, thank you, Ms. Tanner. At your suggestion we did that research. The official rate of inflation since 1973 is 236 percent. We figured the rate of inflation of a square foot of Charmin toilet paper since 1973 at 1,281 percent.

Here's a nasty letter from Jonathan Yardley, the book reviewer of the *Washington Post*, about my comments on celebrities who write books "with" professional writers. He calls me hypocritical because I didnt mention a friend of mine who had help writing a book. Mr. Yardley enclosed a copy of his review of it and then told me I also should have mentioned that Ulysses S. Grant wrote his own memoirs.

Well, thank you, Mr. Yardley. Pointing out Ulysses Grant to me suggests you have a keen sense of what makes good television. If youll send me a resume and more samples of your work, I'll see if I can get you a job interview here at CBS. Meanwhile, dont give up your day job at the *Post*.

Most of this mail here refers to my statement that Matthew, Mark, Luke and John did not know Jesus Christ. I was wrong and I apologize. It seems certain that John and Matthew did know Jesus even though the Gospels bearing their names werent written for many years after Jesus died. Jesus left nothing in writing himself.

Now, none of this has anything to do with the greatness of the Bible as a book.

College Football

We're about at the end of the college football season and theres a big debate about which team is #1 and who should play whom in the Rose Bowl, the Orange Bowl, the Sugar Bowl, the Cotton Bowl, the Liberty Bowl, the Fiesta Bowl, the Gator Bowl and other bowls.

The Rose Bowl used to determine the college champion but now the Rose Bowl is between the best team on the West Coast and the best Big Ten team and theyre not usually the two best in the Country. A lot of good teams come from Florida and none of them are allowed to play in the Rose Bowl.

In 1934 Columbia University was undefeated. They went on to win the Rose Bowl that year by beating Stanford 7 to 0 and they became national champions. Of course, that was back in the days when colleges let the students play on the football team.

There are a lot of arguments this year about who's #1 . . . Nebraska, Florida State, West Virginia . . . several others.

Here's my idea how they should decide which is the best college football team. Invite the ten teams who have won the most games in their regular season. Take twenty-two players from each of those teams, put them on the field and sit them down at desks on the field. When the whistle blew, theyd all start taking a written examination.

The questions wouldnt be too hard. For instance:

Name three colleges besides the ones on your football schedule.

If you were paid $100 a day to dig a hole, would that be more or less than your athletic scholarship pays?

What color was Red Grange's hair?

How many teams are there in the Big Ten? (Thats a trick question because there are eleven.)

When time was up, a group of college professors would mark the exam papers and give each player a score. The scores for each team would be added up and the college team with the best total score would win the National Football Championship.

And if Columbia played this year, theyd beat Florida State, Nebraska and West Virginia.

Shoe Size

Of all our body parts, none is funnier-looking or harder to cover than our feet. I bought a new pair of shoes last week and I dont understand shoe sizes.

My size is 9EEE or wider. Not many companies make shoes that wide. I measured my foot with a ruler. It seems to be about 11 inches long and maybe 4 or 4½ inches wide. And what I'd like to know is this, how come my size is called 9EEE?

Theres a good shoe store on Broadway, in New York City, so I went into Harry's to ask some questions.

ROONEY:

Im curious about sizes. Now I wear a 9EEE. Is that nine inches?

ROBERT GOLDBERG (SHOE SALESMAN):

That would be a 9 wide. Your foot is broader than standard.

ROONEY:

I know but what, what is that nine?

GOLDBERG:

9EEE?

ROONEY:

What does the 9 stand for?

GOLDBERG:

9 is the length of the foot.

ROONEY:

I measured it this morning. Its about 11 inches long. Why a 9?

GOLDBERG:

Thats the gauge according to shoe sizes. In terms of the size that the shoe would match up in terms of the length of the shoe.

ROONEY:

Yeh, but how long is a 9?

GOLDBERG:

Oh, actually, its probably very hard to tell you that.

ROONEY:

Why dont they do it in inches?

GOLDBERG:

Because unfortunately I dont think theres any standardization in the shoe industry that would allow for such an exact measurement.

ROONEY:

I see you have socks over here. Now, I never understood that. I wear an 11 sock. Why do I wear an 11 sock on the same foot that takes a 9 shoe?

GOLDBERG:

Well, sock sizes . . . again. Theres a translation to a sock.

ROONEY:

Why?

GOLDBERG:

I think the two industries never put it together so you could match one against the other identically. I think the sock sizes are just based on the sizes of the sock in terms of . . . If you wear one size shoe, youll wear X size sock. They just translate it. It would be much easier, if you wore a 9 shoe, youd wear a 9 sock.

ROONEY:

I'll say it would. If a woman wears a 9 shoe is her foot the same length as mine?

GOLDBERG:

No. Her foot is on a woman's scale.

ROONEY:

Oh, dont tell me.

GOLDBERG:

Right. So theres another variation, again. And its approximately a two-size differential between a woman's 9 and a men's.

ROONEY:

This is a mess, isnt it?

GOLDBERG:

Well, it does create some level of variation. No one system that applies.

Theres still a lot of work to be done on shoes. They look so good in a store window that we're always tempted to go in and buy a pair. They dont look that good for long. After we've worn them for a few months, they begin to look lumpy and out of shape because the shoes begin to look more like our feet . . . which are not as good-looking as the shoes in a store window.

Theres a battle going on between our shoes and our feet and the result is, our feet hurt.

1994

Classified Ads

I own a house, I have a job and I dont buy used cars, but just for fun I often look through the classified section of the newspaper. The ads are written in a language all their own. These are some papers from around the Country we bought.

For instance, what does this mean: "Sauna & more, 4BR, mostly brk, split lvl, w/fam rm, rec rm . . . "?

Would it have cost them a lot more to have written that out in English?

Here's one: "Tucked away in historic wooded area."

It means the place is in the woods ten miles from town.

"Historic."

That always means the house is old.

"Completely updated"?

The house has electricity and indoor plumbing. Im always suspicious of the house when the ad talks about how good the grounds are.

"Quiet, wooded setting"?

It means theres a tree in the backyard. They abbreviate the word "room" to just "rm."

The word "beautiful" is in half these ads, but they never abbreviate "beautiful." "Beautifully landscaped grounds."

Translation?

Theres a bush out front.

"Lushly landscaped"?

There are *two* bushes out front.

"Beautifully landscaped south garden"?

Theres a bush on the other side of the house, too.

Do you think anyone ever bought a house because the ad says "Must sell!"

And how about this:

"Builder leaving area"?

Would you want to buy a house from someone who was going to take the money and run? Did he have to leave town?

There are always a lot of "charmings" and "cutes" in these ads. Here's a "quaint."

"Quaint" means the house was built without an architect, so the bathroom is off the dining room instead of near the bedroom. Thats "quaint."

This is in the *Houston Chronicle*: "Charming 'Cape Cod.'"

In Texas? If they want to live in a Cape Cod house, they should move to Cape Cod.

If a young person is lucky, he or she'll be buying a house someday. Any school that teaches foreign languages ought to teach kids what the words in real-estate ads mean.

Television Magazine Shows

Im sure youve noticed the proliferation of magazine shows on television. Anytime a television show is successful, there are always imitators and, of course, *60 Minutes* has been successful.

There are other good shows now like *20/20, 48 Hours, Prime Time Live* and some Ive never even seen that are good. And then there are the bad ones . . . all those television equivalents of the supermarket newspapers . . . shows like *A Current Affair, Hard Copy* and *Inside Edition*.

One thing the shows have in common is, they all need stories.

One favorite story is about someone wrongfully imprisoned for murder. You may remember Ed Bradley's story about "Johnny D."

ED BRADLEY:

His name is Walter McMillian, known to his friends as Johnny D. He's been on death row in Alabama's prison for almost six years. Was he, in fact, the man who walked into a dry cleaning store in Alabama in November of 1986 and robbed and murdered the clerk or did they get the wrong man?

ANDY ROONEY:

It was proven that Johnny D didnt do it and Johnny got out after that show.

The problem is, there arent enough stories like this to go around. Most of the people in prison for murder, murdered someone and this doesnt make a good story for a television show.

There are 87,500 people in prison for murder in the United States . . . 82,000 men and 5,500 women. All but a very few wouldnt make good stories for television because they are not innocent. They did it. Theyre in for a murder they committed and they should stay in.

All those murderers in prison make it hard on *60 Minutes* for another reason, too. When Ed gets one guy off, most of the others write him to say they didnt do it, either.

Some shows like *Barbara Walters Specials* interview famous people just because theyre famous. Thats what theyre famous for. It can be interesting but, like someone in prison for a murder he didnt commit, theres a shortage of famous people who are famous enough to make a good interview.

You look at the morning television shows and you know how often theyre scraping the bottom of the well-known barrel. They have famous people on all the time that you never even heard of.

When you come right down to it, what makes it so difficult for the producers of television magazine shows is, most of you Americans arent doing your part.

You go around all day being nice, normal, honest people. You arent movie stars, you dont cut parts off your husband when he's asleep. Most of you have never been in a headline for anything. Youre just good, simple Americans. You dont make good stories for television magazine shows. Thats the trouble with you.

Ex-Presidents

It must be a strange experience to be President of the United States. For a brief period of your life, the whole world is watching every move you make.

Pretty soon youre not President any more but to the day you die, everywhere you go, youre a highly visible ex-President.

There are five living ex-Presidents now. There are that many partly because ex-Presidents are living longer and partly because four of the five served less than the full eight years allowed.

Whether they served two full terms or not, we get our impression of our Presidents from the stories about them and, after a few years in office and thousands of sometimes accurate and sometimes inaccurate stories, thousands of sometimes fair and sometimes unfair stories, we end up with a truer picture of them than they have of themselves.

Presidents almost always hate reporters because . . . you know how it is. When someone takes a picture of you, you wish you were better looking . . . and thats how it is with Presidents. They wish they looked better . . . in pictures and in print.

Most of us have more or less the same feeling about our ex-Presidents. Say you rate them on five things: Intelligence, Honesty, Ability, Likeableness, Decency.

Richard Nixon was smart and capable but not likeable. We arent sure he was decent.

Ford was decent and likeable. Not too smart.

Carter was decent, smart, likeable and honest but strangely ineffectual.

Reagan was likeable. He didnt have much else going for him but that was a lot.

Bush is the last and maybe the most forgettable of the living ex-Presidents. I dont know why that is. He seemed fairly smart, decent enough, sort of likeable and probably honest but for some strange reason he's already less remembered than Nixon or Reagan.

We're still deciding what we think about Bill Clinton and he isnt too happy these days because he wants to make his points with his foreign policy by going to Russia and reporters keep poking him about things that happened back in Little Rock. He doesnt want to talk about that.

There are four kinds of Americans when it comes to how we talk about our President. First, theres the Republican who'd hate any Democratic President even if he was George Washington. Second, theres the Democrat who'd hate any Republican President even if he was Abraham Lincoln. And third, there are people who'd hate any President no matter who he is.

Roman Numerical

Next Sunday in Atlanta at this hour theyre playing the Super Bowl so this is a very big week for Roman numerals. This one is going to be XXVIII. Thats twenty-eight. You probably wont be watching the game next Sunday. You'll be tuned right here to *LX Minutes*, on at the same time.

Roman numerals come up quite often considering that most of us forget what they mean when we see them.

When you pass a building that has a Roman numeral on it, you feel you ought to know when it was built but you usually dont. MCMVIII. I can do that. Thats 1908. Fine but what about MDCLXIV. I looked that up and I think its 1664. Dont tell me this was built in 1664.

Its always pretentious for an architect to put Roman numerals on a building. No one can read them but Romans. What's wrong with just the date? I suppose they think Roman numerals lend class to a building.

They use Roman numerals on clocks and watches, too. They look good on big clocks. A watch with Roman numerals costs more.

Here's *The Wall Street Journal* . . . volume CCXXIII. Thats 223. Why dont they say so?

As a public service tonight, Im going to refresh you on your Roman numerals. Get a pencil. I think you know all these. I, II, III, V, X. XX is 20. XXX is thirty. L is 50. And C is 100. Thats the easy part. It gets harder.

You'd think that if III is 3, IIII would be 4 but it isnt. I guess they thought it was getting too long so when the smaller Roman numeral is in front of a bigger one, you subtract the first from the second one. You dont add it.

That means that IV is 5 minus I which is 4. VI is 5 plus I or 6. L is fifty. X is ten. So XL is 50 minus 10 = 40.

These are the big numbers.

D is 500.

M is 1,000.

V with a line over it is 5,000.

X with a line over it is 10,000.

And all the way up to a million which is M with a line over it.

The Romans didnt have anything for a billion. Our Government, of course, doesnt deal in anything *under* a billion.

The copyright date on this show is MCMXCIV. We think it gives *LX Minutes* a little class.

Byron De La Beckwith

Last week in Jackson, Mississippi, Byron De La Beckwith was sentenced to life in prison for ambushing the civil rights leader Medgar Evers from his hiding place in the bushes across the street from Evers's home in Greenwood.

In its story last Sunday, *The New York Times* said: "After 31 years, blacks say justice has at last been done."

Blacks say justice has been done? The idea that blacks alone rejoiced at the conviction of Byron De La Beckwith is objectionable to this white man who was ecstatic over it.

In 1970, I spent two months producing a *60 Minutes* report with Harry Reasoner on the murder of Medgar Evers.

Before driving the ninety miles to Greenwood to film the houses of Medgar Evers and Beckwith, I checked in with the FBI district chief in Jackson.

"Dont buy gas." "Be very careful," he said. "Dont stop for anything. And whatever you do, dont sleep in Greenwood. They'll know youre there."

To further put us at ease, he said to let him know every few hours where we were.

Back in Jackson two days later, Harry joined us.

When he started his introductory statement on camera in front of the same Hinds County Courthouse where Beckwith was convicted, we were arrested by two redneck sheriffs.

Harry and I were brought into court that day to answer trespassing charges because we had been standing a few feet off the public sidewalk on the courthouse grass. Fortunately, the judge was a fan of *60 Minutes* and he let us off.

The next day I went to the company that employed Beckwith. They made boat trailers and big rigs for carrying picked cotton. We'd been told Beckwith traveled Mississippi as a recruiter for the KKK under cover of his title of salesman for the trailer company. It seemed possible so I asked to see the president of the company.

"Im looking for Byron De La Beckwith," I said. "I understand he works for you."

He looked at me, flushed red and shook his finger in my face. "You mention that boy on your television," he said, "and I'll git you. We got people everywhere and I'll git you."

Well, the report was broadcast and he didnt git me but for months I looked across the street toward the bushes when I was putting the car away at night.

I'd appreciate it if *The New York Times* didnt exclude me and millions more white Americans, many from Mississippi, next time they mention people who thought justice was done when Byron De La Beckwith was convicted of murdering Medgar Evers.

The Spy Game

I have this idea that spies are just people who like to spy. They dont particularly care who they spy on. I dont think spies are great people, either.

This week our Government announced that another Central Intelligence agent, Aldrich Ames, has been caught spying for Russia.

President Clinton was very upset.

"It is a very serious case," he said. "We will be immediately lodging a protest to the Russian Government . . . ."

Now this guy Ames is scum, theres no doubt about that. He's probably responsible for the deaths of ten Russians who were spying for us, but did Ames give the Russians any really important American secrets? I'd like to ask President Clinton two questions:

First. "What were the secrets that Aldrich Ames sold to the Russians?" The Russians already know what they were so why dont you tell us? Second question. "Do we have spies in Russia, Mr. President?"

Well, of course no one answers questions about spies. The Central Intelligence Agency always says, "Revealing that information would endanger our national security."

Ask our spies about cheating on their expense accounts and they'll say, "Answering that would endanger our national security."

We spend 30 billion dollars a year on the CIA and half that money is spent trying to catch the spies of other countries. *They* spend half *their* budget trying to catch *our* spies. What's with all this spy stuff, anyway?

We have forty books on spies in our little CBS Reference Library. Spies make great books and exciting movies but theyve never done much to help the country they spy for.

Intelligence agencies of every country get their money by scaring citizens into thinking someone's about to attack their country. On the advice of our CIA, we've spent hundreds of billions of dollars over the years preparing for an attack by Russia that the Russians never planned.

How come the CIA didnt tell us that the Soviet Union was about to fall apart a few years ago so we could save money? They didnt want their budget cut, thats why.

How come we didnt know Saddam Hussein had a nuclear weapon? Did they find out where Terry Anderson and the other prisoners were being held in Lebanon? They did not. What did we get for our 30 billion?

What we need is more intelligence and less spying. Spying is a dishonest, immoral business that doesnt pay off. Why doesnt the United States get out of the dirty spy business?

Charles Kuralt

We've had a sad time here at CBS News this week. Charles Kuralt says he's leaving. When Kuralt says he's leaving, he isnt dickering for more money—he's leaving.

Its sad for us in television news because we've had a little more class than we otherwise would have with Kuralt in our business.

Kuralt doesnt like to be called Charley but thats what I call him because a person doesnt get to choose his own nickname.

One of the best broadcasts in all television for fifteen years now has been *CBS Sunday Morning*. Charley's done ten thousand things and everything he did was best. He did *On the Road* for many years. He did the best political pieces. He did the best reports from the Olympic Games. He did the best morning show.

The fact is Kuralt does everything in television news better than anyone else. He writes better, he reports better and his presence on camera is better.

If youve been thinking of Charles Kuralt as a warm, simple person who could easily be your best friend, forget that. Kuralt is about as plain and simple as Albert Einstein. I dont know anyone who understands Kuralt and that may include himself.

Im one of his closest friends at CBS and we're not very close. If it had to be his initiative, we might never see each other again. He wouldnt seek me out.

But then, Charley has this great warm friendship with the American people. In spite of all the evidence to the contrary in the news, he thinks people are good . . . and thats what comes through in all his writing.

Everyone wants to know why, with $6 million in salary coming to him if he stayed, he's turning his back on fame and money.

Well, theres been a gradual decline in the quality of television news. That doesnt make television news special. Theres been a decline in the quality of a great many things. Kuralt wouldnt say so because he's a classy person and not the kind of guy who says a lot of negative things about anything but I suspect this decline contributed to his decision to leave television. He has more integrity than a lot of us who believe what he believes but continue to take the money anyway.

Everyone was quick to say in the announcement, "Kuralt's in good health." Well, I dont know. His health may be good but he's sure in terrible shape. He's overweight and I can tell when Charley comes in the office because I can smell the cigarette smoke wafting down the hallway. I see the cigarette butts in the men's room and in the ashtray by the elevator. He's fifteen years younger than I am but I could beat him around the block anytime.

I'll tell you what, Charley. As a going-away present, to show you how much I think of you, Im not going to call you Charley anymore.

Good luck. I hope you find the life youre looking for out there . . . Charles.

Kurt Cobain

(NOTE: The only complaint the business people at CBS have about 60 Minutes is that they say it attracts an old audience. That may be true but when I did this on the occasion of Kurt Cobain's suicide, I got 10,000 angry letters from viewers under 30.)

You know the world has passed you by when your newspaper carries a page one story about the death of someone you never heard of. It happened to me this week. All the papers had it.

"Kurt Cobain," this story says, "who helped to create the grunge rock sound that has dominated popular music, was found dead at his home. Mr. Cobain, lead singer, guitarist and song writer for the influential band Nirvana, killed himself with a shotgun blast to the head."

It isnt bad enough I never heard of Kurt Cobain, I never heard of "grunge rock" or "Nirvana" either.

The story says grunge rock is "the noisy, icon-smashing spawn of punk rock."

Kurt Cobain's death at age twenty-seven doesnt sadden me, it angers me. He must have been a talented person but a lot of people would like to have the years left that he threw away. I'd like to have them.

What's all this nonsense about how terrible life is? A young girl who stood outside his home in Seattle with tears streaming down her face said, "Its hard to be a young person nowadays. He helped open people's eyes to our struggles."

Please, wipe the tears from your eyes, dear. Youre breaking my heart. I'd love to relieve the pain youre going through by switching my age for yours.

What would all these young people be doing if they had real problems like a Depression, World War II, or Vietnam? Do they work at all? Are they contributing anything to the world theyre taking so much from?

Everything about Kurt Cobain makes me suspicious. This picture shows him in a pair of jeans with a hole in the knee. I doubt that Kurt Cobain ever did enough work to wear a hole in his pants. He probably had ten pairs just like these hanging in his closet—all with fake holes in the knee.

All this fake stuff makes me suspicious of his music. No one's art is better than the person who creates it. If Kurt Cobain applied the same brain to his music that he applied to his drug-infested life, its reasonable to think that his music may not have made much sense either.

On a back page of the same newspaper with the Kurt Cobain story, theres an obituary of Samuel E. Thorne who died at the age of eighty-seven. Professor Thorne was a retired legal historian at Harvard.

"Mr. Thorne," the obituary said, "was an authority on English legal history dating to the 12th century. During World War II he was a Navy cryptanalyst in the Pacific. He is survived by two sons and his wife of 50 years."

I'd like to suggest we save our tears for Professor Thorne.

Kurt Cobain Reaction

Im well paid for what I do here on *60 Minutes*, and while the money's nice, its the warm, generous comments I get that make this job a joy to have—like the comments I got after my remarks last week about the suicide of Kurt Cobain, whom I'd never heard of.

"Dear Mr. Rooney, I can honestly say you are the jackass of the nation. I believed all my life God was perfect and has no flaws, but your creation causes me to rethink this." Joey Mulvey, Middle Village, New York.

"You are an old, outdated, blundering boob." Signed, Disappointed, T. Michaels, Memphis, Tennessee.

"I will never listen to another word out of your vile mouth. I hope that on the day your obituary appears, some commentator will correctly describe you as the loud-mouthed, self-important, out-of-touch windbag that you are. Too bad you wont be around to read it." Mark Chamberlain.

Well, I was around to read Eric Mink of the *New York Daily News*, who said I dismissed the pain of a grieving, young Kurt Cobain fan who spoke of how hard it is to be a young person today.

"In other words," Mr. Mink writes, "forget the ethnic brutality revived by the fall of communism in Eastern Europe and Asia. Forget the repressive governments of the Far East, the starving peoples of the Sudan, the warring factions in South Africa, the racial divisions in this Country, and the environmental recklessness that threatens to despoil the planet."

I'll have to admit that I didnt realize these problems were what Kurt Cobain was singing about. Maybe I have been unfair.

Anna Quindlen, columnist for *The New York Times*, wrote that I "brought to the issue of youthful despair a mixture of sarcasm and contempt. After all," she said, "that has long been the attitude their elders have brought to the pain of those far younger than they."

When I said I'd like to relieve the pain of young grunge fans by switching ages with them, Ms. Quindlen said, "I wouldnt. I wouldnt be seventeen again on a bet."

She finishes her column saying that young people who feel an inner agony "often do not reveal themselves because they suspect some adult will scoff and say that what they feel is 'nonsense.'" "Sunday evening," Ms. Quindlen concludes, "some adult did just that—and on national television, too."

The Worst Inventions

We're all familiar with the great inventions that have altered civilization . . . inventions like the electric light bulb, the telephone, the airplane, radio, Coca-Cola.

There are, on the other hand, inventions we'd be better off without. And tonight I'd like to list five of the worst inventions of modern times.

#1. The hot-air hand drier in public bathrooms. These represent the triumph of salesmanship over paper towels. Theyre totally unsatisfactory.

#2. Most books come with a removable paper cover called a dust jacket. Dust jackets do nothing except make books more expensive and harder to handle.

#3. Pop-top cans. Its an unpleasant little task to get your finger under the metal tab so you can pull it open but the worst thing about these things is that you cant close them. No one wants to drink twelve ounces of a sweet soft drink without stopping. Do the people selling this stuff want us to save some for later? No. They want us to throw out what's left and buy more.

#4. Venetian blinds. I'd like to talk to the Venetian who invented blinds. I have them in my office and theyre fine until you try to open them or close them.

#5. I'd like to nominate the ballpoint pen as one of the great failures of the century. The earliest pens needed an inkwell but they were satisfying to use in many ways. You had to have a blotter and then you had to have a pen-wiper when you finished.

So, they invented the fountain pen. Well, they really werent satisfied with the fountain pens either so inventors came up with the ballpoint pen. I dont know whether theres really a ball in here or not.

They have survived because of the credit card craze. The idea is you can bear down hard with a ball point pen so your signature goes through four fuzzy carbons. You get the last copy, of course, which you cant read.

You cant put a ballpoint pen in your pocket or a drawer for any length of time and expect it to work when you take it out, either. I have three of them here and I notice that of the three, only one of them works now.

If these are the worst inventions of modern times, the rubber band may be the best.

Tobacco Company Executives

People in the tobacco and cigarette business have been having a tough time lately. Just last week a poll showed that 83 percent of the American people dont think tobacco companies tell the truth when they talk about cigarettes.

The executives of seven tobacco companies testified before Congress this week.

REPRESENTATIVE RON WYDEN (D-OREGON):
I just cant understand how each of you is engaged in an enterprise that is sure to kill some of our children.

ANDREW TISCH (LORILLARD, INC.):
The data has not convinced me that smoking causes death.

JAMES JOHNSTON (R. J. REYNOLDS TOBACCO COMPANY):
The implication is that we're somehow doing something sinister.

ANDY ROONEY:
I thought there were other more convincing arguments those tobacco executives could have used. For example:

CIGARETTES ARE IMPORTANT FOR NEWSPAPERS AND TELEVISION TOO. CIGARETTES ARE ONE OF THE FEW THINGS ANDY ROONEY CAN SAY TERRIBLE THINGS ABOUT WITHOUT GETTING IN ANY TROUBLE.

And they might say:

IF IT WERENT FOR PATIENTS WHO GET LUNG CANCER FROM SMOKING, A LOT OF DOCTORS WOULD HAVE TO CHARGE OTHER PATIENTS MORE TO MAKE UP FOR THAT LOST INCOME.
DONT FORGET 418,690 AMERICANS DIED OF SMOKING-RELATED ILLNESSES LAST YEAR AND THEY DIDNT JUST UP AND DIE SUDDENLY EITHER. THEY DIED OVER A LONG PERIOD OF TIME AND EACH STEP OF THE WAY PROVIDED WORK FOR DOCTORS AND NURSES AND THE BOOKKEEPERS WHO PAD MEDICAL BILLS.

Another argument tobacco executives could use:

THE SURGEON GENERAL SAYS CIGARETTE SMOKING CAUSES LUNG CANCER. THIS IS FAULTY REASONING, TWISTED LOGIC. WHY ISNT THE SURGEON GENERAL INVESTIGATING WHY PEOPLE WHO ARE GONNA DIE OF LUNG CANCER HAVE THIS UNCONTROLLABLE URGE TO SMOKE?

Cigarette company executives might put out a press release:

RECENT SURVEYS SHOW CIGARETTE SMOKERS ARE LESS LIKELY TO COMMIT SUICIDE, LESS LIKELY TO GET DIVORCED, ABUSE THEIR CHILDREN OR GET AIDS.

You can get away with anything if you can quote a survey. No one checks up on surveys.

OUR WHOLE ECONOMY DEPENDS ON THE TOBACCO INDUS-TRY. HOW WOULD YOU FEEL IF YOU HAD A FAMILY-OWNED COM-PANY MAKING ASHTRAYS IF YOU HAD TO FIRE 37 PEOPLE BECAUSE RESTAURANTS NO LONGER BOUGHT YOUR ASHTRAYS?

I suppose the tobacco companies wont use my arguments and I think I know why. The price of their stocks keep going up. The more bad things that people say about cigarettes, the more money the tobacco companies make.

Medal of Honor

Have you always wanted to be a war hero and march in the Memorial Day parade, wearing medals on your old Army uniform? Well, you can do that now without going to all the trouble and danger of fighting in a war. The Defense Department recently approved the sale of military medals to any-one who wants to buy them. You dont have to show any proof that youre entitled to wear the medal.

It would take a psychiatrist to explain people's fascination with medals. Every country has always encouraged its fighting men by pinning medals to their chests for bravery, but then theyve presented awards for lesser actions, too.

During the Persian Gulf war, there were 570,000 U.S. servicemen and women in the Middle East, and the Pentagon gave out more than four mil-lion awards. Our military leaders decorate their chests like Christmas trees, even though many of them are too young to have fought in any war.

Selling medals on the open market is going to mean new business for the three companies that stamp out our armed services medals.

On the other hand, its going to take away a lot of the honor from anyone who actually won the award on the battlefield if people can wear medals designed to honor bravery as though they were jewelry.

There is still one medal you cant buy, and thats our highest military award—the Medal of Honor, often called the Congressional Medal of Honor.

PRESIDENT RONALD REAGAN:
A nation grateful to you and to all your comrades, living and dead, awards you its highest symbol of gratitude. For service above and beyond the call of duty, the Congressional Medal of Honor.

ROONEY:
In all this Country's history, the Medal of Honor has been bestowed on just 3,401 people. It is given for rare heroism. And although its against the law to claim you have received the Medal of Honor if you havent, there have always been imposters—people who posed as war heroes who were not.

MS. ROZ KARSON (CBS News):
We understand youre a Medal of Honor winner, or a Legion of Honor winner?

MR. DAVID R. VIGIL (Claims to have won medal):
Medal of Honor.

MS. KARSON:
Medal of Honor. And you were at this cutting ceremony at Lakewood not too long ago?

MR. VIGIL:
Yes. Yes, uh-huh.

(Footage of article; footage of Vigil's home)

Roz Karson of *60 Minutes* was asking about an article we read in a California Veterans Affairs publication that referred to David R. Vigil as a Medal of Honor winner. Mr. Vigil had cut a ribbon at the opening of a veterans information booth in Lakewood, California. His home is stacked with war memorabilia, and he loves to talk about his medals.

VIGIL:

These are the medals right here that I received. Fact, like I say, I can take them out and put them on my civilian clothes and—to wear for ceremonies—they generally want the full-size medals. Thats the Congressional Medal of Honor. Tha—thats the new one they have now that you put—you pin on those there. See, the long—theres the—here's the big one here—the . . . (unintelligible) one. This one right here—my pride and joy.

KARSON:

Thats your pride and joy.

VIGIL:

Well, I like it a lot.

KARSON:

And when did you get that?

VIGIL:

I was stationed aboard the carrier Franklin. There was quite a few of us on the Franklin. Was—I think its—five altogether got the medal, and one got it taken away from him, but there was five of us altogether on the ship there. We got hit pretty bad. Ive got the whole history in a book that I got over there. The day I got there it was on my seventeenth birthday, March 18, 1945; I was seventeen years old.

KARSON:

What was your rank?

VIGIL:

Always enlisted. Thats a copy of my Congressional Medal of Honor—wha—what the dates I received it and all the thing on that part there.

ROONEY:

We asked the author of this *Guidebook of U.S. Medals*, Evans Kerrigan, to look at that footage with us.

Now is this a legitimate Medal of Honor?

KERRIGAN :
No, thats actually a copy of a Civil War Medal of Honor, which you can buy as a replica or a copy.

ROONEY:
So thats nothing anyone would have gotten for World War II?

KERRIGAN:
Oh, no. The pad would have been different on the World War II medal and also the medal itself would have been gold-plated—the medal and anchor.

ROONEY:
And what about the wings?

KERRIGAN:
The wings here are Navy aviator wings, and he wouldnt have been a naval aviator if he was enlisted. He would have been air crew.

ROONEY:
There are 194 living recipients of the Medal of Honor. David R. Vigil is not one of them.

A friendly fellow named Joseph O. Gorman lives in this beautiful country club compound in Palm Desert, California. When I approached him outside his home, Joe talked freely about his war experiences.

We understand youre a Medal of Honor winner.

GORMAN (Claims to have won the medal):
Well, Im supposed to be, yeah.

ROONEY:
Yeah. So you are, though. Where'd you win that?

GORMAN:
In more—in Hollandy in New Guinea.

ROONEY:
You were in the Marines?

GORMAN:
No, I was in the United States Army.

ROONEY:
Which group were you with?

GORMAN:
Well, I finally finished out with the 503rd paratroopers.

ROONEY:
Joe even took us inside to see his medals.
Which one is the Medal of Honor?

GORMAN:
The one in the middle.

ROONEY:
That was the Congressional Medal of Honor?

GORMAN:
Mm-hmm.

ROONEY:
. . . and thats the Silver Star, and this is the Purple Heart.

GORMAN:
This one—yeah.

ROONEY:
Where were you wounded, Joe?

GORMAN:
Well, once in New Guinea and once in the Philippine Islands. And then I
got two wounds in—which gives me a battle citation, you know?

ROONEY:

And this is the actual commendation?

GORMAN:

This is the commendation there.

ROONEY:

"To Lieutenant Joseph O. Gorman for valor and heroism in the field." Is this the actual citation for the Medal of Honor?

GORMAN:

No, this is a copy of the citation.

ROONEY:

Well, your name is not in any of the books.

GORMAN:

Well, it—theyre—thats what theyre tracing now. Thats what I said. I was never presented . . .

ROONEY:

Mm-hmm.

GORMAN:

. . . formally with it up—I was given the medal in the field, and it never went any further, and this is what Ive been going through . . .

ROONEY:

I see.

GORMAN:

. . . for fifty years trying to get the recognition for the . . .

ROONEY:

I see.

GORMAN:

. . . for the medal.

ROONEY:

Out back in the garage, Joe Gorman's Cadillac had a special Medal of Honor license plate. He had it made himself. You'll notice it differs from the official plate issued by the state to Medal of Honor winners. Gorman also says he jumped with the paratroopers. The cameraman thought it unusual that a paratrooper had pinned on his master's jump wings upside-down.

Joe Gorman may have been a war hero—I dont know. He did not receive the Medal of Honor.

Its difficult to separate the genuine heroes from the impostors because we all want to believe in heroes—even Presidents.

PRESIDENT REAGAN:

. . . a B–17 coming back across the channel from a raid over Europe, badly shot up by anti-aircraft. The ball turret that hung underneath the belly of the plane had taken a hit. The young ball turret gunner was wounded, and they couldnt get him out of the turret there while flying. But over the channel, the plane began to lose altitude, and the commander had to order, "Bail out." And as the men started to leave the plane, the last one to leave—the—the boy, understandably, knowing he was left behind to go down with the plane, cried out in terror. The last man to leave the plane saw the commander sit down on the floor. He took the boy's hand and said, "Never mind, son. We'll ride it down together." Congressional Medal of Honor, posthumously awarded.

ROONEY:

Well, it was a good story, but it wasnt true. There was no Medal of Honor winner, and President Reagan's story was taken from a 1944 movie called *Wing and a Prayer* starring Dana Andrews.

A man named John M. Iannone, successful in the oil business in Pitts-burgh . . . went to great lengths to establish himself as a hero of the war in Vietnam. We got hold of this official-looking document signed by President Reagan that reads: "For conspicuous gallantry and intrepidity at the risk of his life above and beyond the call of duty in action with the enemy."

Only one trouble: John Michael Iannone was not a hero, and these documents are fraudulent. Theres no record that he ever served in Vietnam or anywhere else. There is one note saying he applied for the Marine Corps and was turned down. Thats as close as John Iannone ever came to being a war hero.

The only woman ever awarded the Medal of Honor was a doctor named Mary Walker, who served during the Civil War.

Knowing she was the only one, we were naturally surprised when we heard about Lucille Hewitt. A story in the Kern Valley Sun in Kern, California, reported that Lucille Hewitt, a Medal of Honor winner, was going to be the honorary marshal and lead the Whiskey Flat Days parade.

We made arrangements to take pictures of that parade, but after word got out that we were coming, Lucille Hewitt did not appear. She is not a Medal of Honor recipient.

We talked about impostors with Mitchell Paige, who was awarded the Medal of Honor as a Marine in World War II.

In retirement, Mitch Paige has been a one-man task force, tracking down

people who claim they have received the Medal of Honor but did not.

Are these fraudulent claims common?

PAIGE:
Today they are, yes. Theyre untold numbers out there, Andy, that—I would suspect right now there are probably 500 or more that have Congressional Medals of Honor that theyve purchased at some gun show or some other place like that.

ROONEY:
How long have you been tracking down these impostors?

PAIGE:
About thirty-five years.

ROONEY:
And how many would you think youve found?

PAIGE:
Oh, well over 1,000.

ROONEY:
Have you ever made a mistake?

PAIGE:
No, not once.

ROONEY:
Mitchell Paige may never have made a mistake, but we found it difficult to get all the facts from people he has accused of being impostors.

When an article appeared in the Oceanside, California, *Blade Citizen*, the reporter said that a man named Dan Owen had told her he had been awarded the Medal of Honor.

We went to Mr. Owen's home. He didnt repeat that claim.

It was too bad this woman said you were a Medal of Honor winner, wasnt it?

OWEN:
Yeah. Yeah.

ROONEY:
She—she just made the mistake?

OWEN:
Yeah.

ROONEY:
Yeah, that was too bad. She just assumed you . . .

OWEN:
Yeah—I guess, because all I'd said was that I had been recommended for it.

ROONEY:
Dan Owen served as a fighter pilot in the Mediterranean in World War II.

Hanging on his wall are two Purple Hearts and the Silver Star. He's had an active life since the war. An article he showed us says he killed a 42-foot, 3,000-pound snake in Brazil and that he took photographs for the *National Geographic*. There are no pictures of the snake, and the *National Geographic* has no record that he ever took pictures for them.

Last May, a pest control expert in Florida named Alan Lorith received a letter from Mitch Paige accusing him of posing as a Medal of Honor recipient.

Where did you spend the—the war?

LORITH:
I was in a Haiphong prisoner-of-war camp in North Vietnam about ninety miles away from Hanoi. Its a death camp.

ROONEY:
Well, how did that Medal of Honor thing all start anyway?

LORITH:
I wish I knew.

ROONEY:
Yeah.

LORITH:
The—even the counselor over at the vet center where I was originally planning on meeting with you, even asked me about it. I says Ive been trying to down it as much as I can, and—like that.

ROONEY:
So its pretty much gone now, though?

LORITH:
I dont know. There are people still—like yourself, just come up out of the clear blue sky.

ROONEY:
Mmm.

LORITH:
And Im just trying to down it as much as I can.

ROONEY:
Mmm. I mean, you never said you were a Medal of Honor winner?

LORITH:
I tried not to.

ROONEY:
Army records dont show anyone named Alan Lorith who was a POW in Vietnam. He is listed in Army records as a driver for the chaplain at an Army base there.

Mitchell Paige is merciless with impostors. I guess I'd be too, if I'd won the medal. But we found ourselves going a little soft on these people we talked to who had made grandiose claims. They were often more pathetic than criminal.

Even so, Mitch Paige is right, of course. Heroism, real bravery, is the triumph of courage over fear. The soldiers who have accomplished that in battle and have been honored for it shouldnt have to share that honor with those who dream of having done brave things in war, but did not.

Sports Seasons

Baseball players are making an average of 1.2 million dollars a year and they objected to the owners' idea of a salary limit . . . what theyre calling a salary cap. There ought to be a profit cap for owners, too.

Both the players and the owners, though, have a nerve. They own the teams. They dont own the game. Baseball fans ought to go out and get themselves some other players and some other owners. That would show them.

To tell you the truth, I thought the baseball season lasted long enough this year. It started April 3 and the strike began August 12. Each team played 114 games. They should know which the best team is by now. Why dont they just declare a winner? I'll tell you why they dont—money, thats why.

All professional sports are lasting too long because of money. Baseball runs into the football season. The Super Bowl is played two weeks later than it used to be. Its winter!

Basketball runs into the baseball season. The first NBA championship game was played on April 22, 1947. This year the championship was played exactly two months later, on June 22.

Hockey's the worst. The first Stanley Cup championship was played in 1918 on March 30. In 1954 it was April . . . 1974 it was May . . . and last season it ended June 14, two months and two weeks later than that first championship. Ice hockey in June, for goodness sake? They should play on roller skates.

The other sports news is that CBS lost the National Conference Football Games to Fox. If you work here at CBS, it changes your attitude toward a lot of things. I always liked John Madden until he left CBS to go to Fox for $32 million. It used to be when Madden did a commercial, he sounded to me as if he was doing a football game. Now on Fox when he's doing a game, he sounds to me as though he's doing a commercial.

If CBS is worried that it may hurt *60 Minutes*'s ratings when the game runs past 7 o'clock on Fox, I'll make them an offer. CBS would start *60 Minutes* the second the game is over on Fox, just the way they did when it was on CBS.

Ive always wanted to go longer. So I'll volunteer to fill the time between 7 o'clock and the end of the game . . . if the owners of CBS will lift my salary cap.

Women's Magazines

There was a story in the paper the other day about a woman who won a suit against a San Francisco law firm for $7 million because one of the partners kept making dirty remarks and wouldnt keep his hands off her.

Women have made a lot of progress. It was too long coming. At CBS News now, almost half the people who work here are women and a lot of women have good jobs. They arent just doing the dog work anymore.

Now, having said all that—and I know Im going to get in trouble for this—but I want you to see the magazine stand downstairs here at CBS. Right here in their main display case. Look at some of these magazines for women. I brought some of them up to the office here.

HOW TO FIND A MAN WHO'LL REALLY LOVE YOU.

A SEXY STOMACH.

LOVE HABITS—WHICH BUILD PASSION, WHICH ERODE IT?

Is this what the women who fought to get ahead in broadcasting are reading?

HOW TO GET THE MAN TO MARRY YOU. You mean, without ever harassing you?

WHY WOMEN PUT UP WITH MEN WHO BEAT THEM. Nice?

BIG BONUS HOROSCOPE 3-MONTH SEX, LOVE & MONEY PREDICTIONS.

SEXIER SEX. THE 3 STEPS TO GREAT LOVING.

Is the person who reads this junk anyone I want to have as my boss?

They have some suggestions in here for what women might want to wear. SHIRT IN SHEER SILK AND POLYESTER $725. She ought to be arrested.

MAKEUP: 4 GREAT LOOKS FROM SEXPOT TO ANGEL FACE.

ADULTERY—DO'S AND DON'TS

Here's a successful woman having a conversation with a guy. His jacket is longer than her skirt. How would it be if his pants were as short as her skirt?

It seems to me feminists ought to start looking around in the ladies' room. The enemy may be in there.

Lawyers

They start picking the jury for the O. J. Simpson trial tomorrow. I hope O. J. is innocent. I dont think he's innocent but I hope he is. And you know something? If I was on the jury, I could be absolutely fair. Fair jurors are not what the lawyers want, though.

And its the lawyers who bother me most. In this trial, for instance, are they trying to find out whether O. J. murdered two people or are they trying to find out which lawyer is smartest?

Its as if the facts in the case dont matter at all. Its which lawyer is cleverest at obscuring the truth. I might find one of the *lawyers* guilty if I was on the jury.

The lawyers are too important in this trial and theyre too important in our lives. Laws should be written simply enough so we could all understand them without hiring a lawyer every time we turn around.

There are plenty of good lawyers. I have a lawyer I'd trust with my life but there are too many bad ones. The good lawyers should do something about the bad ones. There are more bad lawyers than bad doctors.

There are some questions I'd like to ask about lawyers.

— For instance, if a defense lawyer knows his client is guilty of murder, does he try to get him off anyway?
— If a lawyer believes his client is innocent, why should he be afraid to let his client testify?
— And another question: How come so many lawyers get rich on personal injury cases that cost all of us a fortune in taxes and insurance?

The lawyers encourage people to say they got hurt so they can get rich suing someone. But its the lawyers who get rich.

They all say they wont charge if they dont collect.

There are lawyers who specialize in suing doctors for malpractice. The American Medical Association says that 53,000 doctors got sued for malpractice last year.

I asked the American Bar Association how many *lawyers* got sued for malpractice? You know what they told me? They said they dont keep track.

Is that a typical lawyer's answer? You can bet it wasnt 53,000. Its hard to get a lawyer to sue another lawyer.

We have 200,000 more lawyers in this Country than we have doctors. Its enough to make you sick.

Dictionaries

One of the things I like to do least is look up a word in the dictionary. If youre trying to find out how to spell a word, its hard to look it up if you dont know how to spell it. And then you have to wade through all those little symbols and you dont know what they mean.

I looked up the word H-A-R-A-S-S to see whether its spelled with one or two R's or one or two S's and whether its pronounced HArass or haRASS. I still dont know.

Anyone can call a dictionary Webster's. Theres Merriam Webster's Collegiate, Webster's New World, Webster's New World Second College Edition, Random House Webster's, Random House Webster's Concise Dictionary. The concise one is bigger than the one that isnt concise.

One is called The American College Dictionary. For people who are supposed to be word experts, thats not very expert. It isnt a dictionary for American colleges. Its an English dictionary for American college students.

Then theres The American Heritage College Dictionary. Their New College Edition is actually older than the one that doesnt say "New." I have a dictionary thirty years old that proclaims its newness. They ought to print the name with disappearing ink. The word "New" would disappear after ten years. The argument in the dictionary business is whether to explain the proper use of English or whether to tell you how its being used by the most people—often inaccurately. For instance, I never say "If I were smart." I always say "If I was smart." I dont like the subjunctive no matter what the dictionary likes.

The dirty words are in dictionaries now, too. They didnt use to be. This old dictionary, for instance, goes from FUCHSIA to FUDDLE to FUDGE: "a homemade candy."

Its interesting that we dont use words on television that you hear all the time in the movies. Some movies would be lost without dirty words.

And who decides which pictures to put in a dictionary? Here's an umbrella. Why in the world do they think they have to illustrate an umbrella? They show a picture of a circle but they dont have a picture of a square. Here's a picture of Barbara Walters but none of Walter Cronkite. Now thats not right.

Here's a picture of O. J. Simpson. "American football player. First to run over 2,000 yards in a season."

I wonder what Webster's is going to say about O. J. in the next New American College Edition.

Lotteries

The voters of eleven states are deciding on bills that involve gambling Tuesday. Thirty-seven states already have lotteries and twenty-three states have casino gambling. Gambling is the fastest growing business in the Country and the rottenest as far as Im concerned. Twice as much money was gambled last year as ten years ago.

There are very few things that make me as mad as state-run lotteries. Its bad enough when an organized mob steals from people but when our own Government gets into something as bad and stupid as gambling, its seriously wrong.

The casinos give you a better break than State lotteries. You put money in a slot machine and all you lose over the long run is maybe 15 percent. A racetrack only takes 20 percent. The states running these numbers rackets take 50 percent or 60 percent. The suckers get peanuts.

Lottery officials say the money goes to schools, of course. Well, have you noticed that the schools got a lot better in the States that have lotteries? I dont think so. Do you think schools get more money than they would if it werent for the lottery? They do not.

There was a lottery jackpot of $72 million in New York state this week, and the lottery got millions of dollars of free publicity.

I'd make it illegal to print or broadcast the name of one lottery winner unless they also gave the name of every lottery loser.

They said four winners were each getting $18 million. Why didnt they give a million dollars to seventy-two people? Theyre so deceitful. And then they have staged events with the winners. A New York state lottery official supposedly gives a winner a check for $18 million.

He's not getting a check for $18 million. The state keeps the money and gives him a small portion of it every year. They get almost as much interest on what they keep as they pay him. And the sad thing is its the people who cant afford it who do most of the betting. Take a look at the lines of people buying lottery tickets if you think Im wrong.

When states are trying to get gambling approved, they argue that people are going to gamble anyway and the state might as well get in on it. So how come now that New York has a lottery, it spends $20 million dollars a year *advertising*—trying to talk people into gambling more?

MAN #1:
Win for life from the New York Lottery. You keep living. We'll keep paying.

MAN #2:
Hey, you never know.

ROONEY:
Trying to acquire money through luck instead of work is a bad idea to promote and gambling is a business no government should encourage.

Early Christmas

Its still five weeks away but already you can see Christmas coming. You can always tell when its getting close because the morning television shows start doing pieces about dangerous toys. The thing about showing a dangerous toy like that is after seeing it, every kid in America wants one.

When I was young, they didnt have morning television shows so we didnt know the toys were dangerous. I could have swallowed a yo-yo or fallen off a pogo stick and hurt myself because I didnt know they were dangerous.

All this dangerous toy information is released every year by an outfit called the Institute for Injury Reduction outside Washington. Theyve done a good job making the toy industry be more careful about the toys they make and theyve done a good job for themselves too.

The Institute for Injury Reduction, which held a press conference this week, is supported by members of ATLA, the Association of Trial Lawyers of America.

LAWYER:
We look to the courts or we should look to the courts to be bringing sanc-

tions against manufacturers who injure children through unsafe toys through the lawsuits of victims and their families. And more and more not giving adequate awards that will shake up the manufacturers and send them the message that this behavior is unacceptable.

ROONEY:

Bringing dangerous toys to everyone's attention is good business for trial lawyers because when people see that toys can be dangerous, more people decide to sue and more juries, who have also seen the dangerous toys on television, are apt to pay them—and the lawyers, of course—big awards.

If there were no toys, no child would ever be hurt by one. Congressman Newt Gingrich wants more orphanages. Well, in that same Christmas spirit, there are a couple of laws I'd like passed.

Make it illegal for any store to mention giving Christmas presents in an ad until after Thanksgiving. Second, no more than ten Christmas catalogs could be sent to any one house. After ten, theyd be automatically shredded at the post office. Third, it would be against the law to use Santa Claus in any display until the first week in December.

A final bit of legislation. There are already places selling Christmas trees. Make it illegal for anyone to cut down a Christmas tree before the end of the first week in December. The penalty for breaking the law would be—theyd have to come and clean the needles off the rug in your living room.

Old Magazine Ads

Are we any better to each other now in America, any more civilized, than we were when the Puritans burned witches? From day to day, its hard to notice any improvement.

The other day I was looking for an idea and I went through a pile of old magazines from the 1950s. The advertising was a shock.

For instance, there were 100 ads with women in them. In 59 of those ads, the women were wearing aprons. They were often standing in front of a refrigerator, a washing machine or a dish washer. Women did a lot of ironing in the ads. They sorted the laundry.

If the women werent doing housework, they were taking care of the children. There were a few ads showing women at work in an office . . . but they were always secretaries. There wasnt one woman who had an executive job.

The men were always the executives in their suits and neckties. The housewives saw them off to work. There were no pictures of men wearing aprons. No women with desks.

Ads taught kids what their role in life was going to be, too. In a Mazda bulb ad, the little girl dusted the bulb . . . the little boy read by it.

Our attitude toward cigarettes has changed dramatically.

An old ad had Lou Gehrig saying "They Dont Get Your Wind."

"Camels: So Mild You Can Smoke All You Want."

There were even cigarettes in the whiskey ads.

It doesnt seem to some black Americans that theyve made any progress. But I was looking through fifty old magazines and didnt find one single picture of a black man or woman in an ad. Not one!

In a big ad for a cruise ship with a picture of the

Lou Gehrig, baseball star, who prefers Came

ship and the ship's staff there was not one woman, and not one black face on board.

Many ads presented the average American family: six white people. Today they always have at least one black person in every picture showing more than three people.

It isnt much, I suppose, but looking at old ads you'd have to say things have changed for the better in some small ways. Maybe we are a little more sensitive, a little nicer to each other.

Two of Everything

Tonight I'd like to talk about how many of something you should have. We're all aware of the people who dont have anything. We talk very little about those of us who have one of everything . . . and in many cases two of them.

For example, 33 million American families own one car. Thirty-eight million American families have two cars. And a ridiculous statistic: 20 million American families own three cars. How many of something to have is a big decision in everyone's life and it isnt just major items like cars.

Shoes is a good example of something people tend to buy more of than they need. Look in almost anyone's closet. Its full of shoes that they dont wear. I dont know what gets into us when it comes to shoes.

All anyone really needs is a pair of shoes to wear when he or she is dressed up and a pair of shoes to work in. You might possibly need a third pair of sneakers to play a game in but thats it. Three. So why do we buy so many shoes?

Television sets. I know people who have television sets in the living room, the kitchen, the bedroom and the bathroom. Imagine how many theyd have if there was anything good to watch on television.

I have three raincoats. I have no idea why I bought three raincoats inasmuch as a raincoat isnt much help if its raining anyway. You get almost as wet in a raincoat as you do without one.

Pens and pencils. How many pens and pencils do you need? I keep these cups here on the desk filled with pens and pencils. I can only use one at a time.

A lot of families have two bank accounts for no good reason. It makes them think they have more money, I guess.

We have friends who recently had their kitchen done over and they had two stoves put in—ranges. One's gas and the other's electric. What I'd like is two refrigerators. One for the new stuff and the other for leftovers.

Im always buying tools I dont need. And I own four tennis rackets. I always think the new one is finally going to make me a good player.

At Christmas you'd think it would be best to avoid giving someone something they already had several of but thats not true. If people have five of something, the chances are they like it and the thing to give them for Christmas is another one of those.

1995

Democrats vs. Republicans

If you believe in the whole idea of democracy, you have to agree even if youre a Democrat and a sore loser that the American people have spoken and what they have said is, they want more of the things Republicans stand for and less of the things Democrats stand for. The question, of course, is what are those things.

Ive tried to work it out on a chart here. Okay, this is the way I set it up.

	REPUBLICANS		DEMOCRATS	
	FOR	AGAINST	FOR	AGAINST
Welfare		X	X	
Abortion		X	X	
Guns	X			X
Foreign Aid		X	X	
Foreign Trade	X			X
Unions		X	X	
Big Business	X			X
Big Government		X	X	
Crime		X		X
Death Penalty	X			X

Thats pretty broad, of course, and you have to allow for exceptions but if you were explaining the two parties to a foreigner, theyd get a rough idea if you showed them that chart.

Its strange what happened in this last election. For a long time, Republicans were rich people in favor of Big Business. They said that if we all grab as much as we can get for ourselves, it ends up best for everyone—including poor people. In other words, Republicans made a virtue out of greed.

Blue-collar workers and low-level office workers, on the other hand, were always Democrats. They voted for Franklin Delano Roosevelt years ago and the Government got ten times bigger doing things people used to do for themselves. Like saving for old age.

Before Roosevelt, the Government just delivered the mail and fought our wars. Republicans hated FDR and they said Big Government would make things worse because no one would work as hard if they could get money without working.

Liberal Democrats were nicer people. They wanted the Government to help the poor but they were dreamers, too, and what they hoped would happen, didnt happen. Under the Democrats, strangely enough, things got better for Republicans. Big Government worked well for Big Business and worse for Democrats so a lot of Democrats became Republicans. So on Election Day last month, working people joined company presidents and voted the Democrats out of power in Washington.

Or, quite possibly, Im wrong, of course.

Cold Remedies

I feel sorry for a lot of people who have colds at this time of year. Theyre always coughing. They cant sleep nights. Their throats hurt. The only time people who have a bad cold feel good is when theyre taking a hot shower . . . and how long can you stay in a hot shower?

People are about equally divided when it comes to going to work with a bad cold. Half come in. Half stay home. The good guys come in. They share their cold.

I go to a drugstore every year when I get my cold to see if theyve come up with a miracle cure yet. Drugstores have shelves full of new and improved medicines for colds.

Theyre using the same vague words, though. They dont call them cures, they call them "remedies." They dont give relief, they give "temporary relief." And it doesnt relieve your cold, it relieves "symptoms" of a cold.

Tylenol Cough and Dristan Cold say theyre "maximum strength." Well, of course. Who wants "minimum strength"? Give me everything you got, Tylenol.

The Robitussin is "cherry flavored." And the Dimetapp Elixir says it has a great grape taste. I cant taste a thing with this cold and theyre giving me grape-flavored cough syrup.

Theres no grape in it, of course. Cant you see three scientists in a laboratory trying to make phenylpropanolamine taste like grape?

The NyQuil bottle says its "original flavor." It doesnt say what the flavor is, just "original." I use Vicks VapoRub sometimes. You rub it on your chest. It smells so bad and makes such a mess of your pajamas, it must be good for you.

I always think the most expensive medicine is going to be the best. Look at these little devils. Chlor-Trimeton. The smallest package and it was $14.49. They wouldnt dare charge that much if they didnt work, would they? They would?

Sudafed Plus. "May cause drowsiness . . . May cause excitability." I cant tell whether this stuff knocks you out or turns you on.

Someone always asks me if Ive seen a doctor. Doctors cant help a cold. They tell you to go home, drink plenty of fluids and get lots of rest. What do they care if you have to get up to go to the bathroom all night and youre apt to get fired for not showing up for work?

You call for an appointment with your doctor at this time of the year and youre apt to find he's not in the office.

He's home with a bad cold.

Birthdays

Yesterday was my birthday. Im not going to tell you how old I was because I hate being that old but I will tell you its plenty. When anyone comes up to me and says, "Happy Birthday," I just look them in the eye and I say, "You must be kidding."

What in the world is there to be happy about being a year older? Age is a defect which we never get over. The only thing worse than having another birthday is not having another one.

The last birthday thats any good is about twenty-three. Its all downhill from there on out. No one wants to be twenty-four.

People try to encourage you when you get old. They say things like "Wis-

dom comes with age." Thats not true. At twenty-five youre about as smart as youre going to get.

People also try to make you feel good by saying, "Youre only as old as you feel." Thats nonsense. You arent as old as you feel. Youre as old as you are. Thats how old you are.

Its hard to get used to being old. I look out on the world through the same eyes. I dont see myself much. I think of myself as looking the way I looked like in college when I was nineteen. Or how I looked in the Army when I was twenty-two.

I'd tell you what year that was but you'd all sit there adding and subtracting to find out how old I am now and you wouldnt listen to anything else I have to say.

These days when I see someone who looks old, I realize he's my age.

People are mean to old folks. They start calling them "folks" and "elderly" when theyre about sixty. I'll meet someone on the street and they'll say, "You look wonderful." I know what they mean. They mean, "For someone as old as you are, you dont look bad."

They keep saying "still" to me. "Oh, you still working?" "Oh, you still playing tennis?" I get on the bus and pay half fare and the driver doesnt even want to see proof that Im over sixty-five. I'll be carrying a box or a suitcase and someone will say, "Let me help you with that." I should be grateful but I feel like saying, "How would you like a punch in the nose, Fella?"

Theres nothing wrong with being my age. I feel fine. I love working. I love playing. I love life. The bad thing about it is, Im constantly aware that there isnt much of it left. I just signed a new contract with CBS for three years. I suggested four. They didnt tell me why but they thought three was more appropriate than four. I know what they were thinking.

One of the good things at my age is having friends who are older than you are. It makes you feel superior. Thats why I feel so good about having Mike

Wallace as a friend. Mike stands between me and eternity . . . and Mike's got a four-year contract.

The Jury System

Im not as enthusiastic about the jury system as I used to be. In the movies or on television when Perry Mason talked to the jury, the good guy always won and justice triumphed.

It doesnt seem to go that way any more. We've fooled around with the jury system so much that it doesnt work the way its supposed to.

Most countries dont even have juries. Ninety percent of all the jury trials held in the world are right here in the United States. In Sweden, they have one judge and a panel of three or five people who decide. Theyre elected and they get paid.

In Germany, there are three judges and two jurors. Japan, Spain and Israel have all given up the jury system . . . not that I want to live in Japan, Spain or Israel.

In England, they only have juries for murder trials. In this Country, theres a jury for someone accused of stealing an apple from a fruitstand.

Our jury system is a mess, no question about it. If youve ever served on one, you know that. You sit around forever. Then, half the time, the lawyers go out back and settle the case without you.

The jury system is different in every state, too.

In Utah and Arizona, there are eight people on a jury. In Oregon and Louisiana, a jury's decision doesnt have to be unanimous.

Massachusetts pays jurors $50 a day. California pays them $5. In New York, you get $15 and two subway tokens.

Maybe we should have paid experts who decide cases the way they do in Sweden. They could be lawyers. We've got plenty of lawyers.

The deal always was that if you were charged with a crime, you were judged by twelve of your peers—meaning your equals. Sounds great. Well, thats not what a jury is anymore.

Juries now are handpicked by lawyers. How are you going to get twelve average people if you let the lawyers and the person accused of the crime choose them? If the client is Italian, a lawyer wants all Italians. If he's black, the lawyer wants all blacks. If he's white, the lawyer wants a white jury. If we're going to have juries, twelve people should be picked absolutely at random.

The jury in the O. J. Simpson case has six black women, three black men, one half-black, half Hispanic man, another man who's half white and half Indian, and one white woman. They arent O. J. Simpson's peers. Theyve made a joke of the jury system.

Im not one of those people who says he's tired of this O. J. Simpson case. Its fascinating and its not about O. J. Simpson. Its about Justice in America.

Old Farmer's Almanac

We've had a terrible winter in our part of the Country and by "terrible," I mean I hate it when I dont have to shovel snow a couple of times. I even like reading about how Im flirting with a heart attack when I shovel.

There are two kinds of people when it comes to weather. There are those who like to lie around in the sun at the beach getting skin cancer . . . and then there are the people who enjoy trying to beat the elements.

Those people go on camping trips, they sleep in tents, canoe down rivers, sail, climb mountains, ski.

Fair-weather people stay indoors when it rains. They wear scarves when the temperature goes below 50 degrees and they wont go out in the driveway to get their newspaper when it snows.

Theres something satisfying about beating the weather. I get a good feeling when the rain is hitting my windshield and Im all dry inside my car. Even being under an umbrella in the rain is satisfying fun.

Having bad weather *is* good for people, too. We're nicer to each other when theres a deep snow. A flood brings out the best in everyone. People get more done when the weather's cold and miserable than they do when its warm and pleasant, too. They just lie around when its warm.

Look at the places in the world that have tropical weather and look at the countries that have cold weather. See which ones accomplish the most.

I hesitate to single out one of our United States but look at the one with the absolutely best weather. Its Hawaii. Now tell me how many people invented the telephone or built the world's tallest building in Hawaii.

Like it or not, we all want to know what the weather's going to be in advance. There are people who rely on *The Old Farmer's Almanac* and I was looking at how the Almanac did with their predictions this year.

General Weather Predictions 1994–1995
November through March is expected to be extremely variable, with dramatic swings in temperature and precipitation in many areas.

How's that for going out on a limb with a precise prediction?
The Old Farmer's Almanac said that total snowfall for our area was going to be "heavier than usual." All the hardware stores around here stocked up on snow shovels.

Well, if we're going to have a lot of snow, its got to come fast. Last year we had fifty-three inches of snow around New York. This year so far we've had eleven inches. So much for *Old Farmer's* predicting the weather.

Apocalypse

On April 19, 1995, 168 people were killed when a bomb blast destroyed a Federal office building in Oklahoma City.

Im not a person who gets depressed easily, but sometimes, lying in bed at night, especially if I lie on my back, I have dark thoughts. There have always been nuts who predicted that the world was coming to an end, but you cant help thinking that one of these days, it could happen. Ive had most of the years of my life, but what about four grandchildren? They should have something like eighty years ahead of them, but do they? Who knows what's going to happen on Earth before the sun goes out in another million years. There are a lot of ways it could stop or maybe just keep spinning, but without any of us alive on it.

How could anyone smart enough to make a bomb that would do this in Oklahoma City be so evil as to plant it—and under a day-care center?

Oklahoma City is just part of it.

The poison-gas attack in the Tokyo subway was done by the same people—different race, different religion, different cause, but basically the same people. Terrorists tried to take down the Earth's biggest building complex, the World Trade Center in New York. (1995) They had other plans, too. How would you like to be in the Lincoln Tunnel under the river going to New Jersey the day they explode a bomb and let the water in there? Its so discouraging, reading the headlines day after day. What have we done to have spawned so many evil people? We dont like to read bad news, but theres too much of it to avoid. The Russians are selling the stuff with which to make a nuclear bomb to Iran.

How safe does that make you feel?

In Washington, what would happen if the White House and the Capitol were wiped out?

And we can do without the jokes. It doesnt matter much who did it in Oklahoma City. The idea that there are people alive who would do it is what scares you. You look at a crowd and you think, "Am I looking at any of them?" Theyve already beaten us, too; dont forget that. From now on until forever, we're all going to have less freedom, less freedom to go in and out of buildings, less freedom from being watched, less freedom from being searched.

Terrorists have already done that to us in airports, costing us time, money and liberty.

And we relinquish our freedom voluntarily, of course. Thats the worst way to lose your freedom: voluntarily. The bad guys have won because theyve reduced us to their level. Theyve brought out our least attractive characteristics. Our attorney general wants blood . . .

JANET RENO (Attorney General):
(From news broadcast) . . . the death penalty is available, and we will seek it.

Our President demands revenge.

President CLINTON:
(From news broadcast) Justice will be swift, certain and severe.

We all feel that way. They make all of us seethe with the same hate for them that they have for us. I could kill the bastards. Thats the worst thing theyve done to us.

Balanced Budget Amendment

I was noticing the IRS just cashed the check I sent in with my income tax return a couple of weeks ago. It seems like so much to me, but its so little to them. The reason its so little is our national debt.

The national debt is $4.5 trillion. The figure doesnt mean much to any of us, but thats the amount of money our government has borrowed.

It pays $230 billion a year in interest on that loan.

The question is this: Who loaned it to us and who does the government pay that interest *to*? Well, I was looking into that. The Japanese get a lot of it.

The Japanese net $23 million a day for interest or loans they gave us. They loaned us billions. Did you know that?

Twenty-three million dollars a day to the Japanese, every single day of the year, including Christmas and Mother's Day. The British get $10 million, the Germans $7 million.

Ive been trying to think of ways to reduce the national debt. The first idea would be to make everyone's tax return public. We could all read what our neighbors paid, and they could see how much we paid. I dont think people would cheat so much if we all knew. Its one thing to be caught by the IRS and its another to be caught by your neighbor. The President makes his tax returns public and you just know his accountant was careful to pay every nickel because he knew we'd all be watching.

Here's another way the government could raise big money.

Why should Donald Trump and the Indians make all the money on gambling? Why doesnt the government get in on that? Make it so we'd be able to bet on everything. And just like the casinos, the government would take 17 percent of each dollar bet.

We'd be able to go into a government betting parlor, put down money on whether the jury will find O. J. Simpson innocent or guilty of murder; we could bet on whether that trial will ever end. When a bill comes up in Congress, we could bet on whether it'll pass or not. On Election Day, in addition to voting for who they want for President, people could bet on who they thought would be President. The voting machines would be set up to record your vote and your bet at the same time.

Call it parimutuel voting. You could put a few dollars down on the next election right now.

Bob Dole would be the favorite to be the Republican candidate about 3 to 1. The balanced budget amendment was defeated but we've got to find a way to reduce our debt because its killing us.

The ironic thing is, it isnt even doing the Japanese much good. The dollar is worth only a third of what it was worth when they bought all those U.S. bonds, so the Japanese are only getting back about 35 cents for each dollar they loaned us. I feel terrible about that.

The English Language

I was sitting at my typewriter the other day, and I got thinking that maybe the best thing the human race ever invented for itself is language—the written and spoken word. It separates man from other animals. George Bernard Shaw said, "No matter how loud a dog barks, he cant tell you that his parents were poor but honest."

Here are the ten languages spoken by the most people as their native tongue.

Number one is Chinese, spoken by 840 million natives. Number two is Indian, 340 million; the language is called Hindi. Number three is Spanish, 335 million; the population of Spain itself is only 40 million. English is fourth, 325 million. But another 200 million speak English as their second language. English is the most popular second language in the world.

The Japanese are smart about language. They want to sell us stuff, so they learn how to speak English. Americans, on the other hand, are stupid when it comes to learning other people's language. It may account for our trade deficit.

Number five: Bengali, 190 million; lot of Indians speak that. Number six: Arabic, 185 million. Number seven: Russian, 170 million. Portuguese; 170 million people speak Portuguese. Thats a surprise because the population of Portugal itself is fewer than 10 million. I guess the others are in Brazil and Newark, New Jersey. Number nine: Japanese, 125 million; no one speaks Japanese except the Japanese. And last, number 10, German; 98 million people speak German. If theyll pardon me for saying so, German is one of the worst languages.

Do you notice anything strange about this list? Neither French or Italian are among the ten most spoken languages in the world. We're lucky here in the United States because English is the best language. It has twice as many words as any other language.

You can say things quicker, too.

English isnt perfect. We all know how screwed up it can be. For one thing, theres too much difference between the way words are spoken and the way theyre written.

Look at this word, for example: C-O-L-O-N-E-L. How do we pronounce that? "Kernel." So if you were learning English, how would you pronounce this: C-O-L-O-N-I-A-L? You'd think it was "kernial," wouldnt you?

I know this is an unpopular idea to have in a lot of places, but I think that if youve chosen to live in the United States, you ought to learn to speak English. A lot of people think thats a Fascist thought to have and Im sorry, but I have it. Sayonara.

Safety

Congress voted this week to lift its 55 mph speed limit and let the states decide how fast people can drive. Most states have raised the speed limit on major highways to 65 . . . some have not.

Gov. Christine Whitman of New Jersey, for instance, insists on keeping the 55 mph limit.

If you want everyone to be safe, shouldnt you reduce the speed to 45? How about 35? Wouldnt fewer people be killed if no one could drive more than 12 miles an hour? Why dont you make cars illegal in New Jersey, Governor Whitman? No one would be killed. Are you against that?

I drive in New Jersey enough to know that if the Governor gets out there on a highway without a police escort and drives 55 mph, she's going to get run over.

Fifty-five on a highway is asking people to break the law.

Last year 761 people were killed in highway accidents in New Jersey with the 55 mph limit. Is that okay, Governor?

All of us are constantly being inconvenienced by laws and safety measures passed because of a few irresponsible idiots . . . drunk drivers, the ones who weave in and out of traffic at 80 miles an hour. Whatever the speed limit is, theyre going to ignore it. What we need isnt a lower speed limit . . . we need fewer idiots. And how you going to legislate that?

I have here a blade guard for a power saw. A company cant sell a tool without one. It raises the cost of the tool by as much as 20 percent and the first thing most woodworkers like myself do is take it off.

Last year a twelve-year-old boy was hit in the chest by a baseball and he died. It was very sad. Some group of parents organized to try and make every kid in America who plays baseball, wear an expensive chest protector.

Safety caps on pill bottles have saved lives but theyve inconvenienced millions of us every day because of a few stupid parents who didnt keep dangerous medicine away from their kids.

Some people are too dumb to have kids. How about some kind of a limit on them?

Reward

Its popular now to say "I dont want to hear anymore about it."

Well, Im sorry to tell you, but Im one of the people who is not tired of the O. J. Simpson case. Theres still a lot we dont know . . . the jury didnt find him innocent . . . they found him NOT GUILTY.

A lot of Americans, most of them white, are convinced that O. J. got away with murder.

Even when someone is convicted of a serious crime, there are always people who make that person into a hero. After spending six months in prison, Marion Barry was reelected Mayor of Washington, D.C. Over the years, several Congressmen have returned to the Capitol after serving time and Jean Harris, the woman who spent twelve years in prison for murdering Dr. Herman Tarnhower, is a popular, highly paid lecturer now among the same women's groups who are picketing O. J. Simpson's house because he was a wife-beater.

The NOT GUILTY verdict puts a great burden on the Los Angeles police force. We all form our opinions from small, personal experience and I dont like the Los Angeles police force because I was once arrested there for jay walking.

I could swear the cop who gave me the ticket was Mark Fuhrman. He hated Irish-Americans.

Someone killed Ronald Goldman and Nicole Brown Simpson and if O. J. didnt do it, the Los Angeles police force has to stop spending its time arresting jay walkers and find out who did.

Im one of the people who wasnt happy with the verdict. I wish Simpson had gone on the witness stand instead of on the *Larry King Show*. The acquittal is the worst thing thats happened to race relations in forty years. And its worst for black Americans . . . I dont think they know that.

The best thing that could possibly happen would be if white Americans found out we were wrong . . . that Simpson really did *not* murder those two people. I'd love to be wrong in this case.

There have been several rewards offered in this case and I herewith add one of my own. I pledge to you this: To any person who identifies the killer of Ronald Goldman and Nicole Brown Simpson, which information leads to the conviction of that murderer, I will personally pay the sum of one million dollars.

Doctors

Coming to work this morning, nine people said to me, "Good morning. How are you today?" I said "fine" nine times.

Why do we ask this dumb question when no one ever answers it honestly? The fact is, I feel terrible. I have a toothache and my jaw is swollen. I feel like saying, "How do you think I feel, you idiot?"

Sometimes I go for years without seeing a doctor but in the last month Ive seen five.

In September I went to see my all-purpose doctor for a checkup. He

looked me over and said I was fine but you know how that is. Youre always hearing about people who die the day after their doctor says theyre in perfect health.

I dont have any trouble with my eyes but my doctor said I probably ought to see an ophthalmologist. You could spend your life going to doctors and having them check out various parts of your body that they specialize in.

I got a notice from my dentist that its time for a checkup, which I ignored. My idea of when its time to go to the dentist is when a tooth hurts. Well, wouldnt you know it? A tooth started to hurt. I had to go to him and I was afraid he'd be sore because I didnt come in for a checkup.

He took x-rays—I love the way the dentist always leaves the room—and then spoke four of the most dreaded words in the English language. "You need root canal."

He showed me this picture to prove it. Do you ever see what they see in an x-ray? It could be the Rocky Mountains at dusk.

My left knee's been killing me so I went to see an orthopedist. He looked at both knees, twisted them around and told me the knee thats bothering me is fine but that my other knee is in bad shape.

This is exactly why people are reluctant to go see a doctor.

Anyway, if we meet on the street in the next few days, do me a favor, will you? Dont say, "Hi Andy. How are you today?"

Irish

It isnt often that I use this platform I have here on *60 Minutes* for something personal but thats what Im going to do tonight.

Youve probably seen the demonstrations Indians and semi-Indians staged outside the World Series ball parks protesting the use of the nicknames "Indians" for the Cleveland team and "Braves" for the Atlanta team.

Those nicknames seem harmless to me and in no way disparaging of great Indian traditions.

Americans have a high opinion of the Indian minority.

Having said that, though, let me tell you what does bother me personally. In all the statistics, the polls and everything, Im listed as a white American male. Its the worst thing to be these days and Im tired of it. Im considered to be the majority and I dont want to be a majority, I want to be a minority. They always get a better deal.

Women get in on being listed "a minority" even though more than half the people in America are women. What kind of minority is that?

There are 33 million black Americans. Theyre called a minority. There are 27 million Americans of Hispanic origin and they get to be called a minority.

My great-grandparents on my father's side were born in Ireland. We are a proud people, we Irish. We're a minority of just a few million who have one parade a year.

I dont want to be listed simply as "white" or male or American. If everyone else is going to be called something, I want to be called an Irish-American.

For years, we Irish had the great Irish Sweepstakes. You never hear about the Irish Sweepstakes anymore. What I'd like to see is tax-free, Irish gambling compounds established for the benefit of the Irish-American minority in the United States.

And one more thing. I call on all Irish-Americans to boycott Notre Dame football games until they stop using that demeaning nickname, "The Fighting Irish." What do they mean "Fighting Irish"? Is anyone called "The Fighting Italians"? "The Fighting French"? No.

Are they suggesting we Irish are more belligerent than other people? I object!

I want Notre Dame to stop using the term "Fighting Irish." I not only want it stopped, I demand it! If Notre Dame doesnt stop using that nickname, Im going on the warpath.

Oops! I didnt mean to use that word.

Smoke Gets in the Eye

This was written seven years before Enron.

Theres a war going on in Washington between the Democrats and the Republicans. Im personally ambivalent about being a Republican or a Democrat. I can go either way.

Im a Republican to the extent I think theres too much government but Im a Democrat to the extent that I dont think we can do without a lot of centralized power in Washington. For one thing, we need Big Government to protect us from Big Business.

Business is more dangerous than Government because we cant vote business out of office if we dont like it. Even worse, we dont know much about Big Business and cant find out.

Tough reporting on government is good for the Country. Washington reporters dont let politicians get away with much and good local newspaper reporters are always after their politicians. The only danger is that with so much negative stuff, its easy for us to get thinking that all government is bad. We loose our confidence in it. Not true.

Theres no comparable amount of reporting about the evils of Big Business. Investigative reporters can demand access to government records and the thieves and inept politicians are eventually found out and driven out of office. But news organizations have a hard time trying to report on business. Business records are private and its rare that inept management or dishonesty is uncovered.

All I know is, the events of recent years dont make a good argument for business, capitalism or the free enterprise system.

Handicapped Parking

The United States has led the way in making life better for handicapped people. It isnt perfect but its better.

In 1990 Americans were rightfully proud of a new law, the Americans with Disabilities Act. Theres nothing like it anywhere else in the world. Among other things, it orders businesses to provide a certain number of handicapped parking spaces near their door.

The tough question today is this: Are too many parking spaces being set aside for the handicapped and is it really the handicapped who are using them?

I went out with a camera crew to see what we could find.

First we went to an airport parking lot near New York. This was the area marked off for handicapped parking. There seemed to be plenty.

Only three parking spaces were needed. Two cars had handicapped stickers issued in Florida.

While we were there, one more car pulled in and a man walked off towards the terminal. We couldnt detect much of a limp. Maybe his handicap was mental.

The official license plate for a handicapped person's vehicle has on it the symbol of a wheelchair. In eight hours of shooting in half a dozen locations we saw thousands of handicapped parking places, and lots of license plates with wheelchairs on them. We saw only one wheelchair.

At a mall we watched for more than an hour as people pulled in and out of handicapped parking places. If some of them were handicapped, it must have been with a bad cold. Some may have disabilities that dont show of course, heart problems maybe.

We didnt see many legitimately handicapped people who really needed a parking space near the door.

Its one of those maddening things: We do something thats right, by providing handicapped parking spaces and then people ruin it for everyone by abusing the privilege. Being too fat shouldnt qualify a person.

Or, someone else in the family uses the car with the handicapped plate. They might get a doctor to issue a temporary permit for little or no reason. We saw one man park his pickup at a mall before we had our camera set up so we waited until he came out. We thought maybe he'd gone in to buy a wheelchair. We just couldnt tell what his disability was. Maybe it was that he didnt know right from wrong. This seems wrong.

If no one but truly handicapped people put their cars in handicapped parking spaces, there would be a lot more parking for everyone.

Lemon

Considering that its a slang word for a bad car, its surprising how few things in life are so consistently good as . . . a lemon.

Theyre just beautiful fruits.

Well, apparently the companies trying to sell us stuff at the supermarket know how highly people regard lemons because hundreds of companies are trying to associate their product with them.

Take a look at the shelves in any grocery store and you'll see Brillo Lemon, Ajax Lemon, Joy Lemon, Clorox Lemon Fresh and lemon-smelling nail polish remover.

Here's Cascade Lemon dishwashing detergent. And look at the ingredients. Nowhere does it mention that theres any lemon in it. You know why? Thats because there isnt any lemon in it.

Plastic kitchen bags . . . garbage bags. Fresh lemon scent, it says. Do you think one of these bags is going to smell like a lemon after a load of garbage sits in it for two days?

Here's Lemon Jell-O. Now, that seems like a good idea but the truth of the matter is, theres the same amount of lemon in Lemon Jell-O as there is in Cascade Dishwashing detergent . . . none at all. Its artificial lemon flavoring.

It says on the side of the box that they put in something called "Adipic acid and fumaric acid for tartness." Why dont they call it Fumaric Acid Jell-O?

The funny thing is, I bought a one-ounce bottle of fake lemon extract that cost me $2.49. And then I bought a *two*-ounce bottle of *pure* lemon extract . . . twice as much and it cost me only $1.89. The fake was more than twice as expensive as the real lemon. I wonder if Jell-O knows about that?

Lemon Fresh Comet. No lemon, of course . . . except a picture of one.

Parson's Lemon Fresh Ammonia? What in the world does lemon have to do with ammonia? Ammonia has its own smell which is just fine for ammonia but no one wants ammonia that smells like lemon.

A lot of things like that are great one place and wrong someplace else.

Gas in the tank of your car for instance is fine . . . on your hands, its terrible. Gravy is great on mashed potatoes but its ugly on the tablecloth.

Thats the way it is with lemon. Its great in lemonade, iced tea, cake, cookies, squeezed on fish and in lemon meringue pie but lemon in detergent, in nail polish remover or Brillo is gravy on the tablecloth.

1996

Official Holidays

Ive been looking at my 1996 calendar because I wondered what day Christmas falls on this year. Its a Wednesday. That means people will only be working Monday and Friday. Or maybe not at all.

Wednesday is the worst day to have Christmas on. Monday or Friday are best.

Labor Day is early, which will make for a short summer.

There are no official national holidays but most States go by the ten legal holidays for Government workers in Washington.

New Year's Day, Martin Luther King Day, Washington's Birthday, Memorial Day, Independence Day, Labor Day, Columbus Day, Veteran's Day, Thanksgiving and Christmas. Im not going to make almost everyone mad by naming them but we could probably do without several of those.

We dont need both Memorial Day and Veteran's Day. Labor Day is an out-of-date idea. I like Columbus Day but we dont have a day like it for Americans with German ancestry and there have been more German immigrants than Italian. We ought to have one for everyone or none at all. I suppose Italians would say no German sailor discovered America in 1492.

If you keep adding holidays though, you end up with too many. Different interest groups, different religions demand their own.

Most religious holidays in the United States are Christian. We have Jewish holidays and while theyre only celebrated by Jews, they have an impact on everyone who isnt. There are more and more Muslims and theyre going to want their holidays.

In India theyve kept adding holidays for several religions until now they have about forty. Nothing gets done on those days.

Japan has fifteen. April 8 is Buddha's Birthday and September 15 is called Respect for the Aged Day.

My complaint with most holidays is that the person or the thing theyre supposed to honor gets lost and the holiday ends up as an excuse for a day off. How many of us think about George Washington on Washington's Birthday?

August is the only month without a real or a fake holiday. That's because we dont want to waste a day off work during our vacation.

We have a whole bunch of semi-holidays that are not much more than a trick for selling greeting cards and flowers.

Our local drugstore was driven out by a cut-rate giant in a nearby town so now our hardware store sells the greeting cards the drugstore used to sell. I think this means theres more money in greeting cards than in either drugs or hardware.

"Mother's Day," "Father's Day." Any mother who depends on the cards she gets on Mother's Day for evidence that her kids like her, is in trouble but a lot of us dont dare *not* send cards for fear we'll be considered unloving or uncaring.

I can see the day coming when we'll have a National holiday called Hallmark Day—to honor Mr. Joyce Hall. He's the founder of the Hallmark Greeting Card Company.

Your Father's Name

Ive tried the Census Bureau and half a dozen other places but no one seems to know how many boy babies are given their father's name and called "Junior."

The purpose of a name is to distinguish one person from another and I dont want to alienate the affections of millions of parents who have given a kid the same name as his father but it doesnt make sense to do. It happens everywhere in the world. Osama "bin" Laden means "Osama son of Laden." The preface "Mc" in front of an Irish name means "son of." In Russia, Ivan "Ivanovich" is "son of Ivan." Just as soon as two people living in the same house anywhere have the same name, theres confusion.

"George?"

"Yes. What do you want?"

"No. Im talking to your father."

Who needs that ?

It makes it so hard around the house that half the time, the son is called "Junior" instead of by his name. Or to separate the kid from his father, he gets nicknamed "Sonny."

The least a father and mother can do for a kid is give him a name of his own.

The boxer George Foreman carried ego to the extreme by naming all four of his sons George.

Some juniors drop it when their father dies but others keep it forever. There are lots of men in their eighties who are still called "Junior."

There was a difference of opinion about how to refer to Martin Luther King on his birthday. Some people called him "Martin Luther King, Jr." His father is dead so others left the junior off. I prefer it without. "Martin Luther King Jr. Day" is awkward. Making it possessive is very awkward: "Martin Luther King Jr.'s birthday."

In New York, I often take a road named after a well known labor leader, Harry Van Arsdale. The signs read "Harry A. Van Arsdale Junior Boulevard." That's hard to get on an overhead sign on a narrow road.

The word "junior" itself is sort of demeaning. It suggests lesser. Junior varsity. Junior high school.

There have been eleven Presidents of the United States who were given the same first name as their father but I dont think any of them ever called themselves "Junior."

Bill Clinton was not just a junior but a fourth. He was originally named "William Jefferson Blythe the Fourth." That would be political suicide. His father died in a car accident before he was born and when his mother married Roger Clinton, she changed Bill's name to "William Jefferson Clinton." Doesnt seem right. Poor old Bill Blythe.

I realize that most of the millions of people named Junior wont like this and the parents who stuck them with those second-hand names certainly wont like it but giving a kid the same name as his father is dumb. I wouldnt be "Andrew Aitken Rooney" or Andy. I'd be "Walter Scott Rooney Junior." Even worse, our son, Brian, would be "Andy Rooney Junior." How would you like to stick a kid with that ?

The Flat Tax

A great many of you have written asking me to explain the flat tax about which we're hearing so much. Let me read from a letter I received:

"Dear Andy, Please explain what politicians mean when they refer to the flat tax."

Perhaps it would be best if we began by looking into the the word "flat" itself to better understand the phrase "flat tax."

The word has been used in a great many different ways.

The tire with too little air, for example, is known colloquially as simply "a flat." It is, of course, a flat tire. A flat is produced when a nail punctures one of the rubber wheels on your car and the air in it escapes through the hole made by the nail.

When the air goes out of a bubbly drink, we call that flat. If a glass of beer has been standing for an hour, its flat.

Some people have flat feet. Young men who had flat feet couldnt get into the Army because the air had gone out of their arches.

In 1938 there was a very popular song about someone named Floogie who was flat-footed and had a floy floy. The song went: "Flat-foot Floogie with a floy floy."

This famous warship, the Intrepid, is parked in the North River alongside the island of Manhattan and is known as a flat top. That's because its top is flat so airplanes can land on it.

"Flat Top" was also a famous character in the Dick Tracy comic strip.

The Flatiron Building was one of the first skyscrapers in New York City, and for many years the tallest building in the world at twenty-three stories. It is called the Flatiron Building because it is shaped like an old-fashioned flat iron that was heated on top of a stove.

There is also flat silver . . . the tools we eat with . . . and flat bread. Flowers are started in trays with dirt in them called flats.

For what reason I dont know, paint that isnt shiny is called flat.

When a man or a horse runs as fast as he can, it is said that he's going "flat out."

If you want to describe something as being very, very flat, you say its as flat as a pancake.

If someone doesnt have any money, he's called flat broke.

When a singer cant quite make a high note, he is known as flat.

Now, many of you are probably saying to yourselves: "What the hell does all this have to do with a flat tax ? I still dont understand it."

Well, of course you dont understand it. The flat tax isnt supposed to be something you understand. Its a campaign issue.

Tell the Truth

Many of you probably believe that the Montana recluse, Theodore Kaczynski, whose cabin was found to contain a mail bomb similar to the ones that have killed three people, is actually the Unabomber, the man who did it.

You people think its suspicious that FBI agents have apparently found plans in his cabin for making bombs and notes with the names of some of his victims.

You are the same people who think O. J. Simpson murdered Nicole and Ron Goldman just because his blood was found at the scene, because he had beaten her up in the past and because theres no plausible explanation for where he was when they were done in.

Dont forget, in America youre innocent until proven guilty . . . and then you appeal for nine years.

I hate to think of how much its going to cost taxpayers to determine whether Kaczynski is innocent, guilty or off his rocker. The State of Montana has had to beat off lawyers who want to defend him with a stick.

Gerry Spence, the famous defense lawyer in the buckskin jacket, says that just because Kaczynski had these things in his cabin, doesnt mean he's guilty.

Why, of course it doesnt, Gerry. And just because you seem interested in defending Kaczynski, doesnt mean youre a publicity hound . . . but you have to admit, both things would make the average person who doesnt know any better mighty suspicious of both you and him.

Youd think it would be easy to know when someone is lying about committing a crime but it isnt. If an accused person denies something loud enough and often enough, people begin to believe it never happened.

There are whole organizations promoting the idea that the death camps at Auschwitz, Dachau and Buchenwald never happened.

How many people are still alive who saw Buchenwald? Not many. Who's going to say that those people who deny it was a death camp are liars when those of us who saw it are gone?

Of course, we accept a certain amount of lying in everyday life. Courtesy often takes the form of a lie.

We say "You're looking well" to someone who looks terrible.

We had a miserable dinner at the house of a friend in Los Angeles a few weeks ago and, as we left we both said, "It was wonderful, Helen."

Well, it wasnt wonderful. We lied. And her name wasnt "Helen," either. Im lying about her name to keep from hurting her feelings. We all do that a lot.

If they ever invent a foolproof lie detector that lights up when we lie, one should be planted in everyone's forehead at birth. We wouldnt need judges and juries. We'd know for sure who was innocent, who was guilty. We'd know who was telling the truth and who was lying.

It would be a better world.

President Clinton Takes a Trip

President Clinton will be returning from his weeklong trip around the world later tonight.

He's getting in too late to catch *60 Minutes*, which seems like poor planning.

On Monday President Clinton met with the President of South Korea, Kim Young-sam. (Kim is his last name. In Korea, a man's last name comes first. That's the kind of little thing that makes it difficult for Americans to do business over there.)

Then Mr. Clinton flew to Tokyo where he met Prime Minister Hashimoto.

He also met the Emperor Akihito.

The Emperor of Japan is technically the head of Government but actually, he's more a cross between a king and a vice president.

(Prime Minister Hashimoto's wife told reporters she "doesnt interfere

with her husband's business. Not with her mouth, her hands or her legs."
Interesting but curious comment. Bill and Hillary must have had a good
laugh over it when they got back to their room that night.)

The Clintons stayed at the Akasaka Palace in Tokyo. That must be a
strange experience for a couple from Arkansas . . . sleeping in a palace.
Everything's different in Japan . . . even taking a bath is a ritual, community
affair. They're all in it together.

I suppose the Clintons had their own shower at the palace but there are a
lot of little details we never get to know about.

We tried to figure out what this trip would cost a husband and wife who
had to pay for it themselves: These figures are for two people.

First-class air fare, Washington to Cheju Island . . . $5,608.

One night in Cheju Shilla Resort hotel . . . $272.

Flight from Korea to Tokyo . . . $804.

Suite at the Okura Hotel, at $2,300 per night . . . $4,600.

On Wednesday the President flew from Tokyo to St Petersburg. That's the
most expensive. It would run you $8,000 each . . . $16,000.

Cost of visas to enter Russia . . . $100.

The Grand Hotel in St Petersburg, suite . . . $700.

Flight from St Petersburg to Moscow . . . $180.

They met with Yeltsin and some world leaders to discuss nuclear safety
. . . which never makes me feel very safe.

In Moscow, a suite in the Raddison Hotel, two nights . . . $1,888.

Figuring meals is hard. Say they ate three meals a day for seven days . . .
minus two days' meals on airplanes . . . so five days.

Meals arent much in Korea or Russia but in Tokyo, dinner for two can run
you $350. Let's say $300 per day, five days $1,500.

Three phone calls home . . . $37.

Taxis. A cab from the White House to Dulles Airport costs $75. In Japan,
from the airport into Tokyo costs $250. And they have to get back out there.

Let's say for taxis . . . $1,000.

Tips for cabs, doormen,waiters, hotel . . . $300.

That's a total of . . . $33,252.

Its not going to cost them anything for a taxi to get back to the White
House because I understand they left their own car in the parking lot at the
airport.

The Auction

I was reading about the auction held by Sotheby's of the personal possessions of Jacqueline Kennedy Onassis. A total of 5,914 items sold for $34 million dollars.

I have the catalog.

I dont want to wait 'til I die to have someone sell my stuff but I hate to part with any of it while Im alive. Its a dilemma.

Ive been comparing some of the things I have in the office with some of

Jackie's things that were sold. President Kennedy's famous rocking chair went for $442,500. I dont have a rocking chair. Rocking chairs are best on front porches and we dont have a front porch. This is the chair Ive used for twenty-five years now. I can just imagine it properly displayed on the auction block. Its of great historic value but not to anyone but me.

I was sitting in this very chair when I got suspended from my job five years ago. The bidding would probably begin at around $12.

Ive done 500 pieces for *60 Minutes* at this desk which I made myself out of a huge slab of walnut. President Kennedy only used his desk a few times and it sold for $1,432,500. I ought to be able to get a couple of hundred for mine. I'd be willing to sign it.

Three of Jackie's gold watches sold for $140,000. I dont have a gold watch. My Timex cost me $17 six years ago. I suppose that doesnt make it an antique yet. Would it be worth more or less than what I paid for it ?

Several pictures of former President Kennedy were sold.

I have pictures of myself but I dont think theyd bring much.

The Kennedys had a couch that went for $32,200.

I have a couch. If I was up late the night before, I often lie down on it to close my eyes and think.

Jackie got letters from a lot of famous people. They brought big bucks. I have those. Just last week I got a letter from Phyllis Diller.

There were several antique cushions in Jackie's auction.

Ive got cushions from Super Bowl games Ive been to.

Super Bowl XXIX. You talk about antiques.

Jackie had a lot of cups that were sold.

Boy! Do we have cups. For instance, here's a real collector's item, a genuine, original Pat Sajak memorial cup.

Arnold Schwarzenegger bought President Kennedy's golf clubs for $772,500. They'd be heavy to carry but golfers have caddies who do the heavy lifting. Does someone as strong as Schwarzenegger need a caddy to carry his clubs?

I dont have golf clubs but I have a baseball bat, a cricket bat and a Giants helmet.

Here's something I have that Aristotle Onassis couldnt have bought from me with all his money . . . a picture of John F. Kennedy given to me by my friend Harry Reasoner.

I dont have a catalog ready yet for my auction. I think I'll wait a few years until it gets more valuable. Antiques are getting younger every year. I hate an antique thats younger than I am.

The Montana Freemen

The Freemen were an anti-government group who held off Federal agents for eighty-one days in 1996.

Is it okay if Im fed up with those outlaws holed up in that farmhouse in Montana?

Is it okay if I think its wrong for us to be spending a million dollars a day to surround the farm where these idiots are telling the United States to go to hell?

Theyve occupied the full time of 100 FBI agents for forty-eight days now. Certainly the FBI has better things to do with *its* time and *our* money.

I understand why the FBI is gunshy after the fiasco in Waco but I cant believe the FBI doesnt have a way of getting them out and locking them up without killing anyone. What about cuting off their food, water and electricity?

Theyre accused of bank fraud, mail fraud, illegal weapons possession, threatening to kill a judge. We're being too nice to them.

They wont get drivers licenses because they dont recognize the authority of the State. They dont want to pay taxes. This makes them special ? Everyone who loves to stand in line at the license bureau or pay taxes, raise your hand.

They say they dont like the Government in Washington. Well *of course* they dont like the Government in Washington. None of us do. Liking big Government is un-American.

Ralph and Emmett Clark, two of the leaders whose farm theyre staying on, have collected $675,000 in subsidies over the past eight or nine years. They didnt hate the Government so much they wouldnt take the handout, did they?

These people met in an open field with the FBI and laid down all sorts of conditions for coming out. It ought to be made clear to them that they dont get to establish any conditions. They shouldnt be promised anything but a fair trial.

Obviously these people dont understand what it is to be American. They dont understand that there are obligations that go with all the good stuff we have like freedom. We have some unwritten agreements with our politicians.

For example, a lot of us didnt vote for President Clinton and dont like him. A lot of us dont like Bob Dole and wont vote for him . . . but the deal is, after an open and free election, Americans accept the guy who got the most votes as our President whether we like him or not.

We accept our Government. We salute the flag and sing *The Star Spangled Banner,* not because we love the music but because, in spite of everything wrong, we like our Country and its Government better than we like any other.

Apparently the outlaws have plenty of canned food and theres a well so they have water. They can hold out for months. They still have a telephone line going into the farmhouse so they can call home Mothers' Day. The FBI hasnt cut off their electricity so they have television. Theyre probably sitting in there right now, watching a rerun of *I Love Lucy*.

They call themselves "freemen." Well, I dont call them that. Its too good a word for what they are. They arent free anyway. They're prisoners of their own stupidity.

Dr. Jack Kevorkian

Dr. Jack Kevorkian has helped end the lives of twenty-eight painfully ill people. He has been tried and acquitted three times of assisting suicide. I was sitting in my office minding my own business one day when the producer of *60 Minutes* called and asked if I'd go to Detroit and talk to Dr. Kevorkian. I couldnt figure out why he wanted me to do it. I mean all I had was a bad cold. It turns out Kevorkian agreed to the interview if I'd ask the questions so thats what I did. I talked with Dr. Kevorkian and his lawyer Geoffrey Fieger.

ROONEY:
Is there a good way of dying naturally?

DR. KEVORKIAN:
I dont know. I think there is. I think most people would pick sudden heart attack . . .

ROONEY:
In their sleep.

DR. KEVORKIAN:
Right, they would pick sudden heart attack in sleep. We assume thats the best way to die, because youll never know.

ROONEY:
You're too young to get in on this conversation, Jeff.

GEOFFREY FIEGER:
I understand.

ROONEY:
I think I'll call you Mr. Fieger, if I may.

GEOFFREY FIEGER:
You can call me Jeff.

ROONEY:
When do you decide that it would probably be best for a person to go?

DR. KEVORKIAN:
Well, actually, the patient decides when its best to go.

ROONEY:
But is he or she a good judge?

DR. KEVORKIAN:
Only on what—what he or she wants. As a medical doctor, it is my duty to evaluate the situation with as much data as I can gather, and as much expertise as I have, and as much experience as I have, to determine whether or not the wish of the patient is medically justified. The two must then coincide—the wish of the patient, and the medical justification.

ROONEY:
Is—what is the legal aspect of this, Mr. Fieger? Does he tell you what he's going to do?

GEOFFREY FIEGER:
No. Not in advance.

ROONEY:
You're just saying that because you dont want to be . . .

GEOFFREY FIEGER:

Maybe, but I dont think he has committed any crime. He's just doing something thats right. And everybody instinctively understands it. That's why we're winning. This isnt something that we have to teach people a lot about. They understand it. Government has no business telling you when you have to—how much you have to suffer before you die.

ROONEY:

How do you feel about what the Eskimos do? Shove the old people out on an ice floe? Is that a good idea?

DR. KEVORKIAN:

Oh, no, no, thats brutal.

ROONEY:

Well then . . .

DR. KEVORKIAN:

That's brutal.

ROONEY:

Leaving them out on ice floes?

DR. KEVORKIAN:

Well, we're doing the same thing by letting them starve to death, in—in—in hospitals. You recall . . . the Germans did that in the concentration camps. Our Supreme Court has validated it.

ROONEY:

That happens in hospitals, you think?

DR. KEVORKIAN:

Yeah, it sure does. Its legal. And the Supreme Court of the United States, are—our good Supreme Court has validated the Nazi method of execution in—in concentration camps, starving them to death.

ROONEY:

Now, what are you saying? What are they doing in hospitals that you . . .

DR. KEVORKIAN:

They take away their feeding and water, when theyre in coma. And let them die. I mean, youre validated what the Nazis did in concentration camps.

ROONEY:

And, you do not approve of that?

DR. KEVORKIAN:

Absolutely not. That's brutal, that is inhumane. Would you approve of that when—when you say a person should be allowed to die . . . inject then quickly and painlessly. Not let them wither away and starve to death? That is inconceivable, its unspeakable. But our Supreme Court has said, "that is nice; its ethical."

ROONEY:

Dr. Kevorkian, I think I have known doctors all my life. And there has been, I believe, a tacit agreement among doctors, that—that there are times when they have helped people out of this world who were terminally ill, and in—in great pain. And they didnt say anything about it. It was an understanding they all had. Have you ruined that for them?

DR. KEVORKIAN:

I dont think so, but I might have. I dont think I have. But I think that the legal wrangling over this has helped ruin it more than I have.

ROONEY:

And your legal problems have really inhibited you in some sense, from doing it . . . doing it the best way?

DR. KEVORKIAN:

That's true. That's absolutely true. They've inhibited— taken my license away, they suspended it, made it tough for me to get any drugs. And then, when I use gas, they scorn it. Oh, come on.

ROONEY:
You're not a great favorite among doctors.

DR. KEVORKIAN:
Well, I mean, which doctors?

GEOFFREY FIEGER:
Its not "witch" doctors . . .

DR. KEVORKIAN:
Which, which, which—among "which" doctors? Among many Catholic doctors? No. Among many Baptist doctors? No. But, among doctors in general, I think more than half support what Im doing.

ROONEY:
Are you, in any way, religious?

DR. KEVORKIAN:
Well, I might be. But my religion centers in different areas than—than what's considered conventional religion.

ROONEY:
Anybody—any time anybody starts hedging like that, I realize theyre not religious.

DR. KEVORKIAN:
No, no, religion is an internal spiritual world. And I have my own, with my god, Johann Sebastian Bach. I mean, why not? You invent god, so thats my god. At least he's not invented.

ROONEY:
If, what you do, became popular—in other words, if it was accepted legally and ethically, and people in hospitals, who were terminally ill, and in nursing homes or anywhere else, and they died with some help from doctors like you, would this have an effect on the income of—of doctors in hospitals?

DR. KEVORKIAN:

It could. It—if you let every doctor do it, it could. Just like everything else, you let any doctor do it, and some are going to abuse, because you got crooked—some crooked doctors out there.

ROONEY:

Should they let every doctor do it?

DR. KEVORKIAN:

No.

ROONEY:

Well, what—who should do it, and who shouldnt?

DR. KEVORKIAN:

They should be specified. I dont care by who. Not by government, preferably, but by the medical profession, who certifies cardiac surgeons.

ROONEY:

You mean, it should be—something that—would be a certification, just like being a . . .

DR. KEVORKIAN:

Yes.

ROONEY:

Where do you stand on capital punishment?

DR. KEVORKIAN:

Huh, I—I—I was neutral, but I would admit, like Socrates and Aristotle and Plato, and some other philosophers, that there are incidences where the death penalty would seem appropriate.

ROONEY:

What about—what about abortion?

DR. KEVORKIAN:

Absolutely. Woman's choice. Im for absolute autonomy of the individual. And an adult mentally competent woman has absolute autonomy. Its her choice.

ROONEY:

But, is not the fetus a person yet?

DR. KEVORKIAN:

Whether the fetus . . .

ROONEY:

No rights?

DR. KEVORKIAN:

The fetus is . . . if it exists or not, cannot supersede or equal the—the autonomy of—of the mother carrying the fetus.

ROONEY:

I think the American public is puzzled about you; they dont know whether youre a—a medical philosopher or a nut. Which are you?

DR. KEVORKIAN:

Im both. You might say Im a philosophic nut, or a nutty philosopher. It doesnt matter. Words dont mean anything. It—if you dig into anybody's character, you can find eccentricities if you can—you can characterize as nutty.

ROONEY:

You've done some nutty things, though. I saw your picture of you in a— in a pillory. Why would you do that?

DR. KEVORKIAN:

Well, for example these are object lessons. Nothing is more powerful than object lessons.

ROONEY:
You seem abnormally obsessed with death.

GEOFFREY FIEGER:
He's not at all.

ROONEY:

But, Ive seen some of your art. Ive read some of your book. Both your prose and your painting are macabre . . .

DR. KEVORKIAN:
Well, okay. The one on war with a—where you have this body . . .

ROONEY:
Macabre.

DR. KEVORKIAN:
With . . . with the head on the plate in front of it.

ROONEY:
Yeah, I would—I would tend to call that macabre.

DR. KEVORKIAN:
What is war? When you look at that, do you get a good feeling?

ROONEY:
No.

DR. KEVORKIAN:
You look at it—its colorful. Its nice. It draws you to it. And then, which we do to war, and then you go through it and then say, "god, that was macabre!"

That's the feeling Im trying to convey with the painting. I—you look at that painting; you like looking at it. Its colorful, but you hate what youre looking at.

ROONEY:

In view of all these things, and— and how you were viewed by the American public, as somewhat of an oddball, do you think that youre the right guy to have represented this cause about which you feel so strongly? Could someone else have done it better?

GEOFFREY FIEGER:

No.

DR. KEVORKIAN:

Maybe. Sure. Where is he? Where is she? Look at—why criticize me? You're not the poster child for this, fine! The reason Im doing it in a fashion thats not entirely acceptable to everybody, is because of the prosecutor, the—the prosecutor, and the intimidation. They threaten me with jail, and hauled me into court. We've got to hide things.

They come in and confiscate everything in the house. Just get off my back, I'll show you how to do it right. This is almost brutal. Prosecutorial departmentized.

ROONEY:

You havent enjoyed it just a little bit? You look as though, sometimes in court, youre enjoying . . .

GEOFFREY FIEGER:

We enjoy winning.

DR. KEVORKIAN:

What looks like enjoyment is the— is the sneer of contempt. That's not a smile.

ROONEY:

You were sneering?

DR. KEVORKIAN:

Sneering in contempt, right. This last trial, I showed—I had to show contempt, not just say it. Ive showed it.

(Trial footage from 1991, when Dr. Kevorkian was charged in the deaths of two women in Michigan.)

DR. KEVORKIAN:
Tell me Im wrong!

PROSECUTOR:
You're wrong.

DR. KEVORKIAN:
Prove it!

PROSECUTOR:
Easily.

DR. KEVORKIAN:
Prove it! Cite a case of common law of assisted suicide prose—prosecution. Cite it!

PROSECUTOR:
Objection. You were instructed not to ask questions. Speak before you ask . . .

DR. KEVORKIAN:
I dont care. Charge me for contempt, your honor, I dont care.

PROSECUTOR:
Thank you, Judge.

ROONEY:
You advise him against being so contemptuous?

GEOFFREY FIEGER:
Oh, absolutely. He doesnt listen to me. And, of course, I dont listen to him. So we're equal.

ROONEY:

Well now, when you become involved with somebody who is terminally ill, and you agree to help them end their lives, is there a charge for that?

DR. KEVORKIAN:

No.

ROONEY:

No money ever exchanges hands?

DR. KEVORKIAN:

No. No.

GEOFFREY FIEGER:

Youd be in jail.

ROONEY:

Is that true?

GEOFFREY FIEGER:

He'd be in jail if that was true.

ROONEY:

I havent thought of that.

GEOFFREY FIEGER:

He would be in jail.

DR. KEVORKIAN:

First of all, money should—a transfer of money should never be involved in this profound situation. Terminal illness is profound too, but medicine is a business today. Its a business. There is a way to solve it. The doctor who does this must be salaried. Now, what youve done with that, you had two— you create two big advantages; first, theres no incentive for the doctor to do more than he has to do. In fact, he wants to do less now. All salaried people would like to do less for the money.

And second, you—you prevent abuse.

ROONEY:
You have a low opinion of other people in the medical field? Doctors?

DR. KEVORKIAN:
Huh . . . Not of the—some—not of any of the people in the field. I have a low opinion of the organized profession, which I now no longer call a profession.

ROONEY:
What do you do about money?

DR. KEVORKIAN:
I—I—first of all, I saved a little, cause I knew what was coming.

GEOFFREY FIEGER:
Cheap.

DR. KEVORKIAN:
Yeah. And live cheap. Right.

ROONEY:
You dont enjoy good food or any . . .

DR. KEVORKIAN:
No, I dont—I dont enjoy good food. I dont enjoy flashy cars. I dont care if l live in a dump. I dont enjoy good clothes. This is the best Ive dressed in months.

GEOFFREY FIEGER:
Tell him how much that suit cost. He's proud of it. How much did that suit cost? Its a genuine ersatz Armani, isnt it?

DR. KEVORKIAN:
Armani—its an Armani copy, right.

GEOFFREY FIEGER:
Yeah, its cheap—he told me its genuine.

ROONEY:
Now, how much was that suit?

DR. KEVORKIAN:
Fifteen bucks.

GEOFFREY FIEGER:
Who shines that suit, Jack?

DR. KEVORKIAN:
There was an original shine. Fifteen dollars.

ROONEY:
I didnt realize that you two were—were such a team. I mean, youre a pretty good team. I can see that. Has this been good for your practice, or bad?

GEOFFREY FIEGER:
Well, theyve gone after me, just—legally, theyre going after my license, because of my defense of Jack.

ROONEY:
Did you really, seriously worry about going to prison?

DR. KEVORKIAN:
No. Never. Am I a criminal? The world knows Im not a criminal. What are they trying to put me in jail for? You've lost common sense in this society because of religious fanaticism and dogma. You're basing your laws and your whole outlook on natural life and mythology. That wont work. That's why you have all these problems in the world. Name them. India, Pakistan, Ireland. Name them! All these problems. They are religious problems.

ROONEY:
You dont seem to feel very strongly about this issue do you? What do you do for fun, Dr. Kevorkian?

DR. KEVORKIAN:
Huh . . . I irritate people.

In 1999 Dr. Kevorkian was convicted of second-degree murder in the death of Thomas Youk. The judge sentenced him to ten to twenty-five years in prison. I tried to get an interview with him in 2002, but Michigan officials wouldnt allow it. It is barbaric for the State of Michigan to have imprisoned this good man and then isolated him from his world.

Foreign News

The other day we dug out some old CBS News broadcasts . . . a few from ten years ago and some from twenty years ago.

Were they different from the news now? I'll say they were.

The biggest difference was in the emphasis on international news.

Twenty years ago, with Walter Cronkite, almost half the broadcast was foreign news.

CRONKITE:
Bruce Dunning reports from Tokyo.

Even ten years ago with Dan Rather, there was a lot of important news from abroad.

All three network news broadcasts do much less foreign news now. Lots of fluffy feature stories.

ANCHORMAN:
Goats, hundreds and hundreds of goats, trucked into fire danger zones, to chomp away at the dry grass and brush, to clear it away so fire cant take hold.

Interesting but not of great importance if you only have twenty minutes to tell everyone about everything.

Is this the fault of network news people? I suppose some of it is but mostly its the fault of Americans in general.

The networks give them what they want in order to attract the biggest audience and people just dont want much foreign news. Dozens of foreign news bureaus have been closed by the networks. CBS used to have ten foreign bureaus—a bureau in Warsaw, Poland, if you can believe that.

Even the candidates arent talking about foreign affairs because they know Americans just dont give a damn.

A great many Americans hate the whole idea of the United Nations. They didnt approve of President Clinton going there to sign the nuclear bomb treaty this week. If you put it to a vote, a lot of Americans would vote to leave the U.N.

That's so stupid. The U.N. has been poor a lot of the time but its the best hope the world has.

We cant watch the whole world go to hell while we just sit here fat and rich. It matters to us what happens in Bosnia because theyre human beings there. It matters that people are starving in Africa, that there are epidemics all over that could spread to us, that sex abuse of kids is rampant in parts of the world. International crime and terrorism matter to us. A nuclear test ban matters to us.

If we're as nice as we like to think we are, we cant let a few million people starve to death or murder each other and we shouldnt have to prevent those things ourselves. That's what the United Nations can do, with our unqualified support.

Americans are so turned in on themselves . . . selfish really. Just because we were lucky enough to have been born here we dont like to admit the rest of the world exists.

That's my sermon for tonight. The ushers will now pass among you to collect the offerings.

Presidents and the Media

If Senator Dole loses next Tuesday, he says it'll be because reporters are liberal and were unfair to him. Well, if Bob Dole loses this election, it will not be because of the liberal media. And I concede the media is, more often than not, liberal. Bob Dole will probably lose for several reasons that may be unfair, but not because of an unfair media.

First, things are going pretty good; unemployment is down, we arent at war and the economy's humming along. Some of the credit should go to George Bush, but thats not the way it works. Clinton gets the credit. Dole isnt doing well for other reasons.

He has a dour personality. He sounds negative, critical and pessimistic.

So do I, but Im not running for President.

Clinton sounds bright, cheery and optimistic.

Americans have accepted Bill Clinton in spite of his shortcomings. They know he's done some fooling around, and they arent casting the first stone.

And if he doesnt love his wife, and if she doesnt love him, its a great act they put on.

I feel bad about Dole because I like him and he blew it. When this thing started I thought I might vote for him. I was uneasy about Clinton. Dole was capable, experienced and my age. Senator Dole claims the media ignored things that would make President Clinton look bad. Well, the fact is the media has done a better job detailing what's wrong with the Clinton administration than Bob Dole has. Dole gets most of his information about what's wrong with it from the reporters he criticizes.

Attacking the media was a dumb thing for Dole to do, even if he was right.

It sounds as though he thinks his bad showing so far is everyone's fault but his own. There has never been a politician who didnt think the media was out to get him.

Of the millions of words written about Bill Clinton and Bob Dole, some of them certainly have been untrue or unfair. But out of the whole mess, some basic truths emerge, and voters have gotten to know these two men better than they know themselves.

It may not make sense to you, but they seem to like Bill Clinton better than they like Bob Dole. We'll know late next Tuesday. Of course, if Dole wins, maybe the media wont report it.

Time-of-the-Year

I dont want to argue with all the poets who have given spring a good name but I dont care much for this time of year.

For one thing, there are just six more days before the worst day of all. Next Saturday, the days start getting shorter. Sunday will have five seconds less of daylight than today.

That's not right.

The longest day of the year should be at the *end* of summer when our vacations are over. On December 22, when we dont want them long because the weather's bad, days start getting longer.

Vacations are coming up soon now. The best thing about a vacation is planning it . . . getting ready to take it. Maybe you buy a new sports shirt, a bathing suit or a golf club. That's the fun of a vacation.

The vacation itself is never as good as looking forward to taking it. Just as soon as your vacation starts, you begin worrying about how soon it'll be over.

This is the end of the year, too, and endings are sad. Dont tell me New Year's Eve is the end because it isnt. New Year's Eve is right in the middle of the year.

Labor Day is New Year.

That's when things begin and we can start anticipating next year's vacation again. Now, all we can do with this one is take it.

There are some good things about this weather but the effort we make to stay warm in winter is more satisfying than the effort we make to stay cool in summer. Bundling up in warm clothing is a good feeling. You have a sense of defeating the elements.

No matter how little you wear on a warm day in summer, its too hot. And then, theres something wrong and artificial about air conditioning. A burning log in the fireplace is real . . . even a furnace is a consolation compared to the irritating whirr of an air conditioner perched unnaturally and clinging tenuously in a window.

And vacations are so phony. A lot of us who live in the city go to the country for vacation. People who live in the country often go to the city for one.

City people admire country people and country life. On vacation, they pretend to be part of it by wearing country clothes but they arent. They are fake country people intruding on real life in the countryside.

Late spring is the best of times and the worst of times.

Its best because things are growing. The sun comes up early and doesnt go down until late.

Its the worst of times because pretty soon we wont be able to look forward to the days getting longer anymore. We wont look forward to our vacation because it will be over.

Magazine Articles

Every once in a while I get to an airport early and have to spend time checking out the magazine stand.

There's something I dont understand. It costs a fortune to fly these days and what I dont understand is this. Why would anyone smart enough to have the money to buy a ticket read some of these magazines they sell?

Magazine editors are obsessed with numbers.

John Kennedy's magazine *George* carries a story called "THE TWENTY MOST FASCINATING WOMEN IN POLITICS."

Now, *George*, dont you think that number is high. I dont think many people could name twenty women in politics . . . let alone twenty fascinating ones.

The most puzzling thing is why magazines pick the numbers they do.

Smart Money has "THE 14 BEST CAR BUYS." How come fourteen?

Working Woman offers "THE TEN MOST POPULAR MUTUAL FUNDS."

Reader's Digest: "7 TASTY FOODS TO BOOST YOUR HEALTH."

Seven? That's hard to digest.

Prevention: "33 WAYS TO SIMPLIFY YOUR LIFE."

Is there anyone in the world who believes that there are just thirty-three ways you could simplify your life by reading a magazine article about it ?

Modern Bride: "HOW FIVE COUPLES MADE THE MOST OF THEIR BUDGETS." Three of them were probably divorced arguing over money before this issue of the magazine came out.

Cosmopolitan magazine featured an article called "ANSWERS TO THE 10 MOST FREQUENTLY ASKED QUESTIONS ABOUT ORGASM." I didnt read it but Im frankly suspicious of it. I dont think the average person ever asks a question about orgasm, let alone asks ten of them frequently.

Harper's Bazaar: "MORE THAN 200 RUNWAY LOOKS THAT WILL TAKE OFF." Oh, come on, *Harper's Bazaar*. I looked at your pictures . . . They'll be on sale for half price before you know it.

This number thing must sell magazines because some of them wont let up. We got some back issues of *People*.

Look at them:

"THE TEN MOST ROMANTIC COUPLES"

"THE 25 MOST INTRIQUING PEOPLE OF THE YEAR"

"THE FIFTY MOST BEAUTIFUL PEOPLE IN THE WORLD IN 1996"

I'd like to see *People* list the ten worst magazines to see if they were on it.

Mademoiselle: "5 THINGS YOU CAN CHANGE ABOUT HIM."

Redbook has "8 SURPRISING WAYS TO SPICE UP YOUR MARRIAGE."

I can think of two ways I bet *Redbook* doesnt mention. One, stop reading these magazines, and two, pay some attention to the person youre married to.

Sodium-Restricted Diet

Last week I went to my doctor for my annual physical.

Things are looking up for me. My weight is up, my cholesterol is up and my blood pressure is up.

My doctor is also my friend and he was fairly insistent that I lose weight.

As I was leaving, he handed me these two brochures. This one, from the American Heart Association, is called *SODIUM RESTRICTED DIET* and the other was put out by the Morton Salt Company.

With due respect to my doctor, let me say in the nicest way I know how— these pamphlets are ridiculous. If youre going to help someone with a diet, you dont tell them how much salt there is in one ounce of Animal Crackers, 5/6th of an ounce of Shredded Wheat or in half a boullion cube. Its been years since I had half a boullion cube for dinner.

If you followed the advice in this booklet, youd be eating off a scale.

Im suspicious of the Morton Salt pamphlet too. If their business is selling salt, are they really going to help someone use less of it?

And they keep calling salt "sodium." Salt and sodium are the same thing . . . why do they try to make it sound more important by calling it sodium ? You dont notice them calling it the Morton Sodium Company.

They list the sodium content of strawberries. Half a cup of strawberries has one milligram. The average person doesnt have any idea what a milligram is and I am an average person.

And how do you measure half a cup of strawberries? Here's the half cup mark . . . do I mash them down, Morton's?

I like salt. Im the kind of person who puts salt on his sodium. If I followed the advice of Morton's and the American Heart Association, there wouldnt be much I could eat. And if I do take their advice, dont expect to be seeing as much of me in the future because there wont be as much of me to see.

The American Heart Association keeps telling me to see my doctor before I do anything.

"Do not use any salt substitute that your doctor has not recommended. The important thing is to keep in touch with your physician . . . "

Why is the American Heart Association trying to get in good with doctors? Or are they doctors?

My doctor is busy. He doesnt want me hanging around asking if its all right to eat 200 milligrams of low-sodium dietetic peanut butter. He's so busy I'll bet he never even read the pamphlets before he gave it to me to read or he'd never have given it to me.

Caviar is on their list of things that are bad for you. Eleven hundred dollars a pound would make anyone sick.

I must admit, there are a couple of surprises in here.

Listen to this: "You may use carrots and celery sparingly to season a dish—one stalk of celery to a pot of stew."

The other day at a party I ate two stalks of celery so, if Im not on next week because I dropped dead, youll know it was that second stalk of celery that did me in.

Immigration Test

Most of us who are lucky enough to be Americans arent really enthusiastic about letting in a lot more people from other countries the way our grandparents or our great-grandparents were let in.

We no longer take that legend on the Statue of Liberty as literally as we once did. "Give us your poor, your tired, your huddled masses yearning to breathe free." We dont want any more huddled masses. We want to keep what we have for ourselves.

Last year 720,461 people immigrated to the United States . . . there were several ceremonies where thousands were sworn in as citizens at one time.

Last week I went into a little store out in the country in upstate New York run by a couple who came here four years ago from Pakistan.

It was early in the morning—no customers until I came in for the newspaper—and as I opened the door, the woman was saying to her husband, "Who was the first President of the United States?"

I knew the answer was Herbert Hoover so naturally I was surprised when he said, "George Washington."

It turned out that the woman was helping her husband practice for the citizenship test he was going to take the next day.

The test has twenty questions and you have to get at least twelve of them right to pass.

I got hold of some of the questions they frequently ask and here's my idea.

We have all these people who want to get into the United States and a lot of people already here who dont want to let any more in. Let's face it, its getting crowded. In order to make room for immigrants, give this test to every American citizen . . . anyone who fails the test has to leave to make room for one of the new people who does pass the test.

Here are ten typical questions. See if you get to stay here.

You can miss four of them.

1. How many stars are there on the American flag?

2. What do we call a change in the Constitution?

3. Name the two senators from your State.

4. Who is the Chief Justice of the Supreme Court?

5. What's the name of the ship that brought Pilgrims to America and did they land on a dock or a rock?

6. What is the minimum voting age in the United States?

7. What Country did we fight during the Revolutionary War?

8. Here's one that'll send you back to the Old Country. Name ten of the thirteen original states .

9. For how long do we elect Representatives to Congress?

10. Who said "Give me liberty or give me death"?

That's your citizenship test. Each of you who got more than four wrong . . . Get Out!

The Election Is Over

Its safe to say we're all glad the election is over with. Not many of us liked the campaigns this year no matter whose side we were on.

There were no good speeches . . . no graceful phrasing of great ideas.

I enjoy the concession speeches the most. My dictionary says to "concede" means "to acknowledge something as true—often unwillingly."

That's what a politician does late at night on election day.

Hours after everyone else knows he's lost, he gives his concession speech—unwillingly.

Its a hard speech for a politician to make. All day, the candidate has been predicting he's going to win but he must secretly have been thinking about what he'd say if he lost because he's always ready. You never see a losing candidate who doesnt know what to say.

Bob Dole: "Tomorrow will be the first time in my life I dont have anything to do."

Adlai Stevenson quoted Abe Lincoln quoting a boy who stubbed his toe in the dark. "Im too old to cry but it hurts too much to laugh."

George McGovern quoted Stevenson quoting Lincoln quoting the boy . . . but reversed the punch line. McGovern said, "It hurts too much to laugh but Im too old to cry."

One reason I suspect that candidates plan their concession speeches is that theyve usually looked up a quotation to use:

In 1980 when he lost the race for Governor of Arkansas, Clinton quoted Robert Browning. "'A man's reach should exceed his grasp, or what's a heaven for?' Remember me as one who reached for all he could for Arkansas."

I didnt even know Robert Browning was from Arkansas.

If you are a politician, there are certain rules you have to observe in a concession speech.

You have to thank your wonderful family.

Former President George Bush: "Of course, I want to thank my entire family, with a special emphasis on a woman named Barbara."

You have to thank your supporters.

Ross Perot: "I want to thank the staff thats worked tirelessly on this for doing an incredible job."

Geraldine Ferraro: "All of us can go to sleep tonight confident that we did everything we could to win this election."

What Im always thinking is, if everyone did such a great job, how come this guy got beat so bad? Ross Perot even thanked the television crew that made his infomercials.

Perot: "Thank you, Tom and Mike and Bill, and thank the great crew from AMS. You are terrific."

I saw your infomercials, Ross . . . dont leave a space on the bookshelf in your office for an Emmy.

Politicians try to be good losers but it doesnt ring true.

Harvey Gantt: "Im absolutely proud of the campaign that we ran."

The sore losers make the most interesting speeches. They sound honest. The classic sore loser of all time was Richard Nixon after he lost the race for governor in California in 1962.

Richard Nixon: "Just think how much youre going to be missing. You dont have Nixon to kick around anymore."

I like what a candidate did who lost an election in New York Tuesday. This guy was running for Congress and he lost bigtime to a woman. He didnt make a concession speech. He just locked himself in his house and wouldnt speak to anyone. That's what I'd do.

Liquor Commercials

You dont see bottles of liquor on television because years ago distillers, who make these drinks, and the television networks, who make money, voluntarily agreed not to show commercials for hard liquor like vodka, gin, Scotch and bourbon.

Recently the distilleries announced that they want to end that agreement. Sales of this stuff is way down, sales of beer is way up.

Beer companies spent $600 million on TV commercials last year. The liquor companies want to know why they cant advertise if beer companies can.

Its legal to make this stuff, its legal to sell it, its legal to drink it. They want to know why they arent allowed to advertise it.

Its an interesting argument and if everyone in the Country voted on it, Im not sure which side would win.

I know which side Im on.

I drink.

Every night when I get home and before we have dinner, we watch Dan Rather with one drink and then we have a second watching Jim Lehrer. Its a pleasant, relaxing part of the day. And a drink makes the news easier to take, too.

Some nights the news is so bad that I drink both mine during Dan and have nothing left for Jim.

I like a drink so much that people who drink too much make me mad. People who drive when theyre drunk infuriate me. They give a bad name to a civilized custom.

Those who dont think anyone should ever drink make it sound as though everyone who does is a drunk. Its not true.

So, do I approve of commercials for liquor on television? I do not. Its wrong. It shouldnt be illegal, its just wrong.

Liquor is a product for adults and it shouldnt be sold with the kind of shotgun advertising that television provides. A television commercial hits everyone.

There's a lot of advertising that shouldnt be on television but for different reasons.

Some of it is nothing more than a matter of taste. Personal items like toilet paper, sanitary napkins, hemorrhoid cures or even underarm deodorants are nothing anyone wants to sit and watch in their living room. How dare they intrude on our privacy?

Its why we have doors we can close on our bedrooms and bathrooms even though we all know what we do in them.

Being part of civilization calls for us to behave by a code of standards that dont always come naturally to us but should not be subject to law.

We eat with knives and forks.

I doubt if a ban on liquor advertising would stand up in a court of law—any more than a law against eating with our hands would stand up. Not having commercials for liquor on television should be part of a civilized agreement we have among ourselves.

My Eyebrows

What's my problem? Well, nothing really but how would you like to have ten million people staring at you every week the way I do, looking for flaws?

I mean, the money's good but I hate it.

Here's a letter from a fellow named Trainor complaining about my shirts. He says my collars are too small and make my neck look funny. He says I ought to wear longer sleeves so I have more cuff showing.

No one likes to be inspected that carefully.

You know what else he noticed? He asked why I wear my wristwatch underneath my wrist instead of on top of it. Well, I wear it that way because I like it that way, Trainor, thats why I wear it that way.

On radio Don Imus has complained about my eyebrows. Do you know what Don Imus looks

like? I mean, is this man someone youd tune in to watch on an empty stomach?

I like Imus. He's dirtier than necessary but very good. They've started simulcasting his radio show on MSNBC and I was on with him one morning. This guy's in love with the length of his own hair, and he's complaining about my eyebrows?

Imus compared them to those of Pierre Salinger.

Salinger's the guy who went off half-cocked with that old rumor about a missile shooting down Flight 800.

Salinger's eyebrows dont bother me but his comments did. It gives television commentators a bad name.

Letterman even had my eyebrows on his top ten list one night. I dont know what to do. I try to look nice. I comb my hair, have it cut. I tie my tie, I put on a clean shirt and a jacket but I draw the line when it comes to trimming my eyebrows. I could use a face lift too but you ought to work with what you got.

Even the cameraman, Keith Kulin, complains. He's always telling me to pull my coat down in back. It rides up.

Just a few minutes ago, I put on this jacket I keep behind the door. It turns out I wore it to dinner the other night and there was a spot on the lapel.

It has been my experience that spot removers dont remove the kind of spots I get on my clothes. It may change the size or color, or move it around a little but spot removers dont remove spots.

People are so busy criticizing what I look like that I dont think they pay any attention to what Im saying.

Im going to tell you something Ive never said before. I try to be honest with you. My reputation depends on my being honest. My hair is naturally brown. Now, I know that at my age no one is going to believe I have brown hair so, for years Ive been dyeing my brown hair grey so youll think Im honest.

My Crystal Ball

We've come to the end of the year 1996 and there are still a lot of unanswered questions. Someone sent me this crystal ball and tonight its providing answers to the ten most difficult questions.

1—Movies, books and television shows are sexier and more violent than they used to be. Is public morality declining and, if it is, why did it wait until 1996 to do it . . . and what's next?
A: MORE DIRTY MOVIES IS NEXT. THEY MAKE MONEY.

2—Has patriotism been a force for good or evil in the world? The people of every country think their country is best. Is it a good idea to be patriotic even when your country is wrong?
A: YES . . . BUT ONLY IF YOU'RE AMERICAN.

3—Which religion does God like best, Christianity, Hinduism, Buddhism, Islam or Judaism?
A: GOD ONLY KNOWS.

5—Are smart people happier than dumb people?
A: THEY ARE, YES . . . BUT OFTEN THEY'RE TOO DUMB TO REALIZE IT.

6—Is capitalism and free enterprise where everyone takes all they can get for themselves the best system for distributing money fairly among all the people?
A: Its A LOUSY SYSTEM—BUT ITS THE BEST ONE THERE IS.

7—Is life better or worse for people with electriciity, cars, television and two bathrooms in every home than it was for the caveman?
A: ITS BETTER . . . BUT THE PAYMENTS ARE KILLING US.

8—Astronomers are talking about the outer edges of the universe. Does the universe really end . . . and, if it does, what's just beyond the end?
A: MANY SAY BUFFALO.

9—Would it ever be possible to make doing good work the object of our selfish desire the way the acquisition of money and material things is our object now?

A: NO. IT WOULDNT.

10—If God created man, who created God ?

A: I PROMISED NOT TO TELL.

And one last question:

—What happened to question #4?

1997

State of the Union

President Clinton's State of the Union message to Congress Tuesday night was better than his Inaugural address but that wouldnt be hard. That was somewhere in between poor and terrible.

Only about 25 percent of all Americans bothered to watch that. He did better with his audience this week because if you wanted to find out whether O. J. murdered Nicole and Ron Goldman, you had to stay tuned to the President.

It was like having the World Series and the Super Bowl on at the same time.

I dont know why it is but President Clinton talks better than he speaks. When he's off the cuff, he's pretty good.

His speeches, though, dont have any class. Theyre long, dull and filled with speechy-sounding cliches.

A speech shouldnt sound like a speech.

He had some good ideas the other night too but the cliches gave his speech a tired, old sing-song quality that puts people to sleep.

I dont know why the word "challenge" is so popular with speakers. They're always saying we're facing "the challenge of the future." President Clinton used it seven times.

He kept throwing in the word "together" as if it would make listeners feel more like they were in on what he's doing. "Let us work together." "We must work together." ". . . together we can make American education the envy of the world." "Together we must make . . . ". Speechy.

He said "We must" forty-eight times in the speech.

"We must pursue . . . " "We must advance . . . " "We must move strongly . . . " "We must rise . . . " "We must build . . . " "We must never . . . " "We must fight . . . " "We must renew our commitment . . . "

What do you mean "*must*," Mr. President ? Or else what?

If he wasnt saying "we must," he was saying " Let us . . . " "Let us do what it takes . . . " "Let us seize the days . . . " "Let us agree . . . " "Let us work . . . " Mr. President, leave us not forget youre boring us.

If President Clinton writes his speeches himself, he ought to take his own advice and see if he cant find a good writer to hire who's on welfare.

Almanacs

This year's almanacs are out so Im ready for next year. I get both the *World Almanac* and the *Information Please Almanac*. This year I also got the *Universal Almanac* and *The Practical Guide to Practically Everything*.

The almanacs are good reference books. If you forget the name of one of your senators, theyre in here . . . or who won the hundred-meter dash in the last Olympics.

What almanacs are best for is settling arguments. Most of us dont know what we're talking about most of the time and you cant beat a fact.

What baseball player had the best batting average last year? Which company spent more on advertising, Coca-Cola or Pepsi-Cola ? Pepsi did. Who invented the parachute?

These almanacs dont always agree.

The *Information Please Almanac* says the population of Belgium is 10,131,000. The *World Almanac* says 10,170,000. That's a difference of 40,000 people. I suppose it doesnt matter—unless youre one of them.

Afghanistan 22,000,000. Come on, *World Almanac*. We have enough trouble counting Americans with an expensive Census Bureau. Who's counting people door-to-door in Afghanistan? Some of them dont even have doors.

Who was Miss America in 1971? Phyllis George.

What's the name of the newspaper in . . . let's see here . . . Sacramento, California? The *Sacramento Bee*.

The newspaper in New Orleans? Can you name it? The *Times-Picayune*. Des Moines? The *Des Moines Register*.

The Practical Guide to Practically Everything is better than its title but its more a book to read for fun than it is a reference book. How much to tip. Here's advice on CAREERS.

It says "Dont answer every question in a job interview." I wonder if the guy who wrote that ever looked for a job.

"Think twice before giving your boss a Christmas gift."

You wouldnt keep this in a bar to settle an argument between two drunks over how many acres there are in a square mile or who won the Orange Bowl last year.

Here's a section on how to buy apples. "Fruit should be firm . . . should have no soft spots, broken or shriveled skin."

If youre so dumb you didnt know that, you wouldnt be reading an almanac.

If Im ever sent to prison for a year, for pretending to know what Im talking about on television, I'll take these almanacs with me and just read all day in my cell. By the time I get out, I'll know all about everything.

Florida State beat Notre Dame in the Orange Bowl. There are 640 acres in a square mile.

Cloned

I worry about death a lot—mine and everyone else's. My old college roommate, Bob Ruthman, used to worry that theyd find a cure for cancer the day after he died of it.

I hate the thought that theyre going to find a cure for death the day after I die.

The news from Scotland this week suggests they may be making some progress. Dr. Ian Wilmut cloned a sheep. He produced an exact, genetic replica of a sheep, which he named Dolly. The next logical step is to clone a human being. You know, like me and possibly even you.

If we can make duplicates of ourselves, we're going to do it. Dont tell me its immoral or unethical. Human beings always do anything they find out how to do whether its immoral and unethical or not. We made the atomic bomb.

We could start cloning the best of us. It would be nice to have more capable, creative, honest people on Earth.

We'd have ourselves hundreds of men as smart as Stephen Hawking, as straightforward as Colin Powell, as talented as Itzhak Perlman. We could have a bunch of Walter Cronkites . . . lots of men as strong as Arnold Schwarzenegger. We'd clone the defensive line of the Green Bay Packers. We'd have plenty of women as bright as Madeleine Albright who looked

like Candice Bergen. We might clone every college professor. Every Olympic champion.

I'd hope some of us on *60 Minutes* might be cloned so the show could go on forever. I wouldnt mind having a clone stand in for me so I could take a month off without worrying about being replaced.

There's been a rumor that Diane Sawyer's coming back to CBS. If they cloned Diane, she could be on both *60 Minutes* and *Prime Time Live*. They'd have to clone her paycheck.

The big problem with cloning is, who picks the people to be cloned. We couldnt clone everyone. We already have too many people . . . what we need is fewer but better and that raises the specter of Adolf Hitler.

There are a lot of people we wouldnt want two of. Even one of some is too many. We could take two of my old college roommate, but we dont need two of anyone convicted of murder. Someone's bound to suggest we not clone any high school dropouts or illegal immigrants. No one with a traffic ticket. That would leave me out.

So, thats going to be the big problem, who decides who gets cloned.

Cloning is all done with genes in a laboratory. Theoretically, that could mean the end to producing babies the old-fashioned way . . . but I dont think so.

Team Names

Does anyone know who decided every team in sports has to have a nickname?

The college basketball championship game was played Monday and everyone knew the Wildcats were going to win because both teams, Kentucky and Arizona, were called the Wildcats. If Northwestern or Villanova had played, it would have been the same because theyre the Wildcats, too.

Why is "Wildcats" such a popular nickname for a team ? Has one single player on either team ever *seen* a Wildcat? I dont think so.

I called the Arizona Fish and Game Department and when I asked how many wildcats there were in Arizona, the man said there really was no such thing as a wildcat. He said mountain lions and bobcats are wild cats but there is nothing called a plain Wildcat.

The names we give teams are consistently illogical.

In major league baseball there are three birds, the Orioles, the Blue Jays and the Cardinals, and theyre mixed in with animals like Tigers. Shouldnt they all be either birds or wild animals? Why arent teams ever named after nice animals like elephants or golden retreivers ?

Two teams are named after the color of their socks for goodness sake. The Red Sox and White Sox.

The Oakland team is called the Oakland Athletics. What does that mean, Athletics? Shouldnt they be the Oakland Athletes?

They have priests, the Padres, mixed in with the Cowboys. Fish, the Marlins, with mountains, the Rockies. It doesnt make sense.

It used to be popular to name teams after Indians . . . in baseball, there are the Cincinnati Reds, the Atlanta Braves and the Cleveland Indians. In football, the Washington Redskins and the Kansas City Chiefs. They dont name new teams after Indians anymore because the Indians dont like it. I dont know why they care.

Professional basketball teams are a little more original . . . the Utah Jazz, Indiana Pacers, New Jersey Nets.

Sometimes a team has a name they think acts as a sort of an advertisement of a feature of the city they play in . . . the Pittsburgh Steelers . . . Detroit Pistons. The Milwaukee baseball team is called the Brewers because they make beer there. Miami's basketball team is nicknamed the Heat because its warm there, I guess. Never mind the Heat, Miami. What about the Humidity? How would that be for a team nickname: the Miami Humidity?

The newest team name in pro football is the Baltimore Ravens. The owner, who moved there from Cleveland, named the team after the poem called "The Raven" by Edgar Allen Poe because Poe also moved to Baltimore.

What the owner probably didnt know is, after Edgar Allen Poe moved to Baltimore, he turned into a drunk and died broke.

My question to Baltimore fans is this: Is a funky poem about a talking bird with a dirty mouth, written by an alcoholic genius who died drunk on the floor of a local saloon, anything you want to name a football team after ?

What about the Baltimore Wildcats?

Digital TV

Sometimes it seems as though theyre inventing new things faster than we're learning how to use the old ones.

You must have read that we're all going to have to throw away our television sets in the next couple of years and buy new ones because of digital TV . . . whatever digital TV is.

They claim the picture will be much better.

Well, pardon me, but the quality of the picture is not what's wrong with television. What we need is not a clearer pictures but better programs.

Look at some of the television listings:

"Elijah Wood plays an arrogant prep-school student who is suspected of murder."

"Cary-Hiroyuki Tagawa joins *Sabrina, the Teenage Witch* for some kung-fu fighting."

Is digital television going to make *Sabrina* any better?

Its the same with a lot of inventions.

I started using a computer several years ago.

I gave up my old Underwood. Its just for show here now.

CBS has a sophisticated computer system. If I get stuck or dont know how to do something, a computer expert comes up from downstairs and helps me. Sometimes they cant come though, because theyre too busy installing new systems.

I dont know how to use the old system but theyre installing a new one.

Every day I get dozens of e-mail messages on my computer.

Its magic. Its going to make stamps obsolete.

Here's an e-mail message for instance:

"Does anyone know someone who is on a fad diet—that is, the cabbage diet or the grapefruit diet? Please call me." That's from a producer on the CBS *Morning Show.*

I get a lot of happy-to-announce memos. "Im happy to announce that Harvey Nagler has been named general manager, etc."

Now, my question is this. If computers are so much better than this old typewriter, how come the stuff people write on them isnt any better?

Why is progress in one area so far behind progress in another?

Television sets and computers are the same. The trouble is not the delivery system, its the junk thats being delivered.

Too Much Advertising

No one in the whole world sells stuff to each other the way Americans do. There's no question about it, our advertising is the best.

The trouble with advertising is, theres too much of it. No matter what we try to look at, theres an advertisement or a commercial between us and it.

There's a road I take driving home every night and I cant avoid seeing the billboards. One sign in particular is intrusive and insulting. "ITS A WOMAN THING." What does that mean? Its a stupid statement and I dont want it in my face. Half the time I dont even know what theyre trying to sell.

A dealer sells you a car for $30,000 and then puts HIS advertisement on YOUR car by fixing a sign with his name on it to your license plate.

Buses have big, broad sides. No big broad empty space escapes being plastered with advertising.

Trucks on highways carry their messages to the rest of us fighting for our half of the road. The side of some trucks is one big ad.

You pay a fortune for a ticket on an airplane. They tell you to fasten your seatbelts so you cant get out and then they put up a commercial on the screen in front of you.

Magazine ads! *Vanity Fair* costs $3.50. Of the 384 pages in the April issue, 263 of them were advertising. That's 68 percent. The ads are attractive but for this you pay $3.50?

A *New York Times* critic wrote about the proliferation of commercials on television. I opened the daily *New York Times*. It was eighty pages . . . approximately thirty-one of them advertising.

In this thirty-two page travel section, twenty-one were advertising . . . 65 percent.

The late-night movies on television are so loaded down with commercial interruptions that its hard to follow the plot.

The average hour of radio has eighteen minutes of commercials, 30 percent.

On daytime soap operas, 28 percent of the time is spent on commercials.

Commercials have changed the pace of professional football games.

Even this broadcast, *60 Minutes* . . . In 1987 there were nine minutes of commercials in the hour. They've added almost three minutes to that in 1997. Im including the in-house advertising. This year actual program time of *60 Minutes* is about forty-seven and a half minutes. I worry about the day publishers start using the blank pages in books for ads.

Here's my suggestion. The Government insists on warning labels these days. How about this? Every newspaper, every magazine, every radio and television broadcast would have to say, up front, what percentage of the contents was advertising.

WARNING: This magazine is 50% advertising!

WARNING: The broadcast you are about to watch is 27% commercials!

The National Basketball Association

We go through sports cycles in this Country. You dont have to be a fan of the sport to enjoy the World Series, the Super Bowl, the Stanley Cup, the Master's golf, the tennis Open or the Kentucky Derby.

You dont have to be a big basketball fan to get interested in the NBA championship series coming up and for those of you who dont normally follow the game, I have some basic information about the teams and the players.

There are a lot of numbers here so pay attention.

There are twenty-nine teams. Each team has twelve players.

More than half of them make more than a million dollars. Michael Jordan has the highest salary, $30 million for eight months' work. During the season, Jordan scored 2,431 points. That means he was paid $12,341 for every point he scored.

Jordan doesnt have to scrape along on that though because he also does endorsements for a lot more than that.

Of the 348 players in the NBA, 280 are black, 68 are white.

All but ten players are more than six feet tall. Thirty-two of them are at least seven feet tall.

The shortest player is Muggsy Bogues. He's five feet three inches.

The tallest American player is a Mormon named Shawn Bradley.

One of the biggest problems a basketball player has is finding a comfortable hotel room. The bed is never long enough for Shawn. Taking a shower is a problem because he's taller than the shower head. Wherever he walks, he's ducking his head.

Shawn's team, the Dallas Mavericks, isnt in the playoffs this year but it doesnt matter. It is such a certainty that the Chicago Bulls will win the championship again this year that I am going to make another offer. You may recall I offered $1 million reward to anyone who found the murderer of Nicole Brown Simpson and Ronald Goldman. I have not had to pay that amount so Im in good shape financially and if the Chicago Bulls do not win the NBA championship, I will personally write a check for one thousand dollars, made out to O. J. Simpson, to help him pay the $33 million judgment against him.

Little Rock, Arkansas

No hometown ever stuck to a President the way Little Rock, Arkansas, has stuck to President Clinton. Bill Clinton is the reason so much attention was focused this week on the fortieth anniversary of the forced integration of Central High School in Little Rock.

The President was eleven years old when it happened. Now he's fifty-one, and he went back. Mr. Clinton might not recognize his old hometown.

Its citizens are still friendly and incurable boosters of the city and the State they love, but most of downtown Little Rock is in danger of becoming a ghost town. There arent many people on what were once main streets there. The streets are lined with deserted stores, deserted theaters. There are more deserted banks than you could shake a bad check at. Even one of the town's newspapers, a good one, folded.

The trouble is, like so many American cities, much of Little Rock has moved out of town. The rich and middle class, mostly white, have gone to the suburbs. The poor, mostly black, are still living in the city, in the decaying old homes that were once middle class.

I spent some time walking around one of the poor neighborhoods near Central High, once the single biggest high school in the United States. I remember watching my friend Harry Reasoner report the story the day Governor Orval Faubus blocked black kids from going in.

HARRY REASONER:
Do you think there'll be more trouble this year?

UNIDENTIFIED MAN #1:
Yes, sir, I do.

REASONER:
Would you help make it, if you had to?

MAN #1:
Yes, sir, I would.

REASONER:
You dont want Negroes in school then?

MAN #1:
No, sir.

REASONER:
Is that a pretty general attitude? How do you feel about Negroes in school?

UNIDENTIFIED MAN #2:
Well, I dont think Negroes should go to school with the white people. They should stay in their own class.

Compare that conversation that Harry Reasoner had forty years ago with one I had recently with some kids going into classes at Central High.

UNIDENTIFIED WOMAN:
This school has the best of the best in Arkansas.

ROONEY:
It sure is great, considering the school's troubled past, isnt it? I mean, that it should be this good?

UNIDENTIFIED TEENAGER:
Well, it really is. Its consistently ranked as one of the best public high schools in America. And we offer more advanced placement courses than any other high school in Arkansas.

It always interests me to consider whether human beings are basically any better, any more civilized than they were when our ancestors lived in caves.

We've got a lot of good new stuff, like electricity, airplanes, Diet Coke, but are we better people? You read the newspapers, you wouldnt think so. But then you look at what's happened at Central High in Little Rock, Arkansas; you have to believe we're just a little bit more civilized than we were forty years ago.

The Promise Keepers

I wish resolving to do something helped but it hardly ever does. When I resolve to lose weight or resolve to clean out the garage, it never results in me getting thin or in the garage being clean.

The leaders of the organization that calls itself "Promise Keepers" did a lot of resolving in Washington last weekend. They asked God to make the men in the audience better people and they asked the men themselves to resolve to *be* better people.

Asking a bunch of men to promise to be nicer to their wives isnt going to work any better than me promising to clean out my garage and I certainly dont believe asking God to make them better will help, either. God has enough to do.

A lot of television evangelists arent going to like Promise Keepers because in addition to keeping promises, you can bet Promise Keepers will be keeping some of the money the evangelists have been getting.

Promise Keepers wont help the good local churches in town, either. Hometown churches always suffer the most from these religious movements-of-the-moment.

I watched some of the Promise Keepers praying on television and Im puzzled about prayer.

Isnt it sort of insulting to suggest God doesnt know what we want until we tell him ?

And they praise God as if they thought he liked being flattered.

It seems wrong to me for anyone to think that if they pray, they'll get a lot of good stuff from God that the ones who dont pray wont get.

People are always asking God for special treatment. You see football players praying or thanking God after theyve scored a touchdown. What about the poor guys who lost? They didnt pray?

Bill McCartney, the founder of Promise Keepers, even asked his followers to prostrate themselves while they prayed in order to get God's attention. God must have had a good laugh over that.

I always think politicians have a nerve ending their speeches by telling God what to do. Their order is "God Bless America!"

It should be "Please God, bless America."

"By the way, God. While youre at it, would you please bless some of the countries that dont have it as good as we do ?"

Where's the Story?

People send in ideas and the idea they suggest most frequently is for me to do a piece on all the little cardboard things that fall out when you open a magazine.

Please dont suggest that again, would you ? I did that sixteen years ago.

I read a lot of magazines and I enjoy them. Every magazine I see has one or two articles in it that I want to read. The rest I dont want to read. I could save money if I had my own editor who could make me my own, personal *Reader's Digest*.

As much as I enjoy magazines though, editors keep finding new ways to annoy me. For example, theyve started having these foldout ads inside the front cover. This is a very bad start for a magazine.

Half the time, you cant even find the table of contents. There used to be an unwritten rule that the table of contents for a magazine was on the first or second page, inside the front cover. *Time* does it right. Its index is where an index ought to be.

You have to paw your way through six or eight pages of perfume ads and pictures of women sitting around in their underwear before you find the contents. Its easy to forget what you were looking for in a magazine like *Harper's Bazaar*.

Once you find the table of contents, its often difficult to identify the story inside the magazine from the title they give it outside. They dont always coincide. For some inexplicable reason, they will give a story a different title in the table of contents than they gave it on the cover.

Say I want to read a cover story in *Newsweek* called KIDS WHO CANT READ. I look around inside and here's the story on page 56 called WHY ANDY COULDNT READ.

In *People*, MURDER IN A SMALL TOWN isnt called that inside. Its called THE AVENGER.

THE PROZAC ECONOMY. I like the *New Republic* but I look at the table of contents and theres nothing in there called THE PROZAC ECONOMY.

Here's *Forbes*. You want to read a story called GETTING RICH OFF LOW TECH? Well, dont look for it under that title because the headline on the story inside calls it RIDING THE REVOLUTION.

You like Sean Penn and want to read about his next life? Its not under that title in the index in *GQ*. There its called BEAT THE DEVIL.

The New York Times Magazine advertises a story on its cover called EVOLUTION AND THE PROM MOM. Would you recognize that inside? They call it WHY THEY KILL THEIR NEWBORNS.

There ought to be a rule that the title of the article inside the magazine is the same as the title on the cover.

Im awfully proud to be working in television where commercial aspects of the business never intrude on the content of the shows.

Your Nuts

I was in my supermarket last Saturday, looking at mixed nuts, and I got thinking about just how mixed the nuts were. I dont have much to do on Saturdays.

I brought these to the office. This is a twelve-ounce can of Planters Mixed Nuts. It says it has in it peanuts, cashews, almonds, Brazil nuts, filberts and pecans . . . LESS THAN 50% PEANUTS, it says.

I figure they meant less peanuts by weight, not by number, or they would have said "fewer than 50% peanuts." Anyway, I decided to separate the nuts, count them and weigh them.

It was hard to count some of the nuts because, while the picture on the can shows all of them as whole nuts, not all the nuts in the can are whole.

The Brazil nuts, the filberts and the almonds were mostly whole. A lot of the others were in small fragments. The pecans, particularly, were in broken pieces. Not one whole half of a pecan. These little pecan pieces should have gone into cookies. Planters must have gotten a good buy on pecan pieces from someone using whole pecans for something else.

They ought to have some small bits and pieces of nuts in the picture here on the can if theyre going to have so many little pieces in the can.

I counted out the nuts in an eleven-ounce can of Eagle brand nuts, and a twelve-ounce can of Planters and Foodtown.

In the Planters can, there were 35 cashews, 43 almonds, 25 filberts or hazel nuts, 7 brazil nuts and the pecans were in such little pieces I couldnt count them. There were 193 peanut halves and 86 whole peanuts. Planters' Brazil nuts were a lot bigger than the Brazil nuts in Eagle's can.

In the twelve-ounce Planters can, there was a tiny fraction less than six ounces of peanuts . . . amazing precision for a nut factory.

I called a wholesale nut company in New York. They told me pecans are the most expensive and peanuts, of course, the cheapest. Hazelnuts and, surprising to me, Brazil nuts, are also relatively cheap.

You may well ask this question: Does it make any sense to count the nuts in a can of mixed nuts?

Let me ask you this. What did you do last Saturday that was so important?

1998

The IQ of an Audience

A New York advertising agency announced that according to its survey, *60 Minutes* has the oldest audience of any program on television, a median age of fifty-seven.

Shows called *Sister Sister* and another called *Smart Guy* have the youngest audiences, down around twenty.

The implication was that having an older audience was bad.

Now, inasmuch as you, at whom Im looking this minute, are the audience they say is old and suggest is bad, let me ask you a question. Do you feel old and bad?

This is a wonderful position Im in tonight for a change. Everyone watching me now is a watcher of *60 Minutes* or they wouldnt be watching, right, so Im in no danger of making anyone mad when I say . . . people who *dont* watch *60 Minutes* are dumber than people who do. Let me repeat that aanother way for emphasis: People who watch *60 Minutes* are smarter than people who dont.

What we need is a survey showing the IQs of the audiences of all television shows. Highest IQ to lowest. Does this guy who did this survey want to make a bet? I'll bet *60 Minutes* has the smartest audience of any popular television show on the air.

I'll make this surveyor another bet, too. Would he be willing to put some money on which audience has the most money to spend on products advertised on television—*60 Minutes* or, say, *Jenny* or *The Simpsons*? Those audiences are less than half the age of ours.

I dont suppose its overwhelmingly smart or politically correct for me to say but it seems probable that, generally speaking, smart old people have more money than dumb young people.

Thats why *60 Minutes* has such a classy bunch of advertisers. Not an underarm deodorant in the lot.

Differences

There are certain basic things that touch all our lives that we always argue about.

Tonight, in an effort to promote discord, I propose to take a stand on a number of vital issues about which Americans are always disagreeing.

Q: Which is better, shredded wheat or corn flakes . . . coffee or tea . . . cats or dogs . . . skirts or pants . . . big cities or small towns . . . blue or green . . . day or night?

Q: Which is better, Coca-Cola or Pepsi-Cola?

A: Coke was invented first, 1886. I think of Pepsi as a ripoff imitation.

B: Pepsi was made in 1898. In a paper cup, you cant tell the difference between Coke and Pepsi anyway.

Q: Which is the best state to live in, Florida or California?

A: Florida has some of the best weather in the world.

B: Florida has some of the worst weather, too. Half the time, the oranges freeze.

A: While the oranges are freezing in Florida, there are fires, earthquakes and floods in California.

B: Lotta dull people in Florida.

A: Thats because California's got all the nuts.

Q: Which is best—hot or cold?

A: I'd take being cool over being hot anytime. I hate hot.

B: Its easier to stay cool on a hot day than warm on a cold day.

A: Air-conditioning sucks.

Q: Which is best, Ford or Chevrolet?

A: You cant tell one car from another anymore. I bought three Fords because I read that Henry Ford handed out dimes to poor kids.

B: That wasnt Ford, that was John D. Rockefeller.

A: There is no car called a Rockefeller.

Q: Which tastes best, chocolate or vanilla?

A: Chocolate is a bold, strong taste. Vanilla is namby-pamby.

B: Vanilla is more popular.

A: I like chocolate better and I like people who like chocolate better than I like people who like vanilla.

Q: Golf or tennis? Which is best?

A: Tennis is better. Golf takes too long . . . like sailing.

B: Golf is a great sport for life. You can play until youre in your nineties.

A: Its not a sport, its a pastime. Golfers hit one ball, ride a hundred yards in a cart, hit the ball again and take another ride.

Q: Which is best, a hot dog or a hamburger?

A: Theres nothing like a hot dog at a baseball game.

B: I dont like baseball and Im suspicious of anything that needs mustard.

Q: Who's right, Republicans or Democrats?

A: Democrats are knee-jerk liberals.

B: Republicans are just jerks.

If we could resolve these issues that divide us, once and for all, A and B could all live together happily forever after.

Clinton

I say what I think even when Im not thinking—which is too often. My trouble tonight is, I want to say what I think about President Clinton and I cant decide what I think.

The First Lady says theres a conservative conspiracy against her husband. Well, Im neither liberal nor conservative . . . Im part of the middle-of-the-road conspiracy against Clinton. I like him and Im disgusted with him. It isnt as if he was a naughty little boy. He's President.

I was going to apologize for having voted for him but then I watched his State of the Union speech and darned if he wasnt pretty good.

Its still a thrill to have both Republicans and Democrats stand up and cheer when the President of the United States comes into Congress—just because he is President. The Democrats cheered more enthusiastically but the Republicans clapped.

Clinton's been a good President but was he being honest when he answered Steve Kroft on *60 Minutes*?:

KROFT:

Im assuming from your answer that you categorically deny that you ever had an affair with Gennifer Flowers.

CLINTON:

Ive said that before.

Very evasive. Yes or no, Mr. President. Sometimes its a little trick in the words he uses. He first said of Monica Lewinsky "There is not a sexual relationship." Well, *is* not or *was* not, Mr. President? And then, theres apparently some technicality in his mind about what is and what is not a sexual relationship.

We're all clear about what is and what isnt, but our President isnt sure.

Last week we all saw the calculated opportunity he gave photographers to take his picture coming out of church holding Hillary in one hand and the Bible in the other. Please, Mr. President. We werent baptized yesterday.

He's embarrassed his presidency with the tawdry people he's involved himself with. Charlie Trie, Dick Morris, Webster Hubbell.

Linda Tripp worked in the White House and then hid a microphone on herself and got her dear friend Monica Lewinsky to talk about having sex with the President. What are good friends for, right?

Monica Lewinsky now denies it and people feel sorry for this sweet young thing. I dont feel sorry for her. Either she lied on tape when she said she did have sex with the President or she lied when she said she did not. One way or the other, she has done serious damage to our Country. Im unmoved by the argument that she's an innocent twenty-four-year old girl.

Paula Jones, also known as Rebecca of Sunnybrook Farm, is suing President Clinton for what she says was a lewd request he made of her.

President Clinton apparently has the same trouble that President John F. Kennedy had. Its a common problem with men and I have a suggestion.

Im not a doctor but I know that if you have a headache, you take aspirin. If you get pneumonia, you take penicillin.

When I was in the service, the Army slipped saltpeter in the food to alleviate the problem that most soldiers share in common with President Clinton.

I recommend that Bill Clinton stop in at the Pentagon some day and get himself a bottle of saltpeter and keep it in his desk in the Oval Office.

Opinions

Ive been looking through the papers again so I could have some opinons. Thats what I do for a living—have opinions. Im lucky. You probably make only a few friends mad with your dumb opinions. I get to make millions of people mad with mine.

President Clinton says we're going to have the first balanced budget in thirty years. A poll showed that most people would rather make Social Security safe with the extra money than have their taxes reduced.

Public opinion isnt that smart very often. Its really surprising that a democracy works as well as ours does because let's face it, public opinion is usually pretty stupid. If we voted on everything, the average American would be wrong about three quarters of the time. Not me, mind you. Im thinking more of you.

President Clinton plans to get another $65 billion from cigarette companies to help the budget. I dont like that. Either make tobacco illegal or leave smokers alone. If its money the Government's after, why dont they make marijauna and cocaine legal and tax that the way they tax tobacco?

It looks as if we're going to bomb Iraq. Boy, I dont know about that either. Im not for starting a war but you have to figure the President knows more about what weapons Saddam Hussein's got than he's telling us. He must know that Iraq's getting close to being able to wipe us out or wipe someone out. Israel, probably. I still trust the President enough to believe that if we do it, we had to do it.

In Texas they offed a woman named Karla Faye Tucker the other night. She killed two people with a pickaxe and then claimed she got religion in prison. Its amazing how devout murderers become when theyre locked up.

The death penalty is barbaric for a civilized Country but if thats the state law, Karla Faye sure had it coming. For one thing, I favor equal rights for women. In the past twenty-two years, 434 people had been executed in the United States; just one of them was a woman. That doesnt seem fair. Women have a long way to go before they gain equality being capitally punished.

The single best story I read this week was about a new glue doctors have that they can use instead of stitches to put you back together after they operate and open you up.

I hope it works—glue is often a disappointment though. Too often it wont do what they claim it will. Anyone who has ever tried to mend a broken dish or cup knows that.

Ive been sewed up three times now . . . once for my appendix and twice for hernias. Never been glued together.

Valentine's Day

Yesterday was Valentine's Day and I was thinking about how cluttered our calendar is with holidays and special days like that.

Arent there any of these we could get rid of? Having so many special days makes each one of them less special.

Halloween and Valentine's Day arent really important except that next to Christmas, stores sell more stuff on those two days than on any other day of the year.

The greeting card companies have turned love into an industry and some of these cards are ridiculous. Can you imagine sending a sappy Valentine to your son? My son would call to ask if I had lost my marbles.

Here's one for sisters to give each other . . . "Your warmth and thoughtfulness make such a difference in my life." I watched three girls grow up together as sisters and they liked each other but the only warmth they got was when one of them stole the other's underwear.

"To a dear Aunt with love on Valentine's Day." Valentine's Day isnt for aunts.

This one says "From the two of us . . ." You dont go in together with someone on a Valentine. Its a personal thing.

And this is touching . . . you put money in the envelope. Romantic?

Theyre even selling dirty Valentines.

This is one of the milder ones:

". . . Theres this intimate, out-of-the-way romantic little place I'd like to share with you . . . If we go there tonight, we can watch the light reflecting off the water . . . "

Inside, theres a picture of a bathtub.

Look at all this junk they sell though. This bear on a polyester pillow was made in China. I doubt if the Chinese know from Valentine's Day.

When I was in the third or fourth grade, I loved Valentine's Day. We made our own valentines and gave them to the girls we liked. I dont think anyone makes their own valentines anymore. The big thing was, you didnt sign them so the girls werent supposed to know who they were from.

Hallmark wouldnt like it but you cant beat a homemade valentine. I always had trouble trying to draw a heart.

"Heart-shaped" is hard to draw freehand. I dont know where that phrase "heart-shaped" came from either.

If youve ever seen pictures of a bypass operation, you know that hearts are not "heart-shaped." They dont look anything like this "heart-shaped" box of candy or this lollipop.

Love is the ultimate form of friendship—the very best human emotion—and Valentine's Day is a celebration of love. Giving someone a card with a bad poem on it or a heart-shaped box of cheap candy is not my idea of the best way to express that sentiment once youve had your twelfth birthday.

Vans

The big news in the car business is that fewer people are buying cars—theyre buying vans instead.

Chevrolet got itself a lot of publicity recently by giving a monster fifteen-passenger van to the McCaugheys, the parents of the septuplets.

The McCaugheys seem like nice people and it was good of Chevrolet to give them the van but I hope driving big vans and having seven children doesnt become popular in America. If every couple did that, there wouldnt be room enough on our roads for the vans or in our schools for the kids.

We dont need bigger cars OR bigger families. There are already more vehicles on our roads than the roads can handle and more kids in our schools than the schools can teach.

I was curious to see what it would be like to have one of those big vans so I rented one. I wanted to see how it drove.

Now I know how a Greyhound bus driver must feel.

Weekends I do a lot of shopping so I tried parking it at the mall.

I should have qualified for handicapped parking with that thing. It was like trying to dock the *Queen Elizabeth.*

Sometimes I drive to work but when I take the train, I park at the station in our little town in Connecticut. I wanted to see how that would work out. The space was small and I stuck out too far in back to park.

When I buy a new car, I keep it in the garage. Im very careful of it until I put the first dent in it. I wanted to make sure the van would fit in my garage. Here's a play-by-play:

ROONEY (parking in his garage):

I have the magic opener here . . . the door opener, one of the greatest inventions. Now is the van going to go in there? Is it clearing over there, Bob? . . . Maybe I ought to get those skis out of there on the side of the garage for more room . . . shovel, too . . . not making it with the mirror am I? . . . What if I fold the mirror in? What about the bicycle? . . . Is that in the way? I could come another six inches . . . Its not going to make it, is it?

I wish we'd start thinking small in this Country . . . both cars and families.

Olympics

Broadcast rights to the Olympics never should have been sold to anyone. They should be covered by all the networks as a news event. If they did that, the network that had the fewest commercial interruptions would get the most viewers. That would put the pressure on them not to ruin the Olympics for us by having more commercials than events as has been the case this year.

Im a sports fan. I like them all and I have this terrible feeling that sports are choking to death on money. Basketball players making ten million dollars a year. Shortstops signing for $33 million.

During the Olympics, I was sitting in my living room having a good time thinking how great it was that this freckle-faced, all-American kid, Picabo Street, won the downhill ski race—next thing I know, theres Picabo doing a Chapstick commercial. Whatever happened to amateur athletics? Are there any left?

There are some basic problems with the winter Olympics as a television show, anyway. For one thing, too many events arent won in direct competition. Half the time, the winner is decided by a stopwatch or by a bunch of biased judges. Tara Lipinski was great. Michelle Kwan was great. Who says one was better than the other? No one but the judges understand the scoring in figure skating.

How come one skater gets a 5.4 and another a 5.3. Why doesnt one of them get a four and the other a three? What are the fractions and the decimal points all about? Why not just a plain ten for Tara? She was perfect.

The skiing events are settled by ridiculously small fractions of seconds. A skier comes all the way down the hill a mile long and loses by four tenths of a second.

Do you know how long less than half a second takes?

I'd like to see all the skiers standing up there on top of the hill together. The starter shoots the gun, theyd all start down.

The first skier to cross the finish line wins. Never mind four tenths of a second. The ice skaters usually race a few at a time against the clock. They ought to compete against each other, too. Thats the way runners do in track events.

My major complaint about television coverage of all sports events, not just the Olympics, is that producers dont understand how important pauses in the action are for viewers.

They think that when the football players arent hitting each other that fans arent interested. Wrong. Half the fun of watching any game is thinking about what a team is going to do next.

Television ruins it by filling in all the pauses with commercials or chatter from the announcers.

Shut up, for gosh sakes, and let us enjoy the game.

Fred W. Friendly

You get to be my age, friends die.

During the war, I lost friends I grew up with. Obie Slingerland and I were co-captains of our high school football team. At that age, I had not understood how dear a friend Obie was until he died in his fighter plane in the Pacific when he was twenty-three.

But then there were a lot of years when everything just went rolling along. I had the same friends year after year. Now Im losing friends again. Its another kind of war.

All of us at CBS had a great loss this week. It was a great loss for you, too, but you probably dont even know it. Fred W. Friendly died. You know who Fred was? It seems likely that you do not even though he was responsible for a lot of good information you got over the years.

You probably know who Edward R. Murrow was because his fame depended on his having been seen on television as one of the first and best news broadcasters. He's part of television history. You know Murrow, in some part, at least, because Fred Friendly was the producer of much of the work that made Ed Murrow a household name on radio during World War II and then on television when television took hold in about 1950.

Im not calling it the television news business—which it is now—because Fred never thought of it as a business. He thought of it as a crusade. He had the ego to believe he could make this a better Country by informing its people about their world.

He turned this Country in another direction, a better direction, when he and Ed destroyed the tyrant Senator Joe McCarthy simply by revealing McCarthy to the voters for what he was. When people in television news talk about "the good old days," theyre talking about Fred Friendly and the ethical standards of broadcast journalism he established and lived by.

Fred thought words were more important than pictures too.

As a writer I liked him for that. Not everyone liked Fred, though.

I know a man who Fred fired when he worked at CBS. The man got another job, a better job, in public television. When Fred quit CBS because the company refused to preempt its lucrative morning soap opera schedule to broadcast an important news event, he went to the Ford Foundation, which gave large amounts of money to public television and was an important influence on it. Fred had the executive he had fired at CBS, fired again.

I'd forgotten the details and one day last year I was talking to this fellow, also a friend of mine, about what terrible shape Fred was in after several strokes and how bad I felt about it. I didnt get much reaction so I said, "You dont care?"

He paused a second, then said, "How would you feel about someone who fired you twice?"

Its a mistake to have a friend who is your boss. Fred was both to me but a lot more likeable as a friend than as a boss. Even when I cursed him as my boss, I loved him as my friend.

If a democracy depends for its strength on people being informed about the issues, news is important to a democracy. Thats what Fred Friendly believed. Informing people and making them think was the end towards which he devoted his ability and his brain. He had more of both than anyone in television news before or since.

Tobacco

I want to say something about tobacco. We all owe something to the tobacco companies.

Hate is such a satisfying emotion and how many things are there that we all hate as much as we hate the tobacco companies?

In Congress, theyve been arguing about a law that would make the tobacco companies pay $516 billion for a so-called "settlement."

What's to settle?

Smoking cigarettes often leads to death from lung cancer or heart disease. Why is Congress pussyfooting around?

SEN. HOLLINGS:
Because it is very complicated and not very pleasing to everybody.

REP. GINGRICH:

My position is that the money has to go to children's health. Thats the biggest single question I have about the entire tobacco deal.

In Kentucky, President Clinton said he didnt want to put tobacco companies out of business: "We have no interest whatever of putting the tobacco companies out of business. I just want them to get out the business of selling tobacco to children."

Well, why in the world DOESNT he want to put them out of business? I like children but I like adults too. Why is it okay to kill them?

How does the President feel about the Mexican drug cartels? Which weed has killed more people over the years, tobacco or marijuana? Its no contest. Tobacco has.

Marijuana and cocaine are bad for people so they are illegal. Why isnt tobacco illegal?

The idea that the United States Government actually pays farmers to grow tobacco is one of the most outrageous mysteries of our capitalist economy. We should pay them NOT to grow tobacco.

Tobacco companies are trying to make up for the loss of business in the United States by selling more cigarettes in foreign countries. Its no wonder Americans are thought of as the bad guys abroad.

Its no worse to sell a carton of cigarettes to a sixteen-year-old American kid than it is to sell a carton to a sixteen-year-old in Africa, China or South America.

It should be as illegal to export cigarettes as it is to import cocaine.

Smokers make some people mad. They dont make me mad, they make me sad. We've got a couple of them right here at *60 Minutes*. Harry Reasoner was addicted to cigarettes. Morley smokes several packs a day.

The tobacco companies are addicted . . . not to cigarettes. Theyre addicted to money. They cant get enough of it.

Andy Reviews *The Times*

It seems right that newspapers review television shows to give their readers an idea of whether they are good, bad or indifferent.

It seems wrong that television does not review newspapers.

Television doesnt review newspapers because its afraid to, thats why. We dont want to get bad reviews so we are not critical of reviewers who are critical of us.

The New York Times seldom has anything good to say about television. Its been critical of television's coverage of the White House scandal. When the Paula Jones case was dismissed by Judge Wright one reporter referred to a "phalanxes of television pundits." She said a Fox News anchor "intoned" something.

The same reporter says, "Tom Brokaw of NBC weighed in" . . . with something. Tom didnt "weigh in" with anything, he just said it. Television critics are so superior they ought to be President.

Did that *Times* reporter notice that the *Times* editorial writer "weighed in" with 500 words on the same subject that day?

Here the reporter suggested people arent interested in television coverage of the White House scandal.

"Some people said they didnt even bother to turn on their televisions . . ." she wrote.

Does the *Times* think then that no one reads its columnists when they write about it? In the past two weeks, a phalanx of *Times* pundits, Bill Safire, Abe Rosenthal, Maureen Dowd and Frank Rich have mentioned Clinton, Paula Jones and Monica Lewinsky a total of thirty-seven times. Weigh that.

The *Times* has complained that there are too many commercials on TV. Well, of course there are too many commercials, we all know that but have

Times critics looked at their Automobiles section in the Sunday paper recently? It makes commercials on television look scarce. Look at this . . . one half page of editorial copy in this section of the paper and then twenty-two solid pages of advertising. Any comment, television critics?

This is a recent Sunday magazine section of *The*

Times. Do they have any standards of taste for advertisements in this?

If this kind of ad was a television show, there'd be a warning telling kids to leave the room.

And if a guy at *The Times* tacked up this picture near his desk, wouldnt some woman reporter accuse him of sexual harassment?

Here's a full page ad on the back of the section. Calvin Klein is apparently trying to sell underwear. Is underwear the first thing you think of looking at this ad? It certainly isnt going to keep this sweet young thing warm in winter.

Well, if any of you television reviewers are watching, I think you know Im not knocking you or newspapers. This is all done in good fun. Just kidding around.

Kenneth Starr

Tonight Im conducting my own in-depth investigation of the special prosecutor, the investigative Kenneth Starr.

Starr is the kind of person who, when the photographer says

"smile," he smiles even though he has little to smile about.

No one trusts a man who smiles in adversity.

Even at an early age young Kenny Starr was smiling for the photographer . . . here in his graduation picture.

It says something about Kenneth Starr's character that he always sits in the back seat of a car. Ive never trusted a man who sits in the back seat. If I had a chauffeur, I'd sit up front with him to give him driving advice.

We know who this woman is (Monica Lewinsky) kissing the President because we've seen it a thousand times . . . we do not know who this mystery woman is in this picture with Ken Starr.

Kenneth Starr has tried to get a list of the books that Monica Lewinsky has bought recently. We tried to find out what books Kenneth Starr has been reading.

He certainly hasnt been reading the newspapers delivered to his house. We visited and saw the papers piled up outside.

Kenneth Starr is outspoken. Over the past few years, he has frequently and outspokenly not spoken a word about his investigation.

STARR:
I cant comment on specific . . . well, I dont want to comment on what ah . . . I cant speak well. I cant comment on . . . again, I cant answer specific questions, I just cant comment on that . . . Im just going to stay with the comments I previously made.

Ken Starr always says the investigation is proceeding quickly.

STARR:
Well, the investigation is moving as Ive said before very quickly . . . etc. . . . etc. . . . etc. . . .

Nothing about the investigation is going quickly, Mr. Starr, and if you think so, you better get a new watch.

This concludes my investigation of Kenneth Starr, who has spent $40 million trying to prove something about President Clinton that most of us already thought was true anyway.

The Cancer Cure

Theres been more good news in the news lately than we're used to. The economy's good with the stock market way up and unemployment way down.

It must make the job of being President bearable for Bill Clinton.

Do you remember the report that a moderate amount of drinking was good for people?

That was good news for me. I'd been feeling kind of guilty about it for years and I dont have to anymore. Now I think of bourbon as a medicine.

Something else I like that Ive felt guilty about is salt. I use too much of it. So what happened this week? More good news. Not eating any salt can be bad for you. This is the kind of news I live for.

The other medical breakthrough that everyone's talking about is Viagra, the pill that enhances sexual ability in men. It seems somehow wrong to take a pill for that. Most men dont need it—we all know at least one who doesnt.

When you talk about the best news we've had in years, here's a name you ought to learn how to spell: JUDAH FOLKMAN.

Strange name . . . you know who it is? You ought to. Dr. Folkman has discovered a way to inhibit the growth of malignant tumors—cancer in mice—and if it works for people, his name is going to be added to the list of the great names in medical research like Wilhelm Roetgen, discoverer of x-rays, Alexander Fleming, penicillin, Jonas Salk, cure for polio, and Louis Pasteur. Dr. Folkman's name doesnt ring a bell yet but his name could be the greatest of all if this stuff really works.

Someone said that, so far, its only good news for mice with cancer but I have a sneaking feeling from the way they released this report that its better than that. They say it'll be two years before the drug is available but they'll probably get it out sooner than that.

The pressure's going to be tremendous on them.

I was thinking this morning how terrible it would be to discover I had cancer and realize I'd probably just barely miss out on being cured with this stuff. Its called angiostatin and endostatin.

What the drugs have done with mice is cut off the supply of blood to tumors by shrinking the veins or arteries or whatever it is that feeds them so the tumors dont grow, they die.

More than half a million people died of cancer last year, 556,000 . . . its not a good way to go either, so a possible cure is as good as news gets.

We dont need another national holiday but if his discovery is as good as it sounds, the next one should be named Judah Folkman Day.

(Progress in medicine must seem slow if youre dying of something for which theyve announced a cure. Dr. Folkman's work has lead to progress but not a cure in the treatment of colon cancer.)

Visitors with Money

Tourism is not what you normally think of as an industry because the only thing it makes is money. Tourism, though, may be the biggest business in the world.

Every community fights to attract strangers to come to see its sights because tourists come with money and leave without it. If they dont have any sights to see, they invent something like Disney World.

Considering how much cities spend to woo people it seems strange that the name tourist itself has become sort of a dirty word. That may account for the trend towards calling them visitors instead of tourists.

Tourists are so easily spotted they might as well wear signs reading "Kick me."

Their uniform identifies them. They wear shorts in summer, carry some sort of bag . . . or backpack . . . and always have their cameras at the ready. The guidebook told them to wear sensible shoes so they wear sandals, which are not sensible at all.

Tourists need pictures of landmarks to prove to friends back home that theyve been somewhere. They enjoy their trip most after they get back home. They tell friends how wonderful it was—no matter how terrible it was.

In their desperate attempt to attract tourist dollars, cities come up with all kinds of fake attractions . . . gimmicks like imitation antique trolley cars.

Horse-drawn carts that bear no relation to the life of the city they are in are popular with tourists.

Nothing comes cheap for them. In New York, a ride through Central Park behind a smelly horse in a hansom cab goes for $68 an hour.

Every inducement is offered to attract tourists to a city but once they come, theyre treated like cattle.

Several times a day they are rounded up and herded off into a bus to be taken to another location. This gives other business people a chance to get some of their money.

Tourists have no real purpose. Theyre looking for something wonderful in a strange place and they cant find it. Often what theyre looking for doesnt exist. If it does exist, when they get there, its full of other tourists who got there first.

In the cities, they walk out the front door of their hotel and, immediately, theyre lost.

They consult their map but have no point of reference because their hotel isnt on the map.

Foreigners gape from afar at the seat of power here in the United States where our President lives. They strain to get closer for the best possible view of our White House.

Perhaps he's explaining to his friend, that the Lincoln bedroom is on the second floor and is nice—but very expensive.

Tourists are looking for a good time and good times are elusive anywhere. You cant set out to have a good time and expect to find one. In real life, good times most often come unexpectedly.

In spite of the cost, the discomfort, the disaappointment and the inconvenience of travel, no amount of evidence to the contrary can convince determined tourists that they should have stayed home on their vacation and done some work around the house.

Baseball

Even if youre not a baseball fan you have to enjoy the competition between Sammy Sosa and Mark McGwire to see who can hit the most baseballs over the fence.

Its just fun and its so nice to be able to turn to the back pages of the newspaper and find a good, clean story.

Part of the fun is what good guys both McGwire and Sosa seem to be. They even like each other.

Baseball players arent always that sportsmanlike.

The New York Yankees were good enough to send me some used Louisville Sluggers. They are pretty nice bats. This one is broken I notice. George Steinbrenner must have sent me this one. The average player breaks a hundred bats a year.

They break easier now because the handle is so much thinner. Someone told me Babe Ruth used the same bat the whole year.

The owners of professional teams are always making things worse but big league baseball has done at least one thing right. Theyve kept the wooden bat.

Both McGwire and Sosa use Rawlings bats. Rawlings sent us some beauties. Made of ash. Ash is hard, like oak, but it has more flexibility.

Aluminum bats are used outside the major leagues. Thats why you see college scores like 23 to 14.

If the pros hit with those, the ball would come off the bat so fast theyd kill a couple of pitchers every year.

The official baseball costs $12.95 so McGwire and Sosa will cost their teams about $1,800 in balls alone.

When I was a kid we used cheap balls and the cover always came off after a while so we wrapped it with black tape. I'd like to see how many home runs McGwire or Sosa could hit with a ball wrapped with tape.

I cut two balls in half to see the difference between a cheap one and an expensive one.

The cheap ball is solid cork. The major league baseball has what looks like a high-tech, rubber center.

Do you really think Babe Ruth got to hit a ball like this?

Here's what I'd like to do with the ball I cut in half. I'd like to get Mark McGwire to autograph one half . . . and Sammy Sosa to autograph the other half. Then I'd put them together. Wouldnt that be some souvenir baseball?

And, of course, if I ever wanted to play with it, I'd just wrap it with black tape.

Impeach

Most people dont know what theyre talking about when they talk about "impeaching" the President.

The word sounds good so we all use it.

"To impeach" means to accuse someone of having done something wrong. Thats all it means.

This week a committee asked the House of Representatives for authorization to look into the question of whether or not to impeach President Clinton. Kenneth Starr didnt look into the sex lives of the committee members deciding the President's fate.

If the House ultimately votes to impeach the President, that is, accuses Mr. Clinton of committing what the Constitution describes as treason, bribery or other high crimes and misdemeanors . . . it then goes to the Senate.

Its complicated in the Senate. A delegation from the House prosecutes the case like lawyers. It will be a trial just like in a courtroom. It could be more interesting than the O. J. Simpson trial except it doesnt have Johnnie Cochran. The judge will be the Chief Justice of the United States. If the Senate says Clinton is guilty of the impeachment charge, then he's gone.

Its not Clinton's relationship with Monica that bothers me, its his relationship with us. We trusted him and he lied.

He fudged about the draft . . . he fudged about marijuana . . . he fudged about Whitewater . . . he lied about Gennifer Flowers . . . he lied to the grand jury and he lied when he looked us in the eye, shook his finger at us and said he hadnt had sex with Monica.

He says its a private matter between him, his family and their God but I doubt if God wants any part of this mess.

Bill Clinton made fools of those of us who voted for him. I used to hate people who called him "Slick Willie" and I hate it even worse now that I know they were right.

Im almost afraid to say this because of all the nasty letters I'll get but I dont think Clinton should be removed from office. Im not thinking of him, Im thinking of us.

We dont have to drag the Country through this mud.

Maybe he never should have been our President but he IS our President. What would removing him from office do for us anyway? He has serious character flaws but he has a lot of ability, too. He's been a bad boy but he hasnt been a bad President . . . and he's probably more able than the guy we get if he's thrown out.

We ought to impeach him, find him guilty on his last day in office and send him back to Arkansas without his pension.

We're the Good Guys

Its been hard to keep up with all the news this week. You cant pay as much attention to it as you know you ought to and still get anything done in your own life.

Monday we got the news that President Clinton had called off the bombing of Iraq.

None of us would admit it but we had sort of looked forward to that bombing.

We all know that crisis in Iraq isnt over. Saddam Hussein is a bad guy and all that stuff he has is a worry . . . wherever you live, you have to worry about some nut dropping a jar of anthrax in your neighborhood.

Tuesday anyone who cared could have listened to Monica Lewinsky on tape talking to tacky Linda Tripp.

MONICA:
You know its really weird. I keep hearing these double clicks.

TRIPP:
Thats my gum.

MONICA:
Oh, okay.

Kenneth Starr took over Thursday with his testimony.

STARR:
The evidence suggests that the President participated in a scheme.

What President Clinton does about Iraq is more important to all of us than what Kenneth Starr does to President Clinton.

By Friday, with everything going on, we'd just about forgotten the Serbs and the Croats, the Israelis and the Palestinians, and the floods in Central America.

Its no wonder newspapers run comic strips.

Its funny . . . its not funny, its unusual . . . but with all the lying Bill Clinton has done about his personal life, most of us still trust him, as President Clinton. We trust him to handle the mess with Iraq.

Generally speaking though, Americans would be happy if the rest of the world just went away and left us alone. Foreign affairs doesnt interest us. Its probably because we're selfish. We got ours.

Things are going good here and we know it.

Even the poorest among us are better off than the poor in other countries. Even better off than the rich in some countries.

One of the things Americans dont understand—or I dont understand it anyway and Im American—is why everyone hates us. We seem like such nice people to ourselves.

But they hate us everywhere . . . In Pakistan they hate us . . . in Panama . . . the Nicaraguans hate us . . . Clinton is burned in effigy in India. Uncle Sam gets strung up in Jordan.

Followers of other religions around the world hate us . . . not because most Americans are Christian . . . but because theyre American.

Why do they hate us? We've tried to do the right thing . . . in this century, anyway.

In World War II we did the right thing . . . and we were gracious winners too. We put Germany—all of Europe—back on its feet.

When U.S. soldiers were sent to fight in Vietnam, it may have been a mistake but we had good intentions. We didnt do it for any selfish, evil reason. There was nothing in it for us, economically.

We're so good at selling ourselves things with all our advertising . . . why are we so bad at selling ourselves to the rest of the world?

If we bomb Iraq—which seems likely—we ought to mount a major campaign to make it clear to the rest of the world that we're doing it because its the right thing to do.

Im not much of a flag-waving American but we're the good guys here and we ought to make sure that everyone knows that.

1999

Andy Answers His Mail

The price of stamps just went up again and to save money, I thought I'd answer a couple of letters here on the air instead of mailing them.

I was surprised at how many angry letters I got after I spoke about the Christmas card I received from the White House signed by Bill and Hillary. I said that I didnt know if I really wanted a card from Bill Clinton.

People thought I was ungrateful. This letter is typical:

"Dear Andy, Trashing the Clinton's Christmas card which pictured their dining room table with 12 chairs, and your comment that you didnt think they had 10 friends who'd come to dinner, was a cheap shot. Im a friend of the Clintons and would happily accept any invitation to The White House.

"Youve lost me, Andy."

Signed, Ann Landers.

Okay, Ann. I guess I was wrong. That'll be three of you at the table, anyway.

Im surprised at how polarized our Country is in relation to President Clinton. A lot of people dont think he's done anything wrong or, if he has, that its anyone's business but his own.

And then there are the people who hate Bill Clinton. Theyve always hated him and nothing he can ever do will keep them from hating him for the rest of their lives. They call him "Slick Willie." You cant talk to these people.

Im glad everyone else is so sure of what they think about Bill Clinton because I dont know what I think. I do know I like the people who like him, better than I like the people who hate him. Maybe that'll get me back in good with Ann Landers.

Its maddening the way Clinton has acted so imperiously about impeachment . . . as if it was just another rap he's going to beat. Slick Willie.

So help me, I think if he broke down . . . said he was sorry and sounded as if he meant it, we'd all excuse him, Republicans and Democrats alike.

If I were in the Senate, I'd vote against throwing him out of office. As far as censure goes . . . what's censure? He's been impeached . . . thats censure. It will be a black mark on his record for all the rest of history. Thats censure enough.

But I know youre tired of hearing about Bill Clinton and impeachment. Here's a better letter . . . from Tom Brokaw. Tom has a best-selling book out called *The Greatest Generation*. He quoted me in it, used my picture and said my contribution made him feel good. "Dear Andy," Tom wrote:

"Would you please send me the name and address of your favorite charity? I'd like to continue the good feeling by making a contribution in your name."

Well thanks a lot, Tom. Thats very kind of you . . . my favorite charity . . . let me think a minute. I'll tell you what to do Tom . . . why dont you just make the check out to me and I'll handle it from there.

Ingredients

Next to the newspaper, the thing I read most is labels on packages of food. I read more labels than novels or directions on how to do something or how to put together something I bought. Ive probably read words like riboflavin, lecithin, niacin and partially hydrogenated vegetable oil ten thousand times. Ive eaten the stuff ten thousand times and I have no idea what riboflavin, lecithin, niacin or partially hydrogenated vegetable oil is—or are.

Corn flakes have riboflavin in it. Crackers have niacin, thiamine mononitrate and riboflavin. Others have niacin, reduced iron, thiamine mononitrate, riboflavin . . . natural flavor, it says.

White Castle hamburger buns have niacin, mono- and diglycerides, polysorbate 60.

We went to a commercial drug company and bought some food additives to see what they really look like before they add them to anything.

This is a little bottle of the magic potion—riboflavin. Yellow. Looks like curry powder. It says, "KEEP FROM CHILDREN." I dont know why they would say that. They put it in everything that kids eat. If its dangerous to children what are they doing adding it to everything?

Sodium Alginate . . . Polysorbate 20. This is a liquid . . . You could have this on the rocks. It looks like motor oil. I wonder if there was a chemist who failed to be successful because he only came up with Polysorbate 19.

Guar gum is a popular ingredient. A jar of olives has guar gum in it. Why would they put guar gum in olives?

The definition of lecithin in *The Handbook of Food Additives* reads: "Mixture of the diglycerides of stearic, palmitic and oleic acids linked to the chlorine ester of phosphoric acid" . . . Well, sure . . . And its really good for us?

Lecithin is in almost everything you eat. These are cute little devils. They look like jelly beans.

This is thiamine mononitrate . . . iron metal here . . . and it really is iron . . . very finely ground. It tastes a little tinny.

If all this stuff is so good, how come we dont get to use it ourselves when we're cooking?

I looked through the *Joy of Cooking* and *Fanny Farmer*. Not a single word in here about any of these ingredients. Why didnt Irma Rombauer or Fanny use riboflavin in her recipes if its so good ?

Pepperidge Farm cookies. Theyre good cookies but listen to this lyric prose on their label: "STROLLING DOWN A COBBLESTONE STREET TO YOUR FAVORITE EUROPEAN BAKE SHOP. THE AROMA OF OLD WORLD BAKING FILLS THE AIR. PEPPERIDGE FARM BRINGS THAT EXPERIENCE HOME."

Then look at the ingredients on the other side . . . iron . . . thiamine mononitrate . . . riboflavin and partially hydrogenated vegetable shortening. Cant you practically smell that stuff filling the air of a cobblestone street in Europe? The other thing a lot of labels say these days of course is, "ALL NATURAL." You cant expect them to say, "WITH A LOT OF FAKE INGREDIENTS."

America

Ive been trying to put my finger on what's wrong about the mess in Washington. Its pretty good entertainment but something is seriously wrong about it . . . wrong for this Country.

I guess its a healthy thing for people to be suspicious of their Government but they ought to respect it.

Americans are proud that we can say terrible things about ours and not get arrested. We're always reminding ourselves that a lot of people in the world cant do that.

The funny thing about it, considering how much we say we complain about our United States Government, is how much we love being American.

We're the most patriotic people on Earth. Nationalism is like another religion. We're not all Catholic or Protestant or Jewish or Moslem but we're all American. Instead of a cross or a Star of David, the identifying icon and object of our worship is the American flag, The Stars and Stripes.

Our great sound isnt a hymn or The Lord's Prayer, its our National Anthem, *The Star-Spangled Banner*.

And we dont bow down when its being played, either. We stand at proud attention.

We like ourselves and like being American so much, that its offensive to people in other countries. They find us objectionable. We're ugly Americans.

So what's wrong if we're always making nasty remarks about our Government? What's wrong if we say things like, "Theyre all a bunch of crooks?" Probably nothing if we're half-joking but government stands between a disorganized mob of people . . . thats us . . . and chaos.

We pool our tax money to police ourselves through Government. We organize our public services through our Government. The Government fights our wars . . . helps us stay healthy. The Government tries to make sure kids get an education . . . it provides us with some security in our old age.

It isnt good when the basic premise . . . the premise being that Government can do things for us that we cant do for ourselves . . . is undermined. Thats what theyre doing to us now . . . undermining our confidence in Government. Thats what the President has done. Thats what the House and Senate are doing. This mess is more than about an immoral President or elected officials who are putting their political party ahead of their brains. Its about faith in Government. Jokes about the Government are one thing. This is no joke.

They are providing us with evidence that the people we elected to write and execute the rules that control our lives arent good enough to do that.

Thats what's wrong with what's going on in Washington.

Budget Surplus

The next argument the Republicans and Democrats are going to have after the impeachment proceedings of President Clinton is the budget. I hope theyre nicer to each other this time.

The budget is a problem this year for an unusual reason . . . too much money. There was a surplus of $70 billion last year and Congress cant decide what to do with all that money. Its as if they all went to the Capitol cloakroom and found $20 bills in their raincoat pockets that they had forgotten.

Now . . . theres a catch to all this. The surplus sounds great but our National Debt is $5.6 trillion.

A billion is a thousand million. A trillion is a million million. Thats what we owe, $5.6 million million. Of course, its never really clear who we owe it to . . . ourselves, I guess.

But if you piled up a million million dollars in dollar bills, the pile would reach to the moon and back. Im just trying to impress you. I have no idea how high $5.6 trillion one-dollar bills would be. I made that up.

The interest alone on our National Debt last year was $243 billion. Will someone please tell me why in the world we dont start paying what we owe before we start throwing money around?

Politicians looking for votes are even suggesting the Government give the money back to taxpayers.

Rep. Jennifer Dunn: "Next year there will be a $63 billion budget surplus. Mr. President, give it back."

Nonsense, Congresswoman. The rebate wouldnt pay for your hairdo. Why suggest we're rolling in dough when we're deep in debt? Pay off the National Debt while things are good so you dont have to raise taxes when theyre bad.

The median family income is $35,000. Im a little fuzzy about "median" anything. In this Country poor people are the ones who have only one car and no television set in the bedroom. A tax refund of a few hundred bucks is not going to improve their lives . . . they could take the family to the movies more often, thats about it.

There are other things we should do with this budget surplus, too.

Sooner or later the man I voted for twice to be President was bound to say something I liked.

Clinton: "We make the historic decision to invest the surplus to save Social Security."

He almost made me remember why I voted for him.

The Cat Show

Americans like to pledge that we are one Nation, Indivisible . . . but there are a lot of things beside politics and religion that divide us. There is no one thing about which we are more divided than we are on whether we like or dislike cats.

I went to the International Cat Show in Madison Square Garden Friday. About 800 cats showed up too. These are not your average, everyday, common, ordinary alley cats. I never knew there were so many different kinds of cats. Big cats . . . small cats . . . beautiful cats, homely cats.

It is obvious when you watch them together that people who like cats, like cats better than cats like the people who like them. Cats are absolutely indifferent to the most loving owner. Owners find this loveable about cats.

At the show, owners constantly displayed an affection that was not reciprocal. A kiss is just a kiss but a kiss is nothing to a cat. Cats just dont give a damn.

The show was like one big beauty parlor. Obsessive owners groomed their cats incessantly.

Rooney: "How much time do you spend on yourself and how much on the cat?"

Woman: "About an hour and a half on myself and about an hour and a half on the cat. Equal time . . ."

Rooney: "You look better to me."

Owners philosophize about cats . . . projecting their own fantasies into the imaginary psyches of their animals. They endow cats with mystical qualities cats dont have.

Man: "They are more honest than people."

Woman: "You have to earn a cat's love."

Man: "Cats are touchers . . . They touch with the mind . . . they touch with the body."

Man: "They take life on their terms, not yours . . . "

Woman: "Persians are a very laid-back breed . . . "

Man: "There are certain cats that will come to you because you dont like them . . ."

Vet: "That is the mystique of the cat . . . "

In a cat boutique, owners could buy rat-shaped catnip to provide their pets the ecstacy of a vicarious kill. They have toothbrushes with which to clean the cat's teeth afterwards.

A lot of owners gave their cats pillows that looked as if they were made of cat fur to me. Youd think a cat would object. Worse than cooking lamb in its mother's milk.

One woman even had a long sweater of suspect origin. Looked like cat to me.

We didnt stay to see who the top cat was but reading the newspaper the next day, we found we were lucky. We had taken pictures of Nobu, the grandest puddy cat of them all.

The judges all thought Nobu was the cat's meow. I was indifferent.

Monica

I know how tired all of you are of Monica . . . so tired of her that 70 million of you watched Barbara interview her.

Im tired of her myself and just to make sure, I bought the book that so many of you who are tired of her are buying. *Monica's Story.*

While I was at it, I bought *Diana . . . Her True Story* by the same author . . . Andrew Morton.

This is called just *Monica's Story*, not her TRUE story. Maybe it isnt as true. Linda Tripp says it isnt true at all and no one knows more about deceit than the lovely Linda.

I didnt realize Princess Di and Monica were so much alike. Either that or the author makes everyone he writes about seem the same.

Sometimes it was hard for me to remember which book I was reading. Guess which book this paragraph is from:

"The late-night call made plain the couple's undying affection for one another, not least by its sometimes childishly lewd intimacy."

Clinton and Monica? Wrong, thats in the book about Diana. He's talking about Prince Charles and Camilla Whatshername.

Diana and Monica are both insecure in the books.

Diana was "lacking in self-confidence when she should have had lots."

He says Monica's nagging insecurity made her constantly doubt her own worth to . . . him (the President).

"Estep (her therapist) found Monica anxious and depressed, with a very low sense of self-esteem."

Well, if Monica had a low opinion of herself, its one of the few times she showed good judgment.

Morton tries to make Monica likeable but fails. For instance, she babbled to everyone.

"While she was not absolutely sure that the tiny stains in the fabric (on the blue dress) were from the President, she did joke with (her friends) Neysa and Catherine about it, saying that if he was responsible, he should pay the dry cleaning bill."

She read her friends the messages the President left on her answering machine, too. She says "Im from a generation where women are sexually supportive of each other . . . I know all about my girlfriends' boyfriends, for example, and the President was no different."

Is that really true, girls?

Page 125—"I would always leave (his office) with a Diet Coke; it looked a little more friendly and less sexual."

What a great ad that would make for Diet Coke, wouldnt it? I can see it in big letters on billboards everywhere.

DIET COKE: A LITTLE MORE FRIENDLY . . . A LITTLE LESS SEXUAL.

There are so many people I genuinely like who are difficult to keep as friends, that its a relief and a lot easier to find someone I thoroughly dislike.

Thats why its such a pleasure to read about Monica Lewinsky.

Wealth of Information

I get looking around my office every once in a while . . . you know, just staring.

Things are out of control around here. Im inundated with pieces of paper with information on it. We usually clean this up but this is what my desk normally looks like.

Youd think I'd be learning and getting smarter wouldnt you, but Im not. Im not getting dumber . . . Im staying about the same. Im forgetting old stuff at the same rate Im learning new stuff.

They say old people forget but thats not it. The brain can only hold so much. When its full and you try to put something else in there . . . it pushes something else out.

Thats what makes it seem as if old people forget. Their brains are full.

Young people dont forget because their brains are part empty.

Its why young people seem so dumb sometimes. They have one idea in their head and there arent a lot of them up there yet so the idea rattles around and makes a lot of noise.

I get information on my computer, too, but the reason young people are better with computers than I am is, their heads are empty so its easy for them to fill it with stuff about computers.

We're all getting more information than we can handle. Theres simply too much of it.

My bookshelves are overflowing. You know you have too many books when you start putting them sideways on top of each other.

But I know these books. My brain is full of the information in them. Look at this shelf—these are all books about how to use the English language.

Over there . . . more books. World War II mostly. I dont need to know all I know about World War II anymore but I cant get it out of my head.

Just outside my office, we have six more shelves of books . . .

All good stuff . . . Here's *Folklore from Adams County, Illinois*. Over here, we keep the newspapers. I dont have time to read all of one newspaper . . . we get seven every day.

It that wasnt bad enough we must get at least

seven newspapers, we get maybe twenty magazines. Does anyone read *Time*, *Newsweek and U.S. News*? I mean, all three?

The thing that bothers me is all the millions of bits of information coming in and I have no room left in my brain to store it.

People send me books. A professor in California sent me a book he wants me to read. *Social Ethics of Islam*. You tend to like what you already know, and I wouldnt replace what I know about the English language or World War II to make room for the *Social Ethics of Islam*.

Sorry, Professor. Im going to wait and see the movie.

Hitler and Kosovo

When I was in college, Adolf Hitler was trying to take over Europe.

There was a political movement at the time called America First, led by a senator from Montana named Burton K. Wheeler. America First was telling everyone that Europe's problem was none of our business and I agreed.

Some philosopher I'd read in college had written that "Any peace is better than any war" and that seemed true to me. Why should I die for someone else's freedom? I was certain it was wrong for Americans to get involved in any war in a far away place.

The draft board didnt care what I thought and I was dragged out of college and into the Army, kicking and screaming.

After following the tanks and infantry across France and into Germany, as a reporter for *The Stars and Stripes*, I got to a small prison camp in a town named Thekla. About 250 Jewish prisoners in it had been forced, as slave labor, to make wings for German fighter planes.

When the guards heard we were coming, they poured gas on the roofs of two of the barracks and with the prisoners still inside, set them on fire.

Two days later I got to Buchenwald. By this time, I knew how wrong the idea of America First was. Ive never forgotten how dumb I was thinking it was someone else's war.

I smile and shake my head now when I hear a young senator say the slaughter of the Albanians in Kosovo is none of our business. Its not really a smile, I guess. I dont know what it is. Im saying to myself, "I understand, Senator, I used to be as wrong as you are."

The argument against our involvement in Yugoslavia is that we cant correct every evil in every part of the world. Of course we cant but that doesnt make it wrong for us to stop the slaughter in Kosovo.

A doctor doesnt turn you down as a patient because he cant cure everyone in the world.

We have the weapons, we have the money and we have the moral authority. We even have some help from other countries this time.

Theres nothing in it for us . . . no big oil company is going to make money . . . no bankers. All we'll get out of it is the good feeling of knowing we're helping a lot of poor bastards who dont have the power to help themselves.

It didnt seem as if I'd ever say it about him a few months ago, but I trust President Clinton in this matter. I trust my Country to do the right thing.

Mail

One of the good things in life has always been getting a letter. The trouble is, we have a way of ruining good things and mail has become more of a pain than a pleasure.

The original purpose of an envelope was to enclose the message so that its contents were not revealed until it was opened. Always a little surprise. Now, if theres a blank space anywhere in America, someone writes on it and that includes envelopes.

This is from the Tax Department, State of Connecticut. It says, OPEN IMMEDIATELY. Well, dont order me around, Tax Department, State of Connecticut. I'll decide when to open your envelope and I'll take my own sweet time about it, too. Its bad enough that youre taking my money.

You see this on a lot of envelopes when a company wants you to return something to them—like a check. PLACE STAMP HERE, it says. Do they think we're so dumb we dont know a stamp goes in the upper right-hand corner. If they didnt tell us where to put it, do they think we'd put it on the back on the bottom corner?

IMPORTANT, this one says. I have never in my life received a letter of any kind that had IMPORTANT stamped on the envelope that was in any way important. We all look for ways to save time by throwing away junk mail without reading it and, if the envelope says IMPORTANT, you know its safe to throw away.

This one says, URGENT BALLOT.

A union wants me to vote. This is urgent?

People are always sending me letters marked PERSONAL. This one says both PERSONAL and CONFIDENTIAL.

Its from a salesman named Janis Paris who's trying to sell me a car. How much would you make on the deal, Janis? I bet you keep that "personal and confidential."

Some genius from Santa Ana, California, addressed this envelope to "RADIO SHOW 60 MINUTES. ATTENTION: MICKEY ROONEY." Inside the guy writes, "Some random pains make my handwriting jerky." Well, thats not all that makes you jerky, Fella.

This is from the IRS. OFFICIAL BUSINESS PENALTY FOR PRIVATE USE, $300.

Who are they talking to, me? Are they crazy? Do they think I'd use one of their IRS envelopes for a letter to a friends? Thats how to lose a friend. They couldnt pay me to use this envelope to write to anyone.

We all know which mail we read and which mail we throw out without looking at.

Any letter that has handwriting on the envelope, I drop in the wastebasket unopened. Its the letter-writing nuts who write on the outside of the envelope after theyve sealed it.

Here's an envelope, "A SPECIAL THANK YOU FROM HERTZ." Dont try to con me, Hertz. You know and I know what's inside and its not a gift, its a bill for a car I rented.

The post office needs a new rule: Anyone who puts anything but an address on the outside of an envelope has to use two stamps.

Bombs

We've been in so many minor wars recently, its hard to remember them a few years later. Remember Kosovo and Slobodan Milosevic in Yugoslavia?

Sometimes, after a war is over, its hard to tell who won.

I hope that isnt going to be true this time.

Everywhere you go, you hear people arguing about whether we can beat down Slobodan Milosevic with air power alone.

On the Sunday morning talk shows, I hear people who dont know what theyre talking about talking about the absolute necessity of sending in U.S. ground troops.

There is no doubt that we can bring Milosevic down with air power. And when youre talking about the kind of air power we have, the word "alone" is out of place.

Anyone who doesnt believe 1,000 U.S. warplanes can destroy Milosevic's desire to wipe out the Albanians living in Kosovo doesnt understand what bombs can do.

We're better at this than when the B–17s and B–24s were bombing Germany in 1943 . . . and bombing targets in Yugoslavia is not like bombing woods and fields and hiding places in Vietnam.

Consider what it would be like if we were to drop a bomb on your city, wherever you live.

How would you like to have this happen to one of your public buildings . . . your town hall maybe . . . down the block from your house?

Then we'd go after your telephone and communications centers. With modern bombs and missiles, we can destroy the police headquarters down the block without damaging the hospital across the street.

Next we'd go after your bridges. Thats what we've done in Yugoslavia. You probably cross a river on your way to work in the morning. Most big cities in every country in the world are built on rivers. You cant move if we destroy the bridges.

If you live in Pittsburgh, youd have a hard time if they took out your bridges. Pittsburgh would be an empty island without the bridges that feed into it.

Or Chicago.

I often cross the George Washington Bridge from New Jersey to New York.

How would I get to the office if they destroyed the George Washington Bridge?

Youd have a tough time getting gas if all your oil storage tanks were bombed and burned out the way we've bombed and burned out these near Belgrade. The lines we had during the gas shortage in 1974 would be nothing in comparison.

We're just getting started when we take out the bridges. Next we head for the heating plant. And wait until we put the lights out and cut off television.

If NATO sent in the infantry, it would be quicker, not so messy, more humane. Fewer civilians would die. If we dropped one of our good airborne divisions into Kosovo tomorrow morning, the war would be over by noon.

But dont tell me we cant win this little war without sending in troops on the ground.

Of course we can.

We Want Answers
Not Questions

There are a lot of magazines I enjoy reading but I wish theyd just give me the information they have and stop asking me questions all the time. Half the titles of their articles arent statements, theyre in the form of a question.

The *Weekly Standard* says, "THE NEW EUROPE MENACE OR FARCE?"

Ladies Home Journal says, "WANT TO LOSE 10 LBS.?"

Time wants to know whether Hillary will be the senator from New York. SENATOR CLINTON?

I sat down the other day and tried to answer some of the questions I saw on magazine covers.

Vogue asks me, "WHAT'S YOUR FASHION AESTHETIC?" Listen, *Vogue*, I cant answer that question. If I have a clean shirt and two socks that match in the morning, thats fashion aesthetics enough for me. And anyway, all I want from you is some good-looking women in skimpy clothes.

Harper's—"WHO WAS SHAKESPEARE?" Didnt you watch the Oscars?

Insight magazine's cover says, "ELIZABETH DOLE: WILL THIS WOMAN BE PRESIDENT?"

No, *Insight*. Elizabeth Dole seems very nice but she will not be President and it isnt very insightful of you to ask either. Her husband, Bob, has a better chance of being President than she does and he isnt even running.

Scientific American is the kind of magazine that ought to give us answers but it asks whether space is endless. Let me ask you a question, *Scientific American*. If there is an end to space, what's just beyond the end of it?

Newsweek wants to know where it will end. We dont know where it will end. Thats why we buy your magazine, *Newsweek*. We dont want questions, we want answers. If we knew where it will end, we'd buy *Vanity Fair*.

Bill Buckley's conservative *National Review*'s cover asks, IS SEX STILL SEXY? I hope you arent going all soft on us, Bill. That doesnt seem like a very right-wing question to me.

Time magazine asks about the end of the world. "THE END OF THE WORLD?" *Time* wants to know. No, I dont think so and I dont think you think so, either, *Time*. I notice youre still trying to sell us two-year subscriptions for half off.

Business Week asks, "IS GREED GOOD?"

Thats a serious question. Ive always been puzzled about our capitalist, free enterprise system. It works on the theory that things come out best for everyone if we all greedily grab everything we can for ourselves. If thats true, it shouldnt be.

Men's Health wants to know if Im fat. Well, its none of your business, *Men's Health*. I may not look exactly like this guy on your cover who has been lifting weights while Ive been typing and I might look a little overweight to you but my mother always had a good explanation for it. She said I have big bones.

Business Week has another question. "CBS, CAN CEO MEL KARMAZIN REINVENT NETWORK TV?"

Im reluctant to comment on that. Mel is my top boss here at CBS. I like Mel personally and I love my job. I know CBS shows are doing well and the stock is way up but before Mel reinvents television, I wish he'd arrange to get the elevators working better in this CBS office building.

Old Clothes

At least once a year I decide my clothes closet is too full so I go through it to see what stuff I can throw out or give away.

One of the reasons my closet is so full is that, while my intentions are good, most of the time when I go through it, I dont actually get rid of anything.

I brought in a box with some of this year's candidates.

This is a suit I bought twelve years ago. Can anyone tell me why I ever thought this was something I'd wear? It makes me look as though I run a pawn shop.

It fits me fine but in the twelve years Ive had it, Ive only worn it twice and one of those times I kept my overcoat on so no one would see me in it.

This is a corduroy jacket. I like it. When I get something I like, I usually go buy another.

Im afraid I'll run out of them. Here's the other one . . . slightly different color but otherwise the same. Nice, but the trouble is, I only wear a corduroy jacket about three times a year. Here's a 1984 Giants ticket. It gives you some idea of how often I wear it.

Okay . . . now here's a collector's item and Im the collector. There was a great restaurant in New York years ago named the Quilted Giraffe. The owner, Barry Wine, never gave me a free meal but he gave me a jacket. Can you imagine me wearing this jacket to a Giants game?

We all laughed at Imelda Marcus because she had 1,500 pairs of shoes. A lot of us can understand that. I have three pairs of white bucks with red rubber soles because they were trendy when I was in college. I never wear any of them.

No matter how ugly a necktie is, I never throw one away.

Is that an ugly necktie? The trouble is, its nicely made, it doesnt have any spots on it. Tastes change . . . who knows, next year I may think its good-looking.

There was a time years ago when every man bought what was called "a three-piece suit." Well, the third piece, the vest, has gone out of style. I kept this . . . a tattersall vest. I always dreamed of becoming a smart dresser and smart dressers used to wear tattersall vests.

And here's something I could never throw away. Its my Army Eisenhower jacket with the correspondent's patch on it.

I weighed 185 when I wore this and Im 200 now. As a reporter for *The Stars and Stripes*, I think I interviewed Private Ryan in this.

These are all clothes I should get rid of because Im never going to wear them but what Im going to do is this . . . Im going to pack them up, take them home and hang them back in my closet where they belong.

In the News

Ive been going through a lot of out-of-town newspapers again. Its a last resort when I cant think of anything else.

—This is from the *Seattle Post-Intelligencer*. I love that name, *"Post-Intelligencer."* *Intelligencer* isnt in my dictionary. The story says that Bill Gates is giving $10 million to the Seattle Art Museum.

Gates seems like a good guy even though he's rich. Its hard for someone rich to seem good. In the movies, anyone rich is always a bad guy.

—The Toshiba Corporation . . . they made the computer I have . . . has settled a law suit brought by two men over some flaw in their laptops, for a billion dollars.

The story says "Mr. Shaw and Mr. Moon, the two plaintiffs, are to receive $25,000 each . . . their lawyers stand to make $147 million."

The guys who brought the suit get $25 thousand—the trial lawyers get $147 million. This is Justice in America ?

—The World Wrestling Federation sold $170 million worth of stock in itself.

Professional wrestling is a mystery to me. Its so obviously fake I dont know why anyone with any brains would watch it. Of course, I may have put my finger on the answer right there. No one with any brains does watch but that still leaves them a huge audience.

—My favorite sports story was about the New York Giants quarterback, Kent Graham. He took a hit to the head a few weeks ago and had to leave the game.

The doctor told the coach Graham shouldnt go back in because his head wasnt clear . . . he couldnt answer some questions fast enough. One of the doctor's questions that Graham couldnt answer was "How many nickels are there in $1.35?"

That wasnt a fair question. No professional athlete could answer that even when his head was clear. Ask him how many hundred thousand there are in ten million. Thats their kind of money.

—The Coca-Cola Company is testing a vending machine that will automatically raise the price of a can of Coke during hot weather.

In hot weather maybe I'll automatically buy a can of Pepsi.

—In Miami Beach a restaurant added a tip to the bill of a black customer but didnt add the tip to the bill of any white customer. The owner said he did it because black people dont tip enough.

Tipping is a stupid custom we ought to get rid of. The tip should be part of the bill. Black or white doesnt enter into it.

—I wish I needed a job in Houston, Texas. The *Houston Chronicle* has pages and pages of job openings The worst time I ever had in my life was looking for a job. People with jobs are terrible to people who want one. Thats strange because they must have looked for work at some point themselves.

—I dont know how sports teaams in various cities decide what their nickname will be. They arent all as good as the Yankees, the Green Bay Packers or the Red Sox. The hockey team in Albany, New York, has the worst name I ever saw. They call themselves the River Rats. In the same league, Rochester is called the Americans, Albany is called the River Rats, and I come from Albany.

—A columnist in the *Hartford Courant* says HARTFORD'S DEMOCRATS NEED NEW LEADERSHIP. That doesnt make them a very special political group, does it?

—Some police officers in Evansville, Indiana, were assigned to pose as customers in a club where nude dancers were performing. During the show one of the dancers touched an officer's nose with her breasts. After they watched the whole show, the cops arrested nine of the girls.

Cant you imagine a policeman coming home after work from a job like that? He walks in the door, his wife's in the kitchen getting dinner and she says, "What kind of a day did you have, dear?"

He could say, "Had my nose to the grindstone."

By the way, there are twenty-seven nickels in $1.35.

Mr. Rooney Goes to Sea

It was not long ago when there were three things I'd never done in my life.

Tonight, as I sit before you, there are only two. I have now been down in a nuclear attack submarine. I boarded the Miami in Groton, Connecticut.

I stood on a deck they call "the sail" while we left the harbor . . . under the bridge.

All I knew about submarines was from old movies. I was surprised how much it was really like them.

When we submerged, they actually shouted, "Dive! Dive!"

I thought that was only Hollywood.

And they really did look through a periscope . . . they call it "dancing with the one-eyed lady."

I was never more impressed with young Americans than I was watching the men—boys, many of them, with no more than a high school education—run one of the most complicated machines ever designed—a nuclear submarine.

The Miami is 362 feet long . . . stuffed full of machinery and electronics. Its an incredible package and every inch counts.

There are so many things that have to be done to keep humans alive underwater.

All I could think of down there was getting hit by a depth charge and being trapped inside to drown . . . the crew seemed immune to that thought.

Sailor: "Not at all anymore . . . When I first joined I thought about it. But I dont think about it anymore."

Because it has nuclear power, the boat—they call it a boat—can stay out for as long as the food lasts . . . Food is entertainment on board. The guys eat four meals a day.

They are all guys, too. A submarine would be as hard to integrate as a men's locker room. They share one cramped toilet and shower facility.

His bunk is all the privacy a sailor has.

The sailor in the top bunk has the toughest time going to bed. Unlucky submariners sleep beneath ten tons of torpedo. Each torpedo costs one million dollars.

The submarine is a weapon of war and no one forgets it.

Sailor: "A combination of torpedoes and cruise missiles plus we have twelve vertical tubes for cruise missiles out front."

The best part of the trip was coming up. Its just the opposite of landing in an airplane . . . and twice as exhilarating. It makes you happy . . . and a little surprised, to be alive and breathing again.

If you think the younger generation in our Country has gone to hell, you havent been down with a submarine crew. It brought back all the good memories I have of why we won World War II. It makes you forget Columbine.

Where's Abraham Lincoln?

I dont think any of us are as interested in the people who want to be President as the candidates are in themselves. Its ridiculous that theyre out there campaigning every day as though the election was tomorrow. We're sick of them already and the election isnt until November 7, 2000.

There ought to be a one-year law. No candidate could start campaigning more than one year before election day.

Not many of us are excited about any of them, either.

What we're all after, is a giant of a President . . . someone really great. We dont see anyone like that out there.

Where did all the great Presidents go anyway? Its been too long now since we've had anyone whose face we want to carve out of the rock on Mt. Rushmore.

Al Gore, the Democrat frontrunner, and George Walker Bush, the Republican, seem okay but we ought to have someone better than just okay.

Elizabeth Dole is a smart, attractive woman. Dont write to tell me Im wrong—but a lot of women wont vote for a woman.

Pat Buchanan is probably leaving the Republican Party to join the unreformed Reform Party. The Democrats love that.

Pat's not going to get anywhere near Mt. Rushmore.

No one has anything bad to say about John McCain. We know his war record and he's easy to like. If you arent listening closely, you might think he was a Democrat.

The only candidate causing much interest is Bill Bradley, the one people thought wasnt interesting. No matter what you thought, he'll never be on Mt. Rushmore. He's too tall.

There are outsiders trying to get in on the race now because all those people look easy to beat.

Theres been talk that Warren Beatty wants to be President. He played a senator in the movie *Bulworth*. Maybe he could play President.

Donald Trump is a rich person with a bad haircut who marries beautiful women. He wants to be President. Trump names buildings after himself. The White House might be renamed the Trump House. He's interested in the women's movements. Maybe we'd have Miss Universe on the Trump House lawn . . . the winner would get one night in the Trump/Lincoln bedroom.

Of course, its possible some of the candidates ARE really as good as Washington and Lincoln were. We just didnt look into the personal lives of George and Abe the way we inspect the personal lives of our politicians now.

The Bank's Problem

I know you have problems of your own. You dont watch me to hear someone else's but I have a problem and I need advice.

Wednesday I got a letter from the president of the Chase Manhattan Bank, Michael J. Barrett.

I was surprised that the bank president wrote me himself because when I call the bank, I have a hard time even getting a real person, let alone the president. When I call them, this is what I hear: "PLEASE ENTER THE LAST FOUR DIGITS OF YOUR ACCOUNT NUMBER FOLLOWED BY THE POUND SIGN . . . WE'RE SORRY WE DID NOT RECOGNIZE THE INFORMATION PLEASE STAY ON THE LINE . . . "

As if getting a letter from a bank president wasnt surprise enough, the even bigger surprise was that he enclosed a check made out to me for $9,691.92.

My problem is, I cant decide what to do about it. The bank does not owe me $9,691.92. Theyve made a mistake. Ive called twenty times trying to straighten it out and I get nowhere. It usually goes the other way, of course. The bank makes a mistake in its own favor and people have a terrible time trying to get their money back. I owe those people something.

Here's the story. Last May 11 I was in Columbus Ohio. I ate in a forgettable restaurant except I cant forget it because right after I charged dinner on my Visa card, someone started using my card number to buy all kinds of expensive items. They bought a lot of dot-com stuff. AMAZONDOTCOM, BUY-ITNOWDOTCOM.

The charges were so unlikely—THE TENNIS CO. IN SAN DIEGO, $393—that the Visa security people called to ask if I really bought all of it. I said I hadnt. They were very good. They said that when I got my next bill, I should just pay what I really owed. The total charge was for $14,317.92. I paid $2,270 which I owed and, now, here's where I get lost and I think the bank got lost.

They credited me with $12,047 which I had never paid, either.

Dont try to follow this. Just trust me. They dont owe me money.

This month I didnt get a bill at all. I got the $9,000 check from good old Mike Barrett, my favorite bank president. My question for you is this. Im not in dire straits. But would it be stealing if I just cash the check and keep the money?

Andy's World

I dont know what's wrong with me anyway but there arent many days when I dont think about the end of the world. If theres a God, he waited billions of years to put people on Earth and he might get dissatisfied with us and end the experiment.

Of course we're more apt to end it ourselves.

We've put so much junk in the sky we're destroying the filter between us and the sun and the Earth's getting warmer.

The ice at the North and South Poles is melting so the water's rising. The ocean could move in a hundred miles along the shore and leave cities underwater.

One Antarctic iceberg broke off thats the size of Rhode Island.

Or it could just plain get so hot from the sun that people couldnt stay alive. I'd rather freeze to death than burn to death myself.

We could easily end the world by accident.

Remember Bhopal when an American plant leaked insecticide and killed thousands of Indians?

The Russians almost took the world out at Chernobyl in 1986. That little part of the world is practically dead.

The Japanese could have sent us all to kingdom come last week with their nuclear accident. Wherever "Kingdom Come" is.

And we had our own accident at Three Mile Island back in 1979.

And then what happens when some group of nuts does something on purpose?

A doomsday religious sect in Japan released nerve gas in the Tokyo subway in 1995 and killed a lot of people. How hard would it be to poison the whole world?

Forget the champagne for the year 3000.

On *60 Minutes* Steve Kroft had a story about how Russian prisoners have a tuberculosis bug they cant kill. When the prisoners get out, they bring it with them . . . to other countries, sometimes.

And the medical inventors are a big help. They announced theyve found a way to enable older women to have babies. Just what we need isnt it? More people? We can crowd ourselves to death having sex.

No one will ever know what a great place we had for ourselves here on Earth because there wont be anybody to know.

I hope Im not here when the world ends. I like it too much.

Love all my stuff here in my office.

Good books . . . my television set, ready to tell me what's going on. We have a little refrigerator with cold drinks, hot coffee.

I look out my window . . . great buildings . . . people driving great cars . . .

through the streets of a great city. Planes overhead going to other great cities, London, Paris, Los Angeles . . . Toledo.

If the world does come to an end, I hope its not for another couple of years . . . I just bought a new car and its only got 4,000 miles on it.

Bumpers

You might not think that those of us who do *60 Minutes* set out every day to do good deeds and rout out evil and I dont want to sound self-serving but, in addition to trying to attract an audience and making a lot of money for ourselves, we like to think we make things better sometimes.

Recently I set out to do a report on car bumpers. I was dismayed to find that twenty-nine years ago, in 1970, Mike Wallace and producer Joe Wershba did the exact same piece on bumpers that I was going to do in 1999. Here's an excerpt:

WALLACE:
Mr. Niven, why is it that you people in Detroit cant come up with a standard bumper height and size?

NIVEN:
Well, I think that we not only can do so but we have to do so.

Did Mike stir the automobile industry to make better bumpers? Sorry. Mike did no good at all. Car bumpers are worse than ever.

They no longer stand out from the car . . . Theyre built into it now. Hit the bumper, you hit the car. They dont protect anything except the income of automobile parts departments.

The tire hanging on the back is the bumper for some cars . . . it doesnt help.

Bumpers have covers now. The bumper, the

bumper cover and the headlights on a car can cost a thousand dollars ... often more than what the bumper was put there to protect.

The yard of this car repair shop was littered with old bumper covers. What the bumper covers covered was often a piece of plastic ... or fiberglass ... even foam. Very flimsy stuff.

They keep passing laws to make cars safer.

What we need is a law forcing car manufacturers to put every bumper on every vehicle at one standard height off the road. Otherwise youd have to look for another car just exactly the same brand to hit.

If you paid $20,000 for a new car, totaled it and wanted to put it back together again with new parts, it would cost you $125,000. Manufacturers dont lose money in their parts department.

Im sure that by this time next year, the automobile industry will have fixed the problem it has with bumpers and we here at *60 Minutes* will be able to take great satisfaction, once again, having saved the world from itself.

Women on Submarines

There are more interesting stories in the newspapers every day than there is time to read them.

Recently the question of whether or not the U.S. Navy should have women on board its submarines was a story and I was particularly interested because I took a great trip underneath the surface of the Atlantic Ocean on board the nuclear attack submarine Miami, out of Groton, Connecticut. I asked Commander Jim Ransom about women in the submarine service.

SUBMARINER:
Theres some some privacy issues. Its something thats being looked at. I think its been continually studied. But there are some money issues with

that. It costs money to do conversions. Privacy is an issue . . . but it is something that is on the table.

There is a small amount of sexist pig in every man and Im no exception. There are things women should be and things women should not be. Thats my opinion.

For example, there ought to be more women in politics . . . and the women in politics ought to act like women, not like men.

Its a disgrace that we have had forty-two Presidents of the United States and not one woman.

I'll bet—and I hope—we will have a woman as President in the next twelve or sixteen years.

There are about 800,000 doctors in the United States. Six hundred thousand of them are men . . . fewer than 200,000 are women. Being a doctor is something that calls for a woman's best attributes and there should be more of them. They say there are too many doctors but its doctors who say that—not patients.

The question of admitting women sports reporters into men's locker rooms after a men's game has been an issue. Sorry. Ladies, women reporters, should not be in the men's locker room—not unless you want them in yours.

Women do not belong in the boxing ring. Muhammed Ali should take his daughter Laila Ali home, spank her and put her to bed without her supper.

Theres no room for anything extra on a submarine. Sailors often share the same bunk in shifts. Quarters are just incredibly close. A male sailor simply passing a woman in a submarine passageway could be charged with sexual harassment.

Its unreasonable to think that there wouldnt be problems unless they recruited all very homely women and all the guys were eunuchs.

There are places where men should be and where they should not be. There are places women should be and places where they should not be and, torpedo me for saying so, but a submarine is one of the places women should not be.

2000

Too Good To Be True

The other day I read a newspaper story about a homeless man who bought a lottery ticket and won $2 million. Its the kind of story you often see.

For my own amusement Ive written four stories that are closer to the way things are more apt to happen. Here it is.

HOMELESSS MAN BUYS
LOTTERY TICKET
WITH LAST DOLLAR

A familiar figure on the street known simply as "Big John" has been homeless for six years.

Last week Big John took the nickels and dimes he'd begged from passersby and bought a two-dollar lottery ticket.

Yesterday, he was sleeping over a warm sidewalk grill when a discarded newspaper caught on his foot.

He reached down, took the paper and looked at the headline announcing the winning lottery number worth $5 million. Big John took the lottery ticket from his pocket and, with bleary eyes, compared his lottery ticket with the winning number. It was not the one he had, of course, so he went back to sleep two dollars poorer.

Next story.

MEDICAL EXPERTS SAID
BOY WOULD NEVER WALK AGAIN

When he was four, little Eddie Miller fell from the maple tree in his back yard and fractured his pelvis. Doctors said Eddie would never walk again.

Today, when the mile race was run at Central High, Eddie cheered as his younger brother won by four yards. Eddie watched from his wheelchair because, sadly, the doctors were right.

Another story:

TWIN SISTERS APART
FOR FORTY YEARS

Elizabeth and Esther Murray, twin daughters of Ralph and Mary Murray, were six when their parents divorced. It was agreed that the father would raise Elizabeth and the mother would raise Esther.

Ralph Murray's job took him to Paris where Elizabeth grew up and graduated from the Sorbonne and then went into business designing and selling women's shoes.

Back in the U.S., Esther dropped out of high school and failed at several jobs.

Hearing of a new French company opening an expensive women's shoe store in town, Esther applied for a job and got an interview with the store's manager, a woman who had recently arrived from Paris.

When Esther was shown into the luxuriously furnished office, she saw a well-dressed young woman seated behind the desk and felt shabby in her presence.

For just an instant, Esther thought the woman behind the desk was her sister, Elizabeth, but it wasnt and she didnt get the job.

Last story:

FAMILY MOVES WEST

WITHOUT PET RETRIEVER

The Santleys lived for years on a quiet street in Nutley, New Jersey, with their beloved golden retriever, Dirk. Ralph Santley's company moved to Seattle and if he wanted to keep his job, he had to sell his Nutley home and move to Seattle, too.

The Santleys packed up their worldy possessions and prepared to go. When the movers arrived, everything was packed and ready to go except Dirk, nowhere to be found.

The Santleys delayed their departure for two whole days but Dirk never appeared and, heartbroken, they left without him.

On their third day in Seattle, 2,900 miles away, they sat despondently over a cup of coffee in their new kitchen when they heard a scratching sound at the front door and the soft pleading whine of a dog.

Mr. Santley raced to the door, threw it open and there stood a small white poodle that looked nothing like Dirk.

The moral to all these stories is this:

If it sounds too good to be true, the chances are, it isnt true.

What's the Symbolism?

I try not to have a lot of big thoughts that Im not smart enough to think about, but when I read about the Confederate flag over the capitol of South Carolina, I got thinking how important symbols are to us. They occupy a big place in our thoughts. Theyre like shorthand . . . little signs that stand for something more than themselves.

People like to associate themselves with symbols . . . displaying a flag, wearing a cross, putting on a shirt with a team name or gluing a sign to their windshield or the bumper of their car. When someone puts that little round National Rifle Association sticker in the window of his SUV, it tells the rest of us a lot about the driver. Any environmental sticker says the opposite. The swastika was the most effective symbol of the past hundred years.

I dont care much for symbols. I like the American flag and think it should be displayed but not used. Our flag is wonderfully attractive and meaningful. Its good to see people get theirs out on the Fourth of July. Most of us dont have it on a flagpole out in front of our house 365 days a year because we assume people know that those of us inside are American.

When youre saluting your flag, you have to remember that every country on Earth has a flag its people are proud of. A little pride is a good thing . . . too much causes trouble.

Some people in South Carolina are too proud of that Confederate flag. We all know what the symbol means. It means those who put it up there think theyre better than the people who dont like it up there. Thirty percent of the people in South Carolina are black. This symbol is offensive to them and to a lot of South Carolinians who arent black.

The presidential candidates are in on this one now. John McCain, George W. Bush. Bill Bradley got it right.

The Confederate flag as a symbol of bigotry is as offensive to a lot of us as the swastika was and it doesnt belong on the same pole with our Star-Spangled Banner.

Rate the Candidates

I havent decided who Im going to vote for yet. I dont usually vote FOR someone . . . I vote AGAINST most of them and choose the candidate I dislike the least.

Ive drawn up a chart to help me make a decision . . . judging four candidates on seven things—on a scale of ten.

You can make up your own chart if you dont like mine.

The seven categories are LOOKS, BRAINS, what kind of FIRST LADY their wives would make. How theyre fixed for MONEY. How much I'd like to have breakfast with them in a diner during the campaign and last, how their MORAL standards are compared to those of President Clinton. You can fill in the blanks and then add them up to see who you want to vote for.

	BUSH	GORE	BRADLEY	MC CAIN
LOOKS	6	8	4	6
BRAINS	4	5	9	7
FIRST LADY	5	7	7	6
MONEY	9	5	6	5
PERSONALITY	5	5	4	5
BREAKFAST	4	4	8	6
MORALITY	10	10	10	10

LOOKS: Bush looks pretty good . . . although not as Presidential-looking as his father, 6. Gore tall and quite handsome, 8. Bradley, too easy to caricature . . . looked better in shorts, 4. McCain, masculine—if you like that in a man, 6.

BRAINS: Bush not as smart as his father, 4, Gore, no smarter than his father, 5, Bradley, very smart, 9, McCain, 7.

FIRST LADY: Laura seems nice enough, 5. Tipper's a winner, 7. Ernestine Bradley, no beauty queen but a savvy college professor, 7.

Cindy McCain, no college professor but a real doll and rich, 6.

MONEY: Bush, 9. He's made enough to send money home to Mom and Dad. Gore, always a politician, not rich, 5. Bradley, made a lot as a player but not filthy rich, 6. McCain, makes $135,000 as a senator, 5.

PERSONALITY: Bush, not as much as his father, 5. Gore, not as much as his wife, 5. Bradley, if he has it, he hides it, 4. McCain, more than he needs sometimes, 5.

BREAKFAST: Bush, I dont think we'd have much to talk about, 4

Gore, afraid not, 4. Bradley, yeah. I'd like to ask why that Michael Jordan commercial is so bad, 8.

McCain, I'd like to have a pancake with John, 6.

And last their moral standards compared to Bill Clinton's

Bush, 10. Gore, 10. Bradley, 10. McCain, 10.

You add these up and look what happens. They come out even.

Im right back where I started. I was afraid of that. The trouble is, there isnt one really bad guy that you can hate.

I hate that.

The Democratic Process

Sometimes it seems as if the democratic process we're all so proud of doesnt work. The primary elections are over and theres something seriously wrong.

What Im thinking is the possibility that we're going to come up with the wrong person as President. Its happened before.

The big idea of democracy is that there is some collective wisdom that arrives at the right answer when a lot of people, each of whom may individually be wrong, vote what they think.

The good news is that almost certainly the problem isnt with democracy . . . its with primaries.

The candidates who want to be President are picked by too few of us voting as individuals and too many of us voting as part of a group. Political parties demand members vote for their guy. Veterans' organizations, religious groups, anti-abortion activists, pro-choice activists—all vote like one person.

Theres a small group of rich men who buy too much influence over too many people.

If a candidate is endorsed by a big union in a state, the other candidates might as well fold up.

That leaves a lot of us out. It leaves me out because I dont belong to a group. Im not a registered anything. I wasnt even a Boy Scout when I was a boy.

All of you who want the President picked by an organization, please stand up.

In the months left before the election, the two candidates, Bush and Gore, are going to keep telling us what's wrong with the other guy . . . you know, lack of integrity, lack of intellect, their debt to interests outside the interests of average Americans.

Gore will say that Bush is soft on right-wing religious extremists, opposed to gun control, opposed to a woman's right to choose abortion, opposed to a patient's bill of rights and that he has a bad record on environmental issues.

Bush will say that Gore is close to a disgraced President, that he has a forked tongue in relation to campaign finances and spent his whole life as part of the Washington establishment.

You know what I think? I think by election time the rest of us might just decide that by gosh theyre right. Theyre BOTH right. Everything bad they say about each other is true.

We may not be picking the right man for the job in November because he isnt running. Thanks to the primaries, we have two losers, one of whom is certain to win.

The Commandments

Everyone's trying to figure out what to do about the shooting of schoolchildren by other children.

The answer in some communities has been to post the Ten Commandments on their bulletin boards in schools.

The question comes up about which version of the Ten Commandments to use. I have eight bibles and the Ten Commandments are different in each of them. These are the commandments posted outside a school in Adams County, Ohio, but it doesnt seem to me as if they got them right.

The first commandment here reads, "THOU SHALT HAVE NO OTHER GODS BEFORE ME."

That never sounded like anything God would say.

It suggests there *are* other gods but he wants to be first among them. God wouldnt have said that. Moses is supposed to have reported the Ten Commandments originally. Maybe Moses got them wrong. You know how unreliable reporters are.

2—"Thou shalt not worship any graven image." The word "graven" wouldnt mean much to a kid. Or me, either.

3—"Thou shalt not take God's name in vain." Good. I dislike hearing kids behaving like jerks by swearing.

4—"Remember the sabbath to keep it holy." I totally disagree with that. I dont see anything wrong with shopping on Sunday and I dont think God would, either. Go to church if you want but then dont hesitate to go right from church to the mall and shop.

5—"Honor thy father and thy mother." Thats fine. Maybe "respect" would be a better word than "honor" though.

6—"Thou shalt not kill." Well of course . . . but having it posted in school wouldnt have stopped anyone. Several versions have changed that to "Thou shalt not murder." "Murder" instead of "kill" allows room for an Army to fight a war without violating the Ten Commandments, I suppose.

7—"Thou shalt not commit adultery." That doesnt seem appropriate for kids. They arent clear what "adultery" is. For one thing, they arent married.

8—"Thou shalt not steal." Fine.

9—"Thou shalt not bear false witness." Kids wouldnt know what this means.

10—The tenth commandment in one of my bibles reads, "Thou shalt not covet thy neighbor's house, thy neighbor's wife, his manservant, his maid servant, his ox, his ass or anything that is thy neighbor's."

Outside the school, they cut that down to just plain "Thou shalt not covet."

Most kids wouldnt understand the word "covet," either. It means to want something and its impossible for a person to control what he or she wants. They can control themselves from trying to get it but "covet" is the wrong word.

Maybe they should put up a stone with THE SEVEN COMMAND-MENTS and write them in plain English.

They might read this way:

1—DONT PRAY TO A STATUE

2—DONT SWEAR

3—RESPECT YOUR PARENTS

4—DONT SHOOT ANYONE

5—DONT FOOL AROUND

6—DONT STEAL

7—DONT LIE

And at the bottom there should be one more line. "IF YOU DO, YOURE GOING TO GET THROWN OUT OF HERE—ON YOUR OX."

Elian Gonzalez

You know . . . more than anything else, Cuba is sad. It seems as if nothing good has ever happened there and I dont know why.

A lot of Cubans worked as slaves chopping sugar cane when Cuba was Spanish, then a hundred years ago Spain lost a war to the United States and Cuba became independent. Things looked good but independence didnt do Cuba much good.

In 1952 a bad general named Batista took over and Cuba became a cesspool of gambling and prostitution. A lot of Americans were taking the big money out of Cuba and working Cubans werent any better off than when they were slaves.

Then Fidel Castro came along. He was a Robin Hood kind of a guy, hiding in the mountains with his merry men, attacking the bad guys and running back into the mountains. Batista couldnt catch him and in 1956 Castro drove Batista out and we all cheered.

Revolutionaries never do the right thing once theyve won the revolution though and Castro became the Cuban Communist dictator. He's still dictator forty-seven years later. Forget elections. Forget freedom. Forget Robin Hood.

A lot of people who prospered during the Batista regime, good and bad, ran to Miami.

Things are so bad now in Cuba that most people would like to get out. We all know Elian Gonzalez's mother drowned trying to get out with him. You have to be desperate to try this.

Americans were divided about what should happen to Elian.

There are maybe a million Cubans in Miami who vote here now. None of the 11 million Cubans in Cuba vote here so Al Gore said Elian should not be returned to his father.

Gore keeps making it very difficult for me to want to vote for him.

Elian Gonzalez belongs home with his father.

If it had been his father who had drowned trying to take the boy away from his mother, would anyone be saying his mother shouldnt have Elian back?

Its his *father*, for goodness sake. It isnt a stranger, it isnt a distant relative. Its his very own father who wants his boy back.

The people in Miami have spoiled this poor kid rotten with every imaginable toy. Its been a dirty trick played on a little boy. We know he's not going to have it this good in Cuba.

He wont have all the toys but theres one thing he will have that no one can give him here. He'll have his very own father.

My Mail

I like the mail I get from people who like what I do better than the mail I get from people who hate what I do. The spelling is better in the good letters but the hate mail is more interesting.

When someone really wants to hurt me after Ive done a serious commentary, they always say, "Go back to talking about cereal boxes."

The remarks I made about the public posting of the Ten Commandments evoked interesting mail. By which I mean angry.

A lot of people said I was wrong when I suggested God was allowing that there might be other Gods when he said, "THY SHALT HAVE NO OTHER GODS BEFORE ME.

Jon Oakleaf of Moline, Illinois, says, ". . . you fell flat on your face . . . these other Gods take the form of power, wealth, control, sex, technology, instant gratification . . . "

Walter M. Moore of Dayton, Ohio, says, ". . . it seems that you are coming morally unglued . . .

"God has spoken to me many times and has appeared to me five (5) times . . . Jesus has been to visit me 12 times in this lifetime."

It would be interesting to know what Jesus thought of Dayton when he came there to visit with Mr. Moore.

This is from N. I. Annakindt of Daggett, Michigan.

He says, "Since I myself am a member of the Asatry Religion which uses the Nine Noble Virtues rather than the (Ten) Commandments, I petitioned that the Nine Noble Virtues be posted."

I said professional wrestling was fake. Richard Boesken of Lake Placid, Florida, agrees. He says wrestling is like television news.

Thats not nice, Mr Boesken. You have a right to your opinion but dont expect to be invited over to Dan Rather's house for dinner anytime soon.

Marjorie A. King sent me a novel she wrote and wants to know what I think of it.

I havent read it, Marjorie, but the great Samuel Johnson said, "The man who is asked by an author what he thinks of his work is not obliged to speak the truth."

I said Elian Gonzalez should be with his father back in Cuba and got a lot of letters both ways.

Angele Tegnazian of Rockledge, Florida, says, "Please shut up and go back to your cave."

Several weeks ago I had a negative opinion of the census form. The director of the census, Kenneth Prewitt, wrote asking for equal time. He said he wanted to say how important the census is to the American people.

I hope I didnt hurt the census. I KNOW the census is important. Thats why its too bad someone did such a poor job drawing up the census form, Mr. Prewitt. One third of all the people who got one havent answered it. That isnt MY fault, Mr. Prewitt. Its the fault of the Census Bureau.

I get hundreds of letters asking me to send some personal item for what the writer calls "a celebrity auction."

They have to find some other name than "celebrity auction" to interest me in giving. Im a writer, not a celebrity.

I get a lot of mail from prisoners who didnt do it.

Albert Lee, serving a life sentence in Nevada, writes, "Mr. Rooney, my most heartfelt prayer is that by next Christmas I will be reunited with my family sharing the promise of Christ's birth. I can be released soon if I can cover the cost for DNA testing which is between $3,000 and $5,000."

He sends me this INMATE DEPOSIT COUPON for me to fill in for $5,000.

I checked on Albert Lee. He had a long record before being convicted of rape, theft, slashing the woman's throat and leaving her to bleed to death. The woman survived and identified him.

Why does Mike Wallace always get the ones wrongly imprisoned? Someone out there is doing a lot of murdering.

Next week Im going to play it safe and talk about cereal boxes.

Who Do You Hate?

Its getting close to Election Day now and I feel sorry for all you people in the forty-nine states other than New York where Hillary Clinton is *not* running for the Senate. You dont know the fun youre missing.

I read about the race in New Mexico. Does anyone really care whether Jeff Bingaman beats Bill Redmond there?

Daniel Patrick Moynihan, one of the great senators and citizens of the world, is retiring and the President's wife wants his old job. She'll need big feet to fill Moynihan's shoes.

New York newspapers are filled with pictures of Hillary . . . usually doing good things to make her appear likeable. Lots of children, dogs and worthy causes.

You may have noticed that I havent mentioned the name of the person running *against* Hillary Rodham Clinton in this election. Thats because it doesnt matter. He's a man. He's younger than Hillary. He seems intelligent, nice looking, a professional politician. He's already in the House of Representatives and in the polls, he and Hillary are running about even.

His name is Enrico Anthony Lazio. "Enrico" is not a mainline American name, so for political purposes he calls himself Rick Lazio but it doesnt matter. The reason his name doesnt matter is, no one is going to vote for him anyway. He may win the election but no one is going to vote for Rick Lazio.

Every person who goes to the poll is going to vote *for* Hillary Rodham Clinton or *against* Hillary Rodham Clinton.

Like few people who ever ran for office, the Clintons have the knack for evoking love and hate.

Its funny about hate. It doesnt have a good reputation. No moral authority recommends it. The Bible doesnt say "Hate thy neighbor." Hating is a very satisfying thing to do though.

We all enjoy a little of it. Thats why Im having such a satisfying life. I hate so many things.

Hate is one of the strongest emotions we have and it may be a more enduring emotion than love. People stop loving and divorce but they never stop hating. Theres no divorce from that.

We use the word too casually sometimes. Its typical of the way we inflate the English language. When we say we "hate" something, we usually mean we dont like it . . . a lot. We dont really hate it.

So, Im sorry about you Republican voters in the other forty-nine states but on November 7 youre not going to have Hillary Rodham Clinton to hate.

Halloween

I know how much free enterprise and the capitalist system have done for the United States but turning everything into money hasnt been all good. Too many sports now are nothing but commercial ventures. Look at the Olympics. Olympic athletes used to be amateurs.

There are even people trying to make a buck off Little League Baseball.

All our holidays have been turned into sales tools.

We all know about Christmas . . . but look what theyve done to Halloween. I read where retail sales at Halloween are second only to Christmas.

And nothing's real—everything's plastic at Halloween.

Plastic pumpkins. Plastic witches. Plastic brooms,

I was walking past a store the other day and I saw a plastic form for cutting out a pumpkin. It has patterns for marking the face and little tools for cutting it out. The fun of making a face on a pumpkin is that its your own. It may be a mess, but you did it.

When kids come to our house Halloween, I always feel sorry for the ones who have costumes bought in a store. Stores sell ready-made costumes. You can buy a "four-piece children's space alien costume" for $19.99.

It'll cost $26 for your boy to be Superman. Or $24 for the little girl who wants to be Superwoman.

I found a sick little number for $58. Theres something wrong with spending that kind of money on a Halloween costume. It should come out of a trunk in the attic, the basement or a closet.

You dont BUY a Halloween costume. You make one up. If youre lucky, your mother or father helps.

I dont know exactly how to say this but all this Halloween stuff for kids is like what's happening to a lot of things.

On vacation, too many kids dont organize their own fun, their parents take them to Disneyland. Kids go there to look at what grownups have done.

The reason everyone goes to Disneyland or Disney World is, we're running out of good, natural places for kids to play in.

The vacant lots where they used to play have houses on them now so play is organized for them on school grounds.

Yellowstone Park and the Grand Canyon are more crowded than Times Square. At the beach, there are more people than there is sand to sit on. You climb a mountain to get away from it all and what do you find up there? An orange peel and two empty beer cans.

Maybe I'll go out trick-or-treating myself Halloween. I'll scare people by dressing up as mean old Andy Rooney.

Dont Vote

Tonight Im part of the 17 percent that hasnt decided yet who to vote for. It isnt as though George Washington or Abe Lincoln were one of our choices for President.

I think a lot of the people listed as undecided arent really undecided— theyre embarrassed to admit theyre voting for either Gore or Bush.

At least both of them have short names. They have that going for them.

Not many people think either one of them will make the best President the United States could possibly have. The debates were scoreless ties and then when Richard Cheney and Joseph Lieberman debated, most of us thought the vice presidential candidates would make better Presidents than the candidates for President.

About all we can hope now is that whoever wins will turn out to be better than he seems.

Its possible. Theyre both good men.

Even if it does turn out okay this election has made it obvious that we have a flawed system for choosing our President.

Democracy is one of the best ideas human beings ever had but its been screwed up by professional politicians. The Republican and Democratic Parties have taken the election away from the rest of us. Party members hand-pick the candidates. We dont have anything to do with it. All we get to do is choose between the two they hand us.

How did we let this happen?

In the week before Election Day, theres always a lot of talk about getting out the vote.

Its practically un-American of me to say but Ive never liked the idea that democracy works best if everyone votes. If someone is naturally inclined not to vote, he shouldnt be encouraged to go to the poll . . . chances are, he or she is too dumb. The people least interested in voting are the people least qualified to vote. The hell with them. They dont know or care what the issues are. Im not too sharp on some of the issues myself but I sure dont want one of their votes canceling out mine.

In the last presidential election, only 49 percent of all Americans eligible to vote did vote. I wasnt horrified. My reaction was "Good riddance." You can be sure that the IQ of the average person who did NOT vote was lower than the IQ of the average person who DID vote.

So my advice to all of you who dont know what the issues are is this: Next Tuesday, whatever you do, DONT GET OUT AND VOTE! Just get out.

I doubt that many non-voters will be mad at me for saying this because they arent listening. The people too dumb to vote arent smart enough to watch *60 Minutes*, either.

Austin, Texas

I am at a window looking out at the beautiful State Capitol in Austin, Texas. State capitols are at their best from a distance where you cant hear the politicians inside speaking.

Im not frequently at a loss for words here at *60 Minutes*. Tonight I join millions of Americans who dont know what to say, dont know what to think. We've been at a loss for words for all the days since Election Day when our Country failed to decide clearly who it wanted to be its President.

Maybe its God's way of saying he didnt want either one.

Sometimes its possible for a writer to sound smarter than he is by getting information and working on his words. I can do that sometimes. I cant do it with this.

I wrote my essay for *60 Minutes* Wednesday. By Friday afternoon it looked hopelessly out of date and stupid. My boss, Don Hewitt, threw it out and he was right. I was ignoring this tie-score election, one of the great stories in recent American history.

Late Friday I flew to Texas, for a date I had here. Quite by coincidence and totally unintended by me, I am, at the moment of speaking, within a few blocks of where George W. Bush sits, waiting. Or, I dont know. Maybe he isnt just waiting. Maybe he's pacing.

People have a way of assuming there is a solution to a problem if they can only find what it is. Sometimes there is none. There may be no good solution to this problem. As usual, the dumbest among us are sure of what ought to be done and the smartest are trying to figure it out.

It is clear that because of the inept way it handled some of its election procedures, Florida ought to be spanked and put to bed without its supper.

Basically though we have this mess because responsible citizens who voted Tuesday were sharply divided in their opinion of two very different political philosophies. Those philosophies were represented by the Republican conservative George W. Bush, who believes there is too much Government and that people should do it for themselves, and the Democratic liberal, Al Gore, who believes Government can do a lot for all of us and specially for the people who cant do it for themselves.

The results were so close that if it were any less important a contest, it would have to be settled by a flip of a coin. Heads Gore is President, tails its Bush.

You cant say it doesnt make any difference.

It will make a difference.

We are not at a fork in the road. We are on a major highway headed in one direction and if George W. Bush is elected, we're turning off. We'll be taking another road that half the voters plus or minus about four, think will be wider, smoother and less congested.

If you love this Country, you have to look for something good about our dilemma.

What's good is our republic, our great democracy, will survive no matter which man is ultimately determined to be the winner. No one has to be nervous about our future. There is no rebel leader lurking in the bushes, ready to take over. There is no conniving faction in our Army looking for a coup. There is no foreign country so foolish as to think we are so paralyzed to inaction that this would be a good time to attack us.

Our Country has a way of making bad leaders look good and good leaders look bad. Everything's going to be alright whether its President Al Gore or President George W. Bush.

Co-Captains

I wasnt going to talk about the election again but everyone else is and I dont want to be left out.

These are some election notes I made and with everyone so interested, I hate to throw them away.

This note says CO-CAPTAINS. Half the high schools in the Country cant decide who should be captain of their football team so they elect two and call them "co-captains."

Can you see where Im going with this? If its good enough for a football team, why not the Country? Co-Presidents? I can see the two of them now on future dollar bills. They want the job so bad we wouldnt have to pay them the President's salary of $400,000. They could split it. Al Gore hasnt done anything for his salary as Vice President for more than a year now anyway. He owes us. George W. is rich. Two hundred thousand would be walking-around money for him.

We could save the Vice President's salary because we wouldnt need a vice president. The co-first ladies, Tipper and Laura, would come free. It would be funny if they got to be friends, wouldnt it? That would make Al and George W. nervous.

With 132 rooms, theres plenty of space in the White House for two Presidents. In view of the change, it might be a good idea to repaint it—grey . . . or two-tone, black and white.

The Oval Office would be divided in two—it would be half-moon-shaped.

On Inauguration Day, with Co-Presidents, the band will play *Hail to the Chiefs*.

Each President could invite rich friends to stay in the Lincoln Bedroom on alternate nights.

I dont know whether or not the Bushes or the Gores have dogs. I hope not. We dont need a dog fight on the White House lawn.

This second note says just "POLLS." Polls are never going to be dependable because the only kind of people they can count are the kind of people who have so little to do when surveyers call that they dont hang up. They spend ten minutes answering dumb poll questions.

"ELECTION MONEY" is a note I made to myself.

Politicians spent a record total of $3 billion trying to get elected this year. We were bought and its a disgrace.

About 100 million people voted so they spent $30 for every vote they got. I'd rather have had the cash.

The Winner

Tonight, I have just one question on my mind and this is what made me think of it . . . the Christmas card I got from the White House, signed Bill and Hillary Clinton.

My question is this.

Do you think I'll get a Christmas card from the White House NEXT year?

People keep asking me what I think about this election as if I had some thought about it that they havent had.

I think of myself as so normal and average an everyday person that Im always surprised that other people dont think the same as I do about everything.

For months I couldnt decide whether I wanted to vote for George W. Bush or Al Gore. I was like a dimpled chad. Friends who liked Bush couldnt understand how I could even dream of voting for Gore. The ones who liked Gore hated Bush and hated me for saying I might vote for him. No one was undecided and everyone was vicious.

My real opinion is that neither one of them would make a very good President. It isnt Al Gore who lost this election, its the American public.

At the beginning, I was leaning toward Gore but then, during the campaign, he disappointed me more than Bush did.

It wasnt easy for the Vice President of a very successful administration to lose the election but Gore managed to pull it off.

Bush, on the other hand, behaved as though he wasnt the smartest candidate we ever had but he was sort of a likeable bumbler and that didnt hurt him. Everyone loves a likeable bumbler. Im not saying who I voted for though because I want to get a White House Christmas card again next year from whoever won.

The more I saw of Bush and Gore, the worse I felt about our having lost Bill Bradley because he was the best candidate but the worst politician.

The biggest losers werent the Democrats. The losers were the institutions that came out of it with diminished reputations. The whole state of Florida lost. It came off looking as artificial as Disney World.

The Florida Supreme Court favored Gore because the court had a Democratic majority.

The United States Supreme Court came off as the United States Inferior Court. It voted Republican because it had a Republican majority.

It was the rule of law that lost out.

The news divisions of the television networks didnt come off looking any better.

Worst of all, the institution of the Presidency suffered and thats serious because if George W. Bush fails, we all fail.

I sure hope not. Im ambivalent about the virtues of patriotism but my attitude tonight is patriotic: George W. Bush is my President and Im all for him.

Maybe I'll send Al Gore a get-well card for Christmas.

2001

The Great Country

Tonight I wish to correct the impression that Im always negative. Ive made a list of ten things that are good about America.

1. The United States is a great piece of property. It has high mountains, broad plains, wide rivers and there are lakes with water in them that you can drink. We still have forests with trees we havent cut down. Americans have 5,000 miles of seashore they can go to if they live inland.

2. We have free and open elections to choose the people we want to lead us. If we dislike the one who gets elected we grumble but we dont revolt. We accept the decision of the most of us.

3. We are not starving. More of us have too much to eat than too little. The shelves of our supermarkets runneth over.

4. We hear a lot about the homeless but its too bad there isnt any word comparable to "homeless" for those of us who have homes. The great majority of us have one. We built a million and a half new homes last year alone. That brings the total number of homes we have to 119 million.

5. Americans are good about helping those who cant help themselves. We gave $150 billion to charities last year out of the goodness of our hearts—and perhaps a small tax deduction.

6. We have Monday night football, the World Series, the U.S. Tennis Open, the Masters' golf tournament, the Stanley Cup, the NCAA basketball tournament, the Indianapolis 500 and the Super Bowl. No other country can make that statement.

7. We have movies from Hollywood and free television.

8. We have electricity for light when its dark—oil, coal or electricity for

heat when its cold. We complain that gas costs too much but a gallon of gas in England costs five dollars. And thats for regular.

9. We go where we feel like going. Fifty-seven million families in the United States have two cars. We own a total of 200 million cars. Three quarters of our houses have two-car garages . . . although most of us have so many possessions that we store some of them in the garage so theres only room for one car.

10. The news we get is not approved by our government. Sometimes it isnt approved by any of us but we get it uncensored.

So, those are ten good things about the United States of America. And its why about half a million people from other countries chose to come to the United States to live last year.

And why only about nine left to live somewhere else last year.

God Bless America

The last thing most politicians say when theyre making a speech is "God bless America." We like to hear politicians say that because, when they do, we know theyre done and we wont have to listen to them talk anymore.

I have so many opinions about so many things that it seems likely that, sooner or later, I'll express an opinion that so many people find offensive that it will end my career here.

This may be it: I hate it when politicians end their speeches by saying GOD BLESS AMERICA!

What kind of meaningless, self-serving thing is that to say, anyway? The three words are spoken as if they were an order, but I suppose the words are meant more as a request. "Please God" is sort of assumed.

I just dislike the idea of anyone using God's name to get in good with us and I'll bet God doesnt like it, either, even though he's too nice to say so.

And what does "God Bless America" mean?

Does the politician who says it want God to bless America and not any other place else in the world?

If theyre talking about God giving Americans more than he gives the people of other countries, it seems as if he's already done that. We certainly have more than our share of the good things on Earth.

I dont think we're blessed with so much because God likes us best though and he certainly hasnt blessed us because politicians are always asking him to bless us.

Do the people who ask God to bless America believe that a just and caring God who has the power to make things better or worse for a country, would really choose to make things better for Americans than for the people of say, Canada or Botswana? Why would God do that ?

He certainly wouldnt go out of his way to bless America because George W. Bush or Jesse Jackson asked him to at the end of a speech.

If the politicians who are always saying it were as religious as they like to make voters think they are, theyd be saying, "Please God, make available to every human being in the world all the good things you have provided us with here in America."

I have one concluding thought about political speeches, too.

I liked President George W. Bush's inaugural address. It was good but it didnt sound as though he wrote it. I dont think he did. As a writer, I like to see writers get credit for their work.

Every political speech ought to end, not with GOD BLESS AMERICA but with the name of the person who wrote the speech.

The Mystery of High Prices

One of the things about money thats difficult to understand is why the price of everything keeps going up so fast at the same time the government is reporting that the rate of inflation is slow.

I get used to the high price of some things . . . I dont know why . . . but then, the high price of other things surprises and bothers me.

Just a few years ago I was paying $1.19 for a gallon of gas; now Im paying $1.65 but Ive gotten used to that. I dont like it but it doesnt bug me every time I fill up.

On the other hand, I was at the Super Bowl in Tampa and the price of anything in a stadium is crazy. A bag of twenty-five peanuts costs $2.75.

A Coke was $3.50.

A pint of plain water at the game cost $3. If it was gas, that would be $24. If your tank took fourteen gallons, it would cost you $45 to fill it with water. Not even high-test water.

If you wanted to know the names of the players in the Super Bowl, you had to pay $15 for the program.

The cost of going to a movie is hard to get used to.

In New York, its $9.50.

Tickets for senior citizens are only $6, but I hate to ask for one because Im embarrassed that they never demand proof that Im over sixty-five anymore.

The medium-sized popcorn goes for $3.60.

Hotels have gotten expensive. A room at the Crowne Plaza in Pittsfield, Massachusetts, for example will run you between $120 and $210 . . . and you know how that is. There are none of the $120 rooms left. Pittsfield, for goodness sake!

And, dont order room service in any fancy hotel.

At one, plain toast is $4.50.

Corn flakes, $7. I counted the flakes . . . there were about 135 in the box. That comes to five cents a flake—so dont drop any.

For your convenience, they add a 17 percent service charge plus a $3 cover charge and 8 percent tax. All for your convenience.

I was looking at our phone bill for last month . . . directory assistance is $1.99.

I dont get used to the fact a necktie costs $35 to $40. No wonder a lot of guys have stopped wearing them.

Mechanics are expensive. Theyre probably worth $95 an hour but I dont get used to it.

Häagen-Dazs is good ice cream. They get $2.32 for a small cone. As an experiment, I bought eight cones one night and put them in a one-quart container. The quart cost me $20.

Books seem expensive. This book of mine, for instance, is $20. To tell you the truth though, this is one thing that doesnt really bother me. See . . . I get 20 percent.

Teachers and Education

President Bush says one of his most important goals is to improve education in America. I'd like to help the President with two suggestions.

First, dont let schools and colleges close for so many months of the year. If companies closed down for as long as schools, theyd go out of business. Six weeks summer vacation is plenty. Three or four months is ridiculous.

Second, end the teacher shortage. Im talking shortage of both numbers and quality. Every one of us has had two or three great teachers. We've had dozens of teachers who were pretty good and we've had two or three who were so bad they should have been fired. I'll bet good teachers would agree that there are a lot of bad teachers, too.

Now, here's my idea for getting more good teachers. There are 35 million people in the United States over sixty-five years old and 90 percent of them used to work and dont any more. Theyre retired. Theyre finding different ways to waste the hours of the day until its time to go to bed or die.

How did the idea of retirement ever get so popular? People ask if Im going to retire. I am not going to retire and Ive never understood why anyone with all his marbles would. I may not have all of them . . . I still have MOST of my marbles.

One argument is that old people ought to retire to make room for young people. Dumb. It suggests theres a limited amount of work to be done in the world. Theres an unlimited amount of work to be done. We'll never finish it.

Its ridiculous for a smart, successful, educated person to be playing games all day when we need good teachers. They have social insecurity.

There are something like two and a half million teachers in this Country. We should fire 10 percent of them, give the other 90 percent a big raise and hire a million retired people to add to their numbers. Choose them carefully and give them six months training in the business of teaching. A person sixty-five years old might teach for fifteen or twenty years.

Older people with a life behind them would have something to offer young students that the students cant get from anyone else because there are things you only get to know from having lived a long time.

Most News Is Bad News

There were three stories in the news this week that I wanted to talk to you about:

First, we learned that the United States spent several hundred million dollars digging a tunnel under the Russian Embassy in Washington so we could spy on them.

Does this make you proud to be an American?

What in the world are we doing spying on another country? We think of ourselves as being honest and upright. How is any country in the world ever going to trust us if we keep doing sneaky things like that?

And dont tell me everyone does it. Its wrong and immoral and we shouldnt do it whether other countries do or not. Other countries do a lot of things we shouldnt do. And of course it doesnt work anyway.

I'd like to have the CIA or the FBI tell us one single thing of any importance that theyve found out by spying in the last ten years that was good and beneficial to the United States.

The second story is about the heart problem Vice President Dick Cheney had . . . or has. We all hope he's okay and he seems pretty good but if the doctors advise the Vice President to take it easy, he might have to resign. I didnt know this but I read that under the Constitution the President gets to appoint the new Vice President. George W. would probably pick one of his advisers. Wouldnt it be interesting if President George W. Bush appointed as Vice President, his most trusted adviser . . . his father?

The other vice presidential possibility, in the event Dick Cheney was unable to continue, would be a man more qualified by far than any other for that job. President Bush says he wants to make peace with the Democrats. Maybe he could do that by appointing as Vice President, Al Gore.

The third story that annoyed 8 million people in New York City was the weather reporting last week.

ANNOUNCER: "ITS GOING TO BE A MAJOR STORM ... THAT SNOW IS REALLY EXPECTED TO PILE UP. BLIZZARD CONDITIONS WILL HAPPEN WHEN THE SUN GOES DOWN TONIGHT ... AND BAM IT REALLY GETS US TOMORROW EVENING."

We know it isnt an exact science but they kept predicting as much as twenty-five inches of snow.

"THERE COULD BE UP TO 2 FEET OF SNOW BY THE TIME THIS STORM IS ALL OVER WITH ... OVER A FOOT FOR MIDTOWN ITSELF."

They wouldnt quit. What did we get? Almost nothing. New York City didnt even have to order the plows out. What little did come down melted when it hit.

Weather forecasters like to make the weather sound worse than it is because it makes them sound more interesting and important.

The wind-chill factor, making it sound colder than it is, is nonsense.

Maybe meteorologists should be on a contingency basis like schlock lawyers. If they got it right, theyd get paid. If they were wrong, theyd get nothing.

Dirty Words as a Movie

Last weekend I saw the movie *Traffic*, which has been nominated for an Oscar as "Best Picture" of the year. If *Traffic* wins an Oscar tonight as Best Picture, I'll consider retiring on grounds that I no longer understand what the American public wants. In the dark, I scribbled four notes about *Traffic*:

1. Dont understand half of this.

2. Dont like the half of this I do understand.

3. Picture is fake arty. Wrong to set out to produce work of art. Produce something good enough that people will call it a work of art.

4. Language inexcusably dirty. Adds nothing.

The vulgar four-letter F word was used fifty times. Thats the actual number. This is a cheap trick by a writer to attract attention without saying anything.

I never understood how the widely used word for the act of sex ever got to be thought of as the dirtiest, most vulgar epithet in the English language, anyway.

The other night I saw *The Sopranos* for the first time. It was interesting to watch, well acted, well directed. Better than *Traffic* I thought but like *Traffic* gratuitously dirty. It didnt need ninety dirty words in fifty minutes.

It was as if the producers thought that the reviewers would say it was "honest and realistic" if the actors shouted enough filth and profanity.

Civilization is a bootstrap operation. We have to make a point of being civilized. Our best behavior doesnt always come naturally to us so we have imposed restrictions. It is necessary to rise above some of our basic instincts. Some of those restrictions are laws but a lot of them are self-imposed—you know, just good manners.

Dirty words in a movie makes everyone in the audience less civil by reducing them to what theyre forced to think by what they hear together.

I saw *Erin Brockovich*. Now, Julia Roberts uses the F word too but I thought it was artistically justified. It contributed to the plot and helped make her the character that Erin Brockovich was supposed to be.

Football is a rough game with a penalty for unnecessary roughness. There ought to be a penalty for a movie or television show thats unnecessarily dirty.

Union Air

Tonight I have a proposal for airline passengers.

Theres a ticket agents' union, a mechanics' union and a pilots' union. I hereby propose an airline passengers' union to be called the APU.

To become members, passengers will agree not to fly if APU demands are not met by the airlines. The Earth would still turn if we all stayed home.

Here are some APU demands:

If anyone on board finds that another passenger paid less for a ticket, everyone on the flight who paid more will get a refund in the amount of the difference.

After fifteen minutes, an airline would be penalized five dollars for every minute a passenger stands in line buying a ticket.

Tickets would be made so passengers could read them, not in hieroglyphics.

No plane would leave the gate and taxi to the runway until it was cleared for flight, saving the airline gas and the passengers angst.

Flight times in airline schedules would be based on the time between when the door was closed at one airport and the time it was opened at its destination. The average time spent waiting on the runway for takeoff and waiting for a gate to become available upon arrival would be figured as flight time.

Every airplane would have an aisle wide enough to permit a passenger to get past the food cart to the bathroom.

The APU would prohibit annoying announcements. For example, no airline employee would be allowed to thank everyone for their patience after a two-hour delay when passengers were not patient at all. They were mad as hell.

If passengers on the left side of the plane were awakened by the pilot announcing a good view of the Grand Canyon for passengers on the right side the Annoyance Penalty would be five dollars per left-side passenger.

APU members would judge the food as 1) EXCELLENT 2) GOOD 3) ACCEPTABLE 4) POOR 5) INEDIBLE or 6) COULDNT OPEN IT.

If the vote averaged less than ACCEPTABLE, the airline would provide a free meal at a good restaurant in the next city.

If a suitcase goes to the wrong city, the passenger would be entitled to a free flight to that city any time within a year or after he got his bag back, whichever came last.

According to APU rules, the overhead compartment would be the exclusive facility of the passenger sitting directly underneath it. No one else could put anything in it without written permission from that seat's occupant.

If an airline faked a repair problem and canceled a lightly booked flight to save money because their flight an hour later wasnt full either, it would be penalized $100 per passenger.

Some of the terrible things that happen to airline passengers are not the airlines' fault. A lot of the terrible things that happen ARE the airlines' fault. We need to organize!

China

Im always reading stories that dont interest me much about trade deficits with China. Theyve been arguing about it this week in Congress. The Commerce Department says we buy $90 billion more stuff from China than they buy from us.

It made me curious because I didnt know China HAD $90 billion.

You look around though and its surprising how many things there are from China right here in my office . . . here's a leather bag sold by that fine old Oriental company, L. L. Bean of Portland, Maine . . . these sneakers I wear were made there . . . my umbrella . . . this Japanese radio says "made in China" . . . Chinese china, a couple of plates I have. And look at this—a flag! An American company has a nerve selling American flags made in China.

American business has spent $100 million trying to get Congress to give the Chinese a break on import taxes. Why would American business want to make it easier for the Chinese to sell things here ? Naturally I was suspicious.

This is a list of just 350 of the thousands of American companies that do business in China. It includes AOL TIME WARNER, AMERICAN EX-PRESS, CATERPILLAR TRACTOR, COLGATE-PALMOLIVE, GOOD-YEAR, GENERAL MOTORS. How many Cadillacs do you think General Motors sells in China?

I couldnt believe how dumb I'd been when I found out why American businesses like these are in favor of low tariffs on Chinese products. Very simple. Its because a lot of it is *not* Chinese. Theres no $90 billion trade gap. Thats done with mirrors.

American companies *own* the factories in China. They use cheap Chinese labor to make things for $1.10, then they ship the things here and sell them to us for a hundred and ten. The value of the things an American company ships from China to the United States is counted as part of that trade deficit.

A lot of that $90 billion so-called "trade deficit" doesnt go to the Chinese at all, it goes to Americans. Thats okay but let's not call it a trade deficit and make the Chinese sound like the bad guys.

Its all hard to figure out. I was never any good with chopsticks, either.

I Get Letters

One of the few bad things about this job is the good mail I get . . . so many people reaching out and then I ignore them. I simply cannot answer all the letters and have time for any fun.

Two things I said recently drew thousands of letters. One was about politicians who end their speeches saying GOD BLESS AMERICA. The other disparaged retirement and suggested more retired people ought to teach.

John Gautreau, Towson, Maryland:
"YOU SHOW ME A GUY WHO WANTS TO TEACH AT THE AVER-AGE PUBLIC SCHOOL AFTER A LIFE BUSTING HIS HUMP TO GET AHEAD AND I'LL SHOW YOU A SAINT."

Richard Harron, Oshkosh, Wisconsin:
"WORKERS NOT RETIRE? WHAT DO YOU KNOW. YOUVE NEVER HAD A REAL JOB . . . YOU HAVE NOTHING TO RETIRE FROM . . . "

Daniel Yergensen, Visalia, California:

"WHAT I FOUND LACKING WAS YOUR FAILURE TO UNDER-STAND THAT TEACHERS SPEND 20% OF THEIR TIME TEACHING AND 80% ON DISCIPLINE."

Helen Krieger, Colorado Springs:

". . . LET ME SAY THAT NOT EVERYONE WHO IS AN EXPERT IN ANY FIELD CAN TEACH. I WONDER HOW LONG THE UNITED STATES WILL CONTINUE TO BE A WORLD LEADER WITH SUCH A SORRY SITUATION IN OUR SCHOOLS."

Tom Garrett, Tuscon, Arizona:

". . . YOU ARE STUFFED CLEAN FULL OF BLUEBERRY CUPCAKES."

Mary Allsopp, Brick, New Jersey:

"ANDY, IF I HAD YOUR JOB, I WOULDNT RETIRE EITHER."

Carlos Del Bagge, Livermore, California:

"AS A BLUE COLLAR WORKER . . . WHO, DUE TO LACK OF EDUCA-TION, WAS FORCED TO PERFORM WHATEVER JOB HE WAS OFFERED IN ORDER TO SURVIVE, LET ME ASSURE YOU, HAD YOU BEEN IN THAT SITUATION YOU WOULD HAVE RETIRED YEARS AGO."

Myra Cox, Apple Valley, California:

"RETIREMENT IS GREAT. I GET UP WHEN I WANT TO, DO WHAT I FEEL LIKE ALL DAY AND GO TO BED WHEN I WANT TO . . . ITS A LUXURIOUS FEELING TO KNOW THAT 24 HOURS A DAY BELONG TO ME ALONE."

Dawn O'Brien, Hamburg, Pennsylvania:

". . . YOUR BLANKET STATEMENT THAT TEN PERCENT OF CUR-RENT TEACHERS SHOULD BE FIRED IS PREPOSTEROUS." (Okay, Dawn, I'll take that back . . . 20 percent.)

About my objection to politicians who end their speeches with "GOD BLESS AMERICA" . . .

Dolores Fisher, Lake Elsinore, California:
"YOU CAN BE SURE AMERICANS WOULD RATHER HEAR 'GOD BLESS AMERICA' AT THE END OF THEIR ADDRESSES THAN 'HAVE A NICE DAY.'"

Melvin H. Clingan, Carefree, Arizona:
"RETIRE BEFORE YOU MAKE AN EVEN GREATER FOOL OF YOURSELF!"

Carol Deverick, Fresno, California:
"GOD DOESNT BLESS THE WHOLE WORLD BECAUSE HE DOESNT GO WHERE HE'S NOT WANTED."

Gretchen from Faribault, Minnesota:
Now, this is my kind of letter . . . short and sweet . . . .
"GOD BLESS YOU, ANDY, LOVINGLY, GRETCHEN."

Bob Kerrey, Hero?

Former Nebraska Senator Bob Kerrey, not to be confused with Massachusetts Senator John Kerry, won the Medal of Honor as a member of a Navy Seals unit that killed as many as twenty unarmed Vietnamese civilians during an action that took place February 25, 1969. Details of the action, not always flattering to Kerrey, were revealed in a report done jointly by 60 Minutes II *and* The New York Times Magazine.

The most unpleasant news story of recent years is the one about Bob Kerrey and the massacre at Thanh Phong. I hate everything about it. I like Bob Kerrey but I hate the story about him.

Neither do I think its right to suggest that My Lai and Thanh Phong were the same thing.

The details of what American soldiers did in Vietnam are often sickening. It makes the men who refused to go or who fled to Canada to avoid the draft seem righteous.

Think of it—Bill Clinton beat the draft and got to be President and Kerrey's in trouble for fighting the war.

Its always a shock to find that your Country has done something wrong. We were wrong going to Vietnam in the first place but our intention was not an evil one. We are not the bad guys in the world. It was not the business of the Americans who did the fighting there to philosophize about it, either. "Theirs not to reason why, theirs but to do and die." They trusted their Government to have done the right thing when it decided they should fight it.

I feel bad about Bob Kerrey because he almost certainly did a terrible thing even if he did it for a good reason. He must have been at least partly responsible for the death of women and children at Thanh Phong. I watched Dan Rather interview him on *60 Minutes II*. I was on Kerrey's side but it didnt seem to me he was always telling the whole truth.

KERREY:
Let other people judge whether or not what I did was militarily allowable or morally ethical or inside the rules of war . . . let them figure that out. I can make a case it was.

Well, Kerrey didnt come off great in that interview but, pardon me, I still think he's a hero anyway.

It is impossible for anyone who has never been in a war to imagine the position Kerrey and his men were in that night. The possibility of their being killed was everywhere every minute. Some of Kerrey's critics are probably afraid of the dark.

Part of the problem is, we have idealized war and soldiers until a lot of people dont know the truth about either. During the Gulf War, hardly a war at all, the Pentagon handed out six million medals to five hundred thousand soldiers.

The medals often give the false impression, perpetuated by military organizations, that every soldier is brave and heroic. Heroes are as scarce in war as they are in peace.

Tom Brokaw notwithstanding, there was no Greatest Generation. There are a lot of great people in every generation but there are some who arent much good at all, too. A hero is someone who risks his life for someone else and Bob Kerrey risked his life for his Country in Vietnam.

It has been suggested that Kerrey should return the Bronze Star he was awarded for his action at Thanh Phong because he doesnt deserve it. I have a Bronze Star I got in Normandy in World War II. Im proud of it in public but uncertain I deserved it in private. If Bob Kerrey gives back his Bronze Star, I'll send him mine.

Capital Revenge

When they stick the needle into Timothy McVeigh Wednesday, twenty-six people sitting behind glass will watch him die almost instantly.

I personally am not a big fan of watching someone die—even such a bad guy as Timothy McVeigh, but for those who are, I should think watching him die so quickly would be less fun.

Humans have thought up hundreds of ways to put other humans to death over the years and executions have always been crowd pleasers.

Stoning was once common.

Crucifixion was another common method of execution. People gathered to watch the victim die slowly and in excruciating pain, hanging from a cross from nails pounded through their hands and feet into the wood. Jesus Christ was the most famous person in history ever capitally punished.

In 1790 Dr Joseph Guillotine invented the beheading machine named after him. It was the first relatively humane method of execution.

Firing squads are dramatic. The story always was that one of the guns was loaded with blanks so that no one of the squad of shooters knew for certain he had killed anyone. This gave him an out on judgment day.

Hangings have been frequent in the United States. They say the victim's neck is broken when he drops and he dies instantly—but who knows for certain? No victims have talked about it.

The electric chair is the least civilized of the modern methods of killing someone. Supreme Court Justice William Brennan said the electric chair is the contemporary equivalent of burning people at the stake.

Thirty-eight states have capital punishment laws. Twelve dont have any. Since 1930, 4,560 people have been put to death officially in the U.S. Only thirty-nine of those have been women—which doesnt seem fair.

Hawaii and Michigan have never put anyone to death. Texas is a leader in executions and its interesting to note they lead in murders, too. Texas did it to forty people last year alone.

The official methods left are lethal injection, now the most popular, gas and electrocution. Hanging is still legal in Delaware, New Hampshire and Washington but they dont do it. Idaho, Oklahoma and Utah still have firing squads. Some states give the prisoner a choice between being fried, poisoned or shot. I dont think I'd want to choose—I'd rather be surprised.

Revenge is an emotion we all reluctantly enjoy and capital punishment is society's ultimate revenge.

If, as we all hope, people are gradually becoming more civilized, maybe capital punishment will soon be a spectacular of our less civilized past.

Have a nice day.

Busy Day, Busy Day

Tonight I am going to address one of life's most difficult problems.

From the time we get up in the morning until we go to bed at night we are faced with deciding what to do first and what to leave to do later.

The people who decide right are the ones who succeed.

It starts the minute we get up in the morning.

Some of us decide to go to the bathroom, take a shower, get dressed and then have breakfast. Others get up, have coffee, go to the bathroom, take a shower and THEN get dressed. Its what kind of people we are.

I know guys who put their shirt and tie on before they put their pants on.

My line of work is different from yours probably but still, we have the same problems. We all have to decide what to do first. Take last Friday, for an example of my problems.

I came to the office and couldnt decide whether to answer a pile of mail or write my newspaper column.

While I was thinking it over, I made a cup of coffee.

I wanted to get to work but I like to keep up with what's going on in the world so I read the newspaper.

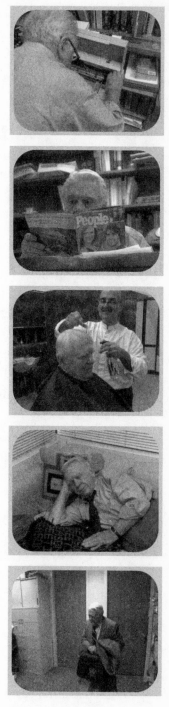

By then I was nervous about all the things I had to do so I made a list. I often make a list of things to do instead of actually doing any of them.

Before I got at the list, I decided to make a couple of phone calls. I made some notes but when I tried to print them I noticed the type was very faint on my printer so I got a new ink cartridge out of our cabinet and changed that. It takes a while but its satisfying to do.

Ive been thinking I ought to buy a new printer so I looked at a catalog that came in the mail with printers in it. Its fun to look through a catalog even if you arent going to buy anything.

Just before I finished looking at the printer catalog, the mail came with this week's issue of *People* Magazine. *People* isnt my favorite but I decided to look at it just so I know what other people are reading. Im up on bare midriffs now.

It was time for lunch so I went across the street to get a sandwich. As long as I was going out, I decided to take my electric razor to get it fixed. The repair place is right near where I get my hair cut so I called to ask if Manny could take me at 1:30. He had an opening so I had my hair cut. Manny is too busy to cut my hair more often than I am too busy to have it cut.

It was a nice day and I walked back to the office. I passed a lot of stores. Ive been meaning to get a suitcase with wheels.

When I finally got back to the office, I'd had several phone calls. I returned those but I didnt sleep well the night before so I closed both my door and my eyes and took a little nap.

After that, it was so late there was no sense starting anything so I packed up and left. Tomorrow Im going to make some tough decisions and go right to work . . . just as soon as I have coffee . . . read the paper . . . and make a few phone calls.

Terror in New York

I dont do it often but I had the television set on in my office. The cameras were focused on the hole where the World Trade Center had been. The phone rang and it was my friend John Sharnik calling to say he didnt have anything to say.

Thats the way I felt. I wanted to talk but I didnt know what to say; I wanted to write but I didnt know what to write. Nothing that came to mind was important enough. Who can explain the inexplicable?

All four kids called. Ellen called from London in tears. Were we okay? They knew we were but it was a time for love.

I stared at the screen on my computer then turned it off and went down to the sixth floor and kissed Judy. I just felt like it.

Maybe you thought New Yorkers dont give a damn. In the elevator two young men said they going to give blood. A third man, staring at the floor, looked up and said, "Radio just announced people have already given so much blood they dont need any more."

I saw the worst of World War II. I watched while the Luftwaffe destroyed most of London. I walked into Buchenwald while they were taking those pictures youve seen so often. Ive seen a lot but no single day in the history of the world exceeds in evil the terrorist attack on the World Trade Center.

We try to get over feeling bad about something by thinking of the good things about it. "At least he didnt suffer," we say of a friend who dies of a heart attack. Its not easy to find anything good about this.

"It could have been worse." You could say that, I guess. They might have released anthrax spores that killed millions instead of thousands.

Our FBI and CIA have been too concerned with their own problems for a long while now to serve the nation well. Donald Rumsfeld was asked if they had advance information about the attack. He said he couldnt answer questions about our intelligence. "No" was probably the honest answer he didnt give.

The CIA and FBI hide behind a convenient veil of secrecy; if this forces them to improve, that will be a good thing to come out of this.

I have often thought of how strange it is that it took something so terrible as World War II to bring out the best in Americans. We worked harder and did more good things from 1942 to 1945 than ever before or ever since.

If this attack produces that same feeling of togetherness in this generation it will not have been all bad.

Take the Train

Some people are afraid of everything. Other people arent afraid of anything. A lot of Americans are afraid to fly now and its ridiculous. Youre more likely to win the lottery than die in a plane crash.

Fear of flying is bad for the airline business—theyve been in financial trouble for years anyway and it got worse on September 11.

Airlines have treated us so badly over the years, its hard to feel sorry for them. You feel sorry for the good people who work for airlines.

Congress has voted to give airlines $15 billion in emergency relief and I dont understand that. Railroads have been in financial trouble for fifty years. Why doesnt Congress give railroads $15 billion?

What ever happened to travel by train anyway?

This Country is dotted with abandoned or little used railroad stations. Cute stores have moved in.

In New York, they tore down the magnificent Pennsylvania Station. Michigan Central Station in Detroit, an architectural gem, was abandoned. Its idle tracks rust away waiting to be boiled down.

There are thousands of miles of empty railroad tracks running contiguously with crowded highways.

Our heavy loads should be moved on steel wheels rolling on steel rails instead of rubber tires on concrete highways. Trucks there play accordion with the cars.

There are 1,345,000 railway freight cars in the United States. Each one can carry several times as much cargo as the biggest truck. Using railroads would reduce our use of oil.

It takes 1,500 gallons of fuel for a plane to fly from New York to Chicago with a hundred people on board. A train with 1,000 people can make the same trip on fewer than three hundred gallons.

The United States is way behind in train travel as anyone knows who's been to Europe or Japan. Trains everywhere are better, faster and more luxurious than ours. Why?

Theres no greater feeling of luxury and satisfaction than being whisked 500 miles closer to your destination while you sleep on a fast-moving train.

Trains are seldom delayed or canceled. They run in sunshine or in snowstorm, oblivious to wind and water.

If the Government is going to give the airlines $15 billion, the government ought to *run* the airlines. Or maybe jump-start travel by giving taxpayers $15 billion worth of tickets to go where they wanted—on a train.

Selling America

Its been satisfying to know we're bombing the hell out of the Taliban. WE all like that. I remember though, how pleased we were in 1993 when the Pentagon showed us pictures of our bombs dropping on Iraq. We were going to bomb Saddam Hussein into oblivion. Well, that didnt happen, did it? We made more enemies than we eliminated.

Its probably possible for us to take out the Taliban government with bombs but then we have to win over a lot of people who hate us.

We do a lot of things well in this Country but theres nothing we do better than sell things. Advertising sells us cars, clothes, pills, breakfast cereals, everything. It sells us the politicians we then vote for.

Right now we ought to be trying to sell America, not cigarettes, to the rest of the world—convince them that we're the good guys, not the bad guys.

Maybe we ought to turn the job over to our advertising agencies instead of the Army. Why dont we try to win them over with words? We have the Voice of America doing a good job with the truth, but the bombs we've dropped on Afghanistan in just a few days have cost more than the Voice of America gets in a year.

President Bush appointed Tom Ridge as director of Homeland Security. How would it be if he appointed another director in charge of selling America to the people of the Middle East who hate us? This person would mobilize our advertising industry to do the job.

We have a great product. We dont have anything to hide. We arent trying to take over any other country. We arent trying to push any religion on them. We're a little selfish and too pleased with ourselves sometimes but advertisers know how to hide the bad stuff and anyway we're decent, peaceful and generous people. Not only that we're genuinely concerned about the whole world. We dont want to see anyone starving, dying of disease or getting killed. The rest of the world ought to know that and it doesnt.

We could put the money we're spending on bombs into radio and television advertising. Inundate those countries with positive information about the United States. Drop good stuff on them, not just leaflets but radios, Hershey Bars, sunglasses . . . new prayer rugs maybe . . . whatever they need. Drop a few million Yankee caps to keep the sun out of their eyes.

But I mean, do good things for them. Make them love us, not hate us.

It seems to that me our advertising experts ought to be able to sell us. We're really awfully nice people.

Dont Mail Me Anything

I got this letter that made me nervous last week. I flattered myself thinking I might be important enough to be the target of a terrorist like Tom Brokaw was.

The envelope was fat and soft and I couldnt read the postmark. Of course, that doesnt make it special. You often cant read the postmark our postal service stamps on our letters.

CBS security people opened it and it turned out to be filled with harmless junk from some nut in California.

Mail isnt as good as it used to be. We've done bad things with it.

Ted Kaczynski killed three people before he was caught mailing bombs.

We've made a mess of our mail in so many ways. The idea of mail being a way for one person to communicate with another is almost a thing of the past. We should never have allowed the mail to be used for advertising. It has made it more of a pain than a pleasure.

Three quarters of all the mail we get now is either trying to sell us something or asking for money. E-mail is not the same as a personal letter. You dont get an e-mail ending in "love."

It isnt like anthrax but when my bank statement comes, the envelope is so full of junk that its hard to find where it says how much money I have. Last week the Chase Bank put fake checks in the envelope.

PAY TO THE ORDER OF ANDREW A ROONEY $5,000, they said on them. Is anyone so dumb as to think a bank is giving them $5,000?

I got two other fake checks last week.

This was for $7,000. This other one was for $25,000.

They were both from car dealers in Connecticut trying to sell me a Jeep. Does a product as good as a Jeep have to resort to such sleazy advertising?

Like a personal letter, a check in the mail is one of the pleasures of life and no one should destroy that by using it in some fake way. I wouldnt buy a car from either of these places if I had to walk to work . . . and thats forty-five miles.

Im sorry to tell you this. But, I wont be opening my mail for a while now . . . and not reading some of it will be a pleasure.

Honesty

Ever since they cloned that sheep, Dolly, in the laboratory in Scotland its been assumed that the scientists are going to be able to make people. Some people are offended by the idea of science moving in on God.

If scientists ever get to the point where they can control what we're like in a laboratory by fiddling with our genes, I hope they forget about making us all good-looking and smart and just make everyone honest. Eliminate the dishonesty gene. Imagine how much simpler life would be if we were all honest.

We wouldnt have to lock the doors every time we leave home.

We wouldnt have those dumb little locks on our windows.

Everyone who comes into the CBS building has to pass through security.

I unlock the outside door of my office . . . then the inside door. A security check and two locks just to get to work.

Some people keep their desk drawers locked.

The maintenance people walk around the CBS building with a ring of keys that weighs nine pounds.

There are stores that sell nothing but locks . . . all kinds of locks. There are more locks than there are thieves.

People get carried away locking stuff. The dumbest locks are on briefcases. If youre going to steal a briefcase, you steal the whole thing—lock and all.

Store owners pull down iron gates when they close up.

There are iron bars on windows.

Some doors are chained shut . . . one of the problems with having a bicycle in the city is finding something to chain it to.

If we were all honest, we wouldnt spend so much time looking for the keys to our cars because cars wouldnt have keys—for the doors or the ignition.

A million and a half cars were stolen last year so we spend $120 billion on car insurance.

Banks spend millions building vaults where they pretend our money is safe behind steel doors. If theyre going to steal it, banks are too smart to take it out of here.

If they could make us all honest, we would have saved forty billion dollars not having 1,578 prisons.

We pay an average of $60,000 a year to keep each one of the two million criminals locked inside.

Every community has its own police force. They cost us $50 billion. New York City alone has 72,000 cops. Thats more cops than some cities have people.

Stores hire their own police to cut down on shoplifting.

The amount white collar thieves steal makes the cost of stolen cars look like peanuts.

If science learns how to control our genes, they could make us so that no one would ever murder or steal again. Everyone would tell the truth, the whole truth and nothing but the truth about everything.

Or . . . do you think thats going too far?

The Stars and Stripes

We simplify life with symbols—designs or images that stand for an idea too hard to say every time. The dollar sign is one . . . the asterisk . . . the cross . . . theyre all quick ways of saying something complicated.

One of our great symbols is the American flag . . . thirteen red and white stripes corresponding to the number of original states, on a rectangular piece of cloth . . . one corner blue with fifty white stars . . . for fifty states.

You see the flag everywhere now. What so proudly we hail. It means the World Trade Center happened to all of us.

"We're proud to be Americans," say flags on front porches in small towns across the Country.

Some homes seem to have been built to fly the flag.

It wouldnt be complete without it. Just perfect.

"We're American too," say the flags inelegantly glued to city apartment windows.

The declaration of patriotic intent is everywhere these days . . . .

Rockefeller Center, with 150 beauties fluttering in the breeze, is in show business . . . a stirring sight . . . although it is unlikely that management there loves our Country any more than the owner of the smallest small business displaying just one tiny flag.

The Annin Flag Company makes most American flags. They have more business than they can do, now.

You dont have to go as far as Annin to buy a flag though.

Flag sales are a street-corner cottage industry. Furtive, illegal street operatives set up shop in big cities . . . to them the buck means more than the banner.

The colors of our flag and the numbers of stars and stripes are ordained but there is no rule regarding dimension.

There are tiny flags on sticks—made in China or Taiwan.

A grand flag is so big on a building in New York that it had to be continued around the corner.

Everyone wants to be associated with the America by hanging their personal flag next to it . . . America and Yale . . . America and Episcopalians . . . America and JP Morgan . . . America and Maxell . . . America and the Ritz Tower.

There are, inevitably, people who are more anxious to *appear* patriotic than to *be* patriotic. They tread a fine line between patriotism and commerce. The flag is everywhere in close proximity to a business interest.

It sells shoes . . . And shoe repair . . . Women's dresses.

The American flag invites diners to foreign restaurants . . . Japanese . . . Italian . . . even Afghan.

There is an official flag code but it is routinely ignored.

It is not proper to use the flag as a tablecloth.

It is not to be used as an awning. Or a canopy.

Or plastered to the hood of a car.

The code says the American flag is not to be used as decorative clothing.

Some find it irresistibly fashionable and we are more amused than mad.

This is how the Star-Spangled Banner was meant to be flown . . . on the end of a pole of its own . . . free to wave majestically in our own free air.

The Sunday Paper

There are several things that need to be invented. I'd like a device with a headset attached to my temples that would scan a newspaper and feed the information directly into my brain without my having to read it.

This is the Sunday *New York Times*, six pounds of it. It may be the best newspaper there has ever been—and it makes me feel terrible. I end every day with a great sense of guilt because I havent read the whole thing.

The *Los Angeles Times, Chicago Tribune, Miami Herald, Washington Post*—all good newspapers but look at the size of them.

This issue of *The Times* alone has 526 pages. If they filled every page with 4,000 words . . . times 526 pages . . . that would be more than two million words. Half the pages are pictures or advertising so cut that in two . . . its still a million words of editorial material.

The average person reads 150 words a minute so, if you read a newspaper for eight hours a day, it would take you fourteen days to read this one Sunday edition of *The New York Times*. By which time, of course, youd have two more papers in the driveway.

That isnt all, either, because before you start *The Times* you have to read your local newspaper . . . to see if your name is in it.

The *Times*, the network television news broadcasts, *60 Minutes* . . . none of them would exist without the money they get from advertising. The paper is fat because they need space to print the ads that pay for writing, reporting, editing, printing.

The *Times* gets about $75,000 a page Sunday . . . multiply that by 250 pages. This edition would bring in $18 million.

What you actually pay for the paper is petty cash for the *Times*.

How did it ever happen that so many good things are so dependent on the business of advertising ?

If you had to pay for a good newspaper, it would probably cost you twenty dollars a day. *60 Minutes* isnt sixty minutes, its forty-five minutes. Without commercials CBS would have to charge you twenty dollars to watch it.

Its all paid for by advertising but dont kid yourselves—you pay for it every time you buy something. Its strange we dont face the facts and pay for things like newspapers directly.

New York City

The rest of our Country has been great to New York since the terrorist attack brought down the mighty World Trade Towers. They have been consoled, sympathized with . . . even loved. Its a strange experience because New Yorkers are unaccustomed to being cared for and fussed over. They hardly know what to make of it.

The biggest change in New York since the terrorist attack is in the attitude of those people who inhabit it. They are nicer to each other. They are saying "Good morning" to neighbors to whom they had not previously nodded in years. They are strangers no longer so strange. The shared sense of loss and bereavement has brought them together.

The best of what has always been in New York is still here unchanged. Culture is rampant and signs of the best of civilization are still everywhere apparent in its world of art, literature and commerce.

New Yorkers still go more places, do more things. The pace is faster. Out-of-towners who are amused at how quickly the city moves often fail to notice that it also gets there first.

There are more people doing more things than in any place on Earth. There are more good restaurants than in Paris . . . more concert halls than Vienna . . . more museums than London or Florence.

If business is bad in the business pages of the newspaper, it isnt apparent on New York City streets where everyone carries a recent purchase.

A woman willing to pay $1,200 for a simple dress does not have to go to Saks Fifth Avenue to buy it. Madison Avenue is filled with small shops with big prices.

Central Park, three miles taken out of the heart of the City, is as busy as ever. New Yorkers use it like a backyard. They run in it, play in it, attend concerts in it. Every morning of its life, the park is awakened by the footsteps of the young and the old, the involved people of the City getting their bodies ready for the work their brains will be doing in an hour.

New York is not the official capital of anything. Those who live here call it simply The City . . . as if there were no other.

They have not fixed on the hole left where 3,273 people died and it is, for the most part, out-of-town visitors, not New Yorkers, who go to view the remains of the World Trade Center as though it were an open casket.

In Dayton or Austin or Atlanta, a visitor is asked, "How do you like Dayton, Austin, Atlanta?"

New Yorkers are indifferent to praise or criticism of their city. They are themselves ambivalent or indifferent to their city's size, excellence or importance at the top of the international rank of cities. They use their city . . . seldom standing back to admire it.

A New Yorker, passing St. Patrick's Cathedral on his way to work, does not look up from his thoughts to admire it. You wouldnt guess from the way we act, but busy New Yorkers have been touched by the attention New York has been given.

There is something just a little off this year about saying to anyone in New York, "Have a Merry Christmas." Perhaps "Have a Christmas" might be a more appropriate greeting and New Yorkers, youll be pleased to know, seem to be having one.

2002

Play Money

A lot of us think the same thing about things and one of the things we've all been thinking is—theyre ruining sports with money.

Half the time the headlines are about how much someone is making not about the game. When the coach of the football team makes four times as much as the college president—something's wrong.

You probably read that television star Katie Couric of the *Today* show signed a contract for an outrageous $15 million a year. Well, do you realize that if Katie Couric played baseball, nine guys would be making more than she does?

These are the nine highest paid baseball players:

Alex Rodriquez: $25,000,000

Danny Ramirez: $20,000,000

Derek Jeter: $19,900,000

Sammy Sosa: $18,000,000

Jason Giambi: $17,142,857

Jeff Bagwell: $17,000,000

Carlos Delgado: $17,000,000

Todd Helton: $15,722,222

Mike Hampton: $15,125,000

None of them played for the Arizona Diamondbacks but the Arizona Diamondbacks won the World Series.

Alex Rodriquez signed a contract with the Texas Rangers to play for $25 million a year. He didnt help. The Rangers won fewer than half their games and A-Rod, as he is known, ought to have to give some of that money back.

I love it when the team that spends the most doesnt win.

Here's a list of how some of the teams' won/loss records compared to how much they spent.

The Yankees spent the most—$112 million dollars–and had the third best won/loss record. Not bad.

The Boston Red Sox had the second highest payroll. But Boston finished fifteenth. Someone should get fired.

The Mets paid fifth most . . . finished sixteenth.

The team that did best and should have been declared the World Series winner was the Oakland Athletics. They had the second best won/lost record in the major leagues and their payroll was next to the lowest.

There are thirty major league baseball teams. Each one of them plays 162 games and all but two of them lost money last year because people arent going to games the way they used to.

There are a lot of reasons people dont go to baseball games anymore. One of them is, the games take too long.

The fifth game of the World Series took four hours and fifteen minutes. Television loved that of course because it gave them so much time for commercials.

Baseball players all have nervous tics that take time. They spend more time getting ready to play than playing. They hitch up their pants, adjust their cap, pull on their shirt—then they step off the mound or out of the batter's box and make fans wait.

The other reason people dont go to games is, teams pay the players so much that ticket prices have to be too high. A good seat for a game in Yankee stadium that used to cost $12 costs $65 now.

If you want a Coke and a hot dog, thats another arm and a leg.

Kids arent baseball fans anymore. They dont play pickup baseball Saturday mornings in vacant lots. There are no vacant lots. They play baseball organized by adults, on school grounds and sponsored by local businesses who sponsor the teams in exchange for the publicity they get.

The great American pastime isnt baseball—its money.

The N-Word

I never thought I'd hear myself say the word but a Harvard professor named Randall Kennedy has written this book called *Nigger: The Strange Career of a Troublesome Word.*

Its a good book because he turns a thousand interesting little ideas in it.

The best way for any of us to get rid of a problem is to hold it up to a bright light and look at all sides of it. Thats what Professor Kennedy does in this book. He takes a lot of the poison out of the word "nigger" while he's doing it.

He even questions whether he's offending people by using it in his title instead of the euphemism "the N-word." It wouldnt be as strong a title.

A book review in *The New York Times* calls Randall Kennedy "African American." I dont know whether he likes that or not. I dont like it. I dont call myself "Irish-American. Im American. Thats good enough for me. Professor Kennedy is American. He's no more African-American than Im Irish-American.

Im called "white" and he's called "black" even though he isnt black and Im not white. So-called "white" people are actually an unattractive pink. His picture looks as if Kennedy is that good-looking shade of brown that pink people try to get to be by sitting in the sun at the beach.

I never understood the American Indian objection to being called "Redskin." It isnt used in a disparaging way. I do agree with them that the tomahawk idea is juvenile and objectionable. I guess if they dont want to be called "Redskin," we shouldnt do it but its silly.

Our thoughts about words change over the years. In 1968 I wrote a television show called *Black History, Lost, Stolen or Strayed* for Bill Cosby. I remember being uneasy with the word "black" because the acceptable word back then was "Negro." Today I wouldnt use "Negro." Its a good, strong word but now it sounds wrong to most of us.

Different ethnic groups of Americans have always had terrible nicknames for each other. I remember hearing them as a kid. You dont hear them much anymore because they always make the person using them sound ignorant.

Italians were "wops," Germans were "krauts." There were "kikes" and "spics."

Irish Catholics were "harps" or "micks."

Mexicans were "wetbacks."

Koreans or Vietnamese were "gooks."

Chinese were "Chinks" . . . "Slant eyes." Arabs were "towel-heads."

Let me read just one paragraph from this book by Randall Kennedy:

As a linguistic landmark, "nigger" is being renovated. Blacks use the term with novel ease to refer to other blacks . . . Whites are increasingly referring to other whites as niggers . . . and indeed, the term both as an insult and as a sign of affection is being affixed to people of all sorts ... "Nigger" as a harbinger of hatred, fear, contempt, and violence remains current, to be sure. But more than ever before, "nigger" also signals other meanings and generates other reactions, depending on the circumstances.

This is the way to get rid of words like "nigger" and all the contemptible ideas that go with it.

The Case for Bigger Government

For a long time now most of us have thought that theres too much Government in Washington. We use "Washington" as though it was a dirty word.

Maybe the pendulum has reached the top and ought to start swinging the other way. Maybe we need MORE government not less.

Something's seriously wrong when the seventh-largest company in the Country, Enron, suddenly goes broke and the president of the company walks away with a couple of hundred million dollars while the employees get zilch.

There are things that need to be done to fix a problem as big as the Enron mess and only the Government is big enough to do it.

The first thing we need from Government is a law that prevents Big Business from buying politicians. Thats a crude way to put it but its the truth. A lot of people in office have been bought with campaign contributions. What is a politician going to say to a businessman who has been responsible for huge contributions to a politician's election campaign when the businessman comes to his office in Washington and asks for a favor?

How did we ever let this happen?

Enron was doing things that were bad for all of us and the Government didnt stop them because Enron had paid to get a lot of politicians elected.

President George W. Bush is doing his best in a hard job but he took half a million dollars for his campaign from Enron.

The Attorney General, John Ashcroft, has excused himself from making any decisions in this case. Ashcroft took $57,000 from Enron.

The head of one of the investigating committees, Senator Joe Lieberman, is relatively clean. He hasnt taken money from Enron since the $2,000 he got in 1994.

Seventy-one Senators and 188 Representatives took money from Enron.

How tough were those seventy-one Senators going to be on them?

This week, speaking about Enron, President Bush finally said that the Government ought to force companies to disclose more of their financial information. Well, I'll say.

What we can see of Enron's books are a mess and a lot of their records are confetti now because they shredded them. I wish someone would make a machine that puts shredded files back together.

The financial records of corporations ought to be open to everyone. If Enron's had been, this never would have happened. We even find out now that Enron didnt pay ANY taxes last year. Why arent we all madder about this than we seem to be?

It might be good if all of us—everyone in the Country—had to say what we paid in income taxes. Dont stop at Enron. I have a neighbor whose tax return I'd like to see. If they published a book of everyone's tax returns, it would be a best seller.

Sometimes it seems as if our Government and everyone in it is dishonest and thats too bad because it simply is not true. It also seems as if everyone in business is out to screw the rest of us and that isnt true either. The fact is, Big Government and Big Business are a lot alike and they both have to be watched . . . by each other and by all of us.

On Being American

Im as proud as anyone to be an American but you may have noticed I dont wear an American flag in my buttonhole. It trivializes a great symbol.

Not only that, I wish we werent treating the Olympics as if it was an American event. Its an international event and its rude and boorish of us, as the host Country, to act as if we were the most important part of it.

We're puzzled over why so many people in the world hate us, then, next thing you know, we're saying to them, "Our Country is better than your Country. Yaaaa."

The television reports from Salt Lake City were dominated by information about how Americans did.

"THE UNITED STATES HAS WON ITS FIRST MEDALS OF THE WINTER OLYMPICS ON THIS THE FIRST DAY OF COMPETITION."

"SHANNON BAHRKE OF TAOS CITY, CALIFORNIA, CAME IN SECOND IN WOMEN'S FREESTYLE SKIIING MOGULS. SHE EARNED THE SILVER MEDAL."

They didnt report who won the race because the winner came from a foreign country. Its as if we were deliberately setting out to make the rest of the world dislike us.

We're always being embarrassed by bumptious Americans who act as though they made this Country what it is today.

Well, none of us living now had anything to do with how great this Country is. We're lucky to have been born here or to have been accepted into the Country. If we've contributed even a little bit to keeping it as good as it is, we can be proud of ourselves but we didnt make it as good as it already was when we got here.

Im not easy, either, with the people, the companies and the charitable organizations trading in patriotism by using the tragedy of the terrorist attacks as a way of calling attention to themselves . . . to a cause or to their product.

I get fund-raising letters every day of the week that mention September 11 just as if their organization had some special connection to the tragedy.

Here's a tacky outfit that calls itself the 1st National Reserve Limited. Historical Ground Zero Vault Recovery. Theyre trying to turn the tragedy into cash by selling $1 worth of silver they claim was found in the World Trade Center basement for $50. Plus $20 shipping.

Major companies are trying to increase sales by associating themselves with the tragedy.

During the Super Bowl halftime, I left my seat because I was uneasy about the show that featured the names of 2,800 people who had died. Some people were touched by it. I found it too close to using the emotion evoked by recalling the event as entertainment.

In our personal lives, we're influenced by other people's appraisal of our behavior. If the friends we hang out with dont like something we do, we usually stop doing it.

The rest of the world doesnt like the way we behave, as if no one else's country is as good as ours, and we ought to stop acting that way—even if we're right.

More Annoying Mail

This is my week's mail. I wish I knew which letters were worth reading before I go to the trouble of opening and reading them.

The wording on envelopes you get often seems too long and repetitious. This is from *Time* magazine. "Time Inc.," it says, "Time, Time & Life Building." At the bottom it says, "An AOL Time Warner Company." Over here, it says *Time* Magazine. Okay, Okay. All right all ready ! So its from *Time*.

Here's another:

UNITED STATES DISTRICT COURT
DISTRICT OF CONNECTICUT
UNITED STATES COURTHOUSE
915 LAFAYETTE BOULEVARD
BRIDGEPORT, CONN.

No wonder our courts are all backed up.

Ive never known what those four extra numbers are after a zip code. This is addressed to me at 10019–2985, my zip code. Thats the area the post office says Im in.

Now . . . there are nine numbers in my zip code. There are 280 million people in the United States. That figure has nine numbers in it. That means every single American could have his or her very own zip code.

Something is wrong here and its obvious zip codes should be a lot shorter.

Postcards are never quite big enough. All the postcards I get are from people who had about two sentences more to say than they could fit on the postcard. Postcards obviously need to be just a little bigger.

This is an old letter from a man in Antioch, Illinois. He lives at 41242

North Westlake. Presumably theres a just plain Westlake Avenue or a South Westlake Street. The almanac says 8,000 people live in Antioch. So, how come they have a street with 41,242 numbers on it? Must be a lot of empty lots in Antioch.

The biggest problem though is the abbreviations assigned the states. Who decided which states would get which letters?

For instance who decided Michigan would be MI. What about Mississippi, Minnesota or Missouri? And why did they give MA to Massachusetts instead of to Maine?

The best ones—abbreviations you cant miss—are ones like FL for Florida, KY for Kentucky and TX for Texas.

Some dont make any sense at all though. For instance, if Oklahoma is OK, which seems OK, and Ohio is OH, why isnt Iowa IO instead of IA? And if Idaho is ID, which it is, logically Pennsylvania ought to be PE not PA.

So . . . if you really want to annoy me, keep those cards and letters coming.

Bigger and Dumber

The papers have been full of it this week. David Letterman may leave CBS and replace Ted Koppel and *Nightline* at ABC.

ABC is worried because surveys show that while about as many people watch Koppel as watch Letterman, Letterman's audience is younger and thats what advertisers want.

We're sympathetic because surveys show that young people dont watch *60 Minutes* either.

Ive taken my own, unofficial survey:

The average IQ of the people who watch *Nightline* and *60 Minutes* is thirty-four points higher than the people who dont watch either broadcast.

My survey also indicates that the people who watch David Letterman and Jay Leno stay up two hours and nine minutes later than people who go to bed at a reasonable hour.

The reason they stay up late is, 37 percent of them dont get up and go to work in the morning because they dont have jobs. They dont have money to buy the stuff in the commercials, either.

The people who stay up late to watch Ted Koppel dont have to get up early because theyre the bosses and they can come to work any damn time they feel like it.

David Letterman's show is on at 11:30 but he tapes it at 5:30 in the afternoon. The reason he does that is simple. Letterman is smarter than 94 percent of his audience and at 11:30 at night, he's home watching *Nightline.*

If CBS loses David Letterman, maybe they could replace him with Congressional hearings. The best thing on television recently has been those Enron hearings.

Jeffrey Skilling, former head of Enron, was a witness. If someone says they dont remember, you cant argue with him.

This is a sampling of what Skilling said: "IN MY RECOLLECTION . . . ALL OF MY RECOLLECTION IS . . . MY ONLY RECOLLECTION OF IT . . . MY RECOLLECTION THAT . . . I VAGUELY RECOLLECT GOING TO JOE AND SAYING . . . I DONT RECALL THAT SPECIFICALLY . . . I DONT RECALL THAT . . . MY RECOLLECTION . . . I DONT RECALL THAT EXACT DATE . . . I DO SPECIFICALLY RECALL . . . I JUST RECALL MY . . . ."

Skilling knows we dont like accountants too so he kept saying he wasnt one. "QUITE FRANKLY . . . I WILL STATE RIGHT NOW THAT I AM NOT AN ACCOUNTANT . . . TO BE QUITE FRANK, I AM NOT AN ACCOUNTANT . . . QUITE FRANKLY . . . AGAIN IM NOT AN ACCOUNTANT . . . QUITE FRANKLY . . . IM NOT AN ACCOUNTANT . . . QUITE FRANKLY . . . I DONT KNOW . . . IM NOT AN ACCOUNTANT."

I never believe anyone is being frank who keeps saying "frankly."

Skilling may be innocent but it seems wrong that a shoplifter who steals a ten-dollar scarf from a store can go to prison for a year when the president of a bank can steal ten million dollars with a bookkeeping trick and never spend a day in jail.

And one last statistic in my survey: the average age of prisoners in the United States is thirty-three . . . too young to be part of the *60 Minutes* audience.

Sex and the Catholic Church

The Catholic church has never officially recognized that sexual desire cannot be suppressed by resolve. Sex isnt something anyone can decide not to have and then never feel sexy. The church was unrealistic when it established rules that put both marriage and sex outside the boundaries of acceptable behavior for priests. The church might as well have ordered church bells not to ring when struck.

The question now, with the revelations about illicit sex in the priesthood so prevalent, is to what extent the lives and protestations of belief by priests are sincere. Can a man who claims special goodness because of his professed devotion to the teaching of Jesus Christ be believed when he ignores basic principles of decency with his personal behavior in society?

Religions have always been concerned with sex and its difficult to understand how so basic a human urge ever got to be considered evil. Religions—Christianity being principal among them—are obsessed with sex. Theyre against it. Adam and Eve were the original sinners. Mankind has been conceived in sin if you take the Bible or the Koran literally.

One of the results of the revelations of unholy transgressions will be the shadow cast on all Catholic priests. The best, most innocent among them are always going to be suspect. No one is going to look at a priest again without thinking: "Does he do it ?"

It wont matter that there is some goodness in the bad priests. We are all better remembered for our exceptional moments, good and bad, than for our everyday accomplishments. The priest taking sexual advantage of young boys might have been a good parish priest but he wont ever be known for that.

I dont know how anyone gets to be a priest. If someone becomes a teacher, a cop, a lawyer, a business person, a plumber, a military leader, an artist or a politician it is probably because he or she showed some ability in that direction and pursued it. It isnt clear why a young man would set out to become a priest now or what steps he would take to get to be one. Fitness for the job is a criterion in most professions but the church is so short of priests, it has almost certainly lowered the standards.

There are 50,000 Catholic priests left in the United States. There were once 100,000. The priesthood has been slowly declining in both number and quality for hundreds of years. There was a time when it attracted intellectuals but as religion was confronted by science, the number of bright young men who wanted to be priests dwindled.

Extinction of the profession was built into the code of behavior demanded of priests. With the prohibition against marriage and sex, it was not a job that was ever handed down from father to son. The fathers of young lawyers are often lawyers. Businessmen bring their sons and daughters into their business. A great many doctors are both the sons and fathers of doctors. Continuity has been one reason for the strength of a variety of professions but the priestly oath of celibacy eliminates, officially anyway, that factor in the Catholic church.

The study of religion is a hobby of mine but I am more interested than knowledgeable about it. Anything can be perceived as religious, no matter how stupid it is, if it is believed by enough people over a long period of time. This accounts for the widespread acceptance of something like genital mutilation by many religions. Circumcision is first among them but in some more primitive religions, the clitoris of women is removed at puberty so they cant enjoy the evil pleasure of sex.

All of us are aware of having done some wrong things—having "sinned"—and a great many sinners who dont want to live with their shortcomings look for forgiveness in religion from a power they perceive to be superior to their own. This is their God. Presumably sinning priests are either rotten clear through or they believe their God has forgiven them.

Palestine and Israel

Of all the people in Government, Secretary of State Colin Powell is one of the hardest to dislike. He's direct and honest. He tells the truth and not some altered version of the truth designed to make himself and the boss look good. He's a Republican but he doesnt act like either a Republican or a Democrat. He acts sensibly.

In 1996, when he was suggested as a presidential candidate, he said he didnt want to be President and that was the end of it.

I like anyone who's smart enough not to want to be President. Thats the kind of President we need.

Colin Powell has been trying to do an impossible job . . . make peace between the Palestinians and the Israelis. You might as well try to reason with a German shepherd and a Doberman pinscher in a dogfight.

Its impossible because no impartial observer whether a diplomat, a reporter or an informed citizen can suggest either side is wrong about anything without making them mad about everything.

The New York Times published a picture of an Israeli soldier beating a Palestinian peace protester. It made the Israeli army look bad and *The Times* got a lot of angry calls saying the paper was anti-Semitic.

Dan Rather spoke about the problems in the Middle East with Larry King. He said, "IN SOME IMPORTANT WAYS THEY BOTH ARE RIGHT. ON THE OTHER HAND . . . IN SOME IMPORTANT WAYS THEY BOTH ARE WRONG."

Dan has a little politician in him.

Hamas and Fatah, the Palestinian terrorist organizations, dont want peace, they want to destroy Israel. Arafat is a poor leader for the Palestinians and he's a toothless tiger who no longer has the power to stop terrorism if he wanted to.

Ariel Sharon doesnt want peace. He loves this war. The Israelis are our friends and the Palestinians are strangers but Sharon is not our friend and President Bush should stop pussyfooting and say so.

Americans and Israelis are hated in the Arab world. Saddam Hussein has offered to give $25,000 to the families of martyrs who kill themselves as terrorists.

How is Colin Powell going to reason with guys who believe that if they kill themselves, theyre going to heaven with seventy-two virgin maidens at their disposal? What's he got to offer that could compare to that?

Who can Powell talk to sensibly? Arafat cant speak for the Palestinians. He has to raise his hand just to get permission from Sharon to go to the bathroom.

Television identifies the weapons used in Israel. Well, the pilot is Israeli but the helicopter is an American Cobra.

The rifles used by the Israelis to kill Palestinians are often American M–16s . . . as are some of the rifles used by Palestinians to kill Israelis. Is this crazy?

Last year, we gave Israel one billion nine hundred million dollars for weapons alone. We gave them sixty-seven helicopters and 337 fighter planes.

If Sharon and the Palestinian terrorists persist with their arrogance, we have the power to save Israel and Palestine from themselves by cutting off both the money and the weapons with which this war is being fought.

Knowing the Score

The New York Yankees beat the Toronto Blue Jays 16 to 3 the other day. It caught my eye in the newspaper because it didnt sound like the score of a baseball game. Every sport has a different scoring system and some are better than others.

Baseball is simple. A player can only score one point at a time. Football is more complicated. A player can score six points with a touchdown . . . three points with a field goal . . . two points with a safety or one point after a six-point touchdown.

It makes the game interesting.

The two worst games for scoring are soccer and ice hockey because they dont score enough. Soccer players run willy nilly up and down the field for ninety minutes and at the end of the game the score is one to nothing. A high scoring game is 2–1.

Same with hockey. Its frustrating to watch on television. The puck is always going to someone who wasnt supposed to get it and often the camera cant follow the action. If the player to whom its directed does get it, he shoots and usually misses the net . . . or the goalie, with pads that cover most of the entry to the net, gets in the way.

Theres too much scoring in basketball. The team with the ball usually scores. Its an exception when the team with the ball doesnt put it in the basket. The Portland Trail Blazers beat the Lakers 128 to 120. You need an adding machine.

Women's basketball is interesting because they pass more. Most of the women arent tall enough to reach up and drop the ball in the basket. There ought to be a basketball league for men five feet ten and under.

The dumbest scoring for a good game is tennis. When the first player wins a point, the score is called fifteen-love.

Why start at fifteen? Why not start at one . . . and what's "love" all about? In tennis, love means nothing.

The funny thing is, tennis wouldnt be nearly as much fun without that crazy scoring system.

Major league baseball is having trouble attracting fans and maybe they ought to change their scoring system.

Players get one run when they cross home plate. It might be more interesting if a player got one point every time he reached a base. If he got to first on a hit, he'd get one point. Second base, two points. A home run would be four points.

The team that crossed home plate the most number of times wouldnt always win. If one team got three men to third base, it would get nine points. If the other team got two home runs, it would only get eight points . . . and lose.

Libraries

I use a computer but twenty words on paper are worth a thousand on a computer. I like books and libraries. Tonight, I have ten observations to make about libraries.

1. The tradition of silence in a library ought to be abandoned. Ive worked in newsrooms with people yelling all over the place and never had any problem concentrating.

   Silence can be more intrusive than noise because you strain to hear the words of every whisper but youre oblivious to a yell or a shout.

2. Publishers should print books in just a few sizes—perhaps three. Look at the mess of books on any shelf.

3. There are too many blank pages at the beginning and end of most books. Authors should be discouraged from taking up a whole page to say something like TO MY WIFE GRETCHEN WITHOUT WHOSE

ENCOURAGEMENT THIS BOOK COULD NOT HAVE BEEN WRITTEN.

Why should we waste our time while the author tries to get in good with his wife?

If you took all the useless pages out of all the books in a library, theyd save miles of shelf space.

4. I have written twelve books now. My only complaint with libraries is, having someone take one of my books out of a library does nothing for me.

5. Publishers should print the title of a book on the back parallel to the shelf, not perpendicular to it.

6. I would exclude books of fiction from a library. A library should be used for information, not entertainment . . . go to the movies! If you want to read a novel, buy one.

7. While I oppose capital punishment, anyone caught cutting a page out of a book in a library should be put to death.

8. I would do away with dust jackets. Dust jackets are a pain in the neck and do not prevent books from getting dusty.

9. Oliver Wendell Holmes said, "Every library should try to be complete on something, if it were only the history of pinheads."

This is my little office library here behind me . . . about 350 books. Forty-seven of them are books on English grammar and usage. This is the head of my pin.

10. It is a sexist thought I know that some of you will object to but mechanics, prizefighters and garbagemen should be men. The best librarian I know is a man but I prefer mothers, nurses and librarians to be women.

Thats what I think about books and libraries.

September 11

We all look for something good about the worst things that happen.

The good thing about what happened September 11 is, it didnt happen to just New York and Washington, it happened to our Country . . . all of us. Americans feel closer together than they did before that terrible day. People to whom New York had been a foreign country suddenly felt an affinity and an affection for it.

Because the mainland of our America had never been attacked before, no one really knew how we would react to an attack. It was possible to imagine millions of Americans panicked and scrambling to flee the danger. In New York, if it was the target, maybe theyd clog the highways headed south and west. Well, they didnt do that. People in New York are going about their business.

We have made heroes of those who died in the September 11 attack and it was the right thing to do. Our attitude has turned the event into an emotional triumph instead of a bitter defeat.

I was working as a young reporter in London in 1942 when the Germans were bombing the city every night. Much of London was destroyed. It was terrible.

The editor of a London newspaper talked about how the English reacted to the bombing. I wrote down his remarks and they were so good Ive kept them all these years:

"Many of us were anxious about the public reaction," he said about the bombing. "We didnt know how the people of London would stand up to it. When the first bombs fell neither the Government nor the newspapers knew what the people who had been hit were thinking and how they would take it. That evening, putting out the newspaper, we decided to assume that they had acted heroically. The next morning we printed all the stories that came in to us of their bravery.

"Right then," the editor said, "the newspapers fixed the pattern of how people ought to behave. Perhaps they would have behaved that way anyway. But there is good and bad in all of us and the right example at the right moment can make all the difference in the way men act."

Our American newspapers and television did the same thing with September 11. They were filled with stories of heroism. Everyone knew what was expected of them and they behaved as they were expected to.

Reinforcing our resolve to be brave and good in adversity is reason enough for all the attention we are giving this September 11 anniversary.

Martha Stewart

We all keep some things to ourselves for the sake of our reputation. I guess I never told you this but I like Martha Stewart. I never told anyone . . . including Martha. I knew I couldnt do anything about it and I didnt want to hurt her.

Actually, we met only once. But, she's good-looking, interesting to talk to and one of the most capable people Ive ever known. Martha Stewart knows how to do things. She does things like CREATE AN AMAZING ARRAY OF DOORKNOBS AND HINGES, MAKE A ROOT BEER FLOAT, CLEAR UP OUR MISCONCEPTIONS ABOUT ALLERGIES TO PETS. She shows us how A LITTLE COPPER WIRE WILL CERTAINLY HELP YOU OUT-SMART THOSE SMART SLUGS IN YOUR GARDEN.

What I cant understand is, if I like her so much why do so many people hate Martha Stewart? They compare her to Leona Helmsley—which is not a nice thing to say about anyone.

Some of the people she works with hate her.

People in the town of Westport, Connecticut, where she lives hate her.

Newspaper headline writers hate her. The nastier the headline the better they like it. Here are a couple: "Grilling Martha," "Martha Gets House Warning," "Martha's Out to Pad Her Assets"

I dont know what Martha's gone and done now. People who are as good at something as she is ought to stay away from money. It only leads to trouble.

Martha sold some stock just before it took a nose-

dive and she's being accused of knowing that was about to happen. Its called "insider trading," which is illegal. We'd all like to get in on a little of that.

Martha says she took advice from a young stockbroker but Im skeptical. Martha doesnt take advice about anything from anyone. When I was on her show I told her how to make good ice cream. Among other things, I told her not to put eggs in it or its frozen custard. She seemed to understand and agree with me.

MARTHA:
There are no eggs which . . . I like that idea a lot.

ANDY:
If you put eggs in it its custard.

Three weeks later Im watching Martha on the CBS *Early Show* and there she is, putting eggs in ice cream.

MARTHA:
And this is vanilla ice cream 101. Its the best recipe that we could come up with. Its two vanilla beans that are cut and split, put six egg yolks into the bowl of a mixer.

So much for Martha Stewart taking advice from anyone.

I hope Martha didnt do anything wrong. I'd hate to see her go to prison the way Leona did. Of course, if she does, you can bet she'll have her cell fixed up real nice . . . and if they had Martha doing time and the cooking, it would be great for the other prisoners.

Attacking Iraq

The polls indicate that we are evenly divided over whether or not we should attack Iraq. Thats what I am—evenly divided.

A lot of good people think its wrong for us to be the ones who start any war. Other sensible Americans think we should attack Saddam Hussein before he attacks us.

Our leaders wont tell us how they'll do it because that would be telling him. Its the most secretive administration we ever had. Donald Rumsfeld, our Secretary of Defense, doesnt ever tell us much of anything.

We have all the weapons we need.

We'd probably start the war by bombing Iraq. We have 1,500 heavy bombers.

We have 1,300,000 soldiers. There are 40,000 colonels alone. Not many of THEM will be getting sand in their combat boots.

A million one hundred thousand of our soldiers are men—200,000 are women.

It seems likely that once weve bombed the hell out of Iraq, we'll drop several thousand of our special forces in there. Try to find Saddam Hussein. These are the guys most apt to get killed.

Its always easier to drop them in than to pull them out.

We have 8,000 tanks . . . and about 24,000 armored vehicles.

We have 9,000 military airplanes . . . 7,000 helicopters.

Iraq barely touches water but our Navy is ready. We have twelve aircraft carriers, eighteen nuclear submarines and fifty-four attack submarines. One nuclear attack sub costs $4,467,000,000. There are a thousand millions in one billion.

Keep in mind, we have all the bad stuff we're accusing Hussein of having, too. We have 2,325 intercontinental ballistic warheads, nuclear warheads. We have stores of anthrax and other test-tube killers. Hussein may have them too. He used mustard gas on the Iranians fifteen years ago but mustard gas is old-fashioned now.

Our military people support the plan to attack Iraq, of course. Theyve lived their whole lives for this. And, if you had all those expensive toys at your command, youd want to play with them too. I must admit, my worst side would enjoy seeing us do it.

Then I get thinking of all the people who are going to die . . . innocent Iraqis, American soldiers. And, I got wondering if we know what we're doing.

President Bush isnt sitting in his private quarters in the White House watching *60 Minutes*, waiting to hear what Andy Rooney thinks but if he was listening, I think what I'd say is, "Dont do it, Mr. President."

About Asking Your Doctor

Ive been pretty healthy most of my life but, even so, not many days go by when there isnt some question I have that I'd like to ask a doctor. The other day I was wondering whether its okay to keep two different kinds of pills in the same bottle.

On television the drug companies make it sound as if you could talk to your doctor anytime you wanted to about anything. They always say, "ASK YOUR DOCTOR" or "TALK TO YOUR DOCTOR."

Well, forget trying to call your doctor. We've all tried to do that.

Usually theres a taped recording that says, "You have reached Internal Medicine Associates. Please make your selection from the following menu. If this is a serious medical emergency or you are a physician, press 1. To leave a non-urgent message for your doctor, press 2."

I understand though. A busy doctor doesnt want to talk to you about whether you should take Plavix or Flonase. He's got sick people to take care of. He's got to make a living, too. Theres no money in talking to you on the telephone.

All doctors must have some patients theyd like to get rid of because they bug them all the time with dumb questions.

Doctors arent doing as well as they did just a few years ago because of HMO's—Health Maintenance Organizations. They have to see more patients to make a living. That gives them less time to have a friendly chat with you about Zocor.

I have someone I call "my doctor." He's good but he really isnt mine. He probably has more than a thousand people who call him "my doctor."

The chances are the person you call "my doctor" doesnt fix what you have wrong with you anyway. I have this carpal tunnel problem in my hand, now. Youve probably heard of it. You can see my hand is swollen. Im having surgery but "my doctor" doesnt do that kind of work. He really doesnt DO anything. He decides what's wrong and sends me to the doctor who fixes whatever it is.

Doctors have become too specialized. My hand surgeon is going to operate on my right hand. Well, my left one needs it too and I'll probably have to get a left-hand hand specialist to do that.

I like doctors though. Not many bad ones. I trust all doctors except the ones who advertise in the yellow pages of the telephone book.

Things have changed for the worse for both doctors and patients. Our relationship isnt what it was. It isnt the doctors' fault and it isnt ours. Its because of HMOs and because doctors have to spend more time on paperwork than on patients. What we need is more good doctors and fewer bad health plans.

Suing for Fun and Profit

Ive been thinking of quitting work and suing big companies for a living instead. Suing has become a popular American pastime and I'd like to get in on some of the easy money. There were more than a million and a half civil lawsuits in California alone last year. Youre talking a lot of lawyer-hours.

A jury in Los Angeles awarded $28 billion to a woman who has lung cancer and says its because the Philip Morris tobacco company talked her into smoking with its advertising. We all hate the tobacco companies but smoking wasnt even a little bit the woman's own fault?

Thats the trouble. Nothing is anyone's own fault anymore. You probably dont remember the name Stella Liebeck, but she was the woman who spilled coffee in her lap in a car and got big bucks when she sued McDonald's because the coffee was too hot.

Every big company gets sued. Kellogg's and Black and Decker got sued by a New Jersey couple who put one of Kellogg's Pop-Tarts in the toaster and then left the house. The Pop-Tart caught fire and did some damage to their kitchen.

We have a cottage on a lake. I tried to buy a new diving board for the dock and couldnt find one. You know why? The companies that make diving boards have practically been sued out of business.

The same with ladders. It costs a company almost as much for insurance as it costs them to make the ladders.

Doctors are leaving Pennsylvania because theyve been sued so often there.

A man named Caesar Barber sued McDonald's, Burger King, KFC and Wendy's because he weighed 270 pounds and claimed he got fat eating their food. He had a couple of heart attacks and said they never told him their food was bad for him.

If someone is killed when his car turns over going around a curve at ninety miles an hour, his family sues the car manufacturer or the company that made the tires. If he hits a telephone pole, they sue the telephone company.

The wife of a man who was murdered sued the company that made the gun. The tobacco companies, the gun manufacturers and the tire companies have it coming but the amount of some of these awards dont make sense.

I know who I'd sue if I quit my job here. I started working at CBS more than fifty years ago—look at the condition Im in! Hair grey, face wrinkled, brain dead, all bent over . . . Im a mess. I didnt get this way anyplace else. CBS did it to me and I'll bet if I get a trial lawyer and sue, I could quit working on *60 Minutes* and retire. I'd split the billions I'd collect 90–10 with the trial lawyer. He'd get 90 percent—I'd get 10.

Russia and Russians

Its no fun reading a story in the newspaper unless you have some opinion about it—usually based on prejudice, or some little experience youve had related to it. I dont know anything about Chechnya but Ive been to Russia three times and I do have an opinion on this tragedy in which 170 people were gassed to death in that Moscow theater.

It hasnt been popular to say in this Country but I like the Russians. Theyre more like Americans than the people in most European countries.

More like us than the French or the Germans, for example. I was in Germany at the end of World War II when our Army met the Russian Army coming the other way on the Elbe River at Torgau.

The huge Hohner Harmonica factory was in Torgau and Russian soldiers broke down the doors and took thousands of harmonicas and accordions. The amazing thing to me was, they all knew how to play. It was a crazy scene.

All the Russians had bicycles too because theyd taken them coming across Germany. A lot of them had the little machine guns, the Schmeisser. Theyd taken those from dead or captured German soldiers. These young Russians were playing the most dangerous game I ever saw. Some of them were riding in circles on their bikes while the others tried to shoot holes in the tires with their Schmeissers.

When the U.S. Army was in Berlin with the Russians, the Russian trucks were always broken down. All the Russians knew how to do was put gas in them. On the highway leading into Berlin good-natured Russian soldiers would stand beside their trucks smiling and waving at Americans as we drove by. Their trucks were broken down but they didnt have a care in the world.

After the war I was in a hotel in Moscow and twenty-three American doctors on a tour had been taken to a hospital with food poisoning. I came into the dining room at three o'clock one afternoon. The sun was streaming in the windows, it was warm and they already had the tables set for dinner four hours later. At each place there was a plate with a piece of fish on it covered with mayonnaise. I knew what had happened to the doctors.

One year I went to Russia for ten days with thirteen black school kids from Atlanta. It was one of the best experiences of my life but it reenforced the opinions that I already had about the Russians. I liked them.

Ive flown on Aeroflot three times, the Russian airline. No one knows their safety record because they dont release information about crashes. I think I know why.

Russia did some great things in space in the 1960s but, like us, they had a lot of help from German scientists.

We seem to be getting along better with the Russians and I hope this theater incident doesnt change that.

They handled it the way theyve handled a lot of things—badly. They do a lot of bungling but the Russians are not bad people.

Hard to Open

We have a crisis in America more serious than any threat posed by Saddam Hussein because it affects the lives of everyone of us every day.

The problem is this: Everything we buy is too hard to open. It doesnt matter whether its a mouthwash, a video cassette, a jar of jam or a bottle of pills . . . theyre all too hard to open. No one wants to spend five minutes working to get the top off something.

Pill bottles are called child-proof but theyre *adult*-proof. The caps on medicine bottles may have saved the lives of some children but theres no statistic on how many adults have died in the middle of the night because they couldnt get the top off a bottle of their medicine.

Everything opens a different way. PUSH DOWN AND TURN TO OPEN.

Sure. "Squeeze sides while turning" is the worst. Like patting your head and rubbing your stomach at the same time. And then some have plastic seals around the top. You have to go at them with a knife to get the plastic off before you start twisting, pressing or turning.

Why should a bag of potato chips be a problem? What are they protecting in that puffy bag, the air? Half the time you end up tearing the bag open with your teeth.

How many small children have died when they got into a bag of potato chips by accident? And what about a quart of milk or a container of orange juice? If there isnt anything dangerous in there, why do they make it so hard to get in one?

Or take a standard box of granola. You fight your way in the box and then you need a pair of scissors to get at the granola itself. I dont eat with scissors.

If you think theres any doubt that things are too hard to open, think of the cottage industry that has sprung up to help you open things. There are hundreds of gadgets designed to help you get into a package, a can, a bottle or a box.

Political Aptitude Test

No one but the candidates paid much attention to the elections this year. Fewer than 40 percent of eligible Americans voted. Theres something wrong with that and I have an idea. Forget voting.

We'd replace voting with a better way of selecting our leaders. Make everyone running for office take a written test. Never mind the political speeches. They wouldnt have to make any and we wouldnt have to listen. Students take S.A.T.'s—Scholastic Aptitude Tests—to get into college. Every candidate would take a P.A.T.—a Political Aptitude Test to get into office.

It would test candidates on their knowledge of the issues and on their basic intelligence. The candidate who got the highest score on the test would win and become the office holder.

Voters have been getting turned off lately and not bothering to vote because there are a lot of things wrong with our elections. To begin with, the average voter doesnt pick the candidates. They get the candidates handed to them by professional politicians. In the primary election, voters choose between several candidates they didnt have anything to do with picking. They were chosen by a small group of professional politicians who run the party organizations. Thats wrong.

This year 98 percent of the candidates already in the House of Representatives were reelected. They won because, as office holders, they are in a position to do favors for people and for businesses who give them money. Thats wrong. Unknown challengers dont have anything to offer.

In New York State three candidates spent $140 million trying to get to be governor. You wonder what's in it for them. Would they spend that much of their own if they didnt think theyd get it back? One business tycoon spent $65 million of his own money trying to buy the election. Thats wrong.

The President didnt go into work on fifty-six working days this year because he was out making speeches for Republicans. He raised $140 million for them. Wrong. Not what we elected him to do. Its not a party matter. President Clinton did the same thing in 2000.

We dont really know what the candidates believe and if we gave them a test, maybe we'd find out. They hate to answer YES or NO to anything because if they do, voters can tell where they really stand on an issue. This Political Aptitude Test would have maybe fifty YES or NO questions.

I put down just a few sample questions.

IF YOU THOUGHT IT WAS NECESSARY, WOULD YOU RAISE TAXES?

SHOULD WE ATTACK IRAQ?

SHOULD THERE BE PRAYER IN SCHOOLS . . . TO THE CHRISTIAN GOD OR TO ISLAM'S ALLAH?

SHOULD WE SPEND LESS ON EDUCATION AND MORE ON THE MILITARY?

SHOULD WE SPEND MORE ON THE MILITARY AND LESS ON EDUCATION?

The test would have questions like those. You can make up your own.

Someone asked me who would mark the tests and give the politicians their P.A.T. score.

I'll do that.

2003

Presidents in General

Americans flaunt their patriotism. They wear flags in their buttonholes but they draw the line on love-of-country when it comes to supporting a President they dont like.

People are vicious about hating a President they didnt vote for . . . and Im not talking about any one President.

When our children were young we had a rich friend with children and she often drove them to a game or a party.

This woman was old enough to remember Franklin Delano Roosevelt and she hated him. When someone gave her change that had a dime with Roosevelt's picture on it, she opened the car window and threw it out.

I have friends now who own a lot of stock but they dislike George W. Bush so much that they hope the stock market keeps going down, even though theyre losing money, just so he wont get reelected.

There was a story on the Internet a while back listing the IQs of the last twelve U.S. Presidents. The study was supposedly done by a think tank called the Lovenstein Institute.

Bill Clinton was at the top of the list with an IQ of 182. Jimmy Carter was second . . . Nixon was the highest ranked Republican at fourth. George Bush was listed at number eleven and George W. Bush was listed twelfth with the lowest IQ . . . the dumbest President.

It sounded possible and I foolishly tried to find the Lovenstein Institute. Well, of course, there is no such thing. It was a hoax by someone who hates President Bush. A vicious trick.

I met Senator Dole and President Clinton downstairs here at CBS last week. It was fun. Clinton was talking about being disliked. He laughed and said, "If I get up and tie my shoes in the morning, someone criticizes the way I do it."

I dont know why people cant simply disagree with a President instead of hating him. I disagree with George W. Bush a lot but I dont hate him. I find him engaging—often wrong but engaging.

The Democratic candidate for 2004 is still anonymous. We dont know who'll run against President Bush but if this anonymous Democrat is elected, one thing is certain: a lot of Americans are going to hate him. They'll say Anonymous is the dumbest President we ever had.

A Ten-and-a-Half-Ounce Pound

There are certain things in life we ought to be able to depend on. We have to trust each other sometimes.

If you get a roll of fifty pennies at the bank, you dont count them. You trust that theres fifty cents in there.

When you buy a container of milk, you trust theres a quart in it.

Tonight is another chapter in our continuing series on how some businesses violate that trust by charging more and giving less for what they pretend is the same.

Our first report was on coffee in 1988. Here's what I said:

"CHOCK FULL O' NUTS HAS NOT ONLY REDUCED THE AMOUNT OF COFFEE IN THE CAN BUT THEYVE ALSO REDUCED THE SIZE OF THE PRINT TELLING YOU HOW MUCH THERE IS IN IT." In 1988 there were only 13 ounces of coffee in a 16-ounce sized can.

Here's the newest update. A one-pound can of Chock Full O' Nuts isnt even as chock full as it was back in 1988. Now its just 11 ounces.

In 1993 I congratulated Martinson's for holding the line at 16 ounces. "MARTINSON'S IS STILL 16 OUNCES. THE CAN IS THE SAME SIZE."

Sorry about Martinson's. Its now down to 13 ounces. If theyre not going to put a pound in it, they should use a smaller can. No one wants to pay for that much air.

In 1988 we had a one-pound can of Savarin.

"SAVARIN AND MARTINSON'S. THEYRE GOING TO STICK WITH THE OLD FASHIONED 16-OUNCE, ONE-POUND HEAVY CAN."

Well, Savarin executives probably got stock options for putting out the lightest one-pound can of coffee on the market: 10.50 ounces. Thats less than two thirds of a pound.

Maxwell House still says its good to the last drop . . . maybe, but there have been fewer and fewer drops over the years.

In 1988, the old can of Maxwell House one-pound came down to 13 ounces.

And here we have the new Maxwell House . . . the last drop was down to 11 ounces.

The only one-pound can we found that still has 16 ounces in it, a pound, may be the best coffee, too. BROWN GOLD.

There are 17 cans here on my desk . . . they hold a total of 13 and a half pounds of coffee. Doesnt that seem like cheating?

Of course I dont really have any right to complain. The actual content of *60 Minutes* is now less than 42 minutes.

The Columbia Disaster

Saturday morning I went out to get the newspaper about seven o'clock. A stranger I passed nodded and said, "Have a nice day."

Well . . . it was friendly of him but it didnt help my day. None of us had a nice day Saturday. At about 9 o'clock we had a death in the family that has brought us together just as the terrorist attack did on September 11. For this brief time at least, there is a warmth among us that didnt exist Friday.

It didnt happen to five men and two women alone—it happened to all of us. President Bush said it, we're together in our grief.

For this terrible time, we are not Republicans or Democrats.

We are not Protestants, Catholics, Jews or atheists. We're Americans together with the same awful feeling in our stomachs.

The purpose of exploring the mysterious space beyond our planet has been to improve life here on Earth. The more we know about what's out there, the easier it will be to change life for the better here. We dont do it often but we're even thinking of future generations.

It has always been the brave men and women who have changed things for the better. The Wright Brothers risked their lives to prove we could fly.

Many of the soldiers who fought our wars were brave men who risked their lives to change the course the world was taking. The seven who died when the Columbia disintegrated were brave men and women.

It isnt bravery when we do some foolish thing for personal glory. The astronauts who waved goodbye and climbed on board the Columbia knew better than the rest of us how dangerous their mission was.

Looking at pictures of them before their flight, its difficult to suppress tears. Great smiling people assuring us that they are not afraid . . . even though they must have been afraid.

If brave men and women never died, there would be nothing special about bravery. Cautious living is comfortable and safe but it is not what made this Nation great. The Pilgrim fathers were not cautious explorers. Caspar Milquetoast was not one of our Revolutionary War heroes. We have lost seven brave people trying to make things better for those of us here on Earth. There is nothing good to say about it.

Built-In Commercials

As Im sure you know, some television viewers tune out when the commercials come on. Naturally, advertisers dont like that because theyre paying for the show youre watching.

A Hollywood producer named Michael Davies is going to do something about it. He's going to make television shows without commercial interruptions because the advertising message will be part of the shows themselves . . . not interruptions. This will make it impossible for people to tune out the commercial if they want to see the show.

Because I dont want to be left behind any new technology in television, I decided to see if I could put commercials in my pieces.

In order to be loyal to our sponsors in this sample piece, I'll use products that have actually been advertised on *60 Minutes*. You should remember them. They are STAPLES, SATURN ION, BREATHERIGHT, CELEBREX, DULCOLAX, LENSCRAFTERS, ZOLOFT, ZOCOR, PEPCID, SERENITY DRY ACTIVE LINERS and THERAFLU.

Okay, now say for example, I wanted to talk about war with Iraq and include commercials in that. Here's how it might go:

"Its my opinion we should not attack Iraq without the support of the United Nations. The trouble with that is, the UN is so tied up with red tape and paperwork, it cant decide what to do. For your paperwork problems and the very in best red tape, visit a Staples office supply store near you."

Here's another built-in commercial:

"President Bush seems intent on taking us to war with Iraq. If we attack, the Army will probably need about 1,500 M-1 tanks. One tank costs about three million dollars.

"General Motors made these tanks. General Motors also makes the Saturn car. You could buy 200 Saturns for what one tank costs the Army. Zero percent financing. Offer ends March lst."

Or this:

"Speaking of Iraq, let me read you something President Bush said in referring to Saddam Hussein: 'I am sick and tired of games and deceptions.'

"Americans are almost evenly divided about going to war. Some approve, others strongly oppose the idea. If the thought of going to war turns your stomach, try Pepcid AC, just one and heartburn's done.

"If you are sick and tired of the thought of war with Iraq, take Zoloft, Dulcolax, TheraFlu, Celebrex or Serenity Guards for urine leakage. Ask your doctor which is right for you."

I want to apologize tonight for my voice. I have a slight cold. I should have worn a BREATHE RIGHT NASAL STRIP.

So, what do you think about integrating commercials into my pieces like that?

On Mixing Flavors

Obviously, I like to eat but I do have some rules. I dont mix flavors. I like vanilla ice cream and I like chocolate ice cream but I dont put them in a dish together.

When I was a kid, I liked peanut butter and I liked jelly but I didnt like peanut butter and jelly sandwiches.

Friday I went to the deli across the street and took a sandwich and a Coke back here to the office. I opened the Coke, took a gulp and almost spewed it over the papers on my desk. I looked at the label and it said VANILLA COKE. Well, I like Coke and I like vanilla but I disliked VANILLA COKE.

Everything's got something else in it. RASPBERRY GINGER CRISP, CRANBERRY ALMOND CRUNCH.

CHERRY VANILLA DREAM WITH PECANS AND CASHEWS. Sounds more like a Cherry Vanilla Nightmare.

ORANGE CAPPUCCINO. They sell HAZELNUT-FLAVORED coffee. What's wrong with coffee-flavored coffee? FAT FREE HAZELNUT COFFEE MATE. The only thing I can figure is, hazelnuts are cheaper than coffee beans so thats what theyre putting in with the coffee to stretch it out.

Soft drink companies take perfectly good water and louse it up with KIWI AND STRAWBERRY. One says TANGERINE-PINEAPPLE-GUAVA. I'd have to be dying of thirst on a desert island to drink that.

SOUR CREAM AND ONION POTATO CHIPS. I guess the sour cream and onions arent even real. It says ARTIFICIALLY FLAVORED.

I have a can of RASPBERRY FLAVORED tea. Down below it says MORE TEA TASTE . . . so what's the raspberry all about if they want it to taste like tea?

Theres a SALT FREE RICE CAKE thats also FAT FREE. A FAT FREE TOPPING. Ive always been interested in the fact that when they dont put something in a product, it costs more. If it doesnt have fat, salt, sugar or any calories in it, its more expensive.

This is a FAT FREE POPPYSEED DRESSING. I always worry about what they do with all the fat they take out of these things. Do they just throw it away? I bet they put it in something else and sell that to us.

Honey is very big in everything now. HONEY NUT CHEERIOS, PLANTERS HONEY ROASTED PEANUTS, HONEY MUSTARD PRETZEL DIP.

Honey doesnt go with either peanuts or mustard. I have an idea that honey is cheap because bees are making it faster than we're eating it.

You know . . . maybe I'll retire and go into business. I'd make an artificially flavored, fat free, honey-coated hazelnut hot dog. You could have it with no-cal French vanilla or chocolate-flavored mustard.

Dying to Kill

This might be a good time to stop and think about how pleased we should all be with ourselves as human beings for the progress we continue to make here on Earth. We've found cures for diseases that enable us to live twenty-three years longer than our grandparents.

We grow food enough to feed ourselves without having to go into the woods to pick it or shoot it.

A thousand years ago most people didnt go much of anywhere because there was just so far they could walk. Now we travel everywhere on wheels and around the world on wings.

The most progress we've made, though, is in the ways we've invented to kill each other.

When one caveman wanted to kill another, he had to get close enough to hit him with a club. The caveman must have worried when someone invented the sling. The sling is what made it possible for David to kill Goliath by hitting him in the head with a rock from twenty feet away.

For hundreds of years, men killed each other with blades of steel—sharp knives and swords. Metal suits were in vogue then, more for protection than good looks.

The bow and arrow was the favorite of medieval times.

The invention of gunpowder was the single biggest help to people killing each other. Men packed the explosive powder in one end of a tube, stuffed a metal ball down the other, then lit the powder to blow it out. They improved on the first cannon by filling a hollow steel ball with powder so it exploded and killed more people when it hit them.

Most of the 600,000 men who died in our Civil War were killed one at a time by a rifle bullet. The handheld gun has been a more popular murder weapon at peace than at war.

World War I brought the first use of chemical weapons like mustard gas. Then we got airplanes and tanks as weapons.

Tanks never really worked out.

There was a proliferation of new weapons for World War II—bombers that could wipe out a whole city, guided missiles, and more recently, nuclear submarines. The United States used the most effective way of killing a lot of people quickly ever devised when we got back at the Japanese for Pearl Harbor. We killed 100,000 of them in no time at all with two atomic bombs. Poof and theyre gone.

Our military leaders assure us that our weapons now are even better.

Human beings on Earth as we know them are maybe 100,000 years old . . . nothing compared to the millions of years of Earth's history without people as we know people.

If we continue our progress inventing weapons capable of wiping ourselves out, Earth could very soon now end up without people again.

The French

You cant beat the French when it comes to food, fashion, wine or perfume but they lost their license to have an opinion on world affairs years ago. They may even be selling stuff to Iraq and dont want to hurt business.

The French are simply not reliable partners in a world where the good people in it ought to be working together. Americans may come off as international jerks sometimes but we're usually trying to do the right thing.

The French lost World War II to the Germans in about twenty minutes. Along with the British, we got into the war and had about 150,000 young men killed getting their country back for them. We fought the Germans all the way across France until the Germans finally surrendered in a French schoolhouse.

Youd think the school in Reims where that historic event took place would be advertised by the French as a great tourist attraction but it isnt. The French seem embarrassed by it. They dont want to call attention to the fact that we freed them from German occupation.

I heard motion picture director Steven Spielberg say the French wouldnt even let him film the D-Day scenes in *Saving Private Ryan* on the Normandy beaches. They want people to forget the price the Americans, the British and the Canadians paid getting their country back for them.

Americans have a right to protest going to war with Iraq. The French do not. They owe us the independence they are flaunting in our face at the U.N.

I went into Paris with American troops the day we liberated it, August 25, 1944. It was one of the great days in the history of the world.

French women showered American soldiers with kisses at the very least. The next day, the pompous Charles de Gaulle marched down the mile long Champs Elysées to the Place de la Concorde as if he had liberated France himself. I was there squeezed in among a hundred tanks we'd given a small force of the Free French Army that we brought in with us. Suddenly there were sniper shots from the top of a building. Thousands of Frenchmen who had come to see de Gaulle scrambled to get under something. I got under an Army truck myself. The tank gunners opened fire on the building where the shots had come from . . . firing mindlessly at nothing. It was a wild scene that lasted maybe ten minutes.

When we go to Paris every couple of years now I rent a car. I drive around the Place de la Concorde and when some French driver blows his horn for me to get out of his way, I just smile and say to myself, "Go ahead, Pierre. Be my guest. I know something about this very place youll never know."

The French have not earned their right to oppose President Bush's plans to attack Iraq.

On the other hand, I have.

Andy vs. Rooney

(In March of 2003, Don Hewitt, the producer of 60 Minutes, hired former President Bill Clinton and Republican presidential candidate Bob Dole to debate each other each week. This was a parody of those debates.)

Im envious of the Dole/Clinton–Clinton/Dole debates because between them, they can take both sides of an issue. If I could take one side for a minute and then take the other, it would be a lot easier for me.

Say, for example, I wanted to argue about being a Republican, or a Democrat.

ANDY:
The trouble with you Democrats is you think the solution to all our problems is more government. Government IS the problem. Let me give you the

titles of just three government jobs we could do without. These are actual positions:

Special Assistant to the Assistant Secretary of Shipping.

Associate General Deputy Assistant Secretary.

Associate Deputy Assistant Secretary of Public Affairs.

Democrats oppose the President's tax cut because they say its good for the wealthiest Americans. Why are Democrats against the rich? What have poor people done for us lately? The wealthiest 5 percent pay more than 55 percent of all income taxes in this Country.

Why tax people for being successful? They ought to be encouraged, not penalized.

President George W. Bush has restored American pride and our prestige in the world by freeing Iraq of Saddam Hussein. He's a great President. We should carve his likeness on Mt. Rushmore while he's still in the White House.

ROONEY:

Republicans like you talk as if they want less Government but every time they get elected, the bureaucracy gets bigger. They fire ten government workers in Washington to make it look good . . . then they hire a consulting firm with 175 employees to do the work of the ten government workers they fired.

You say government should let business alone. Well, it left Enron alone and look what happened. Big Business pretends it doesnt like Big Government but Big Business and Big Government are in business together. The Government is the biggest customer Big Business has.

The economy is down the drain under George W. Bush, the rest of the world hates us and now that our soldiers, most of whom are Democrats, have won the war in Iraq, Bush doesnt know what to do about the peace. Tony Blair makes Bush sound like a high school dropout. You Republicans would be smart if you didnt even nominate him for a second term.

ROONEY: You know one of you is a lot better than the other at this.

The "Coalition"

Ive lived a long while now and I dont remember any more unpleasant times than these. I hate everything about this war except that we're winning it.

You cant even be critical without sounding unpatriotic. Its why Peter Arnett got fired by NBC for speaking on Iraqi television.

Arnett said: "THE FIRST WAR PLAN HAS FAILED BECAUSE OF IRAQI RESISTANCE."

Arnett wasnt being unpatriotic. He was being a jerk—which isnt just cause for being fired.

Im patriotic but I wish our Government would stop treating this war as if they had to sell it to us with slick advertising slogans. The White House web site puts out a daily bulletin about the war with this headline: "OPERATION IRAQI FREEDOM."

Come on, all we want is the news, not a sales pitch.

They called our bombing campaign against Baghdad "Shock and Awe."

After the UN refused to approve the war, our government put together a list of countries it said supported us. They called it "a coalition of the willing."

The generals on television dont talk about "American" soldiers . . . its always "coalition forces."

Reporters have been sucked into it, too.

Its as if there were no Americans there, just coalitions.

The word "coalition" makes it sound as though we're just a few countries short of having the whole world on our side and that isnt true. Most of the world is not on our side. The Administration says forty-nine countries are part of the coalition. I see that Eritrea, Uganda and Iceland are listed as being on our side.

The fact is though we're in this thing with the British, who have 45,000 soldiers there, and the Australians who have 2,000. Thats it. The other forty-six wish us well or let us fly bombers over their country. Big deal.

We've practically bribed some of them. We offered Turkey $15 billion to let our troops go through there to attack Afghanistan but they refused. President Bush wont be sending the President of Turkey anything for his birthday this year.

There arent any good wars but this one is especially bad. We want to win it quickly without more death but we're grown-up people, too. The President, Rumsfeld and the generals ought to stop treating us like children. Tell us the truth. We can take it even when its bad. And the only real good news will be when this terrible time in American history is over.

Illumination

Sometimes when I wake up in the middle of the night, I get thinking things that wouldnt be worth thinking about if I was really awake.

I was lying in the dark the other night and got thinking about what a good job civilization has done lighting everything.

Before Thomas Edison came up with the light bulb, the only way people had of seeing in the dark was with fire. There were campfires. We had kerosene lamps at our cottage at the lake.

Everything's lit with electricity now . . . whatever electricity is. Ive never been clear about it.

Theyre even talking about the time when there'll be a permanent light in the sky . . . a manmade sun hung up there. We'd have twenty-four-hour daytime. Im afraid of the dark but I wouldnt want twenty-four-hour light. We all need some darkness in our lives.

Downtowns everywhere are already lit up twenty-four hours a day. The Great White Way.

We have to pull down the shades in our bedrooms because of the glare of the street light outside.

Flashlights were a good invention. Im a sucker for clever flashlights. The bigger the better. I always want one of the ones with five batteries when I was a kid.

Flashlights bring out the gadget inventors. I'll bet Ive bought a hundred flashlights in my life. I have every kind ever made. But then I can never find one around the house when I really need one.

During World War II the British had those great searchlights scanning the sky over London, looking for German bombers to shoot down.

I always think about what would happen if all but a few thousand people living on some remote Pacific islands were wiped out. Those humans left on

Earth wouldnt know how to make any of the things we have. How long would it take before another Thomas Edison came along and invented the light bulb again?

When I get thinking of something like light in the middle of the night, theres one light that seems perfect. And thats a candle. Its solitary . . . its flicker constantly changes . . . it casts great shadows . . . leaves mysterious dark areas in a room. Candlelight is best for deep thinking.

I'll bet President Bush would make great decisions if all he had for light in the Oval Office was a candle.

Freedom from Advertising

I dont usually follow what's happening in Congress very closely but I was interested recently when New York Senator Charles Schumer got so mad at all the junk e-mail he was getting that he proposed a law making it illegal to send out e-mail sales pitches. The senator's bill is good but it doesnt go far enough for me. We need protection from all kinds of intrusive advertising. Theres no place to hide anymore. Wherever we go, they find us and advertise at us.

The other day I got into a hotel elevator in New York and above the buttons you press for your floor was a television screen with an advertisement running. Theyve got you in an elevator because youre trapped until you get to your floor.

No matter where you are or what youre doing, theres advertising in front of you.

Once a month I get an envelope from my bank with my statement in it. Its important to me. The bank knows Im not going to throw the envelope away unopened so they put a lot of advertising in the envelope that has nothing to do with my money.

That ought to be illegal.

I dont want a vacuum cleaner from my bank. I dont want to borrow ten thousand dollars. I dont want another credit card. All I want in the envelope they send me once a month is how much I have left and where I spent what I dont have anymore.

Newspapers are a pain, especially weekends, because of all the junk advertising they fold into them. Here's *The New York Times* . . . a great newspaper, but isnt there any way for them to pay good editors and reporters without cluttering up the paper with trash that falls out in your driveway when you pick it up ?

Magazines are unpleasant to read for the same reason. You have to tear the junk out of *Time* or *Newsweek* before you can read them. Even a classy magazine like *Harper's* does it.

Our telephones have junk advertising. If you want to call information on 411 you have to listen to a plug for Verizon, the telephone company, before you get your number:

"VERIZON NATIONWIDE 411. MAKE PROGRESS EVERYDAY."

We're all familiar with the car dealers who plaster their name around the license plates on the back of your car. You drive around as a moving ad for them for as long as you own it.

Television is worst of all, of course. They keep moving in on an hour with more commercial time but at least you get something free in return for the junk on television.

Advertising makes the wheels go round in America, no doubt about it. Not only that, it pays my salary but we dont want it in our face all day. What we need, Senator Schumer, is a Freedom from Unwanted Advertising law.

Inside Earth

The Columbia spaceship disaster has caused everyone to look more carefully at NASA, the National Aeronautics and Space Administration. Some have questioned whether its been worth the cost in lives and money.

We spent $24 billion getting to the moon in 1969. It was a remarkable achievement and it provided us with amazing pictures and a great sense of national pride.

The fact is though, it wasnt as big a step as we thought at the time. It led to nothing. The last time we went back to the moon was thirty years ago. It turned out the moon is just one big dull rock in the sky.

Space exploration is different. Even if you cant put your finger on the results or count the advances that we've made in terms of dollars, space exploration is important to the progress of life on Earth. We have to find out more about where we are in relation to the rest of the universe. You never know what's going to happen to this planet. We may have to get off it.

The other thing that seems wrong, or strange anyway, is that we've spent so much time and money exploring *outer* space when we've never been more than a few miles down looking at inner space . . . the Earth we live on. We really dont know much about what's inside it.

Its as if we went two miles into space.

The distance around the Earth—the circumference—is about 24,000 miles. If you went right through the center of it, the diameter is only about 8,000 miles. Here's New York . . . here's Australia on the opposite side of the Earth. Ive always wanted to go to Australia but its too far . . . 12,000 miles from New York. Thats a long time to have your seatbelt securely fastened. If we had a tunnel from the United States to Sidney, a straight line through the center of the Earth, I estimate it would only be about 5,000 miles.

We used to think of heaven as being up and hell as being down. Well, if the center of the Earth is hot as hell—they dont even know that for sure— we should be able to tap into it and use the heat to warm our houses without burning so much oil.

If we ever do dig way down into the Earth, we'd have to find a place to throw all the dirt and rocks we took out.

And thats where the moon might finally come in handy. We could ship the stuff up there and dump it. Eventually of course, we'd have a full moon.

60 Minutes's
Thirty-Fifth Birthday

This is an unusual event—a thirty-fifth birthday party for a television show.

Whales live to be eighty. Owls fifty and elephants live to be seventy. People live to be in their nineties now.

The life expectancy of the average television show is two years. Even the good ones dont usually last more than five.

Arthur Godfrey's Talent Scouts show was #1 in 1951. I was paid $150 a week to write that.

I Love Lucy was # 1 for five years.

Gunsmoke was most popular for three.

The Beverly Hillbillies was the worst #1 show.

All in the Family was #1 for five years and deserved to be. *Dallas* was #1 three times.

Bill Cosby had three great years at the top.

Cheers was the best while it lasted.

Nothing was ever better than *Seinfeld:* #1 in 1994, 1995 and 1997.

All those shows are gone now—this is the only survivor.

60 Minutes has been phenomenally successful for a show that only appeals to adults and smart children. It was the most-watched television show in 1982 and again in 1992 and 1993. It was in the top ten longer than any show in broadcast history.

There are a lot of *60 Minutes* statistics though that no one ever hears. For example, in the twelve years that Lesley Stahl has been on the show she has never worn the same piece of clothing twice.

It seems like a waste considering that Lesley wouldnt look bad in a brown paper bag.

Morley, on the other hand, doesnt spend much on clothes. He has six Turnbull and Asser shirts from London. Theyre all blue checks.

This is his way of making sure no one confuses him with Lesley.

Ed spends more on clothes than Lesley does but his suits are so conservative you dont notice. Ed always wears an earring that goes with his jacket.

Mike and Harry Reasoner were the two original correspondents on *60 Minutes.* I was a writer and producer for Harry. It was very sad for all of us, but especially for me, when Harry died in 1991. I lost my star, I lost my friend.

Mike has done the most reports for *60 Minutes,* more than 1,000. Mike reminds us of Jesus Christ here at *60 Minutes.* When he interviews someone, they get crucified.

Steve is youngest. He doesnt remember the early years of *60 Minutes* because I think he was still in junior high.

Diane Sawyer was on the show for five years. I was briefly in love with Diane—but then she cut her hair.

Some things improve with age. It is my biased opinion that *60 Minutes* has been better than ever in its thirty-fifth year.

Mozart died when he was thirty-five but his music is still played 212 years later . . . good as ever. Old television broadcasts dont stand up that well. I'd hate to have some of the things Ive done shown 212 years from now. They looked funny already.

Don Hewitt, the producer, has made *60 Minutes* what it has been for thirty-five years. Ive known him since 1942 when we met in *The Stars and Stripes* office in London where we were both reporters. Don was young then and the best thing about him is, he never grew up.

This is a special moment that I have dreaded but it seems like a good time to make a personal announcement. Ive been writing for television since there was television. Ive done 800 of these essays in the twenty-five years Ive been on *60 Minutes*.

Ive saved some money . . . I'd like to travel . . . I'd like to spend more time with my family. What I want to tell you is this: Im not going to do any of those things and I'll be back here again next year.

PublicAffairs is a publishing house founded in 1997. It is a tribute to the standards, values, and flair of three persons who have served as mentors to countless reporters, writers, editors, and book people of all kinds, including me.

I. F. Stone, proprietor of *I. F. Stone's Weekly,* combined a commitment to the First Amendment with entrepreneurial zeal and reporting skill and became one of the great independent journalists in American history. At the age of eighty, Izzy published *The Trial of Socrates,* which was a national bestseller. He wrote the book after he taught himself ancient Greek.

Benjamin C. Bradlee was for nearly thirty years the charismatic editorial leader of *The Washington Post.* It was Ben who gave the *Post* the range and courage to pursue such historic issues as Watergate. He supported his reporters with a tenacity that made them fearless, and it is no accident that so many became authors of influential, best-selling books.

Robert L. Bernstein, the chief executive of Random House for more than a quarter century, guided one of the nation's premier publishing houses. Bob was personally responsible for many books of political dissent and argument that challenged tyranny around the globe. He is also the founder and was the longtime chair of Human Rights Watch, one of the most respected human rights organizations in the world.

.   .   .

For fifty years, the banner of Public Affairs Press was carried by its owner Morris B. Schnapper, who published Gandhi, Nasser, Toynbee, Truman, and about 1,500 other authors. In 1983 Schnapper was described by *The Washington Post* as "a redoubtable gadfly." His legacy will endure in the books to come.

Peter Osnos, *Publisher*